Martin Delany, Frederick Douglass, and the Politics of Representative Identity

The
University
of North
Carolina
Press
Chapel Hill
and
London

Martin
Delany,
Frederick
Douglass,
and the
Politics of
Representative
Identity

Robert S. Levine

© 1997
The University
of North Carolina
Press
All rights reserved
Manufactured in the
United States of America

The paper in this book meets
the guidelines for permanence
and durability of the Committee
on Production Guidelines for
Book Longevity of the Council
on Library Resources.

Library of Congress Cataloging-in-Publication Data
Levine, Robert S. (Robert Steven), 1953–
Martin Delany, Frederick Douglass, and the politics of
representative identity / Robert S. Levine.
  p. cm.
Includes bibliographical references and index.
ISBN 0-8078-2323-6 (alk. paper). —
ISBN 0-8078-4633-3 (pbk.: alk. paper)
1. American prose literature — 19th century — History and
criticism. 2. Afro-Americans in literature. 3. Politics and
literature — United States — History — 19th century. 4. Douglass,
Frederick, 1817?–1895. My bondage and my freedom. 5. Stowe,
Harriet Beecher, 1811–1896. Uncle Tom's cabin. 6. United
States — Politics and government — 19th century. 7. Delany,
Martin Robison, 1812–1885. Blake. 8. Stowe, Harriet Beecher,
1811–1896. Dred. 9. Group identity in literature. 10. North star
(Rochester, N.Y.). 11. Slavery in literature. I. Title.
PS366.A35L48   1997
818'.30808093520396073 — dc20   96-9614
                                            CIP

01 00 99 98 97   5 4 3 2 1

THIS BOOK WAS DIGITALLY PRINTED.

For love of Ivy

Contents

Acknowledgments

I am grateful for the assistance I have received from a number of individuals and institutions. My thanks to George Dekker, Neil Fraistat, and John McWilliams for encouraging me to write this book in the first place, and to Beth Loizeaux, Carla Peterson, and Mary Helen Washington for their sage advice and counsel along the way. For their generous and useful readings of the manuscript, I am grateful to Russ Castronovo, Peter Carafiol, Ivy Goodman, and Wyn Kelley. I am particularly indebted to Jonathan Auerbach and Leonard Cassuto, whose meticulous criticisms of the book's penultimate draft pushed me to write a better book. For their wonderfully helpful advice on final revisions, I am also very much indebted to David W. Blight and John Ernest, my readers at the University of North Carolina Press.

Several research grants facilitated the writing and renewed my energy and confidence. I thank the University of Maryland's General Research Board for a Summer Research Award, and the University's Committee on Africa and Africa in the Americas for a Research and Travel Grant. For a Senior Fellowship for University Teachers, I am indebted to the currently embattled National Endowment for the Humanities. Without the year-long grant from the National Endowment, I fear I would still be struggling to make sense of my project.

I did the bulk of my research at the Library of Congress and am pleased to acknowledge the assistance of its expert staff. I am also grateful to librarians at the Carnegie Library of Pittsburgh and at the University of Maryland's Interlibrary Loan Office.

A portion of Chapter 2, in somewhat different form, first appeared in *American Literature* 64 (1992), and a considerably shortened version of Chapter 4 first appeared in *Criticism and the Color Line*, ed. Henry Wonham (New Brunswick: Rutgers University Press, 1996). My thanks to the editors for the early forum and permission to reprint.

The University of North Carolina Press's enthusiastic interest in the book when it existed as little more than an abstract and some sketchy chapters helped to keep me going on the project. For their help at various stages of editorial review and production, I am grateful to Barbara Hanrahan, Sian Hunter White, Pamela Upton, Elizabeth Gray, Kathleen Ketterman, and Nancy J. Malone.

As readers will quickly discern, my book builds on the work of numerous scholars and critics in the field of African American literary and cultural studies. I wish to express my special sense of indebtedness to some of the pioneers in Delany and Douglass studies: Philip S. Foner, Floyd J. Miller, Benjamin Quarles, Dorothy Sterling, and Victor Ullman.

Finally, I am happy to thank my wife, Ivy Goodman, and son, Aaron, for their patience, good humor, and sustaining love.

Martin Delany, Frederick Douglass, and the Politics of Representative Identity

Major Martin R. Delany, ca. 1865
Courtesy of the Moorland-Spingarn Research Center, Howard University

Frederick Douglass, ca. 1855
Courtesy of the Moorland-Spingarn Research Center, Howard University

Introduction

Representative Men

In a speech presented to a convocation of black clergy in 1886, the distinguished African American educator Anna Julia Cooper reflected on the ways in which the (self-)celebration of representative black men could obscure the crucial work of "BLACK WOMAN" in "the regeneration and progress of a race." She remarked of Martin Robison Delany (1812–1885) in particular:

> The late Martin R. Delany, who was an unadulterated black man, used to say when honors of state fell upon him, that when he entered the council of kings the black race entered with him; meaning, I suppose, that there was no discounting his race identity and attributing his achievements to some admixture of Saxon blood. But our present record of eminent men, when placed beside the actual status of the race in America to-day, proves that no man can represent the race. Whatever the attainments of the individual may be, unless his home has moved on *pari passu*, he can never be regarded as identical with or representative of the whole.[1]

Cooper's singling out of Delany as her exemplum is somewhat surprising, for Frederick Douglass was generally regarded as the representative black leader of the time. Celebrations of Douglass usually obscured the achievements not only of black women but of Delany himself. Cooper may have referred to Delany because he had recently died and thus was more in the (African American) public eye. But as the daughter of a slave woman and her mother's white master, she may well have adduced the example of Delany because she was troubled by his politics of race — his notion that he was "representative" of African Americans because of his "unadulterated" African blood. In asserting that the "home" cannot move on with an individual self *"pari passu"* (side by side), Cooper implicitly contested both Delany's politics of emigration and his tendency to figure himself as the incarnation of black Africa.

Delany's insistence on his status as representative and exemplary "black" man has led to his virtual reification as the Father of Black Nationalism — a radical separatist who ultimately sought to lead blacks back to their "native" Africa.[2] But as Paul Gilroy observes, "Delany is a figure of extraordinary complexity whose political trajectory through abolitionisms and emigrationisms, from Republicans to Democrats, dissolves any simple attempts to fix him as consistently either conservative or radical."[3] Born free in Charles Town, Virginia (now West Virginia), the son of a free seamstress and a plantation slave, Delany in the early 1820s was taken by his mother to western Pennsylvania after Virginia authorities threatened to imprison her for teaching her children to read. In 1831 Delany moved to Pittsburgh, where he studied with Lewis Woodson and other black leaders, and by the 1840s he was apprenticing as a doctor and editing one of the first African American newspapers, the *Mystery*. He left his own newspaper in 1847 to coedit the *North Star* with Frederick Douglass. After an approximately eighteen-month stint with Douglass, Delany attended Harvard Medical School but was soon dismissed because of his color. Outraged by Harvard's racism and the Compromise of 1850, he published *The Condition, Elevation, Emigration, and Destiny of the Colored People of the United States* in 1852, and in 1854 he lectured on "The Political Destiny of the Colored Race on the American Continent." In 1856 he moved to Canada and began to plan an African American settlement in West Africa; three years later, after flirting with John Brown's insurrectionism, he toured the Niger Valley and signed a treaty that gave him the land he needed for his project. At around the same time, he serialized his novel, *Blake* (1859–62), and published *Official Report of the Niger Valley Exploring Party* (1861). When his Africa plan collapsed in 1862, Delany commenced recruiting black troops for the Union army, and in 1865 he received a commission as a major. For several years after the Civil War, he worked with the Freedmen's Bureau in South Carolina, publishing a number of letters and essays on the situation of Southern blacks, and during the 1870s he became involved in local South Carolina politics. Ultimately disillusioned with Reconstruction, he tried to help Southern blacks emigrate to Africa and published *Principia of Ethnology: The Origin of Races and Color* (1879). In the final years of his life he unsuccessfully sought a federal appointment in order to finance his emigration to Liberia.

An abolitionist, editor, doctor, novelist, political and racial theorist, inventor, explorer, orator, and judge, Delany was a prolific writer who seems to have been unable to conceive of political action apart from writing. But perhaps because of the prominence modern critics have given his separatist position, he has suffered the typical fate in traditional fields of study of the black separatist: he has been marginalized and for the most part ignored. Indeed, it could be said that Delany as the reified Black Separatist, even with the attention garnered by the 1970 book publication of *Blake*, has been separated from U.S. literature. Astonishingly, the major anthologies of American literature, including the Heath, fail to reprint any of Delany's multifarious and complex writings.[4]

Instead, Frederick Douglass (1818–95) has emerged as the representative black male writer of the period. As is well known, Douglass, the son of a slave woman and a white slave master, spent his first twenty years as a slave in Maryland, escaping to New Bedford, Massachusetts, in 1838. "Discovered" by William Lloyd Garrison in 1841, Douglass became one of Garrison's most valued lecturers, publishing *Narrative of the Life of Frederick Douglass* in 1845. Fearing fugitive slave hunters, Douglass sailed to the British Isles and in 1846 made a celebrated tour of Scotland and England as an antislavery speaker. When he returned in 1847, he established the *North Star*, thus beginning a sixteen-year career as an editor and publisher of three different antislavery newspapers. In the midst of this journalistic career, he printed an expanded version of his autobiography, *My Bondage and My Freedom* (1855), a text that articulated some of the key tenets of his newspapers—temperance and the importance of pursuing black elevation in the United States. During the Civil War, Douglass, like Delany, helped to recruit black troops for the Union army, and from 1865 until his death in 1895 he was a loyalist of the Republican party. For his support, he was rewarded with various public positions, including those of assistant secretary of the commission to Santo Domingo (1871), president of the Freedmen's Bank (1874), and minister and general consul to Haiti (1891). As a celebrity of sorts, he brought out two editions of yet further expanded versions of his autobiography, *The Life and Times of Frederick Douglass* (1881, 1892). Increasingly disillusioned with Reconstruction, near the end of his life Douglass wrote some of his strongest attacks on white racist violence, most notably "The Lessons of the Hour" (1894).

As is true for Delany, the act of writing was central to Douglass's career. In addition to his numerous lectures and essays, he published four versions of his autobiography, a novella, and countless editorials and newspaper articles. Yet despite his massive output, his career shifts from Garrison's moral suasionism to political abolitionism to Republican reconstructionism, and his extensive commitment to journalism, the 1845 *Narrative* has become enshrined as Douglass's representative text and, until fairly recently, *the* representative African American text of the antebellum period. Deborah E. McDowell (echoing Cooper's remarks on Delany) argues that the choice of Douglass as " 'representative man,' as the part that stands for the whole, . . . reproduces the omission of women from view." [5] But in light of Oxford University Press's successful publication of the Schomburg Library of Nineteenth-Century Black Women Writers, which has spawned dramatic curricular renovation (reflected in the prominence given to African American women writers in recent American literature anthologies) and numerous studies of texts by African American women writers, it increasingly seems the case that Douglass's representative status has created a false binarism (Douglass on the one side, African American women writers such as Harriet Jacobs, Frances Harper, and Harriet Wilson on the other) that ultimately omits from view nineteenth-century African American male writers (Henry Highland Garnet, James McCune Smith, William Watkins, Samuel R. Ward, Delany, and many others). Arguably, Douglass deliberately used his representative status to obscure the writings and activities of those men, for he remained virtually silent, in his autobiographical narratives, on his interactions with his black contemporaries. In fact, he did not mention Delany by name in any of his autobiographies, thus prompting the historian Wilson J. Moses to ask in an essay on Douglass as "representative black man," "Had Douglass forgotten his involvement in business with Martin Delany or in politics with the black convention movement?" [6] Guided by Douglass's strong narratives, modern biographers, with the exception of Benjamin Quarles, have barely begun to explore Douglass's relationships with blacks during the 1840s and 1850s.[7] The end result of making Douglass *the* representative black male of the time is to elide some of the most significant dialogues and exchanges of antebellum culture — the very debates out of which Douglass's ideas and writings emerged.

"It is natural to believe in great men," Emerson remarked in *Representative Men* (1850). But he notes as well, "Every hero becomes a bore at last."[8] One of the large goals of *Martin Delany, Frederick Douglass, and the Politics of Representative Identity* is to present Douglass as something other than a towering representative figure (the Emersonian "bore") by studying his politics and writings in relation to his debates and exchanges with Delany. Similarly, I hope to challenge Delany's conception of his own representative status, along with conventional views of him as an unwavering black separatist and emigrationist, by reading his public career in relation to Douglass's. By situating these leaders in relation to each other and by studying the ways in which their ideas and writings emerged from their personal and ideological conflicts, I hope to replace inevitability with contingency, univocal politics with pragmatic (and principled) improvisation. And by paying attention to their overlapping and shared concerns, I hope to challenge reductive binarisms that lead to Delany and Douglass being regarded as unequivocal opponents on the subjects of race and nation.

Emerson remarks in *Representative Men* on the public's need to conceive of leadership in binary terms: "We balance one man with his opposite, and the health of the state depends on the see-saw." The idea of male generational binarism seems especially crucial to African American thought: Booker T. Washington versus W. E. B. Du Bois and Malcolm X versus Martin Luther King are two such pairings that immediately come to mind. In 1967 Harold Cruse argued that the origins of such binary oppositions — and thus of key conflicts in African American culture between integrationism (or assimilationism) and black nationalist separatism — lie "in the historical arguments between personalities such as Frederick Douglass and as [*sic*] Martin Delany." In response to Cruse, Sterling Stuckey maintained that "it is an error to contend that there was not something of the *integrationist* in Delany and much of the *nationalist* in the young Douglass." I share Stuckey's view of the instabilities and overlappings in such key terms as "integrationist" and "nationalist" and thus of the inevitable distortions that arise from an overreliance on binary oppositions to make sense of the ideological commitments of such complex figures as Delany and Douglass. Certainly, if we regard black nationalism as a consciousness among blacks "of a shared experience of oppression at the hands of white people," as a program that "emphasized the need for black people to rely primarily on themselves in vital areas of life," it makes good sense to regard both Delany and Douglass as engaged black nationalists.[9]

But while it is possible in a large historical frame to demonstrate similarities between Delany and Douglass, by the 1850s they regarded themselves as in conflict with each other over issues of absolutely crucial importance. Douglass welcomed Harriet Beecher Stowe's *Uncle Tom's Cabin* (1852) as a text that demonstrated the potential for black elevation in the United States and in 1853 sponsored a national black convention in Rochester, New York, that sought to put the book to use in undermining the increasing prestige of Delany's emigrationism. Delany, who regarded Stowe's novel as the work of a racist colonizationist, attacked what he regarded as Douglass's naïve celebration of Stowe, and in 1854 he sponsored a national black emigration convention in Cleveland. In articulating their conflicts during the 1850s and beyond, Douglass and Delany self-consciously (and perhaps unconsciously) participated in the creation of a binary star, attracting and repelling each other as they pursued their competing political agendas. Douglass's recurrent attacks on Delany's emigrationism suggest that he *needed* Delany as a foil to make his own argument about the crucial importance of blacks pursuing their rights to U.S. citizenship. Delany, as the dimmer star, was perhaps even more in need of Douglass as a foil against which his emigrationist programs could shine forth in all their boldness. If conceptions of Douglass's and Delany's politics are polarized in the historical literature, these leaders must bear some responsibility for the way in which this has come about.

Delany and Douglass seem most clearly at polar extremes, particularly by the late 1850s, on the interrelated issues of race and Africa. In her admiring 1868 biography of Major Martin R. Delany, Frances Rollin refers to his "pride of race, which even distinguishes him from the noted colored men of the present time. This finds an apt illustration in a remark made once by the distinguished Douglass. Said he, 'I thank God for making me a man simply; but Delany always thanks him for making him a *black man.*'" Of interest here are the differing rhetorical uses to which Douglass and Delany could put the same statement. Douglass may not have said precisely those words, but in 1862 he complained similarly that Delany "has gone about the same length in favor of black, as the whites have in favor of the doctrine of white superiority." To Douglass,

Delany's racial pride reinforced the racism undergirding whites' power in the United States and confuted humanistic notions of equality. Moreover, as Douglass well knew, Delany's celebrations of his "African" blood were part of his ongoing efforts to figure himself as more "authentically" black than Douglass and thus—because of his proto–Pan-African commitment to the "race"—as the more representative black leader. Following Delany's cues, Rollin says of Delany, "Africa and her past and future glory became entwined around every fibre of his being; and to the work of . . . exalting her scattered descendants on this continent, he has devoted himself wholly."[10]

In response to Delany's determined self-figurations, Douglass regularly insisted that arguments for blacks' "natural" racial connections to Africa, which he tended to describe as "degraded" and "pestilential," worked only to thwart blacks' pursuit of their rights to citizenship in the United States. In his own ambitious effort to fashion himself as the representative leader of African Americans, Douglass emphasized his native roots in the United States and, more specifically, the fact of his former enslavement and his ability to overcome it. This was a pointed strategy, for unlike Douglass, Delany was never enslaved and thus could be viewed as at an "inauthentic" remove from the experiences of most blacks in the United States. In referring to him as "the intensest embodiment of black Nationality to be met with outside the valley of the Niger," Douglass slyly suggested that Delany would be a more suitable leader of black Africans than American blacks.[11]

Delany's and Douglass's opposition on the claims of race and the place of (black) nation could appear quite stark, but even on the issue of Africa they shared some common ground. As an initiatory model of the kind of analyses that I will be developing in this book, I want to consider briefly a key text by each writer on the subject of Africa. Though Delany and Douglass are not directly debating each other on Africa, each is aware of the other's presence in the culture, and each positions himself rhetorically to make his argument against the backdrop of their debates on Stowe and black emigration.

In 1853 Delany was invited by the Freemasons of Pittsburgh's St. Cyprian Lodge, No. 13, to speak on the topic of the legitimacy of black Masonry. Local white Masonic lodges had refused to sanction the lodge, and the hope was that Delany's speech would convince the Grand Lodge of England to recognize the group. Though Masonic secrecy makes it difficult to trace Delany's relationship to black Masonic organizations, the evidence would suggest that he joined the St. Cyprian Lodge at its founding in 1846—he delivered a funeral oration for a fellow St. Cyprian Mason in 1847—and that at the time of his 1853 address he was still a member of the group (in the prefatory letter inviting him to give the speech, he is referred to as "Companion and Sir Knight"). Douglass had attacked black Freemasonry for "swallowing up the best energies of many of our best men, contenting them with the glittering follies of artificial display."[12] Whatever problems Douglass might have had with Masonic secrecy, pomp, elitism, and self-segregation, Delany, in the tradition of Prince Hall, founder of the black Masons, viewed black Freemasonry as an oppositional response to white racism, one that provided disempowered blacks with a fraternal base on which black community and black leadership could be built.

In his speech, published later that year as *The Origin and Objects of Ancient Freemasonry*, Delany asserts a central truth of Freemasonry (first apprehended, he states, by the ancient Ethiopians): "MAN THE LIKENESS OF GOD." Though the formation of black lodges appears to work against the Masonic ideal that "all men, of every country, clime, color, and condition (when morally worthy,) are acceptable to the portals of Masonic jurisprudence," Delany points out that black exclusivism was forced on blacks by the exclusionary practices of white racist Masons, whose very racism should debar *them* from the Masonic brotherhood.[13]

Delany further attempts to demonstrate the illegitimacy of racist white Masons by proclaiming that "to Africa is the world indebted for its knowledge of the mysteries of Ancient Freemasonry." In a key moment in the speech, Delany asserts that "to deny to black men the privileges of Masonry, is to deny to a child the lineage of its own parentage. From whence sprung Masonry but from Ethiopia, Egypt, and Assyria—all settled and peopled by the children of Ham?" Given that the originators of Masonry were extraordinarily accomplished black people, Delany concludes that blacks have greater claims to Masonry than whites: "Truly," Delany remarks, "if the African race have no legitimate claims to Masonry, then it is illegitimate to all the rest of mankind." He thus demands rhetorically: "Was it not Africa that gave birth to Euclid, the master geometrician of the world? and was it not in consequence of a twenty-five years' residence in Africa that the great Pythagoras was enabled to discover that key problem in geometry—the forty-seventh problem of Euclid—without which Masonry would be incomplete?" By the logic of his argument, white civilization itself has developed from and is dependent on black civilization. Such an argument "legitimates" blacks' place not only in Freemasonry but also in the Western cultures that attempt to exclude and degrade them.[14]

The assertion of the centrality of Africa to the development of Western culture leads Delany to the issue of the transmission of that culture and thus to his own claims to black (Masonic) leadership. According to Delany, Moses, as "the recorder of the Bible," is the person to whom "we as Masons, and the world of mankind . . . [are] indebted for a transmission to us of the Masonic records." Masons owe their beginnings, grandiose purposes, and perpetuity to a "*fugitive* slave" who, Delany argues, gained "all his wisdom and ability" in Egypt, "a colony from Ethiopia," and then transmitted his wisdom to subsequent generations, whose literate leaders persisted in recording and transmitting Masonic truths to the present day. As Delany explains, Masonic wisdom is "handed down only through the priesthood to the recipients of their favors, the mass of mankind being ignorant of their own nature, and consequently prone to rebel against their greatest and best interests." Anticipating Du Bois's elitist notion of the Talented Tenth, Delany credits "the wise men" of Masonry's hierarchical leadership with the group's survival over the centuries.[15] In his lecture — and indeed in his entire career — Delany conceives of himself in the tradition of Moses, as one of those wise leaders whose very knowledge is linked to an Africanist pride in black origins and objects.

Douglass appears to take a similar position on Africa in "The Claims of the Negro Ethnologically Considered," a lecture delivered approximately one year later, in July 1854, to the Philozetian and Phi Delta literary societies during graduation ceremonies at Western Reserve College. Like Delany, Douglass decried what Gilroy terms "the hellenomaniacal excision of Africa from the narrative of civilisation's development." As Douglass himself wrote of "Claims of the Negro" eleven years after the occasion, his 1854 lecture sought to defend "our race" from the demeaning scientific racism of the time by providing a history lesson:

> We traced the entangled threads of history and of civilization back to their sources in Africa. We called attention to the somewhat disagreeable fact — agreeable to us, but not so to our Teutonic brethren — that the arts and appliances and blessings of our civilization flourished in the very heart of Ethiopia, at a time when all Europe floundered in the depths of ignorance and barbarism. We dwelt on the magnificence and stupendous dimensions of Egyptian architecture, and held up the

fact . . . that the race was master of mechanical forces of which the present generations of men are ignorant.

As summarized by Douglass in 1865, "Claims of the Negro" shared much with Delany's *Origin and Objects of Ancient Freemasonry*: its appeals to "our race," its effort to create black community by limning a glorious African past, and its subsuming of white culture to black culture through a "blackening" of Egypt. These similarities are important and worth underscoring, particularly given the emphasis in Douglass studies on his relation to (even love for) white culture.[16]

In the speech itself, Douglass, by arguing for "the unity of the human race," specifically attacks the ethnological "scientific" racism and polygenesis theories of Samuel Morton, Josiah Nott, George Gliddon, and Jean Agassiz, maintaining that "the whole argument in defence of slavery, becomes utterly worthless the moment the African is proved to be equally a man with the Anglo-Saxon." After making scriptural and Enlightenment-based claims for the equality of "the Negro," Douglass demonstrates his pride in "the African" by moving beyond egalitarian arguments to assertions of the greatness, indeed the superiority, of ancient black civilizations. He argues "that a strong affinity and a direct relationship may be claimed by the Negro race, to THAT GRANDEST OF ALL THE NATIONS OF ANTIQUITY, THE BUILDERS OF THE PYRAMIDS"; and, going against the grain of the argument of Morton's insidious *Crania Americana* (1839), he asserts the black African status of the Egyptians: "Greece and Rome — and through them Europe and America — have received their civilization from the ancient Egyptians. This fact is not denied by anybody. But Egypt is in Africa. Pity that it had not been in Europe, or in Asia, or better still in America! Another unhappy circumstance is, that the ancient Egyptians were not white people; but were, undoubtedly, just about as dark in complexion as many in this country who are considered genuine negroes." According to this historical genealogy, which very much resembles Delany's, black Africans were responsible for setting the course of Western civilization — which no longer can be viewed as essentially white — and thus are its proper heirs.[17]

At the conclusion of his lecture, Douglass expresses his desire to reclaim Africa's legacy by regenerating both the "barbarians on the banks of the Niger" and the slaves of the United States. As a former slave himself, Douglass in his person embodies the possibilities of regeneration. He calls attention to this fact, in a deliberate act of self-celebration, by reminding his auditors of his *earned* perspective on the topic of his speech: "I have reached here—if you will pardon the egotism—by little short of a miracle: at any rate, by dint of some application and perseverance." His conception of his own miraculous rise leads him to remark on the degradation brought about by "THE EFFECT OF CIRCUMSTANCES UPON THE PHYSICAL MAN." He complains of the ways in which racists such as Morton supply pictures in their ethnological books of degraded blacks, which they present as representative of the race. If Morton truly wants to present a comprehensive picture of blacks, Douglass insists, he should consider including in his ethnologies portraits of those who "give an idea of the mental endowments of the negro." One of Douglass's suggestions for such a portrait is "M. R. Delany."[18]

Though there exist significant similarities in their lectures and some suggestion of Douglass's admiration for Delany, crucial differences point to Delany's and Douglass's disparate situations (and politics) of the 1850s. Whereas Delany was invited by black Freemasons to address them in secret, Douglass was invited by white collegians to give his speech in public. As the first black keynote speaker at the graduation ceremonies of a major university, Douglass received an enormous amount of publicity for his talk, which, unlike Delany's *Origin and Objects of Ancient Freemasonry*, was widely disseminated and discussed. Whereas Delany addressed a fraternal gathering of Pittsburgh's black intelligentsia and leaders, Douglass in effect addressed whites throughout the nation. Delany's leadership was localized and directed at a specific black constituency; Douglass, as a national figure, aspired to lead blacks and whites alike.

Delany's and Douglass's differing rhetorical and leadership positions were reflected in the politics of their respective speeches. Delany offered a transnational or proto–Pan-African vision of the distinctive qualities of and connections among blacks throughout the world; Douglass demonstrated not the oneness of the "African race" but "the oneness of the human family." And whereas Delany showed himself cognizant of the arcana of black history and Freemasonry, Douglass, in keeping with the university setting, displayed his familiarity with classic white writers, concluding his speech with a quote from Robert Burns: " '*A man's a man for a' that.*' " To be sure, in his 1865 summary of the speech, which he recounted to a primarily black audience, Douglass can seem more of a piece with Delany in the way he pridefully insisted on the accomplishments of "our race."[19] But in 1854 Douglass's main intent in "Claims of the Negro" was to challenge essentialist distinctions between the races. His suggestion that Delany might well serve as an appropriate portrait of the smart "negro" could thus be taken as a backhanded and demeaning effort to lock Delany, unlike himself, into a specific racial category.

I infer hostility here because during the 1853–54 period, when Delany and Douglass delivered their talks on Africa, they were debating the merits of *Uncle Tom's Cabin* and black emigration. Their disagreements became quite vehement and personal. Objecting to Douglass's championing of Stowe and his concomitant organizing of a convention to develop strategies for black elevation in the United States, Delany addressed Pittsburgh's St. Cyprian Masons on Pan-African unity several weeks before Douglass's convention. In doing so, he implicitly countered Douglass's patriotic convention and ideologically legitimated the black emigration agenda of his 1852 *Condition*. Douglass was more explicit in countering Delany in "Claims of the Negro." Having repeatedly attacked Delany's plans for an emigration convention to be held in August 1854, Douglass pointedly refuted Delany's main arguments for emigration in his speech of July 1854, setting forth a biracial vision of the future of the United States: "The black and the white—the negro and the European—these constitute the American people—and, in all the likelihoods of the case, they will ever remain the principal inhabitants of the United States, in some form or other." Consistent with this vision and his equating of "America" with the United States (which Delany would challenge in *Blake*), Douglass, with his prideful demonstration of African Americans' noble past and future potential, only reinforced his opposition to Delany's program to encourage black elites to emigrate from the United States. He concluded his speech with a resounding effort at preempting the mandate of Delany's emigration convention: "All the facts in [the African American's] history mark out for him a destiny, united to America and Americans." [20]

As I hope this brief discussion makes clear, Delany and Douglass were often speaking to and about each other even when they were not engaged in direct debate. And it was often the case that on some matters they were in fundamental agreement, in this instance on the importance of Africa to African American identity, the harmful effects of slavery, and the need for abolition. Though there were also important points of division between the two leaders, what often tended to be at stake in debates between Delany and Douglass was less what was to be done than who was to do it. Their wish to answer the question of "Who?" with "Myself" at times had a determining role on their politics. To make their claims to representative leadership, each man tapped into different sources of legitimation. Broadly speaking, Douglass emphasized his status as a former slave who literally embodied the possibility of black elevation in the United States. Delany emphasized his black skin and blood as signifiers of a "natural" aristocracy that authorized his leadership role as the embodiment of Africa in America. Their rivalry centered on these two very different forms of identity politics, and that rivalry and concomitant politics of representative leadership, I will argue, informed their most important writings.

In his 1845 *Narrative*, Douglass, however modest and disinterested he may seem, takes pains to establish his "consecrated" status as a black Christ, black Jeremiah, and black Moses, concluding his account of his journey from slavery to freedom with the hope, voiced in the text's final paragraph, that both his *Narrative* and his continued antislavery efforts will help to bring about the "day of deliverance to the millions of my brethren in bonds." (Garrison's preface, usually regarded as condescending and intrusive, ultimately works in tandem with Douglass's rhetoric to underscore further his representative identity as a black deliverer.) The sort of self-fashioning that Douglass performed in *Narrative*, wherein by the logic of the typological appeal to Exodus there can be only one "consecrated" figure leading his "brethren" to a "day of deliverance," inevitably bred rivalries, as black men (and some black women, such as Maria Stewart and Harriet Tubman) made their claims to be that deliverer.[21] In the case of black male leaders in particular, these rivalries, not only between Douglass and Delany but also between Douglass and Ward, Douglass and Garnet, Delany and William Wells Brown, Delany and James Holly, and Brown and Garnet, could become all-consuming concerns that risked putting the ego of the leader above the concerns of the black community. In this respect, Anna Julia Cooper's assertion that "no man can represent the race," though directed specifically at Delany, conveyed as well, I think, her resentment at the way nineteenth-century African American male reformers tended to position themselves as heroic deliverers of the race. As opposed to black women, who, Cooper argued, undertook their moral-reform work in the "homes, average homes, homes of the rank and file of horny handed toiling men and women . . . (where the masses are)," black male leaders, particularly before the Civil War, tended to fashion themselves as Mosaic leaders whose programs promised to bring about the liberation and elevation of their people. For

Cooper, who associates representative identity with the masses, Delany's specific claims to representative identity suggest that he is not, in fact, representative, though as we shall see, Delany, through his novelistic persona Blake, attempts to make precisely the claim for himself that Cooper made about black women reformers: that "the whole *Negro race enters with me.*"[22]

Recent scholarship by Frances Foster and Carla L. Peterson follows Cooper in regarding African American women as less self-aggrandizing than African American men when undertaking antislavery and antiracist cultural work; and it is tempting to want to chide Delany and Douglass for their patriarchal politics, their exploitation of their wives (who were saddled with child rearing and domestic responsibilities while their husbands were on the road), their reinscription of "conventional" bourgeois cultural formations, and so on. But such a disciplining critical practice fails to take into account the ways in which nineteenth-century "narratives of masculinity" inevitably became narratives of personhood for black males of the period. And such a practice does scant justice to Delany's and Douglass's complex attitudes toward gender. Their quest to forge a place for black males in U.S. political and economic institutions surely had the potential to work transformations on a racist and nonegalitarian society that would have benefited black women as well. Moreover, within the context of nineteenth-century culture, the two leaders were actually rather progressive on questions of gender. One of the slogans printed on the masthead of their coedited *North Star*, after all, was "RIGHT IS OF NO SEX," and it is well known that Douglass supported and attended numerous women's rights conventions, including the epochal gathering in Seneca Falls in July 1848. Despite his debate with Elizabeth Cady Stanton and Susan B. Anthony on the Fifteenth Amendment, which gave voting rights to African American men, Douglass never abandoned the struggle to enfranchise women. Delany, according to Gilroy, was committed to the notion that "women were to be educated but only for motherhood," but in *Condition* and other works, Delany wrote of the need for women to take up business enterprises, he encouraged the participation of women (including his wife) at all the emigration conventions he sponsored, and, true to his sense of women as political entities in their own right, he presented the reader of *Blake* with actively engaged women revolutionaries.[23]

Though I will be addressing Douglass's and Delany's gender politics on occasion throughout the book, I am taking as a given that theirs was a rivalry that for the most part worked within the conventional patriarchal discourses of the time. Instead of raising or lowering Delany and Douglass from the pedestal, I will be presenting two African American men who were in the position of leadership and who struggled with the vagaries and implications of that position, constructing concepts of representative identity along the way, shaping and reshaping each other's vision. Considering Delany and Douglass together, with Stowe as a prominent example of the cultural forces that helped to mold their changing vision of black representativeness, this book is a study of two (gendered) embodiments of (gendered) cultural forces and thereby a study of the processes by which representative identity and cultural memory are formulated over time.

Inevitably, it is also a study of the ways in which minority discourses and perspectives posed a challenge to the dominant national narratives of nineteenth-century U.S. culture, especially those which made universal, as opposed to particularist, claims for the availability of equality and freedom to the nation's citizenry. Contesting the very social arrangements that, as Donald E. Pease puts it, "produced national identities by way of a social symbolic order that systematically separated an abstract, disembodied subject from resistant materialities, such as race, class, and gender," Delany, Douglass, and many other African American writers revealed that various sites of seeming cohesion in the culture were in fact "sites of contestation, exclusion, and repression." This study will thus address some of the issues currently debated in transnational and "postnational" cultural studies: the location of the (black) nation, the function of borders, the question of difference and otherness, the tension between integrative and resistant narratives. Homi K. Bhabha writes, "Counternarratives of the nation that continually evoke and erase its totalizing boundaries — both actual and conceptual — disturb those ideological manoeuvres through which 'imagined communities' are given essentialist identities."[24] In their writings and politics, Delany and Douglass participated in just such a demystifying cultural project. At the same time, they both found much that was appealing and seductive in the national ideology and thus at various moments in their careers pragmatically sought to make use of that ideology to forge a place for blacks in U.S. culture. More regularly than Douglass, however, Delany concluded that such a pragmatics of U.S. place was futile for blacks; his efforts to challenge and cross borders emerged as one of the fundamental points of difference between himself and Douglass in their debates on black leadership and community.

The two leaders were not always at odds. In Chapter 1 I examine Delany's and Douglass's coeditorship of the *North Star*, focusing on Delany's travel letters to Douglass, which I regard as a major "text" of the period. At this point in their careers the coeditors shared much in common on the value of pursuing black elevation in the United States. Their liberal pragmatics, their efforts to appropriate conventional bourgeois discourses to encourage black uplift, remained central to their politics, even after they split on the issue of black emigration. In Chapter 2 I look at their interrelated debates on Stowe's *Uncle Tom's Cabin* and black emigration, paying close attention to the ways in which issues of representative leadership informed their debate on blacks' place in the Americas. In an effort to consolidate his status as exemplary African American leader and to underscore his politics of antiemigrationism, in 1855 Douglass published *My Bondage and My Freedom*; Chapter 3 offers an extended reading of Douglass's thematics of temperate revolutionism and representative (American) identity in this complex work.

Harriet Beecher Stowe was not a passive bystander to African Americans' reception of her novel. In response to black debate on *Uncle Tom's Cabin*, she changed her views on colonizationism. Though deliberately occluded by the title of my book, for I want to suggest her subordinate place in Delany's and Douglass's debates, the triangulation of influences among Delany, Douglass, and Stowe, the dialogue among these two black men and one white woman, is one of the subjects of *Martin Delany, Frederick Douglass, and the Politics of Representative Identity*. But given the necessarily delimited focus of my study, that triangulation should be taken less as an assertion of a hermetically conceived nexus of influences than as a microcosm of the possibilities of black-white cross-fertilizations in antebellum culture. In Chapter 4 I move beyond triangulation (and subordination) to consider Stowe's engagement with a wide range of African American discourses for the creation of her "other" antislavery novel, *Dred* (1856), which has at its center the "representative" figure of an insurrectionary black leader. The possible influence of that novel on Delany's novel of black insurrectionism, *Blake*, is addressed in Chapter 5, in which I develop a detailed reading of Delany's novel in relation to his rivalry with Douglass and his emergent Pan-Africanism. In the Epilogue I briefly consider Delany's and Douglass's writings after the Civil War, focusing on their debate in the 1871 *New National Era* on Reconstruction and black representativeness.

This book provides extended readings of three major (and relatively neglected) antebellum literary texts — Douglass's *Bondage*, Stowe's *Dred*, and Delany's *Blake* — texts that emerged from the career rivalry between Delany and Douglass and that have at their centers accounts of heroic (and representative) black male leaders. In addition, I provide readings of important (and relatively neglected) lectures, letters, journalistic writings, and convention proceedings. African American newspapers have an especially central place in my study, as it is primarily from the newspapers — the *North Star, Frederick Douglass' Paper, Douglass' Monthly,* the *Provincial Freeman,* the *Weekly Anglo-African,* and the *New National Era* — that I have been able to recover Delany's and Douglass's debates on what they regarded as the pressing issues of the day. In the chapters that follow I attempt to involve the reader in the process of examining these debates as they unfold, and one of my methods for doing this, I may as well say at the outset, is narrative storytelling. The story begins in 1847, when Delany and Douglass first meet.

Chapter 1

Western Tour for the *North Star*

Debating Black Elevation

 In the summer of 1847, several months after Douglass returned from his triumphal British tour, William Lloyd Garrison decided to capitalize on Douglass's celebrity by undertaking with him a Western tour for the *Liberator*. Invited by the Western Anti-Slavery Society to speak at New Lyme, Ohio, Garrison planned a route that would take them through western New York, Philadelphia, Harrisburg, Pittsburgh, and eventually to several cities and towns in Ohio. It was his hope that such a tour would help to bring new subscribers to the *Liberator*. Additionally, we may speculate, he hoped that by spending several months on the road with Douglass he could keep his renowned speaker from straying from the fold. For in April of that year Douglass had informed Garrison that he intended to use the approximately two thousand dollars raised by his British supporters to establish his own antislavery newspaper. Under intense pressure from Garrison, Douglass rethought his decision, and in the *Liberator* of 9 July 1847 he announced that he had relinquished his newspaper plans. Perhaps aware that he appeared to be submitting to Garrison's pressure tactics, Douglass wrote a follow-up letter, printed in

the 23 July 1847 issue, in which he asserted, "I have acted independently, and wholly on my own responsibility." Applauding Douglass's "independence," Garrison noted (somewhat hypocritically) in a letter to Douglass printed in the same issue, "It is quite impracticable to combine the editor with the lecturer, without either causing the paper to be more or less neglected, or the sphere of lecturing to be severely circumscribed."[1] Shortly after this exchange, Garrison and Douglass departed on their Western tour.

The tour began auspiciously enough with rousing meetings in Norristown and Philadelphia. In Harrisburg, however, Garrison and Douglass were attacked by a mob, barely escaping serious injury. Four days later, on August 13, they met a very different reception in Pittsburgh, a town, like Philadelphia, with a number of prominent black leaders. In the first of five meetings to be held in Pittsburgh, Garrison and Douglass addressed an enthusiastic crowd in Temperance Hall. As Garrison reported to his wife, "The place seems to be electrified, and the hearts of many are leaping for joy." In his own report on the Pittsburgh meetings, printed in the *Pennsylvania Freeman*, Douglass similarly exulted in the enthusiastic response and went on to comment on the black leader of Pittsburgh who most captivated his attention, "that nobel [*sic*] specimen of a man, Mr. Delany. He is one of the most open, free, generous and zealous laborers in the cause of our enslaved brethren, which I have met for a long time." Garrison was equally taken with Delany, describing him to his wife as "editor of the Mystery, black as jet, and a fine fellow of great energy and spirit," who "spoke on the subject of prejudice against color in a very witty and energetic manner."[2] So impressed were Garrison and Douglass with Delany that they invited him to speak with them in New Brighton, Pennsylvania, before heading on to their engagements in Ohio.

By all accounts, the meetings in Ohio were as "electrical" as those in Pittsburgh. "The whole Western Reserve is now in a healthy state of Anti-Slavery agitation," Douglass reported in the 9 September 1847 *Standard*. "We are having a real Anti-Slavery revival." But the revivalistic rhetoric of consensus concealed a growing tension between Douglass and Garrison. In late September Douglass once again changed his mind on his newspaper plans and announced the establishment of a newspaper that, according to the prospectus printed in the *Anti-Slavery Bugle* and the *Standard*, would "attack slavery in all its forms and aspects — advocate Universal Emancipation — exalt the standard of public morality — promote the moral and intellectual improvement of the Coloured People —

and hasten the day of Freedom to the three millions of our enslaved countrymen." Two months later Delany was publicly named coeditor of the paper. Had Douglass secretly recruited Delany during their meetings in Pittsburgh and New Brighton? That would seem to have been the case, for Garrison remained uninformed about the publishing venture until he read Douglass's prospectus. In a letter of 20 October 1847, Garrison remarked bitterly to his wife: "It will also greatly surprise our friends in Boston to hear, that, in regard to his project for establishing a paper here, to be called 'The North Star,' he never opened to me his lips on the subject, nor asked my advice in any particular whatever. Such conduct grieves me to the heart. His conduct . . . has been impulsive, inconsiderate, and highly inconsistent."[3] Such conduct, to consider things from Douglass's perspective, was precisely what was necessary to free himself from Garrison's benevolent paternalistic control.

In keeping with his desire for independence, Douglass set up his paper in the "western" city of Rochester, New York, at a considerable remove from Garrison's Boston-located *Liberator*. William C. Nell joined Douglass there to serve as publisher; an Englishman, John Dick, served as printer. As announced in the inaugural issue of 3 December 1847, the coeditor of the paper was Martin R. Delany. Delany probably traveled to Rochester sometime in October to coordinate plans for the newspaper and then returned to Pittsburgh to attend both to his ill daughter and to his own newspaper, the *Mystery*, which he eventually sold to the AME Church. His absence from Rochester would have suited the coeditors' initial plans, for it was decided that Delany, rather than being involved in the day-to-day chores of bringing out the newspaper, would concentrate on extending the *North Star*'s influence (and subscription list) to whites and blacks west of the Alleghenies by undertaking what he termed a "Western tour for the *North Star*."[4]

The full measure of Delany's participation in the *North Star* has been obscured by Douglass and by biographers sympathetic to Douglass. Though Delany told his biographer Frances Rollin that his "brilliant and useful editorial career . . . with the North Star" came to an end in June 1849, which meant that he participated in the newspaper for eighteen months, Douglass's most influential modern biographer, Benjamin Quarles, mistakenly cited the date as June 1848, thereby shrinking Delany's involvement to a mere six months. Following Quarles's lead, Philip Foner and Nathan Huggins, among others, have likewise referred to Delany's six-month tenure at the *North Star*. Huggins's rhetoric is particularly revealing for the ways in which it diminishes not only Delany's tenure but also the nature of his relationship to the paper (and Douglass): "By June 1848 Martin Delany was dropped as coeditor [of the *North Star*]. He . . . was proving to be of little support." As I will argue in this chapter, it is unclear whether Delany was "dropped" or chose to resign; further, whatever the circumstances surrounding the termination of his coeditorship, the fact is that Delany was a tremendously productive corresponding editor. William S. McFeely asserts that "despite repeated pleas from Douglass, he [Delany] contributed only occasional letters."[5] But while on his "Western tour," Delany, in addition to speaking regularly at antislavery meetings, sent Douglass one or two substantial letters a month, for a total of twenty-three letters, plus nine essays, all of which were published in the *North Star*. Even after relinquishing his coeditorship, Delany continued to submit essays and a number of other significant letters on a range of topics. Neglected by virtually all commentators on antebellum black literature and culture, Delany's writings for the *North Star* merit close attention and revaluation.

In this chapter I will focus on Delany's dispatches to Douglass, which, taken together, constitute one of the finest (and most distinctive) travel narratives written by an African American during the antebellum period.[6] This "text" consists of the letters Delany wrote Douglass between 14 January 1848 and 24 February 1849 as he toured the "West" — Pittsburgh, Columbus, Cincinnati, Cleveland, Detroit — in search of free black subscribers for the *North Star*. A travel narrative by a free black that addresses the situation of antebellum free blacks, the letters of Delany's "Western tour" are considerably different from the slave narratives that have come to be regarded as the representative African American texts of the period.[7] In these letters, Delany discusses his travels to the struggling free black communities of what is now the Midwest, describing his visits to schools, churches, and other institutions he conceives of as central to blacks' moral, spiritual, financial, and political elevation. Calling on his free black readers to work industriously and temperately to elevate themselves in U.S. society, Delany at the same time keeps a highly critical eye on the political developments, institutions, and racism of the dominant white culture that thwart these efforts. And so the letters, in the tradition of the travel genre, "journey" widely: from accounts of black music schools to analyses of recent elections, from personal comments on friends he meets along the way to discussions of the black convention movement, from a meditation on slave suicides to a legal discussion of a famous court case—all culminating in a spectacular "transcendental" letter in which he describes, as he crosses the Allegheny Mountains, his apprehension of his likeness to God. At the dramatic center of the letters is an attempt on Delany's life, as he is nearly lynched by drunken whites in Ohio. Alternately ironic, hortatory, genteel, prophetic, dramatic, and poetic, Delany emerges as a shrewd participant in and a critical observer of antebellum culture.

But though my focus will be on Delany's "Western tour," this opening chapter should be regarded as a study less of Delany than of the Delany-Douglass collaboration. Central to Delany's and Douglass's collaborative enterprise was their commitment to black elevation. A month before publishing the first issue of the *North Star*, Douglass wrote to a friend that he wanted his newspaper "to elevate and improve the condition of the nominally-free coloured people in the United States." In one of his early letters to Douglass, printed in the *North Star*, Delany likewise stated, "The elevation of our race . . . is the ultimatum of our aim, and whatever respectfully and honorably contributes to this end, is among the means to be used for its accomplishment."[8] For many African American reformers, black churches, conventions, and newspapers were regarded as the most effective forums for promoting uplift among the free blacks of the North. These institutions became important proving grounds for the black male leaders of the period. And yet, as I contend in the next section, no clear consensus emerged on the means and ends of black elevation, and competing impulses and desires came to inform virtually all antebellum statements on black uplift. Militance can be discerned in apparently assimilationist pronouncements, and vice versa. Given the complex and sometimes contradictory nature of the discourses and practices of black elevation, we need to resist a binary interpretation of the eventual split between Delany and Douglass as that between the militant black separatist and the "color-blind" assimilationist. An increasing conflict over their claims to representative leadership, rather than any stark ideological differences, may have been the principal reason for the consequential parting of the ways of the *North Star*'s coeditors.

Elevating the Race

At the 1831 "First Annual Convention of the People of Colour, Held by Adjournments in the City of Philadelphia," a convention whose very existence posed a radical challenge to white hegemony, the Committee on the Condition of the Free People of Colour of the United States reported "that, in their opinion, *Education, Temperance*, and *Economy*, are best calculated to promote the elevation of mankind to a proper rank and standing among men."[9] According to many black reformers and abolitionists of the period, the free blacks' achievement of "*Education, Temperance*, and *Economy*" would serve the antislavery cause by demonstrating that blacks could be as productive in the marketplace as whites, thereby refuting the proslavery argument that blacks were better off on plantations. African American newspapers had a crucial role in promoting these behavioral ideals, and an interplay between conventionality (or seeming complicity in the dominant culture), on the one hand, and resistance, on the other, is particularly resonant in black journalism of the period. For example, in a March 1837 editorial in the *Colored American*, the most important black newspaper prior to Douglass's (and Delany's) *North Star*, Samuel Cornish wrote in fairly conventional terms of the need for free blacks to elevate themselves morally and economically: "On *our* conduct and exertions, much, very much depends. . . . Should we prove unworthy [of] our few privileges, we shall furnish our enemies the strongest arguments, with which to oppose the emancipation of the slave." Though Cornish can seem to be absolving a racist slave culture by placing the burden for black elevation on blacks themselves, the large implication of the editorial was to suggest the value, and existence, of a black community that can and should speak for itself: "No class of men, however pious and benevolent, can take our place in the great work of redeeming our character and removing our disabilities." In numerous other editorials he regularly argued that white racism contributed to black "disabilities." As he remarked in July 1837, "The colored people of these 'United States' are the involuntary subjects of a social and political despotism, alike unrighteous and cruel; the guilt of which lies, WHOLLY at the white man's door."[10]

It is crucial to recognize the pragmatic interplay between the conventional and the subversive in the discourse of black elevation—a discourse that ultimately sought to "elevate" blacks by asserting their rights to participate as equals in the nation's social, political, and economic institutions.[11] Otherwise, we risk making capitalism the domain of "whiteness," thereby (unwittingly) reproducing the arguments of white racists who sought to exclude blacks from the burgeoning free market economy in the United States. The militant David Walker may well have felt "hatred of the spirit of capitalism," as Sterling Stuckey suggests, but in his *Appeal ... to the Colored Citizens of the World* (1829), Walker devotes a considerable portion of his text to underscoring the importance of education and economy to black elevation. Responding to an older black man's pride in his son's apparent literacy, Walker queries, "Can he post a set of books in a mercantile manner?" When the responses to this and other questions about the son's abilities prove to be in the negative, Walker, in the manner of a Jeremiah, laments that the son "has hardly any learning at all — he is almost as ignorant, and more so, than many of those who never went to school one day in their lives." We see equally conflicted attitudes in the 1840s writings of Henry Highland Garnet, who, despite the militancy of his 1843 "Address to the Slaves," argued that the elevation of blacks depended on their ability to adopt "temperance, industry and frugality."[12]

But in a culture dominated by whites, how possible was it for blacks to be so self-reliant? According to the Philadelphia-based champion of black elevation William Whipper, who helped to establish the influential American Moral Reform Society at the 1835 Fifth Annual Convention for the Improvement of the Free People of Colour in the United States, blacks needed to work hand in hand with whites to improve their situation in the United States.[13] During the late 1830s and 1840s no black leader was more vociferous in contesting Whipper's noncomplexional, consensual politics than the Pittsburgh-based Lewis Woodson. In a series of ten letters signed under the name "Augustine," which were printed in the *Colored American* between 1837 and 1841, Woodson attacked what he perceived to be the self-defeating assimilationism of Whipper's reformism, maintaining that blacks' lowly condition in the United States was causally related to color — that insidious racist beliefs and practices were the main reasons for blacks' degradation: "Slavery has its source in the *corrupt moral sentiment* of the country, and . . . the almost entire means of its abolition, is the correction of this corrupt moral sentiment." In some respects, then, Woodson turned against one of the principal contentions of black-elevation discourse — that the "moral elevation" of blacks in the North would lead to the abolition of slavery in the South. From this more skeptical and pessimistic position, Woodson proposed a plan to bring about black elevation in ways quite different from Whipper: through racial separatism. He explained, "I would have them [free blacks] leave the cities where they are now 'scattered' and 'mixed' among the whites, whose prejudices exclude them from equal privileges in society, churches and schools, and settle themselves in communities in the country, and establish society, churches and schools of their own." In doing so, arguably, blacks would constitute their own "nation" within U.S. national borders.[14]

Delany, who developed his own black separatist program in the 1850s, almost certainly would have been familiar with Woodson's critique of Whipper, as Woodson was one of his most important mentors during the 1830s and 1840s. First meeting Woodson when he moved to Pittsburgh in 1831, Delany was inspired by Woodson's advocacy of education and self-help and in 1832 helped to found the Theban Literary Society, an Africanist version (with its evocation of ancient Egypt's Thebes) of Ben Franklin's Junto. With Woodson, he joined the biracial Pittsburgh Anti-Slavery Society in 1833, and in 1836 he and Woodson also joined the Pittsburgh auxiliary branch of Whipper's American Moral Reform Society. Attending meetings of a group that encouraged blacks to challenge racism and slavery by improving their condition, Delany practiced what he preached, for it was at this time that he began his medical education, working as an apprentice to the white physician Andrew N. McDowell. By 1837 he had the following listing in the *Pittsburgh Business Directory*: "DELANY, MARTIN R. Cupping, Leeching and bleeding." Yet Woodson's break with Whipper and the American Moral Reform Society must have had a significant impact on Delany, for by the late 1830s he was much more the political activist (and even the emerging black separatist) than he had been just a few years earlier. Dismayed by the 1838 decision of the Pennsylvania state legislature to rescind blacks' right to vote, Delany in 1839 toured Texas and surrounding areas to investigate whether these locales would be a suitable place for black "emigration." Because he saw firsthand that white adventurers were anything but anti-slavery, he returned to Pittsburgh with a renewed commitment to political abolitionism, supporting Dr. Francis J. Lemoyne of the Liberty party in his unsuccessful quest for the governorship of Pennsylvania. Additionally, he offered his support to the Pittsburgh Philanthropic Society, a stop on the Underground Railroad.[15]

Perhaps the best indication of where Delany and Pittsburgh's black community stood on the issue of black elevation in the early 1840s is provided by the proceedings of the 1841 Convention of the Colored Freemen of Pennsylvania, held in Pittsburgh in August of that year, a meeting organized by Delany and others to protest the 1838 disfranchisement. Resisting the militant rhetoric that would come to the fore in Henry Highland Garnet's famous address of 1843, Delany and his associates conveyed their continued belief in the centrality of moral reform to black elevation: "No honest condition is so hopeless, but that it may be improved and elevated." Accordingly, a large part of the proceedings was devoted to discussing how blacks could achieve such elevation. While the convention's notion of moral "improvement" was fairly similar to Whipper's—education, temperance, and industry were emphasized throughout the proceedings—the delegates announced themselves as willing to work apart from whites to improve their situation, particularly by developing their own newspapers. Insisting that newspapers tended "to inspire public spirit and enterprise," the delegates maintained that it would be better that "our children should eat plainer diet, and dress in coarser apparel, than to be deprived of the use of a well conducted newspaper." And yet because Pennsylvania itself was lacking in what it needed, "a newspaper conducted by the colored people, and adapted to their wants," the delegates advised Pennsylvania's blacks that "until we can establish a newspaper of our own in this state, the COLORED AMERICAN be considered our general public organ."[16]

Convinced of the centrality of newspapers to the development of black community and desirous of filling the gap left by the demise of the *Colored American* in 1842, Delany established Pittsburgh's first black newspaper, the *Mystery*, in 1843, even as he continued his medical apprenticeship. In the prospectus he promised that his paper would contribute to "the Moral Elevation of the *Africo-American* and African race, civilly, politically and religiously," while supporting "no distinctive principles of race." That same year, true to the racial egalitarianism of his paper, he married Catherine Richards, the daughter of a white Irish immigrant woman and a wealthy black butcher.[17]

Though Delany's noncomplexional commitment to the principles of moral elevation suggests the residual influence of the American Moral Reform Society on his editorial position, the stronger influence of Woodson informs his portrayal of the struggles facing the "Africo-American" in overcoming prejudice against color. For example, in "Not Fair," one of the few extant editorials from the 1843–47 run of the paper, Delany insists on blacks' rights to a substantial period of freedom before they should have to prove themselves "equal" to whites. Given that whites continue to demand that blacks demonstrate their equality, Delany can only conclude that "more is asked of us, than ever was asked of any other people, and if it is expected that with all the disadvantages with which we are surrounded, that we should still equal the other citizens, . . . it is a tacit acknowledgement, that we are naturally superior to the rest of mankind."[18] In addition to revealing a David Walker–like irony in his assertion of black superiority, the repeated use of "us" and "we" conveys the black nationalist politics at the heart of the paper. That politics took on a more aggressive cast in 1845 when, inspired by Garnet's "Address to the Slaves," he changed the motto of the paper from an Afrocentric celebration of black intellect—"AND MOSES WAS LEARNED IN ALL THE WISDOM OF THE EGYPTIANS"—to the militantly Byronic "HEREDITARY BONDSMEN! KNOW YE NOT WHO WOULD BE FREE, THEMSELVES MUST STRIKE THE BLOW!"[19] And yet the extent of Delany's militancy in the mid-1840s is debatable, particularly given his readiness to embrace the moral-suasion politics of the *North Star*. So that we might better assess points of agreement and disagreement between the coeditors, I now want to take up Douglass's politics of black elevation during the 1830s and 1840s.

Though by the mid-1840s Douglass would emerge as the preeminent black Garrisonian, there are important pre-Garrisonian sources of his antislavery thinking. In his 1845 *Narrative*, Douglass emphasized the importance of having read in Caleb Bingham's *The Columbian Orator* (1797) the "Dialogue between a Master and a Slave," a text that, in its portrayal of the ability of a literate slave to use rational means to convince his owner to free him, provided a model of influence that stayed with Douglass at least to the 1850s, when he sought to use rational means to convince Harriet Beecher Stowe to fund a black mechanics institute. Perhaps even more important to his emergent moral-reform philosophy was his involvement, in the years before his escape from slavery, in the East Baltimore Moral Improvement Society, a group of free blacks who met to discuss the ways in which they could improve their condition. This society exposed Douglass not only to the rhetoric of abolitionism but also to the rhetoric of black elevation. After escaping from slavery in 1838 with the help of Anna Murray, a free black from Baltimore whom he married that year, Douglass settled in New Bedford, whose approximately one thousand black residents, however much they hated slavery, had to deal with the more immediate daily struggle of competing and surviving in racist Northern society. Disturbed by the segregationist practices of the mostly white Elm Street Methodist Church, Douglass began attending Reverend William Serrington's Zion Chapel of the African Methodist Episcopal Zion denomination. As McFeely observes, moral reform and self-improvement, not antislavery, were the major topics addressed at church discussions.[20] Perhaps it was the church's relative neglect of slavery that led the former slave eventually to attend antislavery meetings. When in 1841 he was "discovered" by Garrison and made a paid lecturer for the Massachusetts Anti-Slavery Society, he began to focus more on excoriating the practice of slavery than on developing strategies for black elevation, telling the story of his enslavement to buttress and authenticate Garrison's moral-suasion politics.

We need only briefly rehearse Douglass's 1841–47 participation in Garrison's society. As is well known, tension developed between Douglass and the group, particularly after the publication of his *Narrative*, as his celebrity increased and he gained confidence in his ability to talk about slavery on his own terms. Thus he resented Maria Weston Chapman's decision to monitor his speeches and expenses during his British tour of 1845–47; thus, as he stated in his 1855 *My Bondage and My Freedom*, he resented the Garrisonians' efforts to control the content of his speeches; and thus he must have resented Garrison's attempt to stifle his newspaper project. What needs to be emphasized here is that even while working as a faithful advocate of basic Garrisonian tenets — moral suasion, a proslavery reading of the Constitution, anti-Unionism, the immorality of direct participation in the political process — Douglass was somewhat conflicted in his support for these positions. His account in *Narrative* of his use of violence to oppose the slave breaker Edward Covey's domination makes clear just how inappropriate he thought "moral suasion" was to the slaves. That same year, in "American Prejudice against Color," Douglass explicitly worked against his moral-suasion politics by celebrating Madison Washington for engaging in "physical warfare" to liberate his fellow blacks on the slaver *Creole*. Anticipating Delany's efforts in the 1850s to challenge Stowe's racialist stereotyping of blacks as passive homebodies, Douglass asserted that Washington's actions, as well as the heroic patriotism of blacks who participated in the American Revolution, disproved the claims of those who believed that "none but those persons who have a mixture of European blood" were capable of distinguishing themselves through militant action.[21]

Though an increasing suspicion of Garrisonianism marks his discourse during this period, Douglass tended to remain true to his announced moral-suasion politics. At the 1843 National Convention of Colored Citizens held in Buffalo, for example, he opposed Garnet's appeal to the slaves to use violence against their masters, eventually contributing the deciding vote against adopting "Address to the Slaves of the United States" as recommended policy. As paraphrased in the convention's minutes, Douglass stated that he feared Garnet's advice "would lead to an insurrection. . . . He was for trying the moral means a little longer." Concerned about the growing appeal of the Liberty party, which had gained the support of Delany, Garnet, and other prominent black leaders, Douglass at the 1843 convention also made the case, on Garrisonian grounds, against political abolitionism, arguing "that the constitution of this country was a slaveholding instrument, and as such denied *all* rights to the colored men." But though Douglass retrospectively can appear timid and doctrinaire at this particular convention, there was nothing timid or doctrinaire about a Garrisonian moral suasionist participating in a blacks-only convention that was dedicated, as the chairman Samuel H. Davis put it, to "the elevation of our own people."[22]

According to the 1843 convention's "Report of the Committee upon the Press," the establishment of a national black newspaper was crucial to the quest for back elevation. Such a newspaper, the committee reported, would "not only counteract the influences against us, but be made an instrumentality to promote positive good, the tendency of which would be to elevate the people." The subject of a national black press was taken up as well at the National Convention of Colored People held in Troy, New York, in October 1847. As recorded in the proceedings, Garnet supported such a press, maintaining "that the most successful means which can be used for the overthrow of Slavery and Caste in this country, would be found in an able and well-conducted Press, solely under the control of the people of color." Although Douglass agreed on the value of black newspapers, he opposed establishing a national newspaper, for he feared that it "would soon dwindle down to be the organ of a clique. . . . He was in favor of sustaining the 'Ram's Horn, National Watchman, and Northern Star.'" Now, given that Douglass had decided just before the Troy convention to establish his own newspaper, the first issue of which would appear but six weeks after the convention, there was something disingenuous about his decision at Troy to lead the opposition to a national black press. Although he lost the vote on this issue—the convention's delegates overwhelmingly supported the proclamation that a national black press could be regarded as "our Declaration of Independence"—he won the war: Douglass established the *North Star* on precisely the rhetorical grounds put forth by the 1847 convention, and then one year later, at the Colored National Convention held in Cleveland, he received a resounding vote of confidence from the convention's delegates in Resolution 23: "Resolved, That among the means instrumental in the elevation of a people there is none more effectual than a well-conducted and efficient newspaper; and believing the North Star, published and edited by Frederick Douglass and M. R. Delany at Rochester, fully to answer all the ends and purposes of a national press, we therefore recommend its support to the colored people throughout North America."[23]

In the next chapter I will address the question of the representativeness of Douglass's newspaper(s), particularly on the issue of black emigration. Taking as my cue the 1848 delegates' terming of the *North Star* as a joint production, I first want to explore the nature and consequences of Douglass's and Delany's efforts at collaboration. Given that Delany in the 1840s had "combined militant abolitionism with less fiery activities on behalf of political antislavery, black suffrage, and the more amorphous principles of moral reform and the 'elevation' of the race," and given that Douglass's own commitment to moral reform and black elevation led him at times to embrace the rhetoric of militant abolitionism, there would appear to have been more in common between Douglass and Delany at this time than most commentators have allowed.[24] At least that is how Douglass and Delany presented themselves to their readers in their initial writings in the *North Star*.

These writings suggest both Delany's influence on Douglass and Douglass's on Delany. We can discern the influence of Delany (and perhaps Woodson) on Douglass's editorial "Our Paper and Its Prospects," printed in the *North Star*'s inaugural issue of 3 December 1847. Claiming that in establishing a black antislavery newspaper he means to display "no unworthy distrust or ungrateful want of appreciation of the zeal, integrity, or ability of the noble band of white laborers," Douglass maintains, as Woodson and Delany maintained in the early 1840s, that blacks must develop their own institutions. For Douglass, as for his coeditor, the need to disseminate black perspectives on slavery is also of paramount importance: "The man who has *suffered the wrong* is the man to *demand redress*." As he elaborates in a later column, "Colored Newspapers": "Facts are facts; white is not black, and black is not white. There is neither good sense, nor common honesty, in trying to forget this distinction."[25] Delany could not have put this any better himself.

And yet Douglass is hardly absolutist in his demands for black antislavery actions and perspectives, allowing in the early issues of the *North Star* that white actions and perspectives are also of value to the cause. He thus remarks in "Our Paper and Its Prospects" that blacks "must be our own representatives and advocates, not exclusively, but peculiarly—

not distinct from, but in connection with our white friends."[26] By reputation, Delany is the champion of black separatism; yet as we shall see, his *North Star* letters to Douglass often speak well of white abolitionists. This is not to suggest that tension did not develop between the coeditors on precisely the issue of white involvement in black elevation. What can be said is that there is no evidence in the pages of either the *North Star* or (later) *Frederick Douglass' Paper* to suggest that Delany and Douglass began their dispute on the place of whites in antislavery reform prior to the 1852 publication of *Uncle Tom's Cabin*.

What we note instead in the opening issues of the *North Star* is consensus, especially on the importance of black elevation to antislavery. Delany speaks to his own sense of consensus in his farewell letter to readers of the *Mystery*, a letter which probably first appeared in the final issue of the *Mystery* (no longer extant) and which was reprinted in the 21 January 1848 issue of the *North Star*. He writes in glowing terms of his new alliance with Douglass: "We leave the Mystery for a union with the far famed and world renowned FREDERICK DOUGLASS, as co-laborer in the cause of our oppressed brethren, by the publication of a large and capacious paper, the NORTH STAR, in Rochester, N.Y., . . . which cannot fail to be productive of signal benefit to the slave and our nominally free brethren, when the head and heart of Douglass enter into combination." Elaborating on his prior role as editor of the *Mystery*, Delany remarks: "The position that we assumed, was . . . that whatever is necessary for the elevation of the whites, is necessary for the colored. In order more fully to illustrate the truthfulness of this position, we had frequently to touch subjects that at once affected the pride and interests of our brethren, who often in consequence, looked upon us as an injurer than a friend." Douglass likewise, in an editorial printed in the first issue of the *North Star*, points to his encouraging and admonishing relation to "our oppressed fellow countrymen": "While advocating your rights, the *North Star* will strive to throw light on your duties: while it will not fail to make known your virtues, it will not shun to discover your faults."[27]

Although consensus is assumed in these opening statements, consensus itself becomes one of the foregrounded subjects of the twenty-three letters which Delany sent to Douglass from his "Western tour" and which were printed in the *North Star*. But rather than staging a full-fledged debate between Delany and Douglass, these letters suggest that Delany is at times debating with himself or even that the discourse of black elevation, as articulated by Delany, is debating with itself on the "duties" of free blacks in a slave culture. Though I shall at times focus on what I read as Delany's implied and emergent debate with Douglass in the letters, the extent of that debate can be exaggerated by proleptic leaps to Delany's and Douglass's more heated debates of the 1850s and beyond. Signing his letters to Douglass "M. R. D.," Delany presents himself less as an imperial self than as a participant in the shared enterprise of the *North Star*. In this respect, his letters to Douglass need to be regarded as a collaborative effort of sorts, dependent as they are on both the material context of the *North Star* and the role of the addressee.

Western Tour

The first sentence of the first of Delany's letters to Douglass to appear in the *North Star* reads as follows: "I am still in Pittsburgh, getting ready, as fast as possible, to start out on my Western tour for the *North Star.*" Douglass himself, several weeks before the 28 January 1848 publication of this letter, elaborated on Delany's travel plans, noting that Delany "will probably remain absent from Rochester during the present winter, as he intends to travel and hold meetings in Cincinnati, and many towns in the State of Ohio before his return." From Douglass's perspective, Delany's role as lecturing/subscription agent for the *North Star* would be similar to Douglass's role as lecturing/subscription agent for the *Liberator*. What he wanted most from Delany was for him to spread the word of their publishing venture to those western states and territories to which Delany, as a "westerner" himself, would have special access. But while Douglass may have viewed Delany's coeditorship primarily in terms of its potential cash value, Delany, as becomes increasingly clear from his letters, saw himself as engaged in an enterprise equal in importance to Douglass's editorial role. In several of his early letters, Delany appears intent on redefining his letter-writing project against Douglass's more limited expectations. Thus he declares that "I will write you once a week" (actually he averages a letter every two and a half weeks) and that "I prefer . . . to give you a summary of passing events, than one long article on the subject of Slavery." In short, he will be composing a travel narrative, the subject of which is his "western tour for the North Star."[28]

The nineteenth-century travel narrative, William W. Stowe notes, "served as a meeting place for various narrative voices, literary styles, levels of speech, and kinds of subjects, combining disparate modes of discourse without necessarily generating any tension between them or forging them into a 'higher unity.'" In this sense, Delany's letters are typical of the travel writings of the period.[29] But we might also think of his letters as similar to contemporaneous political dispatches. Whereas the midcentury travel narrative was often marked by geniality and bourgeois therapeutics, the dispatch had a more urgent commitment to describe, analyze, and intervene in the pressing social and political debates of the day. The narrative of the time most like Delany's "Western tour" is Margaret Fuller's "Dispatches from Europe," a series of letters published in the *New York Tribune* between 1846 and 1850. For Fuller, the revolutions of the late 1840s spoke to her desire to see republican institutions and freedom spread throughout the (Western) world; for Delany, similarly buoyed by the revolutionary energies of late 1840s Europe, the letters of his tour conveyed his desire to see republican freedom spread to the free and enslaved blacks of the United States.[30]

I want to begin my analysis of Delany's "dispatches" by looking at the ways in which he initiates and defines his letter-writing project in his opening six letters to Douglass, written between 14 January 1848 and 22 March 1848 and published in the *North Star* between 28 January 1848 and 7 April 1848. The first five letters are sent from Pittsburgh, Delany's hometown, as he delays beginning his tour because of an illness in his family; the sixth letter is posted from New Lisbon, Ohio, shortly after he departs on his tour. In these letters Delany announces a number of the issues that he will address over the next fourteen months, and he tries out several narrative voices and personae. But perhaps most important, in these opening letters he foregrounds as a subject his relationship with Douglass—the addressee of the letters—through the use of what I call "collaborative rhetoric." The first instance of such rhetoric occurs in the first letter, when Delany, in the midst of a discussion of Pittsburgh's emerging black professional class, reports on the Pennsylvania bar's failure to admit his lawyer friend George B. Vashon. Delany's response to this racist exclusionism is rhetorical fury, as he compares the "proscription and intolerance" of the Pittsburgh bar to "the lava bursting from the crater of hell." True to the travel narrative genre, the voice that he adopts here is considerably different from only a few paragraphs earlier, when he ironically muses on the frequency of steamboat explosions: "None of these boats, however, I am proud to acknowledge, are of Pittsburgh build, but belong 'below.' The slaveholders make nothing good but *slaves*: these they appear to be better at manufacturing than anything else." While the ironic voice implicitly assumes the existence of readers who, because they share his antislavery beliefs, can discern the force of the irony, Delany, at the moment when he expresses his rage at the Pittsburgh bar, more forcibly works to implicate Douglass (and the reader) in his anger through an actively stated assumption of shared beliefs. "How stand the law, then, and lawyers, when favoring the oppressor!" he exclaims. "I know that you will answer, They are supporters of tyranny and despotism."[31]

Delany's "knowing" assertions, here and elsewhere, of Douglass's support for his views make the coeditors appear to be anything but antagonists. Indeed, on the evidence of Delany's opening six letters, it would be reasonable to conclude that Douglass and Delany are coeditors in spirit as well as in name. In a letter of 6 February 1848 Delany remarks that he finds the initial copies of the *North Star* "all that I could desire — a paper of vast interest and usefulness." In the same letter he praises several of Douglass's recent speeches and essays: "Your 'charge' upon the Mexican War, and comments upon the Colonization speech of Henry Clay, are a triumphant vindication of right upon wrong." Fueled by and anticipating Douglass's writings on similar topics, Delany in a letter of 21 January 1848 attacks Clay's support for Liberian colonization, and in a letter of the following week calls the war in Mexico a "devilish" plan that "would lead to further degradation of nonwhites." Read in the context of the *North Star*'s surrounding letters, speeches, and editorials, Delany's letters would seem to be one of the many voices of the paper's harmonious chorus.[32]

And yet, Delany's at times overinsistent use of collaborative rhetoric raises questions about the avowed consensus. In the 6 February 1848 letter that praises the *North Star*, for example, Delany suddenly seems aware, in the course of attacking Pittsburgh's newspapers for printing announcements of fugitive slaves, that Douglass may not approve of his verbal anger, and so he remarks, "In this animadversion, you may account me severe." But the possibility of Douglass's censure suddenly appears of little concern to Delany, who addresses Douglass once again, now using an assertion of Douglass's (and God's) collaborative support, to legitimize his vitriolic rhetoric: "You being my helper, and God the mainstay of us both, I will never cease to cry aloud, and spare not." Though Delany may assert collaboration here, his confidence in their shared politics seems to break down at the end of the letter when he advocates using violence to resist enslavers. "Tell me," Delany enjoins the moral suasionist Douglass, "when the ruthless slaveholder has fully prostrated before him his struggling victim in the person of my wife, mother, or sister, piteously crying, 'Help! help!' that I should stop to address him with a kind of formal politeness or placid arguments, lest I only aggravate him and fail in my effort? Do you subscribe to doctrine such as this? Tell this to others, but tell it not to me. Should I not arrest his outrageous grasp, by any effective means within my power, in which the laws of Nature's God would justify me?"[33] On the evidence of his actual experience in resisting such tyrants as Covey, the former slave Douglass surely would have responded to Delany's question in the affirmative. By implying Douglass's hesitancy, Delany, who, unlike Douglass, was never in the position of having to resist a slave master, attempts to outflank Douglass, as he presses Douglass specifically and the reader of the *North Star* generally—both of whom are aggressively embraced by Delany's "you"—to adopt his militance as their own.

Yet it may also be accurate to say that the coercive aspects of Delany's rhetoric are directed partly at Delany himself. Thus, rather than labeling Delany on the basis of such rhetoric as more radical or militant than Douglass, it would make better sense to see him (as we might see Douglass) as wavering between moderate and militant positions. Despite his militant rhetoric, once his travels get under way and he begins to report on the struggles of the free blacks west of Pittsburgh, he presents himself as sharing Douglass's politics of moral suasion. In a March 1848 letter to Douglass on "the respectable and praiseworthy" black farmers of New Garden, Ohio, Delany asserts in a Garrisonian mode that he is "a Moral Suasion Abolitionist"; and two months after that, in a letter of 7 May 1848 on the prospering black merchants of Cincinnati, he rejoices that "the colored people are beginning to receive the moral suasion doctrine with much more favor than formerly."[34]

As Delany's hopeful comments on the achievements of black "westerners" suggest, black elevation emerges as his large desideratum in the opening six letters of his tour. He explicitly announces his commitment to black elevation in his third letter to Douglass. Using communitarian rhetoric in an apostrophe to his readers, Delany declares: "Colored People! we want more business men among us; farmers, mechanics and tradesmen. We must, in order to be respected and gain our lost rights and privileges, use the means necessary and adequate to the accomplishment of such a desirable end. Let our people put their children—first to school, next to trades. This must be done." In urging blacks to take to business, Delany aligns himself with the tradition of black elevation discourse that puts pressure on blacks to demonstrate to whites their ability to achieve in the marketplace, an argument, as in Whipper's writings, that emphasizes "condition" over "color." His injunctions are also consistent with the recommendations of the 1847 National Convention of Colored People, whose "Report of the Committee on Commerce" declared that "commerce is the great lever by which modern Europe has been elevated from a state of barbarism and social degradation, whose parallel is only to be found in the present condition of the African race." Delany departs from Whipper and, to a lesser extent, from the 1847 convention not in asserting the value of Africanness (in the letters of his tour he can seem as Western as Douglass or Whipper) but rather in urging blacks, as Woodson did in the early 1840s, to work toward their moral and economic elevation through self-empowerment — the creation of their own cultural and economic institutions — to develop, as Nell Painter puts it, "collective self-respect." [35]

Delany's tour perfectly serves this ideological mission, allowing him, beginning with his sixth letter, when he finally takes to the road, to describe the strengths and limitations of the various free black communities he visits in the Midwest, even as he continues to deploy collaborative rhetoric to involve Douglass (and the reader) in a "collective" project of racial uplift. Between March and June of 1848, Delany reports that the "colored families" of Hanover, Ohio, are "all of the most respectable and praiseworthy kind"; he extols the blacks at Cyrus Settlement as "industrious and respectable"; he proclaims that the "respectable colored mechanics in Chillicothe [Ohio]" are doing "more towards elevating us, than all other human efforts this side of Mason and Dixon's line"; and he praises the few blacks living in Hamilton, Ohio, for "the neatness and cleanliness of their handsome little cottages." So impressed is he by the example of Hamilton's blacks that he offers the following peroration: "Of all things in this world, for heaven's sake, give me cleanliness. Let circumstances be what they may, I see no good reason why people may not be cleanly about their houses and with their persons." [36]

With his paeans to industry, temperance, and cleanliness, Delany can at times sound rather prissy. This morally didactic and elitist voice is regularly employed by Delany to address two interrelated issues that engage him throughout his travels: blacks' need for education, on the one hand, and the relative lack of industry and initiative among the younger black generation, on the other. Like David Walker, who in the *Appeal* offers what he terms "the very heart-rending fact, that . . . school-boys and young men of colour in different parts of the country" are ignorant of "the most simple parts of Murray's English Grammar," Delany presents himself as equally concerned about the ways in which blacks' failures to gain an education ultimately handicap them in their efforts to rise in the United States. In the manner of Walker, he places considerable blame on the dominant white culture, focusing in particular on Ohio's iniquitous black codes. He also blames white educational philanthropists for training blacks simply to perform by rote. While acknowledging the laudable intentions of Hiram Gilmore in creating a high school for blacks in Cincinnati, he laments that students of the school seem mainly to be "taught for the purpose of exhibiting." The end result of the school's failure to prepare students for practical concerns, Delany maintains, is a diminishment of black self worth. He neatly makes his point through a grammatical allegory: "Many of them . . . after having 'finished' (!) their education, as it is termed by many, when putting their hand to paper, write as though there was no such letter as capital I." [37]

Lacking a sense of "I," younger, poorly educated blacks remain ill equipped to improve their condition. As Delany remarks later that year, "Seldom can be found in our country towns and small cities, a colored youth or maiden who can practically apply to business purposes the arithmetic they have learned at school, or who is able to write a correct sentence." But inadequate education is only part of the problem. A recurring concern in Delany's letters and essays in the *North Star* is that younger free blacks are failing to contribute to the uplift of the race not only because they are poorly educated but also because they are lacking in their parents' initiative. Again and again in his letters Delany adopts the persona of a hectoring Jeremiah concerned about the dissipating forces of fashion and luxury on the lives of the young. He praises the "useful and respectable attainments" of the older black generation of Zanesville, Ohio, while reporting that "the young men and women generally do not appear to have an ambition above a private-house, hotel-table, or body servant!" He reports on similar problems in Cincinnati. In the later Eastern swing of his tour, he notes that Harrisburg's black "young people" fail to hold onto the real estate bequeathed them by their more industrious parents; and in a letter from Wilmington he urges young black women who complacently work in domestic service to "gather in groups of four, six or more, as conveniency will admit of, each leisure evening in the week, for the purpose of mental and moral improvement." [38]

Delany succinctly sums up his position on black elevation: "Whatever is necessary for others, is necessary for us."[39] Anticipating that readers might interpret his Jeremiadic injunctions as calls for blacks simply to accommodate themselves to white culture, Delany asserts to Douglass, in a letter recalling his *Mystery* editorial "Not Fair," that "when it is borne in mind that we are but in a primitive State — a people, as it were, who, like the ancient Greeks and Romans, when visited by the *literati* and philosophers of Africa, are just beginning to receive the germs of enlightened civilization; then the appropriateness of the course will readily be acknowledged."[40] In suggestive ways, African culture is imaged here, as in his 1853 Masonry pamphlet, as that which helped to create "white" civilization; in this sense, Western culture and the economic systems driving and perpetuating it are not so white after all. One of Delany's few references to Africa in his *North Star* letters, these remarks point to the ways in which he will use Africa in his late 1850s and 1860s writings: to encourage blacks' economic elevation by calling attention to the glories of ancient African civilizations.

Delany's invocation of Africa serves (temporarily) to locate blackness outside the United States and thus to challenge the consensual U.S. nationalistic notions of black uplift implied by his status as a black Jeremiah.[41] Given Delany's and Douglass's eventual debate on black emigration, it is tempting to posit that an underlying point of conflict between the coeditors, as with Woodson and Whipper, centered on the issue of black-white relations in the United States, with Delany favoring black separatism and Douglass interracial cooperation.[42] But though Delany in the letters of this tour regularly praises black institutions, we see more agreement than disagreement between the coeditors on the importance of black-white interactions. In his remarks on the blacks at Hanover and the Cyrus Settlement, for example, Delany describes the ways in which their "industrious and respectable" behavior promotes social exchanges with whites: "It is no unfrequent occurrence for the colored residents to receive the civilities of their white neighbors to attend parties and weddings, and *vice versa.*" Similarly, in his discussion of Cincinnati's black artisans and chemical workers, he points to the economic advantages of such high-status jobs: "Occupations such as these bring men into intercourse with the first business men of the place, and establish an acquaintance and secure a confidence that nothing else will." Depicting Cincinnati's whites as mostly "kind and courteous," Delany laments that "the colored people themselves have never taken advantage of the opportunities they have of being sociable with them."[43]

In the context of Delany's calls for black self-help and interracial co-operation, Douglass's major lecture of the period, "What Are the Colored People Doing for Themselves?," which was printed in the 14 July 1848 *North Star*, can be regarded as a central collaborative statement of the paper's coeditors. Like Delany, Douglass insists that the "main work" of black elevation must be "commenced, carried on, and concluded by our-selves." Applauding the example of European revolutionaries, who are "in various ways making their wishes known to the world," he laments that U.S. blacks, by comparison, can seem lacking in self-determination. Nevertheless, the overarching message of the lecture is that the free blacks, through a combination of "hard toil" and the building of alli-ances with "our white friends," can effect their elevation. He proclaims, "Our oppressors have divested us of many valuable blessings and facili-ties for improvement and elevation; but, thank heaven, they have not yet been able to take from us the privilege of being honest, industri-ous, sober and intelligent." In the context of what Michael Rogin has termed "the American 1848," Douglass's hopeful suggestion here, as in Delany's most optimistic letters of the spring and summer of 1848, is that blacks' honesty, industry, temperance, and intelligence, as marshaled by representative black leaders, promise to bring about a revolutionary (and bloodless) "day of deliverance" in the United States.[44]

And yet as upbeat as Douglass might sound in "What Are the Colored People Doing for Themselves?," his mention of "our oppressors" sig-nals his awareness of the counterrevolutionary, or reactionary, forces he knows full well are working in the culture to thwart blacks' liberation. A similar awareness of reactionism permeates the letters of Delany's tour, as his travels increasingly expose him firsthand, in the very act of travel-ing in white racist culture, to the forces blacks will have to overcome to improve their condition in the United States. In an April 1848 letter to Douglass about his travels to Cincinnati, Delany provides a striking image of the white racism that threatens to become an insurmountable barrier to black elevation. Describing himself surrounded by taunting whites, Delany presents his situation on the National Road as a meta-phor of blacks' situation in the United States: "Hallowing, disparaging, and frequently vulgar epithets, gestures, the pointing of the finger full in one's face, and such like, and even in several instances throwing stones and blocks, are among the indignities a colored person meets with from these National Road turnpike American Republican Christians!" White women shout at Delany, " 'Come, here goes a *nigger!*' " Of the children, Delany wryly observes, "Poor little dears — the manner which they spread their innocent little mouths and showed their teeth manifested evidences of great emotion for the absence of their mother's *brains*." [45]

This portrait of the faces of racism anticipates Delany's stunning portrayal of the frightful mob he encounters in Marseilles, Ohio. In one of the most vivid and finely crafted letters of his tour, Delany, writing on 1 July 1848 from Sandusky City, Michigan, briskly narrates his recent travels, moving from scene to scene without giving a hint of the troubles to come. After participating in two conventions in Ohio, he arrives at the small town of Marseilles with his friend Charles Langston, where they hope to lead an antislavery meeting. Ominously, the "principal men of the place," who are "pitching quoits" in the middle of the street, abruptly stop their game at the arrival of the abolitionists. When Delany and Langston later walk to the meetinghouse, they are followed by a group of "men, lads and boys . . . [who] scoffed and used disrespectful language"; at the meeting itself, Delany realizes that of the fifty or so people there, perhaps only a handful are committed to antislavery. His perception is corroborated by Langston, who informs Delany that he has learned, because he was "mistook . . . to be what is called 'white,' " that there is a "scheme" in the works to sabotage the meeting. Delany thus declines to speak to the crowd, whereupon a man rises from his seat to declare, "I move that we adjorn [*sic*], by considering this a *darkey* burlesque." [46]

Delany's harrowing account of the mob scene that follows dramatically portrays white racists' efforts to make the meeting over into a version of a minstrel show. His account therefore provides a black perspective on minstrelsy as it was evolving at midcentury. Eric Lott has brilliantly argued that minstrelsy enacts "a *carnivalizing* of race," in which strict demarcations between the races break down, "interracial solidarity [is] briefly and intermittently achieved through male rituals of rivalry," and "murderous fantasies barely conceal the vulnerability they mask." Lott's remarks specifically address the public staging of Northern minstrel shows in which whites perform in blackface. Delany turns that version of the minstrel show on its head by describing not only Langston's problematic relationship to events — he is a "black" who looks white — but also by describing whites' efforts to stage a "*darkey* burlesque" by "blacking" black abolitionists. [47]

Employing the instruments typical of minstrel performances — "a brass drum, tamborine, clarionet, violin, jaw-bone of a horse, castanets" — the frenzied mob, after chasing Delany and Langston back to their rented room, lights a bonfire in the middle of the street and begins chanting to the music: " 'Burn them alive! — kill the niggers!' " Viewing the mob's performance as theatergoers of sorts — "Our position was such that we could look down upon them, reconnoitre their every movement, and hear all that was said" — Delany and Langston, through their very act of watching, in effect transform the racist attack into a white burlesque:

> Then came the most horrible howling and yelling, cursing and blas-
> phemy, every disparaging, reproachful, degrading, vile and vulgar epi-
> thet that could be conceived by the most vitiated imaginations, which
> bedlam of shocking discord was kept up from nine until one-o'clock
> at night. . . . Hallooing, cursing, and swearing, blackguardism — the
> roaring of drums, beatings of tamborines, blowing of instruments and
> horns, the rattling of bones, smashing of store boxes and boards for the
> fire — all going on at once and the same time, incessantly for the space
> of four hours, by far exceeding anything of a similar nature which I
> have ever witnessed.

In Delany's version of minstrelsy, whites become "blackguards." And yet, however much Delany suggests a carnivalization of race in this scene, the emphasis of the letter is on the ways in which minstrel burlesque enacts the desires of those in power to purge the body politic of blackness. True to his persona as a civilized man among the brutes, however, Delany portrays himself as troubled more by the mob's vulgarity than by its potential for violence. Never losing his cool or betraying unseemly emotions of cowardice, Delany simply waits until morning for the storm to pass. He concludes his account with the somewhat anticlimactic remark, "We left this place unharmed, and even unfrightened."[48]

Delany's relatively dispassionate response to the scene at Marseilles is typical of most of the letters of the Western tour. Downplaying the personal, Delany presents himself more as a representative black leader than as someone whose "private" life has any great relevance to the events being described. Because of his desire to retain a magisterial analytical poise, Delany's letters, considered as a travel narrative, can appear to be very different from those romantic (or transcendentalist) travel narratives of the 1840s and 1850s that, according to Lawrence Buell, charted "spiritual travel, an exploration of one's own higher latitudes."[49] Arguably, that sort of travel was a luxury for an antebellum black traveler concerned with the emancipation and elevation of his people. Yet Delany's letters culminate in a great passage on his spiritual longings; and the personal and spiritual have an important place in a number of the letters of his tour. Even so, Delany takes care to link the personal to the political and (for the most part) to sustain his collaborative rhetorical strategies.

One of the most moving of Delany's early letters, for example, describes his April 1848 visit to an asylum for the blind in Columbus, Ohio. Pridefully comporting himself as a dignitary of sorts, despite the fact that he is visiting a white institution, Delany is led through the facility by a young student at the asylum, Lucinda Shaw, who, though herself blind, is presented as having triumphed over her disability. Because he regards her as model of self-help, someone whose hopefulness and energy have allowed her to overcome difficult obstacles, Delany describes at length Lucinda's "facility [as] she trips from room to room." But in the midst of his description of the tour, which is intended to show how Ohio's "black codes" exclude blacks from such a model institution, the personal abruptly intrudes when Lucinda sings for her visitor. Delany writes:

> Her singing was painfully effective — her first air being the 'Rose-bud,' some of the words of which lamented its being 'nipped in the bud,' coming as it did in the instant of the reception of the intelligence of the death of my dear little daughter, appeared like piercing my heart with a *golden* spear, or riddling my breast with *precious* stones! It seemed as though the innocent and unconscious young Lucinda selected that song intentionally. It was painfully singular how I enjoyed it. I would that she had sung it again, and yet I would that she had not sung it at all. The institution is well-conducted, well-furnished and handsome; the pupils all well dressed, clean and cheerful. But whatever the other merits of this institution, the poor blind colored young can find no sympathy there.

The personal erupts and is then contained by Delany, as he quickly moves from his masochistic desire for even more pain — suggestive of the guilt and sadness he must have been experiencing for having left behind his critically ill daughter — to commentary on the asylum's blindness to blacks. The news of his daughter's death, which bursts to the center of Delany's consciousness on the occasion of Lucinda's singing, also bursts upon the reader, who, because Delany only vaguely referred to a family illness earlier, has not been prepared for having to deal with Delany as a bereaved family man.[50]

Intent on portraying himself as a poised public leader, Delany manifests this sort of personal emotionalism only rarely in his letters. Mostly, as in a letter to Douglass of 20 May 1848 from Cincinnati, he puts his emotions to the service of the larger aims of his tour. In this letter, portions of which I have already considered, Delany praises Cincinnati's black entrepreneurs, points to the limits of Gilmore's high school, and angrily notes the existence of a separate black cemetery. Through all this Delany presents himself as an observer concerned primarily with a measured recording of critical observations. The tone shifts dramatically, however, in the concluding portion of the letter, when he refers to recent news from Covington, Kentucky. Delany tells of how a particular slave family—a mother, father, and twenty-month-old child—had been sold to a slave trader, who planned to keep the child while selling the parents "down the river." Learning of the impending separation, the parents, in a move anticipating the more famous Margaret Garner case of 1856, decide to act. With his daughter's recent death no doubt informing the urgency of the account, Delany describes the events as they unfolded in a "*slave-prison.*"

> The frantic and heroic mother—God bless her! asked her husband for his pocket-knife, which was very small—cut the throat of her child— held her neck to her husband while he deliberately cut her throat— then—O! yes, then like a man and a hero, deliberately cut his own throat, but owing to the smallness of the knife, did not succeed in quite taking his own life. A noble woman!—more deserving of fame than the Queen of the Amazons, or a Semaramis—worthy, thrice worthy to be associated in history with the noble wife of Asdrubal!—Most noble man!—a Virginius!—the manly and heroic deed that thou hast perpetrated shall live in the heart of every true friend of humanity and lover of liberty!

Though the range of references preserves Delany's status as elite historian of the "invisible" reality of slavery, the emotional pitch suggests an investment in the slaves' act of resistance, an act that makes his recurrent calls for elevation among the free blacks seem mundane, if not irrelevant.[51]

The emotional pitch also suggests Delany's awareness that in celebrating acts of (self-)violence, he is violating the spirit of moral-suasion philosophy. And so at the end of his meditation on the heroism of this slave family, he turns to collaborative rhetoric. After attacking slave traders as "infamous dealers in human flesh [who] shall only be remembered to be despised and derided," he offers a two-sentence appeal to Douglass (and readers of the *North Star*), which stands as a single short paragraph: "Do you call this severity! 'Oppression maketh man mad!' "[52] The adducing of a paraphrased line from Robert Browning's *Luria* (1846) suggests that Delany fears he has lost his equanimity here, and so he recovers himself, in elite fashion, through citation. But perhaps the full implication of these lines is that anyone who faults the slave parents or Delany's enthusiastic celebration of them has failed to see that it was the slave system itself that produced such bloody resistance in the first place. Viewed thus, the Browning quote can be regarded as a sop for the timid, a rationalization of emotions and actions that, Delany makes clear, are in no need of apology.

Through his recourse to the experiential and personal, Delany shows how white racist institutions — social, economic, legal — work to undermine the goals of black elevation. The overall effect of Delany's travel reportage, surprisingly, as it goes against the grain of the announced purpose of the letters and the millennial spirit of "What Are the Colored People Doing for Themselves?," is to suggest that when everything is taken into account, blacks in the United States may well be facing too many obstacles to overcome. In some respects, then, the "Western tour" letters anticipate the emigrationist stance of Delany's 1852 *The Condition, Elevation, Emigration, and Destiny of the Colored People of the United States*, wherein he demonstrates the function of racist legal codes in keeping blacks from becoming "an essential part of the *ruling element* of the country in which they live."[53] With his scathing remarks on the slave prison and Ohio's black codes, Delany similarly points to the ways in which the law serves the ends of white racists.

Delany's most sustained analysis of the racist workings of the law appears in a lengthy letter to Douglass of 14 July 1848 discussing the Crosswait trial, which he attends as an observer at the U.S. Circuit Court of Detroit. Delany provides the facts of the case: A family of fugitive slaves, the Crosswaits, fled the Kentucky plantation of Francis Giltner in 1843 and took refuge in Marshall, Michigan, where they had become respectable and industrious members of the community. Thus when Giltner and his fugitive slave–hunting associates attempted to return the Crosswaits to Kentucky by force, a number of the community's whites came to the aid of their black neighbors. These whites were now the accused party of the lawsuit brought by Giltner, who was suing "for damages for payment by the [fugitive slave] law of '93." Presiding over the case was Judge John McLean, known for his antislavery views. Delany's "dispatch" focuses on McLean's betrayal of those views, as he reports what he regards as the proslavery logic of McLean's instructions to the jury: "It was not necessary to the offence that the person interfering with the rights of the slave-catcher should *know* that the person or persons so claimed were slaves. If the slave-catcher did but *assert* his intention, declaring that the persons so claimed were his property, . . . it was sufficient." In addition to reporting McLean's words, Delany subjects them to critical scrutiny: "In the position assumed by Judge McLean, common sense is set at naught, and philosophy at defiance. Though, says the Judge, a person aims at the rescue of a freeman from the hands of a kidnapper, he must be responsible for an unlawful interference between *master* and *slave*!" One of the rhetorical goals (and achievements) of the letter is to present Delany as more competent than McLean to make sense not only of the moral but also the legal issues surrounding the case.[54]

Delany concludes his analysis of the Crosswait case on a note of incredulity and outrage: "Truly, this is the law of the land—law by which you and I must abide!" Until this outburst, Delany for the most part has dispassionately described and analyzed the case. But by the end of the letter he seems to have sunk to a new level of despair at the workings of the U.S. legal system. After all, what is the point of black elevation in the United States when, as Delany puts it, "kidnapping, by the act of Congress and the decision of American judges, has been legalized"? For just this reason, then, despite the fact that one juror holds out against conviction, Delany asserts to readers of the *North Star*, "I declare that every colored man in the nominally free States . . . is reduced to abject slavery." That being the reality of the present situation, he proclaims his willingness to use force to resist such enslavement: "In an attempt, under such pretext, to seize upon the person of myself, I shall know no other law than that suggested by the first impulse of my nature—self-protection!" Because Douglass himself during the 1845–48 period had on occasion adopted such militant rhetoric, there is no reason for Delany to have thought that he was breaking with Douglass on the issue of the legitimacy of force to resist enslavement. Yet the charged rhetoric of this particular letter suggests that Delany saw himself as aggressively challenging black readers of the paper (and Douglass) to assent to doctrine more radical than the moral-suasion line of the *North Star*.[55]

In this respect it is worth remarking that though Delany here and elsewhere sustains his commitment to black elevation, he does so on his own distinctive terms. Indeed, over the course of his tour it can seem that he is pressing Douglass toward a position that would demand some form of action other than injunctions to blacks to adopt industry and frugality (as it can seem he is pressing free black readers of the *North Star* toward a position that would demand some "representative" leader other than Frederick Douglass). For what emerges from the letters is a sense that black self-help, in the larger context of a slave culture whose racism is sanctified by the law, risks helping to sustain that culture. Thus, rather than culminating in a millennial picture of the possibilities of social change, the letters of the tour build to a depiction of white lunacy and self-destructiveness that cannot but pose a challenge to the collaborative project of the moral-suasionist *North Star*.

In what would turn out to be the final dispatch of his tour, Delany, in a great letter to Douglass of 24 February 1849, describes the eventful journey to Pittsburgh of newly elected President Zachery Taylor. Delany, who himself is returning to Pittsburgh as he completes his circuit, comments on how "Gen. Taylor, of Florida-war, Indian murder, bloodhound, and Mexican-slaughter notoriety"—the appropriate president, he implies, for a nation of violent racists—"was to be in the city." On his way to Pittsburgh, Taylor "stops at all slaveholding intermediate ports," where he is greeted by mobs who wish to celebrate his greatness. As historical commentator, Delany observes that desires to glorify "military crusaders" led to the downfall of Rome, "that haughty, insolent empire and commonwealth," thereby implying that a similar fate may befall the United States. Shifting to a reportorial stance, he then presents a frenzied picture of such adulation as a form of national dismemberment and suicide: As white admirers rush to greet Taylor along the way, "at Memphis, Tenn., one man had his arm shot off; at Louisville, Ky., one man lost his life; at Cincinnati, there was one wounded; at Covington, Ky., one had his arm shot off; at Nashville, Ky., another lost an arm." The logical finale of the journey occurs in Virginia, where Taylor injures himself falling from a sleigh and thus has to cancel the rest of his itinerary. Delany gleefully reports on Taylor's fall: "I suppose at the moment when the old non-surrender was tumbling over the declivity, he felt more like *going to* ———! than 'giving the Mexicans hell!'" Whatever Taylor felt, he becomes the victim of his cannibalistic admirers, who consume all the food aboard his ship, "actually depriving the President of three meals." Delany offers an ironically understated summation of Taylor's abortive journey: "Thus did [Americans] not only show their high regard and love for the general, by killing several persons, but were well nigh killing him by starvation and dashing him to pieces."[56]

In contrast to the violence against self and others that we view here and in earlier letters, Delany presents his own travels, in an unusually romantic moment, as culminating in a mystical, spiritual apprehension of his likeness to God. Returning to Pittsburgh via the Allegheny Mountains after a stopover in Philadelphia, Delany, more in the mode of an eighteenth-century traveler than a mid-nineteenth-century one, provides a "picturesque" description of the mountains as "well worthy the pencil of the most accomplished artist." But then, in a move reminiscent of Emerson's shift in the opening to "Nature" from the picturesque to the spiritual, he abruptly experiences a different — a higher — order of consciousness:

> The tediousness [of traveling in the Allegheny mountains] is lost in contemplation of the scenery around. The soul may here expand in the magnitude of its nature, and soar to the extent of human susceptibility. Indeed, it is only in the mountains that I can fully appreciate my existence as a man in America, and my own native land. It is then and there my soul is lifted up, my bosom caused to swell with emotion, and I am lost in wonder at the dignity of my own nature. I see in the works of nature around me, the wisdom and goodness of God. I contemplate them, and conscious that he has endowed me with faculties to comprehend them, I then perceive the likeness I bear to him. What a being is man! — of how much importance! — created in the impress image of his Maker; and how debased is God, and outraged his divinity in the person of the oppressed colored people of America! The thunders of his mighty wrath must sooner or later break forth, with all of its terrible consequences and scourge this guilty nation, for the endless outrages and cruelty committed upon an innocent and unoffending people.[57]

An abolitionist mélange of the Bible, Shakespeare, Milton, Byron, and Emerson — and in their apocalyptic tone anticipating the conclusion of Stowe's *Uncle Tom's Cabin* — Delany's meditations from on high "signify" on a key trope of romantic travel writing: the sublime embrace of nature from the mountaintop, what Bruce Greenfield has termed "the 'discovery vision' trope." In much U.S. travel writing of the early to mid–nineteenth century, as Greenfield observes, an ascent to the mountain, "upon whose summit [the traveler] achieves an almost mystical state of identity with what he surveys," allows for a visionary embrace that enables the appropriation of landscape (of real estate) central to "Euro-American empire building."[58] What for the white explorer serves the ends of appropriation, for the black writer serves the ends of reappropriation, a taking back, via the gaze, of what white racist culture has wrested from its free and enslaved blacks—a connection to land, nation, and self. Delany, who in some of his other writings would disparage conventional Christianity, suggests here, from the elevated perspective of the Pisgah-like Alleghenies, a spiritual and nationalist underpinning to his antislavery work for the *North Star*, thereby spiritualizing, through an act of literalization, the "elevation" in black elevation.

But literal descent is inevitable, and the letter concludes with Delany's return to Pittsburgh and his renewed commitment to the work of black elevation. Though there is a compelling personal dimension in the spiritual aspect of the letter, the final paragraph suggests his continuing collaboration with Douglass: "I intend to hold a series of meetings among the colored citizens here, and shall write once more previous to my setting out for Rochester; where I shall give you an account of the state and condition of people and things about Pittsburgh." Whether Delany ever made his way to Rochester is unclear. As for his account of Pittsburgh's blacks, such a discussion eventually appeared in the *North Star*, not as a letter to Douglass but rather as a two-part essay on the "Colored Citizens of Pittsburgh."[59] Though we are left with an image in the final paragraph of Delany's ongoing black community–building efforts, no additional letters from Delany to Douglass are printed: the "Western tour for the *North Star*" has come to an end.

Division of Sentiment

The end of the tour heralded the end of the *North Star* collaborative project. Three months after Delany's last letter to Douglass on his tour, one week after printing two Delany pieces—"Colored Citizens of Cincinnati" and "Southern Customs"—and one week before printing the first of the two articles on Pittsburgh's black citizens, Douglass, in the issue of 29 June 1849, printed the following announcement:

After the present number, by a mutual understanding with our esteemed friend and coadjutor, M. R. DELANY, the whole responsibility

of editing and publishing the NORTH STAR, will devolve upon myself. . . . I am happy to state, that while the copartnership which has
subsisted between myself and M. R. DELANY, is now terminated, his
interest in the success of the enterprize remains unabated; and he will
continue to contribute by his pen, as formerly, to the columns of the
NORTH STAR; and do all, consistently with his other duties, towards
making the paper prosperous to its editor, and valuable to its readers.[60]

Though Douglass suggests that their collaboration will continue, the fact
is that he published only three additional Delany essays after this announcement, including the two essays on the blacks of Pittsburgh, which
he probably already had on hand.

Guided by their knowledge of Delany's and Douglass's public contro-
versies of the 1850s, most commentators assume that a dispute between
Douglass and Delany on major ideological issues led to the end of their
North Star collaboration.[61] Insofar as my interpretive reading of Delany's
letters posits an emerging split on the possibilities of black elevation in
the United States, I am participating in this proleptic interpretive position. Yet Delany's letters to Douglass, the materials printed in the North
Star surrounding the letters, and even Douglass's private writings reveal little *explicit* evidence of ideological tension between the coeditors.
It may well be, then, that Delany left the North Star for relatively un-
dramatic practical and personal reasons: a desire to be with his family, a
concern about the financial burden of the "enterprize," a renewed commitment to his medical career. And yet conflict clearly did arise between
Delany and Douglass, a conflict, I would suggest, that centered more on
the issue of black leadership than on strategies of black elevation. In
order best to take account of this conflict, we need to return to a crucial
moment that is both part of and distinct from Delany's tour: Douglass's
and Delany's participation at the September 1848 Colored National Convention in Cleveland.

As mentioned, over the course of his tour Delany typically sent Douglass a letter every two to three weeks. There is one significant exception to
this practice: two months elapsed between the letter he wrote Douglass
from Cleveland, posted on 24 July 1848, and the letter he wrote to the
"Star," posted from Philadelphia on 25 September 1848. Delany made
the North Star the addressee of the letter because at the time he was with
Douglass in Philadelphia attending a "most glorious" antislavery meeting. In his letter Delany refers to "my unflinching and faithful colleague,

Frederick Douglass," and in perhaps the most moving account of consensus in any of his letters, he describes the ascension to the podium of important black male leaders of the day, who, at least for the moment, seem in total harmony on their mission: "Here, before this meeting closed, Garnet, Douglass, Remond, and myself, all had the pleasure, for the first time in our lives, of meeting and shaking glad hands together! This was a meeting the remembrance of which can never be effaced. Truly, the God of Liberty, in this instance, was lavish with favors." Inspired by this grand collaborative moment, Delany hopefully proclaims: "With the master-grasp of Garnet, Remond, Douglass, Purvis, and others, who are nobly fighting side by side with us, upon his infernal throttle, with the host of noble men and women at their backs, with the feeble aid that I shall render, the monster now staggers, and must soon fall." Interestingly, Delany downplays his own role in the antislavery struggle, suggesting an ideal of community in which individual personality is subsumed to the larger cause. Linking black elevation to the revolutionary struggles in Europe, adducing the Haitian Republic as a positive example of black self-determination, and (true to form) attacking young blacks for not properly investing their money, Delany, buoyed by the millennial mood of the meeting, asserts that U.S. blacks can bring about the end of slavery should they have "but one mind, one purpose, one cause, and one determination—yea, and but one watch-word—Let my people go!"[62]

Douglass no doubt would have applauded this hopeful vision, for the millennial spirit of 1848 informs the *North Star*'s accounts of the antislavery conventions and meetings that Delany and Douglass jointly attended in the late summer and early fall of 1848. For example, in an August letter to John Dick on his and Douglass's participation at the Free Soil Convention in Buffalo, Delany relates how Douglass was praised "as one of the great instruments by which this event was brought about, when there went up *three cheers for Frederick Douglass*." Two weeks later, in a short piece, "In the Lecturing Field Again," Douglass describes holding a series of successful public meetings with Delany. In agreement, Douglass asserts, on the central Garrisonian doctrine of appealing "directly to all the better feelings of the human heart . . . in order to convert the whole nation," the coeditors then traveled to Cleveland to participate in the Colored National Convention—a convention where Delany and Douglass did clash on the issue of black elevation. Yet it was a clash that, on the evidence of Delany's aforementioned letter to the *North Star*, seems to have had little impact on their later meeting in

Philadelphia. Nor did it apparently have much of an impact on Douglass, who in his paper has this to say about the Cleveland convention: "Whilst there was manifested a variety of views, warmly set forth and insisted upon by the various speakers, there was a commendable toleration and forbearance towards each other . . . quite surpassing any convention we ever attended." [63]

The Cleveland convention of 6 September 1848 had been promoted for several months in the *North Star*. In a letter of June 1848, Delany announced the call for a "GREAT NATIONAL CONVENTION OF COLORED FREEMEN of the United States, [to] be held in CLEVELAND," signing it "by request of Illinois, Indiana, Michigan, and Ohio, the Western parts of New York and Pennsylvania being ready," but including only his own name: "M. R. Delany." [64] Yet despite Delany's input and the western setting, Douglass served as president of the convention. Delany's professed willingness to subsume himself to the cause was put to the test at the Cleveland convention, with Delany's resentment erupting not in immediately subsequent letters but nearly two years later in a letter to Samuel Ward on Douglass's failures as a black leader. Before turning to that letter, I first want to consider the issues that Douglass and Delany debated in Cleveland.

The transcript of the convention's "Proceedings," printed in the 29 September 1848 *North Star*, one week before Douglass resumed printing letters from Delany's tour, provides evidence that a difference of opinion had arisen between the coeditors on how best to pursue black elevation. Delany proposed a resolution excoriating blacks who accepted menial positions in white households, a declaration that risked insulting those (particularly women) pressed by circumstances to take such domestic jobs. According to the proceedings, one J. D. Patterson objected to Delany's proposal, arguing "that those who were in the editorial chair and others, not in places of servants, must not cast slurs upon those, who were in such places from necessity. He said, we know our position and feel it, — but when he heard the Doctor [Delany] say, that he would rather receive a telegraphic despatch that his wife and two children had fallen victims to a loathsome disease, than to hear that they had become the servant of any man, — he thought that he must speak." It was left to Douglass to mediate the dispute between Delany and Patterson. From his more dispassionate, presidential perspective, Douglass, as described in the proceedings, "took the floor. He thought as far as the speakers intimated that any useful labor was degrading — they were wrong. He would suggest a Resolution so as to suit both parties, which he thought might be done. . . . He said: Let us say what is necessary to be done, is honorable to do — and leave situations in which we are considered degraded, as soon as necessity ceases."[65]

Now, considerable evidence indicates that Douglass shared Delany's views on the risks of blacks taking on menial jobs in white households and that Delany shared Douglass's views on the ways in which pragmatic necessity can at times compel blacks to accept demeaning positions.[66] Given their eventual break and (perhaps most important) Delany's outburst in 1850 against Douglass as black leader, I would speculate that what was at stake in their debate on "menial" jobs was less the issue itself than the question of leadership style. Delany in all probability was annoyed by Douglass's intervention in his debate with Patterson, particularly as Douglass's lordly style helped to reinforce his status as the convention's preeminent black leader. Delany's fiery and rather abrasive rhetoric, offensive to the convention delegates, was no doubt offensive to Douglass as well, who generally chose to avoid such rhetoric for fear of undermining consensus and alienating possible white supporters.

Whatever resentments might have arisen from the conflict between Douglass and Delany, however, were contained by the convention itself, which endorsed resolutions on the subject of jobs that incorporated both Delany's and Douglass's perspectives into the "Proceedings": "That respectable industrial occupations, as mechanical trades, farming or agriculture, mercantile and professional business, wealth and education, being necessary for the elevation of the whites; therefore those attainments are necessary for the elevation of us"; "That the occupation of domestics and servants among our people is degrading to us as a class, and we deem it our bounden duty to discountenance such pursuits, except where necessity compels the person to resort thereto as a means of livelihood." The resolutions thus preserved in the "Proceedings" that sense of debate that I have been arguing is a constitutive element of the discourse of black elevation; the convention forged, rather than simply assumed, consensus. The forging of consensus may also be discerned in the delegates' resolution on black violence, which blended Delany's (and Garnet's) militant resolve on violence with Douglass's hesitant allowance of violence for self-defensive purposes. Somewhat ambiguously, the resolution urged free blacks to "use all justifiable means in aiding our enslaved brethren in escaping from the Southern Prison House of Bondage." (Delany had proposed a resolution, which was defeated, that blacks should attempt to master the "science" of "military tactics.")[67]

Douglass's keynote speech, "An Address to the Colored People of the United States," also attempted to forge consensus. Like Delany in his "Western tour" letters, Douglass in the "Address" conceives of black elevation in the North as a way of helping the slaves in the South: "It is more than a mere figure of speech to say, that we are as a people, chained together." And like Delany, he calls on free blacks to "dispense with finery" and to "educate your children." But a large emphasis of the speech, which goes somewhat against the grain of Delany's letters of the period, is to advise blacks to work pragmatically toward their elevation by adopting whenever possible a policy of racial color blindness (even as Douglass takes pains to point out that such will not always be possible): "Act with all men without distinction of color. By so acting, we shall find many opportunities for removing prejudices and establishing the rights of all men. — We say, avail yourself of *white* institutions, not because they are white, because they afford a more convenient means of improvement."[68] In several of his early *North Star* letters, Delany put forth similar ideas, but by late 1848 he had begun to argue, more often than not, for the impossibility of avoiding white racism and thus for the importance of a prideful black self-sufficiency. Whether Delany at the time of the convention dissented from Douglass's "Address" is impossible to say. But it is worth noting that though Douglass's speech was co-signed by the convention's various committee chairs — Henry Bibb and several others — it was not signed by Delany, who chaired the Business Committee.

In the 15 September 1848 *North Star*, Douglass printed a squib announcing that henceforth he will sign his editorials with his initials and that Delany "will probably append his initials in articles written by himself." As Douglass explained, "This arrangement is adopted solely to gratify our readers, and not because there is the slightest division of sentiment between ourselves." The timing of the announcement, along with its general defensiveness, would suggest that Douglass was not being completely candid with his readers, though I would caution against reading too much significance into the announcement, particularly in light of Delany's rapturous remarks on Douglass in his letter of 25 September 1848. Delany continued to speak well of Douglass through 1848 and 1849, and he continued to contribute his writings to the *North Star*, though only sporadically after the announcement that he was stepping down as coeditor. As for Douglass, in 1849 he turned his attention more to Samuel Ward and Henry Highland Garnet. In the summer of 1849 he debated Ward on the nature of the Constitution, taking the Garrisonian position that it was a proslavery document; and on several occasions in 1849, culminating in an extended letter in the 17 August 1849 *North Star*, he attacked Garnet for advocating black emigration. Viewing these exchanges from the sidelines, Delany addressed the contention for power and leadership that he saw as lying behind these debates, arguing in a letter to the *North Star* that such contention was not for him and was hurtful for black people: "I detest that dog-in-the-manger ambition. . . . No, thank God, I have a different object and higher aim in view—the elevation of our race—I care not by whom it be effected so that it be properly done." As for his own participation in such efforts, Delany stated, "I have determined to remain in the seclusion of obscurity."[69]

But how well suited was Delany for "obscurity"? Victor Ullman remarks that by the late 1840s Delany "was an ambitious man and had become accustomed to leadership."[70] As coeditor of the *North Star*, however, he was suddenly cast in Douglass's shadow; and at the 1848 Cleveland convention he would have been especially aware of his subordinate status to Douglass, not only because he was relegated to a subcommittee but because he lacked Douglass's magisterial style as well. If Delany continued to harbor desires for leadership, this would have been difficult to detect, given his 1848 celebrations of Garnet, Remond, and Douglass and his 1849 avowal of his wish for "obscurity." And yet, in Delany's repeated articulations of his outsider status, one senses a growing rage, repressed over a nearly two-year period, at Douglass's commanding position as representative black leader. How else can we explain the excesses of his letter to Samuel R. Ward of 13 June 1850?

To sketch in the background of the letter: In the spring of 1850 Douglass, who several times in 1849 had cordially debated Ward on the nature of the Constitution, published a series of letters, including an "extra" edition of the *North Star*, attacking Ward for speaking at an antislavery rally in a Philadelphia church where blacks, according to the handbill, were denied seating in the lower pews. For Douglass, who had fought against discriminatory seating in New England trains and was continuing the fight against race-based institutions, Ward's putative complicity in these seating arrangements played into the hands of "the revilers and slanderers of our people."[71]

Though Douglass's anti-Ward rhetoric was quite severe, Ward remained silent on the controversy. It was Delany who saw something insidious in Douglass's attack on Ward, and in a letter to Ward, printed in the 27 June 1850 *North Star*, he berated Douglass for what he portrayed as his divisive and well nigh pathological attempts to advance his ambitions at the expense of "his people." Delany begins his letter to "MY DEAR FRIEND" by declaring that he cannot believe Ward would actually have capitulated to such a segregationist request, and even if he did, "it must have been 'an error of the head and not of the heart.'" Thus he argues that even if Douglass's charges are true, he should apologize for the ways in which his "rash manner" of attack would have given comfort to the (white) enemy: "A people wholly oppressed, all making struggling efforts for liberty and elevation among their oppressors, have no time to spend in personal hostility towards each other, especially among their leaders. *We cannot afford to be divided—it costs us too much.*" Delany then praises Ward for "bearing a living representation of those divine-like philosophers who originated mysteries in Ethiopia" and for conducting one "of the only two existing secular newspapers devoted to the elevation of our race."[72]

Two years earlier, in the course of his tour, Delany had implicitly played off his own "pure" blackness against Douglass's mixed blood by commenting on whites' praise of Henry Bibb's antislavery lectures in Dayton, Ohio: "Whatever merit there is in Mr. Bibb, they have always found it very applicable to attribute it to his *whiteness*—that is, they say that his talents emanate from the preponderance of *white* blood in him. This it will puzzle them to say of me!"[73] The veiled suggestion here is that Douglass, unlike Delany, similarly is acclaimed for his "whiteness." In this respect, the references to Ward's blackness (his Africanness) and newspaper work in Delany's June 1850 letter, given his pride in his blackness and his former newspaper work, suggest that he has come to identify with Ward as an "Africo-American" who has claims to black leadership greater than those of the mulatto Frederick Douglass.

Because of his personal investment in Ward's position, Delany's letter to Ward reads like a vituperative letter from Ward to Douglass—the letter Delany wished Ward had written. Comparing Douglass's attack on Ward to "the uncivilized, vulgar attacks of the Mississippi ruffian Foote, of the U.S. Senate, . . . upon the hoary sage of Missouri—Benton," Delany warns that Douglass's "personal ambition" could ultimately undermine the revolutionary struggle for black elevation in the United States. He rhetorically asks: "Supposing Washington, Warren, Hancock,

Jefferson, and other great men, leaders among their people, had ceased their mutual counsel and co-operation . . . what would have become of the common people, both civil and military, and the cause of American liberty?" Having invoked the Revolution, Delany declares that Douglass may prove to be a false revolutionary—a type of Benedict Arnold. Like the ambitious Hungarian revolutionary Arthur Görgëy, who, failing to wrest leadership from Lajos Kossuth, "betrays Hungary into the grasp of the enemy," Douglass similarly would be willing to betray blacks, Delany asserts, to attain his desires for leadership. (This is precisely the charge Delany will be making against Douglass in 1853 for championing Stowe's *Uncle Tom's Cabin*.) As for himself, Delany maintains that he simply possesses a disinterested concern for the elevation of his people. Restating the sentiments of his letter of October 1849, he avers, "I had rather remain in obscurity as I am, than attain such a position at the expense of another's destiny."[74] It does not take too much interpretive ingenuity to conclude that the informing animus behind Delany's letter is his resentful belief that Douglass's ascent to prominence has occurred at Delany's expense.

In his response to Delany, Douglass comes off as the more measured and community-concerned writer. Pointing to the contradiction inherent in Delany's act of writing a vitriolic letter on the divisive effects of vitriol, Douglass states, "One must be struck, on reading [Delany's] letter, with the appropriateness of his advice, if applied to himself." He then instructs Delany on the value of "difference of opinion" and "free expression" among friends; he mildly expresses his displeasure at the way Delany compares him to Foote (while ignoring the more tendentious comparison to Görgëy); he provides a short history of his high regard for Ward; and he remarks on his recent dispute with Ward (and by implication with Delany): "If we differ with him now, it is not that we *love him less*, but freedom and equality more." Perhaps chastened by Douglass's remarks, Delany, in an apologetic public letter printed two weeks later, praises Douglass's "talents and ability" and reasserts his commitment to "our people at large and the cause in which you have embarked."[75]

And so we conclude our examination of Douglass, Delany, and the *North Star* on a tenuous note of consensus, with discordant rumblings on the politics of black representative identity being written off as mere misunderstandings in the larger collaborative project of black elevation in the United States. These rumblings can be discerned in one additional letter that Delany wrote Douglass in 1850, an attack on Lewis Woodson for appealing to white rather than black witnesses to settle a dispute with the New York black editor Thomas Van Rensselaer. In addition to the racial partisanship exhibited in this letter, it may also be taken as a sign of Delany's unhappiness that his former mentor was now working with Douglass to form an American League of Colored Laborers.[76] Though in the abstract Delany would have applauded a program that sought to educate blacks in the industrial arts, he must have resented Woodson's decision to link himself with the man whom he viewed, at least at the time he wrote the letter, as willing to betray the cause of blacks to further his ambition for leadership.

Delany might also have been disturbed by Woodson's apparent abandonment of his black separatist position in favor of Douglass's integrationist views. Although in his "Western tour" letters Delany for the most part seems uninterested in pursuing the sort of rural separatism that Woodson advocated in the late 1830s, in a July 1848 letter to Douglass from Cleveland, Delany raises (and avoids) the issue of black separatism in its most radical form: emigration from the United States. In this letter, Delany describes his visit to Oberlin College, where he is favorably impressed by an African woman student, "one of the Amistad captives, preparing to act as a missionary in her own dear native land, among her benighted brethren." He concludes the letter with an offhand remark on his evening's plans in Cleveland: "Tonight, Mr. Fitzgerald holds an emigration meeting among his colored brethren. I shall be there; and to-morrow leave for Rochester."[77] Subsequent letters have nothing to say about this particular meeting or emigration in general. In 1854 Delany would preside over the most important black emigration convention of the antebellum period. The trajectory from his exploratory interest in emigration to his advocacy of emigration, in the face of Douglass's shrewd appropriation of Stowe's *Uncle Tom's Cabin* to mount his strenuous opposition, will be the subject of the next chapter.

Chapter 2

A Nation within a Nation

Debating *Uncle Tom's Cabin* and Black Emigration

 In a much discussed moment near the end of *Uncle Tom's Cabin*, the light-skinned "black" George Harris, after having spent nine years away from the United States, chooses to embrace what he terms "an African *nationality*." He maintains that those of "the African race" have "peculiarities"—domestic attachments, lack of social competitiveness—that promise to bring forth in Liberia an "essentially . . . Christian" nation far superior to the nominally Christian United States. For this to occur, he claims, that nation must have "a tangible, separate existence of its own" on "the shores of Africa." Harris thus links race to place in ways similar to the Liberian colonizationists, who sought to remove blacks from the United States, even as he distances himself from the racism of the American Colonization Society by theorizing that God's providential hand lies behind Liberia's founding. But the fact that many of the novel's former slaves end up going to Africa suggests that Stowe uses George Harris as a mouthpiece to forward her own colonizationist views that blacks belong in Africa, whites in America.[1]

Yet Harris makes his back-to-Africa argument in the larger context of a social critique of the failure of the United States to live up to its political ideals and moral obligations, particularly given the crucial role African Americans have played in the development of the nation. He declares: "We *ought* to be free . . . to rise by our individual worth, without any consideration of caste or color; and they who deny us this right are false to their own professed principles of human equality. We ought, in particular, to be allowed *here*." Harris's rhetoric is similar to that used by Douglass and Delany in the *North Star*, and it is of a piece with the rhetoric Douglass would continue to use during the 1850s to challenge colonizationists and emigrationists alike. Stowe herself, in a rarely commented-upon moment in the closing pages of the novel, would also seem to have distanced herself from George Harris's African nationalism when she lists, "on the authority of Professor C. E. Stowe," a number of former slaves who have gone on to live economically successful lives in the United States. These enterprising African Americans, she declares, testify to "the self-denial, energy, patience, and honesty, which the slave has exhibited in a state of freedom." Rather than using her examples to support colonizationism, she enlists them to show that blacks have the capacity, particularly when treated in Christian fashion, to rise in the United States to "highly respectable stations in society. . . . Douglas [*sic*] and [Samuel] Ward among editors, are well known instances." By adducing on the last page of the novel the example of Douglass in particular, Stowe, it is worth underscoring, links herself with the African American who, for the past decade or so, had most passionately contested the notion that blacks "belong" in Africa.[2]

This brief discussion of race and nation in *Uncle Tom's Cabin* suggests that the novel remains conflicted on these interrelated issues. On the one hand, Stowe develops providential and racialist arguments for encouraging U.S. blacks to "return" to Africa; on the other hand, she proffers moral-reform ideology to suggest that blacks can and should prosper in the United States. Given the novel's own conflicted allegiances, it is not surprising that the response of literate free blacks of the North was equally conflicted. Outraged and despairing over the Fugitive Slave Law, a number of blacks, most notably Frederick Douglass, regarded *Uncle Tom's Cabin*, as Richard Yarborough puts it, "as a godsend destined to mobilize white sentiment against slavery just when resistance to the southern forces was urgently needed." Many other blacks, however, most notably Martin Delany, were resentful that such massive cultural authority was bestowed on a white woman who, so they argued, was at heart a racist colonizationist.³ But ironically, even as Delany attacked Stowe's colonizationism, he set forth the racialized view that blacks should consider leaving the United States through a program of voluntary emigration. For Douglass, who endorsed Stowe's moral reformism, Delany's criticisms of Stowe and his development of an emigrationist politics were shortsighted and contradictory; for Delany, Douglass's embrace of a novel (and a nation) that ultimately wanted to rid itself of blacks revealed the fatal consequences of a politics of accommodation.

In short, some of the key debates of the early to mid-1850s on race and nation were spawned by the African American response to *Uncle Tom's Cabin*. Stowe's novel worked with and contributed to what Floyd Miller characterizes as "the basic instability of black ideologies at this time." According to Miller, this instability manifested itself in the 1850s in the debates between black emigrationists (such as Delany) and antiemigrationists (such as Douglass), particularly in the way the positions of these opposed groups "often intersected and overlapped." Delany and Douglass, for example, proclaimed in the early 1850s that blacks in the United States were "a nation, in the midst of a nation" (Douglass), "a nation within a nation" (Delany).⁴ Douglass, who viewed the black "nation" within the United States as the result of whites' racial prejudices, persisted in underscoring the importance of black newspapers, conventions, and self-help as pragmatic means toward improving the situation of African Americans. In contrast, by 1852 Delany sought to empower that black "nation" by locating it outside the boundaries of the United States. In his advocacy of black emigration, which he presented, as opposed to colonizationism, as black-led and a matter of free choice, Delany pushed the debate on blacks' condition in the United States beyond the stark binarism of Liberian colonizationism versus black elevation by imagining for African Americans possibilities in a third place that was within the Americas but not a part of the United States — Central and South America and the Caribbean.

My focus in this chapter, a study of the intersection of literary reception and cultural (re)action, will be on the ways in which Delany's and Douglass's conflicting responses to Stowe's novel came to inform their writings and politics of the 1852–55 period. Douglass and Delany debated Stowe's novel partly because they had a principled disagreement over its politics and partly because each wanted to be the main voice for the black community. Their differences fed on themselves on intertwining personal and political levels, serving to drive the former coeditors further apart and into opposing camps. Douglass continued to lay claim to black leadership through his representative status as the embodiment of African Americans' possibilities in the United States. Delany, over the course of his early 1850s debates with Douglass, increasingly came to lay his own claim to black leadership through a very different sort of representative identity: as the mystical and biological embodiment of *black* possibility in the Americas. I will turn first to Delany, whose *Condition, Elevation, Emigration, and Destiny of the Colored People of the United States*, published in April 1852, one month after the book publication of *Uncle Tom's Cabin*, helped to initiate Delany's and Douglass's debates on *Uncle Tom's Cabin* and black emigration.

The Conditions of Emigration

Central to binary constructions of the conflicts between Delany and Douglass is the notion that Delany the Black Separatist distrusted whites much more than Douglass the Accommodationist.[5] Yet in 1849 Delany expressed his delight with (and actually took credit for) the decision of the white philanthropist Charles Avery to build and endow a coeducational college for Pittsburgh's blacks. On a more personal level, Delany remained indebted to the white doctors who had taken him on as an apprentice and, in 1850, wrote letters of support for his applications to medical schools.[6] Although he was refused admission to numerous schools because of his race, his letters of support from the doctors — and from several white ministers testifying to his moral character — convinced Dean Oliver Wendell Holmes to admit Delany to the winter 1850–51 term at Harvard Medical School.

Delany's large-scale disillusionment with white abolitionists occurred in the fall of 1850, the result of the near simultaneity of the passage of the Compromise of 1850, with its infamous Fugitive Slave Law, and his horrific experience at Harvard. Addressing an antislavery meeting in Allegheny on 30 September 1850, twelve days after the passage of the Fugitive Slave Law, Delany declared that he would use violence to keep his wife and children from being taken into slavery. He justified his actions in terms of the nation's political ideals: "Whatever ideas of liberty I may have, have been received from reading the lives of your revolutionary fathers. I have therein learned that a man has a right to defend his castle with his life, even unto the taking of life." Shortly after delivering this speech, Delany set off for Massachusetts with his letters of recommendation, was admitted to Harvard, and there experienced what historian Floyd Miller has termed "the event that was probably most directly responsible for intensifying [his] alienation." In Massachusetts, a hotbed of resistance to the Fugitive Slave Law, the majority of students at "liberal" Harvard petitioned the medical faculty to dismiss Delany and two other black students because, as the students put it, "we deem the admission of blacks to the medical Lectures highly detrimental to the interests, and welfare, of the Institution of which we are members, calculated alike to lower its reputation in this and other parts of the country."[7] Guided by advice from the faculty, Holmes informed the black students that they would have to withdraw at the end of the winter term. As a result, Delany fell short of obtaining his degree. He left Boston in March 1851, three months before Stowe's novel began to appear serially in the *National Era*.

Delany's activities over the next year or so before the April 1852 publication of *Condition* are difficult to document. What emerges from the surviving evidence is a picture of a peripatetic man looking for a focus for his interests and skills. During this period he lectured in New York and Ohio on comparative anatomy. In late 1851 and early 1852 he resided in New York City, where he attempted to obtain a patent for an engine component enabling trains to haul freight up steep grades. Enlisting Douglass's friend, the physician James McCune Smith, to forward his cause, he soon learned that blacks could not legally obtain patents. Meanwhile, even as he was pursuing the patent, Delany was elected mayor of Nicaragua's Greytown.[8]

According to Delany's contemporary biographer Frances Rollin, in 1851 David J. Peck, a friend of Delany's, journeyed to Greytown, where he helped to organize an election that unseated colonialist whites and brought the indigenous peoples back into power. But how democratic could the election have been if a noncitizen like Delany could learn, early in 1852, while still in New York, that he had been "duly chosen and elected mayor of Greytown, civil governor of the Mosquito reservation, and commander-in-chief of the military forces of the province!" If such an election had in fact taken place, we would have to assume that Peck and his friends, and not the Miskito Indians, had made up the bulk of the electorate. Delany nonetheless decided to accept the government position, though his efforts over the next eight months to convince African American leaders to accompany him to Greytown came to naught.[9]

Several things are worth highlighting about Delany's Central American "involvement." First, the account of Nicaraguan politics Delany offered to Rollin, however truthful, has an air of wish-fulfillment fantasy in the way it places him at center stage of a government at odds with the United States during a time when he felt especially disempowered in the nation of his birth. Second, there is a fundamental elitism underlying his plans for governance. Rather than turning to Nicaragua's native peoples for help in developing the government, he wanted to import African Americans with the education and skills he believed necessary to run a successful state. Third, a colonizing, or imperial, desire guides his Central American vision, one not so very different from that of the filibusterer William Walker. One of the significant differences between Delany and Walker, of course, was that Walker served the proslavery interests that Delany fiercely contested. Another difference was that the militaristic Walker actually went to Greytown, whereas Delany remained in the United States. That Delany should have done so during this time suggests that in 1852 a certain hesitation, or conflict, was inherent in his politics of emigrationism. Despite the passage of the Fugitive Slave Law, his experience at Harvard, his failure to obtain a patent, and his Central American ambition, Delany may not have given up hope for blacks in the United States. It is this conflicted sense of possibility and disillusionment, rather than his immediate response to Stowe's *Uncle Tom's Cabin*, that informs and complicates the emigrationist politics of *The Condition, Elevation, Emigration, and Destiny of the Colored People of the United States*.

Rollin reported that Delany wrote *Condition* over eight months, between 1851 and 1852. In the text itself Delany claimed to have written the book in less than one month while in New York City. Whether written in one month or eight, the simple chronological facts argue against reading the book as a "response" to *Uncle Tom's Cabin* — Stowe's book was published late in March 1852, only several weeks before Delany's, and the African colonizationist chapters did not appear in the *National Era* until March and April of that year.[10] Though Delany was no doubt aware of the growing popularity of the serialized novel, I would suggest that if any particular writer was on his mind while writing *Condition*, it was Frederick Douglass. Setting forth a politics of black emigration that drew on the ideas of such notable theorists as Paul Cuffe, Samuel Cornish, Lewis Woodson, Henry Bibb, Henry Highland Garnet, and many others, the "obscure" Delany attempts in this text not only to propose ways of improving the lot of blacks throughout the Americas but also to redefine and redirect Douglass's black-elevation agenda.[11] He does so by relocating the black nationalist project of self-help from within the borders of the ever-expanding United States to the larger terrain of the Americas, specifically Central and South America and the Caribbean, and by emphasizing the ways in which race challenges the very idea of the bordered nation.

"Sincerely Dedicated to the American People, North and South, By Their Most Devout, and Patriotic Fellow-Citizen, The Author," *Condition* at the outset has nothing to say about black emigration.[12] Instead, Delany announces that his book intends to inform whites and (especially) blacks about the true situation of blacks in the United States circa 1852. Not only are blacks enslaved in the South, but for all intents and purposes they remain de facto slaves in the North, occupying "the very same position politically, religiously, civilly and socially (with but few exceptions) as the bondman occupies in the slave States" (14). In fact, Delany argues, freemen in the North constitute "a nation within a nation" (12), for "there are no people . . . so poor and miserable" (39) as America's free blacks. In a key chapter of the text's first half, "Means of Elevation," Delany rather bluntly places a good deal of blame for the free blacks' misery on the blacks themselves. He paternalistically berates black men for "permitting their mothers, sisters, wives, and daughters, to do the drudgery and menial offices of other men's wives and daughters" (43); and he excoriates blacks in general for their passivity. The challenge facing the free blacks who want to elevate themselves in a market culture, he maintains, is to become producers — in business, science, agricultural, the arts, "and all other attainments" (45). And Delany insists, in what may well be an attack on Stowe's emerging cultural authority, that blacks should attempt to improve their situation through their own efforts, rather than through the assistance of whites, who "are not . . . their representatives" (10).

Though suspicious of whites, Delany nonetheless suggests early on in *Condition* that black elevation can and should be pursued in the United States: "Here is our nativity, and here have we the natural right to abide and be elevated through the measures of our own efforts" (48). Blacks have a "right" to pursue such elevation because they have contributed as much to the development of the nation as have whites and thus are entitled to what Robert M. Kahn terms "regime-level protections of citizenship." To support this claim, Delany provides a massive compilation of evidence attesting to blacks' commitments to U.S. ideals and institutions and attesting as well, considering the circumstances of their racial oppression, to their genius in literature, science, and business. Among

the numerous achievers he celebrates are the relatively well known—
Phillis Wheatley, Benjamin Banneker—and the relatively obscure—the
lumber merchant Stephen Smith and the daguerreotypist J. Presley Ball.
It is noteworthy that Delany instructs his readers of this long section of
Condition that many of the successful blacks he describes "are those of
pure and unmixed African blood" (87). He emphasizes such "purity" not,
as would be the case in his 1854 "Political Destiny," because he wishes
to make any special claims about the superiority of black blood but because he wants to make clear, in response to the "scientific" racialists of
the period, that blacks are as enterprising and intelligent as whites. He
points to the politics of his rhetoric: "The equality of the African with
the European race, establishes the equality of every person intermediate
between the two races" (87).[13]

With his overview of "representative" successful blacks and his racial
egalitarianism, Delany makes a powerful case for blacks' rights and abilities to rise in the United States. But then an odd and arguably contradictory moment occurs in the text, about three-quarters of the way through,
that seems to turn against what we have read so far: Delany calls on African Americans seeking to elevate themselves to emigrate to Central and
South America or to the Caribbean Islands, where (he states) blacks constitute the ruling classes. Coming at this late point in the text, his call for
black emigration, rather than standing free and clear as an untroubled
manifesto, gives the book a conflicted feel, reminiscent of Crèvecoeur's
Letters of an American Farmer, where the author withheld his accounts
of the horrors of slavery and revolution until nearly the end of his text
and then, in introducing these unsettling realities, seemed to turn against
his earlier idealizing chapters.[14] So Delany now seems to turn against
the sense of possibility implicit in his overview of African Americans'
achievements by presenting the Fugitive Slave Law, hitherto unmentioned in the text, as having brought about the "National Disfranchisement of Colored People" (147). Seeing no immediate hope for the repeal
of the Compromise of 1850 and thus no hope for blacks in the United
States, Delany contemplates, as did Crèvecoeur in the 1770s, flight from
a nation he claims once to have loved: "What can we do?—What shall we
do? . . . Shall we fly, or shall we resist?" (156). From Delany's perspective,
flight, or emigration, unlike colonization, is a voluntary form of black resistance having a typological analogue in the flight of the biblical Jews
from Egypt (and the Puritan emigration from England).[15] The goal of such

a movement would be to destroy slavery by giving rise to a powerful black nation, a city upon a hill, as it were, whose existence would testify to both the immorality and the economic misguidedness of U.S. slave culture.

Drawing on the millennial rhetoric of Manifest Destiny, Delany argues that the blacks of the United States specifically, and those of Central and South America generally, are a chosen people whose destiny it is to bring forth a great civilized nation in the Americas. In making this utopian claim, Delany emerges as somewhat more of a racialist than the Enlightenment universalist of *Condition*'s first half. As he takes care to show, however, his emphasis on color has much to do with whites' legal practices in the United States, which, he explains, contribute to a "corruption of blood. . . , that process, by which a person is *degraded* and deprived of rights common to the enfranchised citizen" (154). Delany hopes to resist such degradation by relocating U.S. blacks, particularly those "of great worth and talents" (206), to a place where they will have a central role to play in a nation's social and political institutions. As opposed to his earlier biblical insistence "that 'God has made of one blood all the nations'" (36), Delany, in linking race to place, argues for a "familial" oneness among the "colored" peoples of Central and South America, who, he maintains, are "our brethren—because they are precisely the same people as ourselves" (181).

As with his putative Nicaragua governorship, Delany, in his desire to encourage emigration among African American elites of *"intelligence"* (161), seems deliberately unconcerned about the fact that particular countries have particular local histories and cultural practices that may make them resistant to his plans to develop in these regions "a glorious Union" (182) of black states.[16] He also ignores the fact that the populations of countries of Central and South America consist of a variety of peoples of color—native-born Indians, such as the Miskitos of Nicaragua; black Africans; and, of course, the Creoles resulting from the historical mix of Indians, kidnapped Africans, and white imperialists and enslavers. Why would these peoples want to be governed, or guided, by African Americans? Delany's omission of these resistant realities suggests that at this point in his career his emigrationism remains strictly utopian. Central and South America, en masse, emerge in *Condition* as a symbolic place that promises to put into practice the egalitarian ideals of the American Revolution that he celebrates in the text's first half.

Delany's utopianist emigrationism thus allows him to be simultaneously ideally inside and practically outside "America," with the irony being that his project threatens to reduplicate the European "founding" of America, with all that it portended for natives and other subjugated groups. As Delany advises his readers, "Go not with an anxiety of political aspirations; but go with the fixed intention — as Europeans come to the United States — of cultivating the soil, entering into the mechanical operations, keeping of shops, carrying on merchandise, trading on land and water, improving property — in a word — to become the producers of the country, instead of the consumers" (187). Should blacks have any doubts about the ethics or prospects of such a project, Delany reassures them, in an echo (or appropriation) of contemporaneous Manifest Destiny rhetoric, "We can see the 'finger of God' in all this" (172).

With his mystical insistence that the destiny of U.S. blacks lies not in a return to Africa (as the colonizationists would have it) but in developing what Paul Gilroy terms "an autonomous, black nation state" in Central and South America, Delany works with and against two major speeches of the late 1840s on blacks' "destiny": Garnet's "The Past and Present Condition and the Destiny of the Colored Race" (1848) and Douglass's "The Destiny of Colored Americans" (1849). Garnet and Douglass both argue, as Delany does in *Condition*, that there appears to be something providential about the fact that blacks, in Garnet's words, "have been transplanted in a foreign land" and thus something unproductive about yearning for a return to "our [African] fatherland." But whereas Delany's providential vision includes the southern regions of the Americas, Garnet and Douglass, in their 1840s speeches, like Delany in the first half of *Condition*, insist on the United States as the proper home for those blacks who, Garnet states, were "planted here." "America is my home, my country, and I have no other," he proclaims, while Douglass similarly asserts, "*We are here*, and here we are likely to be. . . . This is *our* country." Central to Garnet's organicist metaphor of transplantation is an optimistic vision of renewal, growth, and entanglement. As he remarks, blacks have "grown with their oppressors, as the wild ivy entwines around the trees of the forest," to the point that mutual dependency, even "love," can be said to characterize the relationship between the two races — races that are destined to become "*a mixed race*." Douglass likewise argues that it is "a settled point that the destiny of the colored man is bound up with that of the white people of this country; be the destiny of the latter what it may." [17]

In the final chapters of *Condition* Delany revises Garnet's and Douglass's views of transplantation and racial entanglement to suggest the possibility of perpetual transplantation and thus perpetual growth and renewal through acts of (racial) disentanglement. Dependent on a mystical "Pan-African-American" vision of blacks' "destiny" in the Americas, Delany's ideas on transplantation draw as well on a Lamarckian sense of the heritability of habits and attitudes (the heritability of *condition*) that informs his book throughout. Concerned that the degradation of blacks brought about by slavery in the South and racist practices in the North would be transmitted from generation to generation, thereby contributing to a perpetuity of degradation, Delany urges blacks to break the "system of regular submission and servitude, menialism, and dependence . . . [which] has become almost a physiological function of our system, an actual condition of our nature" (47–48).[18] Just as impoverished Irish and Germans have renewed themselves through transplantation to the United States, Delany argues, so blacks of the United States can renew themselves through transplantation to a more inclusive political and economic system. As he observes about the European immigrants, "Their physical condition undergoes a change, which in time becomes physiological, which is transmitted to the offspring" (207).

In the context of his Lamarckian arguments on generational transmission, there is a renewed urgency near the end of the book in Delany's injunctions to blacks to adopt a work ethic that will help to elevate not only themselves but also future generations. As the actual specifics of his emigrationist project begin to move into the background in the text's final few pages, Delany, as in the letters of his "Western tour," berates his black readers, in a somewhat genteel (and Jeremiadic) manner, for their love of fashion, their lack of "good Penmanship" (193), and their failure to educate and motivate themselves. He places a special emphasis on the need for black women to aspire to something more than menial or domestic work. "No people are ever elevated above the condition of their *females*," he writes, "hence, the condition of the *mother* determines the condition of the child" (199). True to his call for blacks to become "a business people" (193), he yearns for the day when women, rather than "transcribing in their black books, recipes for *Cooking* . . . [are] making the transfer of *Invoices of Merchandise*" (196).

Deeply concerned about the psychophysiological condition of oppressed blacks in the United States, Delany in *Condition* calls for a black nationalist consciousness and emigration program that promises to revitalize blacks' condition in the Americas. Yet he (disingenuously) concludes his text by playing down his own interest in pursuing a leadership position in any emigration movement that might ensue: "The writer is no 'Public Man,' in the sense in which this is understood among our people, but simply an humble individual" (201). As the conflicted utopianism of *Condition* suggests, one reason that Delany may have been reluctant to press his claims for leadership was that, like Douglass, he continued to believe there were possibilities for black elevation in the United States. In fact, in late 1851, while attending an emigration convention in Toronto organized by Henry Bibb, Delany advocated an antiemigrationist position; and in April 1852 he chaired a meeting in Philadelphia that endorsed resolutions urging blacks to continue to regard the United States as their nation of destiny. Significantly, the report of that meeting, which he prepared, appeared in the 29 April 1852 issue of *Frederick Douglass' Paper*.[19]

As conflicted as Delany may have been in *Condition* and as disinterested as he presents himself at the text's conclusion, he was stung by the harsh reviews the book received in the abolitionist press. His anger, which can seem disproportionate to what set it off, signaled his increasing awareness of the cultural authority granted to Stowe's *Uncle Tom's Cabin* at the expense of texts written by blacks. If he did not write *Condition* with Stowe immediately in mind, he certainly defended his book — and came to understand his own position in the cultural scene of the 1850s — in relation to Stowe (and Douglass's championing of Stowe). Delany conjoined *Condition* and *Uncle Tom's Cabin* in an angry reply to Oliver Johnson's review in the 29 April 1852 *Pennsylvania Freeman*. Johnson had attacked *Condition* for its emigrationism and suspicion of whites, paternalistically concluding, "We could wish that, for his own credit, and that of the colored people, it had never been published." For Delany, Johnson's condescending review revealed the hypocrisy of white abolitionists. As he maintained in a letter to Johnson printed in the 6 May 1852 *Pennsylvania Freeman*, the review betrayed a fear of black self-empowerment that "is in keeping with Mrs. Stowe's ridicule of Hayti, which you very adroitly avoid in your apology for the objectionable portion of her work." Disturbed by Johnson's reluctance to challenge Stowe's unsympathetic depiction of black revolutionism in San Domingue (or her colonizationism), Delany declared his contempt for and independence from Johnson and his ilk: "I therefore despise your sneers and defy your influence."[20]

In the *Liberator*, Garrison spoke more respectfully of *Condition*, allowing that "it contains many valuable facts and cogent appeals." But he remained troubled by its "tone of despondency" and its advocacy of emigration. Like Douglass, Garrison saw little difference between emigration and colonization, and thus he called on Delany to rethink his politics of disentanglement: "We are desirous of seeing neither white nor black republics, as such." Frustrated that Garrison hailed Stowe's colonization-ist novel while attacking his emigrationist treatise, Delany nonetheless wrote a temperate, albeit ironic, response to Garrison's criticisms: "I am not in favor of caste, nor a separation of the brotherhood of mankind, and would as willingly live among white men as black, if I had *an equal possession and enjoyment* of privileges. . . . But I must admit I have no hopes in this country — no confidence in the American people — with a *few* excellent exceptions — therefore, I have written as I have done."[21]

Meanwhile, Delany was wondering what Douglass would make of *Condition* in *Frederick Douglass' Paper*. But Douglass never reviewed the book and was to comment on it only in passing in a letter exchange with Delany in 1853. As angered by Douglass's silence as by Johnson's sneers, Delany wrote a letter to Douglass, dated 10 July 1852, which was printed in the 23 July 1852 issue of *Frederick Douglass' Paper*. Though Stowe is never mentioned in the letter, her presence is implicit in Delany's criti-cism of Douglass for ignoring him in favor of white writers. Specifically, Delany complains that blacks seem more interested in white views on Central America than in black ones, despite the fact that blacks have a personal stake in (and racial connection to) affairs of that region. Delany himself, as he informs Douglass, has been thinking about blacks' rela-tionship to Central America "for more than seventeen years" and has recently refined and developed his views in *Condition*, "a copy of which I sent you in May." That being the case, Delany demands to know why his book has "never been noticed in the columns of your paper." And he supplies his own answer: because of the color of the author's skin. He declares: "You heaped upon it a cold and deathly silence. This is not the course you pursue towards any issue, good or bad, sent you by white persons." If there is a lesson to be learned from all this, Delany asserts, in a jab at Douglass's claims to black leadership, it is that blacks should wean themselves from paternalistic whites *and* from those blacks unable or unwilling to do so: "We have always adopted the policies that white men established for themselves without considering their applicability or adaptedness to us. No people can rise in this way. . . . I am weary of our miserable condition, and [am] heartily sick of whimpering, whining and sniveling at the feet of white men, begging for their refuse and offals."[22]

One year later, Delany more specifically would be accusing Douglass of "begging for . . . refuse and offals" at the feet of Harriet Beecher Stowe.

Using *Uncle Tom's Cabin*

Why did Douglass ignore *Condition*? Perhaps because he so profoundly disagreed with its politics of black emigration. But Douglass typically refuted ideas that displeased him in the pages of his newspaper. Perhaps he ignored *Condition*, then, because he found it personally condescending and demeaning. For whereas Delany accorded over fifty lines of text each to James McCune Smith, Samuel Ward, Henry Highland Garnet, and many others in the chapters devoted to accomplished black leaders, he accorded Douglass, squeezed into the middle of chapter 11 ("Literary and Professional Colored Men and Women"), a mere seventeen lines, the same amount as J. Presley Ball, "the principal daguerreotypist of Cincinnati" (118). Even more condescending was that while Delany acknowledged Douglass's fame and writing abilities, he nonetheless referred to him as the editor not of *Frederick Douglass' Paper* but of the "organ of the 'Liberty Party' in the United States" (118), thereby presenting him as the lackey of his white patron, Gerrit Smith. But even allowing that Douglass would likely have been alienated by the politics and personal animus of Delany's text, it may well have been that the main reason he chose not to review *Condition* was because, faced with the two principal (and politically opposed) antislavery works of spring 1852, he decided to invest his cultural capital and prestige in promoting the book he believed had the greatest possibility of improving the condition of blacks in the United States: *Uncle Tom's Cabin*.

Douglass's championing of a racialist and (arguably) colonizationist novel by a white woman distrustful of black militance otherwise appears to make little sense. For, as was the case with Delany, Douglass's outrage at the Compromise of 1850 and its Fugitive Slave Law pushed him toward a greater militancy in his views on black resistance. In a defiant speech delivered in Boston in October 1850, Douglass proclaimed that fugitive slaves should be "resolved rather to die than to go back"; and in "Resistance to Blood-Houndism," delivered in Syracuse in January 1851, he rhetorically demanded, "Are we not invited to the work of slaying kidnappers?"[23]

But while Delany by late 1851 was urging blacks to keep their distance from whites, Douglass remained indebted to his white supporters and financial backers, especially Gerrit Smith, the philanthropic Liberty party man who helped finance Douglass's transformation of the Garrisonian *North Star* into the more politically activist *Frederick Douglass' Paper*. Early in 1851, as Smith was arranging to merge the *North Star* with Smith's *Liberty Party Paper*, Douglass wrote Smith to thank him for his financial support and to assure him that he was moving toward the antislavery reading of the Constitution central to the Liberty party's platform.[24] In May 1851 Douglass publicly jettisoned Garrison's moral-suasion philosophy in favor of a political abolitionism grounded in an antislavery reading of the Constitution and a commitment to Unionism. His break with Garrison over the nature of the Constitution may have been motivated in part by economics, but that is not to diminish the intellectual rigor and practical considerations underlying his transformation.[25] Adopting Smith's antislavery interpretation of the Constitution provided Douglass with a powerful rationale for continuing to work for black elevation in the United States. From this new perspective, setbacks to the antislavery cause, such as the Compromise of 1850, could be viewed as aberrant rather than authentic expressions of American principles, mere legislative acts that ultimately could be abrogated by social and political action. Douglass also came to regard Smith's politics as offering a fuller commitment to the enslaved blacks than Garrison's dis-Unionism. In short, Smith's political abolitionism legitimized and encouraged social action that was more pragmatically grounded than Garrison's moral-suasion immediatism. Because political abolitionists were more willing to work with established institutions to bring about social change, they remained more hopeful about the prospect of reforming the United States by restoring the nation's commitment to its putative egalitarian ideals. A text that could mobilize Americans to support the causes of both the free and enslaved blacks was therefore to be embraced, not simply for its "immediatist" power of moral suasion but also for its potential to spawn specific antislavery and antiracist reforms.

Convinced that Stowe's novel had the power and vision to do just that, Douglass over the next two years set aside numerous columns in *Frederick Douglass' Paper* to publicize, promote, and shape the reception of Stowe's novel. At first glance, the articles can seem to be a fairly miscellaneous assemblage. The same is true of the four-page newspaper itself, much of which was devoted to reprinting antislavery speeches from Congress, antislavery news from a wide range of newspapers and journals, and the proceedings of numerous black, abolitionist, and women's rights conventions. Yet as Benjamin Quarles notes (and as its name unambiguously indicates), *Frederick Douglass' Paper* "was to an unusual degree the product of one man's thinking."[26] The strong personal stamp that Douglass put on the paper should be kept in mind when we turn to the various letters, articles, and editorials on *Uncle Tom's Cabin* that he began to publish. These writings reveal Douglass as a creatively appropriative reader of Stowe's novel. Though many of the pieces appearing in his newspaper were reprinted from other sources, Douglass had an enormous amount of material to choose from; his selection process needs to be considered as a central part of his efforts to shape a particular way of reading and using Stowe's novel.

The first mention of *Uncle Tom's Cabin* in *Frederick Douglass' Paper*, however, was an in-house review of 8 April 1852, which may have been written by Douglass but more likely was the work of his English comrade, financial supporter, and managing editor, Julia Griffiths, who wrote most of the reviews in the weekly "Literary Notices" section. Because of its importance in staking out the paper's position on the novel, I quote the review in its entirety:

> This work has not yet reached us, from the publishers, but when we hear that the first edition of five thousand copies (issued on the 20th of March,) was sold in four days, we are not surprised at the delay.
>
> This thrilling Story, from the accomplished pen of Mrs. Stowe, has appeared week after week, by installments, in the *National Era*, and has been perused with intense interest by thousands of people. The friends of freedom owe the Authoress a large debt of gratitude for this essential service rendered by her to the cause they love.
>
> We are well sure that the touching portraiture she has given of *"poor Uncle Tom,"* will, of itself, enlist the kindly sympathies, of numbers, in behalf of the oppressed African race, and will raise up a host of enemies against the fearful system of slavery.
>
> Mrs. Stowe has, in this work, won for herself a chief place among American writers. — She has evinced great keenness of insight into the workings of slavery and a depth of knowledge of all its various parts, such as few writers have equalled, and none, we are sure, have exceeded. She has wonderful powers of description, and invests her characters with a reality perfectly life-like. Fine as she is in description,

she is not less so in argumentation. We doubt if abler arguments have ever been presented, in favor of the *"Higher Law"* theory, than may be found here. Mrs. Stowe's truly great work, is destined to occupy a niche in every American Library, north of "Mason and Dixon's Line."[27]

This initial review, of course, is not a review of the book proper but of the serialized novel, which, despite the reviewer's assertion of the book's social impact, had a relatively limited audience in the *National Era*. The rapid sale of five thousand copies of the published book would hardly have indicated the full extent of its eventual popularity and influence. Still, the moral and aesthetic evaluation of the "truly great work" is very much tied to the reviewer's sense of its social function: Stowe's descriptive powers, realism, fine characterizations, and "argumentation," we are told, cannot but "enlist the kindly sympathies of numbers" to the antislavery cause. Sympathy is a key concept here—in her preface to the novel Stowe announced that she wanted "to awaken sympathy and feeling" for the slave—and it should be emphasized that Douglass, as his *Narrative* and subsequent remarks on *Uncle Tom's Cabin* reveal, believed that the ability of a writer to create in the white reader a sympathetic identification with the plight of the slave was central to a text's potential to bring about social change. Perceiving the impact of *Uncle Tom's Cabin* to be potentially decisive to the antislavery cause, Douglass, by printing and possibly authoring this review, conveys his belief that Stowe deserves "a large debt of gratitude" from the "friends of freedom," be those readers (so it is implied) white or black. "Cultural work," to use Jane Tompkins's helpful term, is what the reviewer perceives Stowe's novel to be undertaking, a subversive and revolutionary sort of work in that it encourages readers to honor a *"Higher Law"* than that of the federal government.[28]

Whether or not Douglass authored the review, the virtues of *Uncle Tom's Cabin* celebrated therein—sympathy, realism, social influence— would continue to be celebrated in *Frederick Douglass' Paper*. In part, the willingness of Douglass to promote the novel uncritically owes much to his commitment to Enlightenment egalitarian ideals. As Waldo E. Martin Jr. remarks, for Douglass "the liberating spirit of humanism ideally subsumed and eventually overrode the stifling spirit of race." Despite that commitment, two subsequent pieces on *Uncle Tom's Cabin* in his paper did address matters of racial politics and difference in ways that anticipated Delany's criticisms of the novel in 1853. In a letter printed six weeks after the initial review, William G. Allen, who identifies himself as "a free black teacher," praises Stowe's "wonder of wonders" of a novel but then challenges the glorification of Tom's Christlike heroism. "If any man had too much piety," he remarks, "Uncle Tom was that man," for "there should be resistance to tyrants, if need be, to the death."[29] Approximately one month later Douglass printed a column on the reception of *Uncle Tom's Cabin* in New York City. The piece, signed "Ethiop" and authored by William J. Wilson, one of Douglass's regular contributing editors, expresses amazement at the extraordinary impact of *Uncle Tom's Cabin* on a city "hitherto so faced over with the adamant of pro-slavery politics." But that impact, Wilson warns, threatens to become less transformative than narrowly commercial. Where once were "exhibited in their windows Zip Coon, or Jim Crow . . . shopkeepers are now proud to illume these very windows through the windows of my *Uncle Tom's Cabin*." Wilson's cynical sense of the *Uncle Tom's Cabin* phenomenon as a white phenomenon — a white author appropriated by white businesspeople for white consumers — leads him to wish that it had been a black who had written the first acclaimed antislavery novel, for he fears that black antislavery novelists will inevitably be subsumed by the (marketplace) tradition headed by Stowe.[30]

Ultimately, Wilson begs the key question that Delany himself had raised in his response to the negative reviews of *Condition*: Can a white writer such as Stowe faithfully represent the black experience in slavery? The question would not be raised explicitly in the pages of *Frederick Douglass' Paper* for nearly a year, and then with a vengeance in an epistolary debate between Douglass and Delany. Instead there emerged two large motifs in the articles on *Uncle Tom's Cabin* (re)printed by Douglass: the unprecedented impact of the novel, not only on readers "north of 'Mason and Dixon's Line'" but in the South as well; and a concomitant near-hagiographic celebration of Stowe's moral and literary virtues.

A front-page article in an issue of August 1852, reprinted from the *New York Evening Post*, was the first of many testimonials to the representational authority and moral influence of *Uncle Tom's Cabin*. "I am a slaveholder myself," writes a New Orleans citizen who was given Stowe's novel by a family friend. "I now wish to bear my testimony to its just delineation of the position the slave occupies." Douglass's hope was that the novel could influence enough people, North and South, to bring about the end of slavery. As he assessed the situation, influence could come from within and without; thus he also printed numerous articles on the marshaling power of *Uncle Tom's Cabin* overseas. With an article printed in the December 1853 issue on a meeting of the Glasgow Emancipation Society to "testify to our gratitude and approbation under providence to Harriet Beecher Stowe," Douglass initiated his practice of reprinting formal testimonials from British antislavery groups. Two articles on the front page of a March 1853 issue presented discussions of the popularity of *Uncle Tom's Cabin* in Paris and Moscow, thus enlarging the sphere of Stowe's influence. As Douglass remarked editorially after reprinting yet another such article, "Uncle Tom has his mission in Europe, and most conscientiously is he fulfilling it."[31]

As flameholder for the cause, Douglass took it upon himself to defend Stowe from all who might challenge her reputation as a truth teller.[32] His most significant effort to counter criticism of Stowe's novel from a "respectable" source, prior to his debate with Delany, occurred over the course of two issues in early 1853. Responding to an attack on Stowe by George R. Graham in the February 1853 *Graham's Magazine*, Douglass remarks that it "is the most unjust, the most ungenerous and the least refined review of the world-renowned book we have ever read." And it is a review, Douglass makes clear, that is thoroughly informed by racism: " '*We hate this niggerism*,' " Douglass asserts, is Graham's "solution of the whole matter." Evidently content that Graham damns himself with his own words, that his vituperations "will be greeted as THEY DESERVE TO BE," Douglass, in a front-page article of March 1853, reprinted the entirety of Graham's angry rejoinder to several of his critics, which has this to say about Douglass: "Mr. Fred. Douglass has read our article 'with disgust,' and says it may be accounted for thus: '*we hate niggerism!*' He is mistaken. . . . We rather like Fred. himself . . . but we hate the present negro literature—especially that of Fred.'s, which by abusing the white, is intended to elevate the black man."[33]

Patronizing as they are, Graham's comments touch on a crucial issue that continued to be debated among abolitionists: how to "elevate the black man." Given Stowe's emphasis in the second volume of *Uncle Tom's Cabin* on the need to educate U.S. blacks, Douglass came to regard her as a fellow believer in the importance of black elevation (despite the fact that the educated blacks of her novel end up living in foreign countries). His conviction of their shared vision was only strengthened when in March 1853 she invited him to her home in Andover, Massachusetts, to sound him out on how best she could help America's free blacks to improve their situation. This was not the first time Stowe had requested information from Douglass. Two years earlier, as she was planning the

Legree sections of the novel, she had written him in the hope that he could supply her with firsthand information on the workings of a cotton plantation. In the same letter, after praising his newspaper, she declared her intention to "modify" his views on "two subjects, — the church and African colonization," though she focused mainly on defending the church (and hence her family) from charges of being proslavery. There is no evidence that Douglass responded to or even received the letter, but his decision in late 1852 to reprint three articles on Stowe's controversy with the Presbyterian minister Dr. Joel Parker — wherein Henry Ward Beecher, Calvin Stowe, and Harriet Beecher Stowe herself challenged Parker's public accusation that a reference in *Uncle Tom's Cabin* to his putative proslavery views was libelous — may well have been an ironic rejoinder to her defense of the church and the clergy.[34] The reprintings would have spoken as well to his camaraderie with Stowe the novelist on the issue of church complicity in slavery, an author-reader camaraderie that would develop into a tentative friendship following his March visit.

Douglass's articles in *Frederick Douglass' Paper* on his visit to Stowe and its aftermath can be taken as a further effort to orchestrate a social-transformative reading of *Uncle Tom's Cabin*. In an article of March 1853 titled "A Day and a Night in 'Uncle Tom's Cabin,'" Douglass assures his readers that his visit to Stowe, while providing him with the spiritual bliss of meeting with someone "like Burns or Shakespeare," was primarily intended to benefit the free blacks. For because she wrote "the *master book* of the nineteenth century," Stowe has become quite wealthy and thus has "the ability to command and combine the means for carrying . . . forward" what he believes the novel itself calls on whites to do: help to bring about "the improvement and elevation of the free people of color in the United States." She can accomplish this shared goal, he discloses one month later, through the "founding of an INSTITUTION, in which our oppressed and proscribed youth, MALE and FEMALE, may obtain a plain English education, and a practical knowledge of various useful TRADES."[35]

Douglass believed that such an institution, by teaching free blacks the mechanical skills currently denied them by racist apprenticing practices, would provide blacks with the education necessary for leading temperate and productive lives and thereby help end slavery. As he explained privately to Stowe in a letter of March 1853: "The most telling, the most killing refutation of slavery, is the presentation of an industrious, enterprising, thrifty, and intelligent free black population. Such a population I believe would rise in the Northern States under the fostering care of such a college as that proposed." Confident that Stowe would turn over funds to him so that he could establish just such an institution in his hometown of Rochester, Douglass devoted numerous columns to her six-month visit to Great Britain, repeatedly reminding his readers of its supposed practical goal: "the establishment of some institution, which shall be of *efficient* and *permanent* benefit to the colored people of the United States."[36]

But should blacks place themselves under the "fostering care" of a white philanthropist, particularly one who in her novel appears to be advocating not black elevation in the United States but Liberian colonization? That was one of the concerns troubling Martin Delany, whose anger at Douglass for failing to review *Condition* and whose latent resentment of Douglass's status as representative African American leader informed a series of disputatious letters to Douglass, which Douglass printed, along with his rejoinders, in *Frederick Douglass' Paper* during April and May 1853. Of course Douglass could have chosen to ignore Delany's letters, just as he had chosen to ignore Delany's book. By publishing them, I would suggest, he signaled his awareness that Delany raised issues of fundamental importance about Stowe's ability and willingness to help U.S. blacks. And as Douglass waited for Stowe to offer assurances that she *would* be providing the funds he so urgently desired, he may well have shared some of the suspicions of her paternalism that were voiced so vociferously by Delany. Printing Delany's letters would have allowed Douglass to convey through Delany any doubts he may have had about his response to *Uncle Tom's Cabin*, while putting those doubts, at least on the pages of *Frederick Douglass' Paper*, to rest.[37]

Delany's first letter appeared in April 1853, approximately one month after Douglass's meeting with Stowe. In it, Delany addresses the crucial question of how the free blacks should go about the task of elevating themselves. In *Condition*, Delany had stated unequivocally, "Our elevation must be the result of *self-efforts*, and the work of our *own hands*" (45). His letter to Douglass reasserts this dictum, as he worries over blacks' (especially Douglass's) tendencies to depend on whites for their elevation: "Now I simply wish to say, that we have always fallen into great errors in efforts of this kind, giving to others than the *intelligent* and *experienced* among *ourselves*; and in all respect and difference [*sic*] to Mrs. Stowe, I beg leave to say that she *knows nothing about us,* 'the Free Colored people of the United States,' neither does any other white person — and, consequently, can contrive no successful scheme for our elevation; it must be done for ourselves."[38]

In his prior and subsequent writings, Douglass came close to agreeing with Delany on this point. "We must rise or fall, succeed or fail, by our own merits," he had declared in 1848. In the first published version of his famous "Self-Help" lecture (1849), he had allowed whites only a limited role in blacks' efforts at self-improvement, asserting that "equality and respectability can only be attained by our own exertions." And in an 1855 article in *Frederick Douglass' Paper* calling on expatriated blacks to return to the United States, Douglass would proclaim as a central truth: "THAT OUR ELEVATION AS A RACE, IS ALMOST WHOLLY DEPENDENT UPON OUR OWN EXERTIONS." That "almost," though, speaks to a key difference between Douglass and Delany at this time, because Douglass, especially during the mid-1850s when political developments seemed so grim, was willing to take help wherever he could find it. Moreover, unlike Delany, he was not so sanguine about the existence of a cohesive black community that could elevate itself on its own. Thus he writes in response to Delany, in a letter printed on the same page: "To scornfully reject all aid from our white friends, and to denounce them as unworthy of our confidence, looks high and mighty enough on paper; but unless the back ground is filled up with facts demonstrating our independence and self-sustaining power, of what use is such display of self-consequence?" As for Delany's doubts regarding Stowe's sympathies for black people, Douglass testily remarks: "The assertion that Mrs. Stowe 'knows nothing about us,' shows that Bro. DELANY knows nothing about Mrs. Stowe."[39]

In the same letter, Douglass makes the strategic argument that can best be made by those possessing a modicum of power, an argument that would come to characterize the Douglass-Delany debates over the next several years: that Delany is a divisive figure among those committed to black elevation in the United States. In a sense the implication is that to disagree with Douglass, who throughout the 1850s styles himself as *the* representative black leader, is to set oneself in opposition to the struggles of African Americans. Douglass writes that he is "all the more grieved, that at a moment when all our energies should be united in giving effect to the benevolent designs of our friends, his [Delany's] voice should be uplifted to strike a jarring note, or to awaken a feeling of distrust." Having raised these concerns about Delany, he finally brings himself to mention *Condition* in his paper, portraying it, for all its merits, as the confused and disruptive text of a man lacking legitimate claims to black leadership: "When Brother DELANY will submit any plan for benefiting the colored people, or will candidly criticize any plan already submitted, he will be heard with pleasure. But we expect no plan from him. He has written a book — and we may say that it is, in many respects, an excellent book — on the condition, character, and destiny of the colored people; but it leaves us just where it finds us, without chart or compass, and in more doubt and perplexity than before we read it."[40]

Four weeks after printing this exchange, Douglass printed a cantankerous, actually rather humorous, letter from Delany insisting that if the former slave Josiah Henson is "the real *Uncle Tom*," then he should be granted a "portion of the profits." Perhaps even Douglass himself, Delany adds, should be granted profits, for "I am of the opinion, that Mrs. Stowe has draughted largely on all the best fugitive slave narratives . . . but of this I am not competent to judge, not having as yet *read* 'Uncle Tom's Cabin,' my *wife* having *told* me the most I know about it." Though he claims not to know much about the book, he does know that Stowe places special value on black religiosity and nonviolence, the very traits he had warned blacks against relying on in his 1849 "Domestic Economy" essays in the *North Star*. In the second of those essays, he admonished a hypothetical slave for turning to "prayer and supplication for deliverance from the iron grasp of a hard-hearted task master" rather than adopting physical means of resistance. Thus in his April 1853 letter to Douglass he comments that he would have been much happier with Stowe had she celebrated blacks who "buried the hoe deep in the master's skull."[41]

Concerned that Stowe's idealization of Tom's religiosity would serve mainly to perpetuate black subserviency and degradation, Delany, in his final letter on the novel, printed in the 6 May 1853 issue of Douglass's paper, offers his most substantial criticisms of Stowe's racial politics. Allowing that in his earlier letter he was being "ironical" when he claimed that whites knew nothing of blacks — what he meant was that "they knew nothing, comparatively, about us" — he goes on to address the interrelated issues of sympathy and paternalism. Just because Stowe "pathetically portrayed some of the sufferings of the slave," Delany asks, "is it any evidence that she has any sympathy for this thrice-morally crucified, semi-free brethren any where, or of the *African race* at all?" Adducing the comments of a black man who claimed that a "very indifferent" Stowe had asked him "why he did not go to Liberia," Delany portrays her as a racist huckster comfortable only with blacks who are "subservient to, white men's power."[42] This anecdotal account, whether true or not, casts light on a Delany letter to Douglass on the famous black singer Eliza Greenfield, known as the "Black Swan," which had appeared two weeks earlier in *Frederick Douglass' Paper*. Delany argued that because Greenfield's greedy white manager, Colonel Wood, an "*unprincipled* hater of the black race," regularly had her sing before exclusively white audiences, Greenfield herself should be regarded as "the merest creature of a slave, in the hands of this fellow, Wood, and his associates." Penned in the midst of his debate with Douglass, Delany's letter meant to imply that Douglass himself stood in relation to Stowe as Greenfield to her manager: as a "creature of a slave" to a white racist. For this reason, to return to his letter on Stowe, Delany portrays Douglass's proposed mechanics institute as potentially dangerous to blacks, for in all probability, Delany warns, Stowe, "a hater of the black race," will demand "the entire employment of white instructors."[43]

Having accused Stowe of racism and paternalism, Delany then moves to consider perhaps the most troubling issue for black readers of the time (and beyond): Stowe's apparent advocacy, in the final chapters of *Uncle Tom's Cabin*, of Liberian colonization. In a letter printed in the *Pennsylvania Freeman* shortly after the publication of the novel, Robert Purvis disclosed that he felt "unprepared for the terrible blow which the closing chapter of this otherwise great book inflicted. . . . The imposture in the chapter referred to should cause its condemnation as pernicious to the well-being of the colored people in this country. It is *African Colonization unmasked*." Similarly, Delany asks about the novel: "Is not Mrs. Stowe a *Colonizationist?* having so avowed, or at least subscribed to, and recommended their principles in her great work of Uncle Tom."[44] In his writings for the *North Star* and in his comments on the subject in *Condition*, Delany had linked his denunciations of white-dependent Liberia to his celebrations of independent black Haiti. Equally worthy of his censure in *Uncle Tom's Cabin*, therefore, are Stowe's "sneers at Hayti—the only truly free and independent civilized black nation as such, or colored if you please, on the face of the earth." With the clear implication that a woman so lacking in sympathy for blacks, so distrustful of black nationalist aspirations, so enamored of black religiosity and nonviolence, and so insistent on blacks' "proper" place in Africa must therefore be a racist colonizationist, he states that if "Mrs. Stowe be what I have predicated—which I hope her friends may prove, satisfactorily, to the contrary—we should reject the proffers of Mrs. Stowe, as readily as those of any other colonizationist." That said, Delany concludes his letter on a note of ironic joviality, maintaining that he is prepared to work hand in hand on "any good measure attempted to be carried out by Mrs. Stowe, if the contrary of her colonization principles be disproved [sic]."[45]

Delany's attack on Stowe as a colonizationist marked only the third time the colonization issue had been broached in *Frederick Douglass' Paper*, which is surprising given that Douglass himself was such an outspoken opponent of the American Colonization Society. As he had fairly recently argued in "Henry Clay and Colonization Cant, Sophistry, and Falsehood" (1851), the large aim of colonizationists is "*to get rid of us*," when the fact of the matter is that "we are here, have been here, and we are to stay here."[46] Because Douglass was so insistent on blacks' rights and duty to remain in the United States, particularly for the sake of the Southern slaves, he saw little difference between colonization and emigration. Thus, in his response to Delany, he alludes to *Condition* in pointing to contradictions in Delany's politics, while purporting, on pragmatic grounds, not to care about Stowe's: "He says *she* is a colonizationist; and we ask, what if she is?—names do not frighten us. A little while ago, brother Delany was a colonizationist. . . . Yet we never suspected his friendliness to the colored people." For Douglass, the large issue is precisely that of "friendliness," particularly as it translates into usefulness: "Whoever will bring a straw's weight of influence to break the chains of our brother bondmen, or whisper one word of encouragement and sympathy to our proscribed race in the North, shall be welcomed by us to that philanthropic field of labor."[47]

Douglass, it should be noted, was hardly naïve about the colonizationist implications of the final chapters of *Uncle Tom's Cabin*. In fact, using much the same language of his 1851 attack on Clay, he had broached the issue with Stowe in his letter of 8 March 1853 when he linked his plan for an industrial college to his abhorrence for colonizationism: "The truth is, dear madam, we are *here*, and we are likely to remain. Individuals emigrate—nations never. We have grown up with this republic, and I see nothing in her character, or even in the character of the American people as yet, which compels the belief that we must leave the United States." What is appealing about Douglass's interactions with Stowe is his working assumption that he could shape her politics and actions. With Delany, however, he remains censorious and dismissive. Terming Delany's letter "unfair, uncalled for," he announces: "We shall not . . . allow the sentiments put in the brief letter of GEORGE HARRIS, at the close of Uncle

Tom's Cabin, to vitiate forever Mrs. Stowe's power to do us good. Who doubts that Mrs. Stowe is more of an abolitionist than when she wrote that chapter?" And perhaps she *was* "more of an abolitionist," perhaps she *was* stung by criticism from Douglass and other black (and white) abolitionists, for that same month she reportedly sent a note to the New York meeting of the American and Foreign Anti-Slavery Society declaring, in the paraphrased words of the proceedings, "that if she were to write 'Uncle Tom' again, she would not send George Harris to Liberia."[48]

The belief that whites have the power "to do us good"—a power, as Douglass understands it, very much dependent on the ability of blacks to put that "good" to use—centrally informs another response to *Uncle Tom's Cabin* in *Frederick Douglass' Paper*: Douglass's novella "The Heroic Slave." Serialized in the paper early in 1853, several weeks before the Douglass-Delany debate, the novella can be read as a proleptic response to Delany's criticisms of Stowe. It can also be read as a critical revision of *Uncle Tom's Cabin*. An account of the slave Madison Washington from 1835 until he led a successful revolt on the slave ship *Creole* in 1841, the historical novella challenges the racialism of Stowe's novel by presenting the reader with a rebellious slave, "black, but comely," who is willing to adopt, as Delany argues blacks must, the worldly means of revolutionary violence to achieve worldly ends.[49] Unlike Stowe, who bifurcates her blacks into "white-blooded" rebels and "black-blooded" docilities, Douglass merges the two character types in the person of Madison Washington. "A child might play in his arms, or dance on his shoulders. . . . His broad mouth and nose spoke only of good nature and kindness," Douglass writes of Washington's Uncle Tom–like attributes. And yet, like George Harris, "he had the head to conceive, and the hand to execute. In a word, he was one to be sought as a friend, but to be dreaded as an enemy" (103). But though Douglass's novella revises elements of Stowe's characterizations, significant parallels exist between the two works: both make use of temperance themes, particularly in delineating the moral degeneracy of slave owners; both idealize the transformative power of sympathy; and both temper their portrayals of black violence.[50] Douglass tones down the violence of the slave rebellion by having the revolt on the *Creole* narrated by a white sailor, who not only remains unconscious during most of it but also twice has his life saved from militant slaves by Washington's intervention. Unlike the vengeful Babo of Melville's "Benito Cereno" (1855), Washington simply desires the liberty of his people. Presenting him as a temperate revolutionary, Douglass hopes to find a receptive audience among those white readers who might otherwise be alienated by representations of black rage.[51]

These same contemporary white readers would probably also admire the portrayal of Listwell, the white Ohioan who, in sympathetic response to Washington's opening soliloquy, converts to abolitionism and comes to play a key role in the novella. Five years after overhearing Washington speak in a Virginia forest of his desires for freedom, Listwell, with the help of his wife, smuggles Washington aboard a steamer in Ohio bound for Canada. In a subsequent letter to Listwell, Washington addresses him thus: "My dear friend, — for such you truly are" (323). When Washington, after a failed effort to free his wife, is recaptured in Virginia and put on a slave ship headed for New Orleans, Listwell again offers his assistance. Washington exclaims to the slaves, who are startled by Listwell's friendly overtures: "We are all chained here together, — ours is a common lot; and that gentleman is not less *your* friend than *mine*" (332). Listwell's initial response to Washington's dire situation is to counsel him to become, in a sense, an Uncle Tom (or, Delany might say, the typically unworldly religious slave): "Put your trust in God, and bear your sad lot with the manly fortitude which becomes a man" (335). On second thought, however, Listwell decides to act: he purchases "three strong *files*" (337) from a local hardware store and, just before the slave ship departs, manages to slip them into Washington's pocket.

In a searching critique of the novella, Yarborough expresses his concerns about Listwell's prominence. Compared with other accounts of the *Creole* revolt — by William Wells Brown, Lydia Maria Child, and Pauline Hopkins — Douglass places "the greatest emphasis upon the role played by whites in the protagonist's life." Perhaps, Yarborough suggests, the granting of near heroic stature to Listwell "reflects [Douglass's] desire to reach and move white readers." But the end result is this: "He implies that even the most self-reliant and gifted black male slave needs white assistance."[52] The problem with Yarborough's reading is that it overgeneralizes and to some extent dehistoricizes. Douglass's point is surely not that at every time and place — whether in the American 1840s or beyond and elsewhere — blacks need the assistance of whites but that in Madison Washington's particular situation — or in the blacks' particular situation in the American 1850s — there can exist a sympathetic response to suffering that crosses the lines of race and has an instrumental value. Additionally, and this seems to me the crucial point, Douglass suggests that the white sympathy and material assistance that help to produce the slaves' revolutionary action in no way compromise the self-reliance or heroism of such action and are in fact the products of a black's influence on a white: it is Washington's opening soliloquy, after all, that converts Listwell to the antislavery cause and makes him so eager to help the slaves.[53] Nevertheless, in his presentation of the slave revolt in the final section of the novella, Douglass, consistent with his conception of the key role of black male leaders in bringing about a "day of deliverance," stresses that the blacks are liberated not by Listwell but by their own efforts as mobilized by "the triumphant leadership of their heroic chief and deliverer" (348).[54] Although the novella revises Stowe's conception of black heroism by portraying an actively revolutionary hero with black skin, I would maintain that parallels between Douglass's and Stowe's discourse of sympathy and community outweigh the revisionary strain, and that the large thrust of the novella is to counter the views of those, like Delany, who were reluctant to grant that whites could genuinely sympathize with the plight of the slaves and who therefore viewed white "beneficence" as only further contributing to black docility, subordination, and degradation.

For Douglass, the ability to sympathize and to act on such sympathy was a key indication of one's humanity, and those who he believed possessed capacities for sympathy—such as Stowe—were viewed as *nearly* transcending the limits of race (Douglass never closed his eyes to racial difference). Sympathy allows for the possibility of dialogue and influence; and I do not think it too farfetched to read "The Heroic Slave," in part, as an allegory of Douglass's relationship to Stowe, particularly if we take Listwell's overhearing of Washington's soliloquy and subsequent conversion to antislavery as analogous to Stowe's reading of Douglass's *Narrative* and eventual authoring of *Uncle Tom's Cabin*. In this model of influence as I hypothesize it here between Douglass and Stowe and as Douglass in "The Heroic Slave" presents it between Washington and Listwell, power is shared and mutually constitutive. From this perspective, Douglass, in his championing of *Uncle Tom's Cabin*, cannot be regarded (pace Delany) as a dupe or a lackey, for he himself had a role in the production of the novel and continued to play a significant role in its cultural reproduction.

Central to that cultural reproduction was Douglass's emerging plan to organize a national black convention infused by the spirit of *Uncle*

Tom's Cabin. Desirous of assuming "the triumphant leadership of their heroic chief and deliverer," Douglass, in yet another "response" to *Uncle Tom's Cabin* in *Frederick Douglass' Paper*, began in the spring of 1853, in the midst of his debate with Delany, to promote a national black convention that would endorse his social-transformative reading of *Uncle Tom's Cabin*. This was not Douglass's first effort at mobilizing blacks. In 1849 he proposed the formation of a National League, which he hoped would consist of "*the intelligent and philanthropic of our people*." Like Delany, who wanted only selected groups of educated blacks to participate in emigration movements, Douglass manifested an elitist temperament when addressing matters of black leadership. In fact, one of his deepest concerns about emigration programs was that they would siphon from the United States its most intelligent and talented black leaders. Thus he confessed to Gerrit Smith in a letter written shortly before the publication of Delany's *Condition*, "I really fear that some whose presence in this country is necessary to the elevation of the Colored people will leave us — while the degraded and worthless will remain behind — to help bind us to our present debasement."[55] The publication of Delany's book exacerbated Douglass's anxieties along these lines and added to the urgency of his efforts to convene an antiemigrationist convention in order to forestall any movement that Delany might lead.

I want to return for a moment to Delany's and Douglass's epistolary exchange on Stowe, in which we can see their debate on a possible black convention unfolding under Douglass's watchful editorial eye. In his first letter, Delany had called on blacks, specifically "the most competent among *their own* brethren," to meet together to set their own agenda for action at a "National Consultation of our people." Though Douglass would seem to have dismissed such a suggestion in his remarks on Delany's divisiveness, one week later he ran a squib, "A National Convention of the Colored People," that audaciously attempted to implicate Delany in his own plans for a black convention: "Colored men, what say you; shall such a Convention be held? H. O. Wagoner, of Chicago, and M. R. Delany, have already spoken, and are quite in favor of the measure. What say you on the subject?" In a similar vein, Douglass, in his 6 May 1853 response to Delany's final letter on Stowe, cagily expressed a "willingness on our part to occupy an obscure position in such a movement," and he beseeched him, despite their differences, "Will not friend Delany draw up a call for . . . a Convention, and send it to us for publication?"[56]

However "obscure" Douglass said he wished to remain, shortly after asking Delany to write up a call for a convention, in the 20 May 1853 issue of his paper Douglass printed his own "Call for a Colored National Convention," wherein he maintained that the Fugitive Slave Law, colonizationism, various other racist practices, "and withal the propitious awakening to the fact of our condition at home and abroad, which has followed the publication of 'Uncle Tom's Cabin' — call trumpet-tongued for our union, cooperation and action in the premises." He shamelessly listed Delany as one of the cosigners of his "Call" for a Stowe-inspired convention. In a letter of response to Douglass that was printed the following month, Delany complained that "my name was attached to it [the "Call"] without my consent or knowledge," and he asked that the July convention be delayed until late August so that blacks from the West (presumably those receptive to Delany's emigrationist position) could more easily attend.[57] Douglass's response was to drop Delany's name from subsequent printings of the "Call." The convention took place as Douglass scheduled it: in July 1853 in his hometown of Rochester, New York.

The *Proceedings of the Colored National Convention*, published by Douglass in *Frederick Douglass' Paper* and as a separate pamphlet, conveys a remarkably optimistic outlook for the possibility of social change in the United States. Calling for a "National Council of the Colored People," a "Manual Labor School" or "INDUSTRIAL COLLEGE," black suffrage, the right to participate in jury trials, and the repeal of the Fugitive Slave Law, the delegates, through the report of the "Committee on Social Relations and Polity," predict that in the "presence and progress of such polity, all forms of prejudice and hatred would disappear; wicked and oppressive laws become dead letters upon the pages of our statute-books; societies for our removal become extinct." Though Douglass, in his keynote "Address of the Colored National Convention to the People of the United States," warns that change will not come easily as long as "all the powers of slavery are exerted to prevent the elevation of the free people of color," the large message of the speech, of the various committee reports, and of the convention's final resolutions is that blacks should continue to strive after "civil and social privileges [equal] with the rest of the American people" and that their efforts will be facilitated and enabled by Stowe.[58]

Stowe is everywhere in the *Proceedings*. While the prefatory "Call" (reprinted in the proceedings) talks of the "propitious awakening" brought about by the publication of *Uncle Tom's Cabin*, it refers as well to the need to discuss "the disposition of such funds as our friends abroad, through Mrs. Harriet Beecher Stowe, may appropriate to the cause of our progress and improvement." At the midpoint of the proceedings appears Douglass's 8 March 1853 letter to Stowe in which he asks her for financial support for his industrial college. By inserting this private letter into the public transcript of the convention, Douglass can elaborate his plans for a mechanics institute without having to address or debate the delegates directly. Presenting the institute as the best possible way to help urban free blacks improve their condition, Douglass assures Stowe (thus confirming some of Delany's worst suspicions) that "I leave the organization and administration to the superior wisdom of yourself." As in *Uncle Tom's Cabin* (and "The Heroic Slave"), sympathy allows "friends" to move beyond culturally imposed boundaries of race, class, and gender. The convention's resolution on Stowe's novel enunciates a spiritual view of the power of sympathy: "Resolved. That we recognize in 'Uncle Tom's Cabin' a work plainly marked by the finger of God, lifting the veil of separation which has too long divided the sympathies of one class of the American people from another." [59]

The Rochester convention of 1853 was enormously successful in many respects, as it enabled black leaders opposed to colonization and emigration to articulate their agenda for black elevation in the United States. As Douglass hoped and expected, the convention also helped him to consolidate his position as the preeminent black leader of the time, despite the fact that black and white Garrisonians, stung by his defection, had stepped up their attacks on his character, accusing him, among other things, of having an adulterous affair with Julia Griffiths.[60] And yet despite his crowning "Harriet Beecher Stowe convention," Douglass's specific plan to beget a black mechanics institute from *Uncle Tom's Cabin* failed to transpire. Although Stowe, in a letter to Garrison of December 1853, declared that Douglass's "plans for the elevation of his own race are manly, sensible, comprehensive," one month later Douglass announced in the pages of *Frederick Douglass' Paper* that "Mrs. Stowe, for reasons which she deems quite satisfactory, does not, at present, see fit to stand forth as the patron of the proposed institution." Putting the best possible face on the situation, he remarked, "It is equally our duty to state that Mrs. Stowe desires the work to go forward in the hands of the National Council; and we doubt not she will, in the end, be found among the principal friends of the Institution." [61] Perhaps because she thought such a school would be difficult to operate and finance or because she was aware of criticisms of the "segregationist" project from other blacks,

Stowe lost interest in the project while in England. "Thus cold-watered," Quarles reports, "Mrs. Stowe's money-raising efforts realized the meagre sum of $535. This she turned over to Douglass for his personal use."[62]

Despite the collapse of Douglass's project, the evidence suggests that his relationship with Stowe remained cordial and that his admiration for *Uncle Tom's Cabin* remained undiminished. Douglass proclaimed in an 1857 speech reprinted in his paper that "the name of Harriet Beecher Stowe can never die while the love of freedom lives in the world."[63] And his retrospective remarks on Stowe in *Life and Times of Frederick Douglass* (1881) are consistent with his position of the 1850s: "In the midst of these fugitive slave troubles came the book known as *Uncle Tom's Cabin*, a work of marvelous depth and power. Nothing could have better suited the moral and humane requirements of the hour." Yet when he describes in his 1881 autobiography how he learned upon Stowe's return from England that her financial support would not be forthcoming, his disappointment, even after nearly thirty years, is palpable: "I have never been able to see any force in the reasons for this change. It is enough, however, to say that they were sufficient for her, and that she no doubt acted conscientiously, though her change of purpose . . . placed me in an awkward position before the colored people of this country, as well as to friends abroad."[64]

Though restrained, a sense of betrayal informs these late observations on Stowe, as her change of mind would have made Douglass appear "awkward" in the eyes of Delany and his supporters. Because of the publicity surrounding the possible Douglass-Stowe project, Stowe's eventual refusal left Douglass vulnerable to the charge that he had naïvely put his faith in a white woman who, at bottom, perhaps did lack full sympathy for African Americans, as Delany claimed. In Douglass's defense, it can be argued that by attempting to enlist Stowe to the cause of his industrial college in the name of her novel, Douglass sought to make *Uncle Tom's Cabin* do the cultural work that he wanted it to do. Douglass's refusal to give up on Stowe for her racialist and colonizationist ideas — and even for her refusal to fund the black mechanics institute — speaks well for his prescient perception of the cultural forces that could impinge on even the most sympathetic of white Americans. His efforts to persuade Stowe to rethink her colonizationist stance and (through "The Heroic Slave") her racialism suggest that Douglass came to believe that the publication of a text — even one with so massive an authority as *Uncle Tom's Cabin* — does not foreclose the possibility of dialogue between authors and readers, blacks and whites, oppressed and oppressors, when glimmers of mutual sympathy can be discerned.

The Destiny of the Race

But perhaps I am putting an overly bright or Douglass-centric gloss on these biracial possibilities. Let us therefore return to the July 1853 convention's idealization of a "happy brotherhood" between like-minded blacks and whites to reconsider what it meant from Delany's perspective to be cast by this group as an outsider. Although I can tell a somewhat upbeat and sentimental story of Douglass's efforts to see past Stowe's racialism to her sympathetic core, it must be said that central to his appropriative response to *Uncle Tom's Cabin* was an attempt to maintain hold of his leadership in the face of Delany's strongly articulated dissent. Viewing the debate on Stowe and black emigration from Delany's perspective presents us with a less attractive picture of Douglass as a calculating egotist who may well have been the dupe of a white racist. Viewing the debate from Delany's perspective also helps us better to understand the challenges and frustrations attending his efforts to set forth a political position different from that put forward at Douglass's Rochester convention.

Having boycotted the July 1853 convention, Delany one month later issued a "Call for a National Emigration Convention of Colored Men" to be held in Cleveland in August 1854. Challenging Douglass's equation of colonization to emigration, Delany attacks the colonizationists' racist "expatriating scheme," while celebrating the self-reliant character of black emigrationism: "We must make an issue, create an event, and establish a position *for ourselves*." In a passage that underscores his sense of the limited agenda of (and Douglass-imposed constraints on) the Rochester convention, he proclaims at the midpoint of the "Call":

We are friends . . . and ever will stand shoulder to shoulder by our brethren, and all *true* friends in all good measures adopted by them, for the bettering of our condition in this country. . . ; but as the subject of emigration is of vital importance, and has ever been shunned by all delegated assemblages of our people as heretofore met, we cannot longer delay, and will not be farther baffled; and deny the right of our most sanguine friend or dearest brother, to prevent an intelligent enquiry to, and the carrying out of these measures, when this can be done, to our entire advantage, as we propose to show in Convention.

As with their debate on Stowe, in their debate on emigration the issue of who constitutes a *"true"* friend remains a sticking point between Delany and Douglass. Also worth noting is Delany's suggestion that Douglass and his conventioneers had "shunned" debate on emigration at their convention and thus could be regarded as having engaged in a form of censorship. In response, Delany proposes his own form of exclusionism: he invites to his convention "all colored men in favor of emigration out of the United States, and *opposed* to the American Colonization scheme of leaving the Western Hemisphere," while at the same time banning those who fail to demonstrate "their fidelity on the measures and objects set forth in this Call."[65]

Printing Delany's "Call" in *Frederick Douglass' Paper* approximately one month after he printed the Rochester proceedings, Douglass, in the same issue, ran a related piece attacking Delany's proposed convention for its "cowardly" avoidance of debate on emigration and for its possible divisiveness: "Our enemies will see in this movement a cause of rejoicing, such as they could hardly have anticipated so soon, after the manly position assumed by the colored National Convention held in this city. They will discover in this movement a division of opinion amongst us upon a vital point. . . . Looked at from any point the movement is to be deprecated." As Douglass's ability simultaneously to print and to attack the "Call" reveals, Delany took enormous risks in challenging the leadership position Douglass assumed at the "manly" Rochester convention. For Douglass could (and did) bring to bear the weight of the renowned *Frederick Douglass' Paper* against Delany's proposals. In October 1853, for example, he reprinted in his paper a resolution from the Illinois Colored State Convention attacking Delany for his "spirit of disunion"; and the following month he printed a lengthy letter from a Chicago correspondent, who rhetorically asserted: "If M. R. Delany . . . and others wish to leave the United States for Africa, South America, the Antilles, or any other portion of the globe, why not make their arrangements by private correspondence, and leave in a quiet and peaceable manner and not attempt to give their little movement a *national character*, and by this means create dissensions amongst the colored people."[66]

Incensed by Douglass's unsubtle attacks, Delany, in a November 1853 letter to Douglass printed in *Frederick Douglass' Paper*, asks why he, and not Douglass, should be seen as responsible for "the *spirit* and design of *disunion*." He ironically remarks on Douglass and his associates, "We have no quarrel with those who love to live among the whites better than the blacks, and leave them to the enjoyment of their predilections." In a squib printed immediately following the letter, Douglass terms Delany's remarks "dictatorial, uncharitable, hasty." The squib both intensified and hastened the end to their epistolary debate. In a letter printed two weeks later in Douglass's paper, Delany asserts to Douglass that "all I ask is not to be misrepresented. I more than ask it — I demand it." He then wrote to Howard Day's *Aliened American*, a black newspaper published in Ohio, to complain about Douglass's misrepresentations of his emigrationist views. Perturbed by Delany's use of another black paper to voice his criticisms, Douglass, in an article of January 1854 titled "M. R. Delany," announced his plans to do to Delany in *Frederick Douglass' Paper* precisely what Delany proposed to do to dissenters at the emigration convention: exclude him. As he rhetorically puts it, "Why does [Delany] ask us to be freer in our columns than he means to be in his Convention?"[67] Though Douglass would several times more attack the emigrationists (and Delany by implication), his evolving strategy was to downplay the movement by appearing to ignore it himself. Instead, he left the job of attacking the emigrationists to his other writers and editors, particularly William Watkins, who wrote numerous letters and articles for the 1854 volume of *Frederick Douglass' Paper* on the dangers that the emigration movement posed to black elevation in the United States. Unwilling to print Delany, Douglass nonetheless did publish the letters of Delany's friend, the poet James M. Whitfield, who defended black emigration from Watkins's attacks. In this way, debate on emigration, albeit under Douglass's tight editorial control, was aired in his newspaper before, during, and after the 1854 emigration convention.

Meeting from August 24 to 26 in the "western" city of Cleveland, at a remove from Douglass's power base in Rochester, the 1854 emigration convention had a regional feel to it: only three of the 101 delegates were from cities or states east of Pittsburgh; nearly half were from Pittsburgh itself; and (unlike at Douglass's all-male convention), approximately one-third were women. Though he served not as president but as chairman of the Business Committee, the convention was, in every respect, Martin Delany's. James Holly remarked years later on the centrality of the occasion to Delany's career: "All other events in his life, before then, culminated in the part he took in that movement. All events of his life, after the convention, took their point of departure from the principles which he sustained and promulgated there." [68] As a statement of Delany's principles at mid-decade, then, and more generally as a statement of the principles of a sizable group of African Americans who dissented from Douglass's 1853 Rochester meeting, the convention's proceedings deserve our close attention.

The *Proceedings of the National Emigration Convention* are presented to the black reader as a sacred text of sorts, expressive of African Americans' true feelings: "Let every black person keep by him a copy of these Minutes, and hand them, in lieu of an argument, to his oppressor or well wisher, who may there read the living sentiments as they teemed from the black man's heart." Central to the proceedings, as opposed to the Stowe-inspired Rochester convention, is a nearly unrelenting characterization of white antislavery benevolence as both a manifestation of the "self-interest central to Anglo-Saxon dominance" and a risk to black self-determination. Yet despite the racial assertiveness of many of the convention's resolutions, there is, as in Delany's *Condition*, a certain contradictory quality to the proceedings that reveals significant tensions in the emigration movement. For example, though blacks are warned against putting their faith in white-sponsored institutions, the convention does pass a resolution praising "the indefatigable labors of the Rev. Charles Avery, in erecting a College for the education of colored youths." [69] And though a large aim of the convention is to support Delany's Central and South American emigrationist program, the delegates never abandon the values—temperance, thrift, hard work, education—that for the past twenty years or so had centrally informed programs for black elevation in the United States.

Consider, for example, the following resolution approved by convention delegates:

That according to the present social system of civilized society, the equality of persons is only recognized by their equality of attainments, —as with individuals, so it is with classes and communities;—therefore we impress on the colored races throughout this Continent and the world, the necessity of having their children and themselves properly qualified in *every* respectable vocation pertaining to the Industrial and Wealth accumulating occupations; of arts, sciences, trades and professions; of agriculture, commerce and manufacturers, so as to equal in *position* the leading characters and nations of the earth, without which we cannot, at best, but occupy a position of subserviency.[70]

In the tradition of the more conservative, or "assimilationist," black conventions of the 1830s and 1840s, the delegates place a special burden on blacks to demonstrate their ability to achieve in the ways valued by whites. Unquestioned or undefined in this resolution are such key terms as "civilized," "respectable," "attainments," and "commerce." But would these same "Industrial and Wealth accumulating" values appeal equally to the native peoples of Central and South America or to the native peoples of the Caribbean islands? As in *Condition*, assumptions are made about what is best for the natives of the countries to which the delegates intend to travel—assumptions that reveal the delegates' attachments to some of the cultural and economic values of the nation they plan on leaving behind.

Delany takes aim at any lingering attachments to the United States in his keynote address, "Political Destiny of the Colored Race on the American Continent," one of the great black nationalist documents of the antebellum period. Printed at the end of the proceedings, it was delivered (reportedly over a period of seven hours) during the second day of the convention, where it was "unanimously received." In his championing of black emigration, Delany emphasizes the duplicity and malevolence of white racist culture in the United States, and the black disempowerment that inevitably results from such racism. Even free blacks, he argues, are in effect slaves, not only because the Fugitive Slave Law poses an imminent threat to all Northern blacks but also because blacks lack access to legal, social, and political forms of power. As he argues in *Condition*, so he argues in "Political Destiny": blacks can call themselves free only when they "constitute an essential part of the *ruling element* of the country in which they live." For just this reason, Delany warns, in what has to be taken as a response to Douglass's embrace of Stowe, blacks should regard seemingly philanthropic whites as oppressors who, by encouraging dependency, share in racists' desires "to crush the colored races wherever found."[71]

Stigmatizing the efforts of white philanthropists (even, implicitly, Avery), Delany, in this document dedicated "to the Colored Inhabitants of the United States," attempts to forge consensus on the issue of black emigration. In addition to working against the *Proceedings*' moderate resolution on white philanthropy, Delany, in what is perhaps his boldest and most notorious move in the speech, also seeks to create black consensus by positioning himself against the racial egalitarianism asserted in the first resolution of the convention's platform (and in most of *Condition*): "*Resolved*, That we acknowledge the natural equality of the Human Race." For as Delany argues in "Political Destiny," blacks have "inherent traits, attributes, so to speak, and native characteristics, peculiar to our race" that make them different from whites. "The truth is," he maintains, "we are not identical with the Anglo-Saxon, or any other race of the Caucasian or pure white type of the human family, and the sooner we know and acknowledge this truth, the better for ourselves and posterity." He argues that blacks and other peoples of color in the southern regions of the Americas should therefore conceive of and constitute themselves as "one country." Detecting " 'the finger of God' " behind the fact that so many of African descent have been brought to the Americas, he asserts, as in *Condition*, that an autonomous black nation is destined to emerge outside the boundaries of the United States but within the Americas: "Upon the American continent, then, we are determined to remain, despite every opposition that may be urged against us."[72]

Perceiving Douglass as having turned against his black identity by pandering to Stowe and taking an assimilationist position at the Rochester convention, perceiving U.S. cultural practices as increasingly devoted to thwarting black elevation, and perceiving scientific racialism as gaining in cultural prestige (1854 saw the publication of Josiah C. Nott and George R. Gliddon's insidious and influential *Types of Mankind*), Delany attempted in "Political Destiny" to fuel the emigration movement by setting forth an essentialist view of race that would foster black pride and solidarity. In crucial ways, then, his racial thinking needs to be regarded as a form of ideological combat in the sense that, as Barbara J. Fields has argued, white constructions of black racial inferiority made race "the ideological medium though which [African Americans] posed and apprehended basic questions of power and dominance, sovereignty and citizenship, justice and right."[73] His racial thinking also needs to be regarded as central to his efforts, which would come to the fore in the late 1850s, particularly in his novel *Blake*, to privilege "full-blooded" blackness as a way of championing himself as a more representative black leader than Douglass.

And yet, in using black racialist ideology to combat white versions of the same, Delany to some extent reproduced the racialist essentialism and millennialism informing the controversial conclusion of Stowe's

Uncle Tom's Cabin.[74] George Harris, of course, rationalizes away the racism of Liberian colonizationists through his conviction (arguably shared by Stowe) that God plans for world redemption to be achieved through the agency of religious and civilized blacks in Africa. Advocating voluntary (and selective) emigration over forcible colonization, Delany in "Political Destiny" challenges Harris's (and Stowe's) desire for blacks to achieve their destiny in Africa, setting forth a proto–Pan-African diasporic vision that disconnects blacks from the actual place of Africa, even as he insists on blacks' essential oneness as an "African" people. In doing so, however, he shares a good deal with Stowe's George Harris, for he similarly makes the case for blacks' "peculiarities," insisting that they "have the highest traits of civilization . . . [and] are civil, peaceable, and religious to a fault." Given their accomplishments and their potential to bring forth a new world order of morality, civilization, and peace, blacks, according to Delany's logic, would be betraying their obligations to the world community were they to surrender their "original identity" as a racial people. As Delany puts it, again in the mode of George Harris, "There is no doubt but the black race will yet instruct the world."[75]

In his 1853 *Origin and Objects of Ancient Freemasonry*, Delany asserted that "all men, of every country, clime, color and condition (when morally worthy,) are acceptable to the portals of Masonic jurisprudence." One year later, however, in "Political Destiny," a greater sense of urgency, along with a desire to underscore his claims to black leadership, impels him to privilege "color" over the "worthy." His transnational vision of the "West Indies, [and] Central and South America" as "but one country, relatively considered," speaks not only to a Masonic sense of the ways in which fraternal and civilized ideals can cross national ideologies and boundaries but also to a pragmatic sense that only by putting such ideals into practice in a particular place can blacks mount an effective challenge to U.S. slave culture.[76] In the early to mid-1850s Delany thought such a place was in the southern Americas; by the decade's end he would change his mind, insisting that the best place to develop black nationhood was in Africa.

Appropriating and inverting white racialist and millennialist discourses and infusing "Political Destiny" with a Masonic transnationalism, an Afrocentric pride, and a pragmatics of nation and place, Delany inspired the 1854 Cleveland convention to achieve consensus on his emigrationist program, thereby ratifying his claims to black leadership and bringing emigration to the center of black political debate during the

1850s. According to *Proceedings of the National Emigration Convention*, the enthusiasm for the speech was such that, after the vote, the Reverend A. R. Green of Ohio "took the floor, saying that a document of such importance should not be permitted to pass the Convention by merely adopting it, and proceeded in a strain of thrilling eloquence and masterly power, to review and eulogize the document, as being a paper of unusual merit and ability." As a result of Delany's overall efforts at the convention, the group voted to establish a National Board of Commissioners (a counterpoint to Douglass's National Council), which was intended to aid U.S. blacks' efforts at emigration. And it voted to establish its own periodical (a counterpoint to *Frederick Douglass' Paper*), which was intended to instruct the black masses and thereby shape "the future destinies of the race."[77]

Meanwhile, Douglass, who for the most part had been trying to ignore Delany and his movement, felt obliged, because he was threatened, to respond to the Cleveland convention. True to his desire to play down the significance of the emigration movement, he ran only a short paragraph on the convention, observing that the "Colored Emigration Convention" approved "two measures—a Board of Commissioners, and a *quarterly periodical*" and voicing the hope that the periodical would "be started in the United States, for we cannot spare the mental power capable of conducting a quarterly from the immediate conflict of the slave power in this country." Otherwise, Douglass did not have much more to say about the emigrationists, at least not directly. Indirectly, he continued to attack them by encouraging others to do so and then printing the attacks in his paper. His chief man for the job was Delany's former friend George B. Vashon, a lawyer from Pittsburgh, who himself had experimented with emigration by moving to Haiti in the late 1840s. Vashon's most trenchant attack, "The Late Cleveland Convention," appeared in the 17 November 1854 issue of *Frederick Douglass' Paper*. Never mentioning Delany by name, Vashon lambastes the "combatants" for their racialism, insisting that a belief in "a natural distinction between the white and colored races" only legitimates the racism of blacks' oppressors. Like Douglass, Vashon regards Delany's convention as playing into the hands of the colonizationists by "devising gigantic, but impracticable schemes of emigration to other countries." Turning a key phrase in "Political Destiny" against itself, Vashon concludes that it would have been far more beneficial for blacks to have developed strategies for becoming " 'an essential constituent in the ruling element' of their native land."[78]

Douglass could always rise above the fray, recruiting and reprinting others to make his arguments. But as I have been suggesting, Douglass was not so far from the battle as he might have wanted to appear. Because of his commitments to black elevation in the United States and his rejection of Delany's racialized (biological) notion of black nationhood and leadership, he felt a distinct threat from Delany's emigrationist movement, as evident in his preemptive "Harriet Beecher Stowe" convention of 1853, the various articles he printed between 1853 and 1855 attacking emigration, and, as I will argue in the next chapter, his decision in 1855 to bring out a revised, expanded, and reconceptualized version of his autobiography. He even set forth his own "emigration" program in 1854, calling for "an enlightened body of black freemen" to move from the eastern states to the Kansas territory to help make it a free state.[79]

As all his writings of the period indicate, Douglass thought it essential to the cause of antislavery that "enlightened" free blacks remain in the United States to work for the freedom of the slaves. As one antiemigrationist letter writer to *Frederick Douglass' Paper* put it in 1853, these free blacks are heroic because *"they have remembered their brethren in bonds, as bound with them, and instead of fleeing like* COWARDLY POLTROONS *from the great moral strife waging between liberty and slavery, they have enlisted on the side of freedom, resolved to free their country and countrymen from the curse of slavery,* or SHARE THEIR FATE." In Douglass's mind, no one was more heroic in these terms than himself, and it is precisely this sense of moral and fraternal heroism that informs his self-representation in *My Bondage and My Freedom*. Waldo Martin writes of Douglass that "while fully aware of the distinctive collective identity of black Americans, his vision of racial, or ethnic, nationalism remained subordinate to his vision of American nationalism."[80] Linking his "enlightened body," through a patriotic rhetoric of exemplariness and representativeness, to the body of the nation, Douglass in his 1855 autobiography posits an antiemigrationist politics of temperate revolutionism as the best possible hope for black elevation.

Chapter 3
Slaves of Appetite

Temperate
Revolutionism in
Douglass's *My
Bondage and
My Freedom*

 In this chapter I read *My Bondage and My Free-
dom* in the context of Douglass's unfolding career
as representative African American leader, placing
a particular emphasis on the work he wanted the
text to do in its publication year of 1855. In re-
telling his journey from slavery to freedom in the
middle of the decade, less than a year after the Cleveland emigration convention, Douglass was responding implicitly to the arguments of Delany
and other emigrationists that in the foreseeable future blacks would remain slaves, or de facto slaves, in the United States—arguments that
would appear to have gained added currency with the passage of the
Kansas-Nebraska Act in 1854. Central to Douglass's continued hopefulness about blacks' prospects in the United States, despite such obviously
negative developments, was a renewed commitment following his 1851
break with Garrison to the informing ideals of the nation's originary,
revolutionary documents. As he remarked in his 1854 speech "Slavery,
Freedom, and the Kansas-Nebraska Act": "The only intelligible principle on which popular sovereignty is founded, is found in the Declaration of American Independence, there and in these words: We hold these

truths to be self-evident, that all men are created equal and are endowed by their Creator with the right of life, liberty and the pursuit of happiness."[1] In *My Bondage and My Freedom*, Eric J. Sundquist observes, Douglass signals his "entry into America's revolutionary tradition." Thus he presents himself in his 1855 autobiography, as John Ernest puts it, as "a national representative, fighting not only for its moral and political principles (as he does in the 1845 text) but for the very civilization that served as foundation for the development of those principles."[2] Douglass's sense of what was at stake in such a fight may be discerned in his famous lecture of 5 July 1852, "What to the Slave Is the Fourth of July?"

In one of the best-known passages of the lecture, Douglass inquires rhetorically: "What, to the American slave, is your 4th of July? I answer: a day that reveals to him, more than all other days in the year, the gross injustice and cruelty to which he is the constant victim. To him, your celebration is a sham; your boasted liberty, an unholy license; . . . your denunciations of tyrants, brass fronted impudence; your shouts of liberty and equality, hollow mockery." Douglass's conception of the American Revolution as unfinished, or corrupted, was of a piece with numerous other antislavery writers' conceptions of the event. Though some African Americans, most notably David Walker, went so far as to suggest that the Revolution was simply a power play by racists and slaveholders (such as Washington and Jefferson) to perpetuate slavery, the dominant view was that the ideals of the Revolution were worthy of celebration and could therefore be enlisted to legitimate the antislavery cause as a patriotic fight to redeem *American* principles. The logic of the analogy between the Revolution and abolitionism was meant to press white Americans into confronting their betrayal of the Revolutionary heritage and, perhaps more important, to press them into developing a historical awareness of what it meant to be a revolutionary. As Douglass reminds his auditors in "Fourth of July," the rebels of the 1770s, like antebellum abolitionists, were regarded by many "in their day [as] plotters of mischief, agitators and rebels, dangerous men."[3]

The violence of the patriots could therefore be invoked, again through analogy, to legitimate black violence against white oppressors. David Walker concluded his 1829 *Appeal . . . to the Coloured Citizens of the World* by quoting from the "Declaration, made July 4, 1776," thus implying that the violence of the "first Revolution in this country" could be used to endorse the violence of a *truer* revolution in which blacks would "kill or be killed." Similarly, Henry Highland Garnet hailed the black rebels Denmark Vesey, Nat Turner, Madison Washington, and Joseph Cinque as "patriotic" figures who "struck for liberty and death"; William Wells Brown celebrated Toussaint L'Ouverture as a black revolutionary who fulfilled "the glorious sentiments of the Declaration of Independence"; and Martin Delany, in his novel, *Blake*, championed black insurrectionists as "soldier[s] of the American Revolution." In the light of this rhetorical and ideological tradition, what is unusual about Douglass's "Fourth of July" speech, particularly given its post–Compromise of 1850 context, is its muted attitude toward revolutionary violence. Instead of invoking heroes of the Revolution so as to encourage black violence, Douglass, perhaps swayed by the pacifist vision of Stowe's *Uncle Tom's Cabin*, praises them for being "peace men" deeply committed to the transracial ideals of "justice, liberty, and humanity." When he does address the violence of the American Revolutionaries, he takes care to present their actions as the self-defensive maneuvers of rational combatants intent on maintaining their self-control. "Your fathers were wise men," Douglass says to his audience, and though "oppression makes a wise man mad," the Revolutionaries "did not go mad"; instead, "they became restive under this treatment." As restive as they might have become, when the patriots opt for war, they are imaged, in Douglass's telling, as unaggressive to the point of martyrdom; they are described as having bared the "bosom to the storm of British artillery."[4]

Though in several speeches of the 1850s he defended the use of violent means to resist enslavers, Douglass ultimately conceived of violence as a sort of intoxicant that threatened to bring about in justifiably resistant blacks what it brought about in the British oppressors of the American colonists: an imbruting "madness." Viewing the "circumspect, exact and proportionate" actions of the heroes of 1776 as a model for resistance in the 1850s and convinced that temperate self-control, in conjunction with political antislavery, could effect a revolutionary transformation of U.S. society, Douglass promulgated a politics and poetics of what I call "temperate revolutionism." Douglass was not alone in linking temperance and antislavery, for as I noted in Chapter 1, temperance was central to the antebellum black-elevation movement from the time of the first black national convention. Like Benjamin Franklin, who during the Revolution counseled the colonists toward temperate self-help as a way of resisting and thus highlighting the immorality of "intemperate" British power, so Douglass and other African American leaders committed to the "uplift" of the free blacks viewed market-oriented temperance capitalism as serving the revolutionary ends of freedom. Praising the bravery and heroism of the patriots of 1776 at a time when blacks faced new legal and social constraints imposed by the Compromise of 1850, Douglass saw as equally brave and heroic the efforts of African Americans to participate as equals, as self-possessed individuals, in the nation's burgeoning economy. In *Bondage*, he figured himself as the exemplary representative of such efforts at self-elevation — efforts that he hoped would bring about for blacks and whites alike what in "Fourth of July" he messianically termed "your great deliverance."[5]

Responding to the threat posed by Delany and other black emigrationists, then, Douglass's 1855 *Bondage* artfully (albeit problematically) brings together discourses of revolutionary violence and temperate self-help in the service of perpetuating Douglass's status as the nation's representative black leader. William L. Andrews remarks that *Bondage* "is the work of a man who is working his way toward the center of a new group identity from the margins of his Garrisonian past."[6] But to historicize *Bondage* in such a way is to reproduce the rhetorical argument (and politics) of Douglass's narrative. Eliding from the national stage the very existence of contending black leaders, Douglass makes his representative identity as temperate revolutionary synonymous with African Americans' "group identity"; his rhetorical effort to enforce such a connection between himself and the group will be one of the focuses of my discussion of *Bondage*. Before turning to the autobiography, however, I first want to explore how temperance discourse provided Douglass and other antislavery reformers with compelling ways of talking to blacks *and* whites about bondage and freedom in the United States.

Intemperance and Slavery

In his influential *American Slavery as It Is* (1839), Theodore Weld set forth a standard abolitionist position on slavery's tendency to promote "intemperance" among the masters: "Arbitrary power is to the mind what alcohol is to the body; it intoxicates. Man loves power. It is perhaps the strongest human passion; and the more absolute the power, the stronger the desire for it; and the more it is desired, the more its exercise is enjoyed; this enjoyment is to human nature a fearful temptation, — generally, an overmatch for it." For Weld, Garrison, and numerous other abolitionists and temperance reformers of the period, individuals, when bestowed with "arbitrary" power, found themselves incapable of maintaining rational control over the mind or body. Governed by an appetite for power, individual enslavers, like alcoholics, could be viewed as enslaved to their own corporeal desires. In this rhetorical conception of things, the slave master emerged as a sort of "victim" of a system proffering a temptation — absolute power, "a fiery stimulant," in Weld's words — that most people would find difficult to resist. After all, as Weld explained, "the whole history of man is a record of real interests sacrificed to present gratification."[7]

The conception of intemperance as a form of slavery remained central both to antislavery and temperance discourse during the antebellum period, helping white and black abolitionists to develop a trenchant critique of slave owners as "intoxicated" by, or "enslaved" to, the unlimited power vouchsafed them by their culture. For black temperance writers and abolitionists in particular, the image of the slave owner as a beast enslaved to appetite was an attractive one, as it allowed black writers to turn upside down the proslavery stereotype of blacks as brutes in need of restraint. But an obvious problem with the trope of the "drunken" or "enslaved" master, at least as considered by black temperance abolitionists, was that it failed to regard African Americans as potentially active agents in the culture. Numerous black reformers therefore argued that not only white temperance but also black temperance was in order — a concerted effort by Northern free blacks to abstain from drinking so that they could more lucidly and energetically devote themselves to the project of self-elevation. "No oppressed COLORED AMERICAN, who works to occupy that elevation in society, which God has designed he should occupy," Samuel Cornish instructed his readers in an 1837 issue of the *Colored American*, "should be intemperate or even touch, as a beverage, intoxicating drinks." Sharing these assumptions, Martin Delany, who in 1834 helped organize a black temperance society in Pittsburgh, drafted the resolution at the 1841 State Convention of the Colored Freemen of Pennsylvania calling on blacks to adopt "TOTAL ABSTINENCE" as a way of gaining "the esteem of all wise and virtuous men." For, as Stephen Meyers put it in the 10 February 1842 issue of his temperance/abolitionist newspaper, *Northern Star and Freeman's Advocate*, "Whenever it can be said (and not gainsayed) that the free blacks are a sober, industrious and intelligent people, capable of self government, the only argument in favor of slavery falls to the ground."[8]

As suggested by the reference to "self government," black temperance rhetoric and ideology had important sources in the Revolutionary period. In the writings of Franklin, Benjamin Rush, and Anthony Benezet, for example, it was regularly argued that British desires to maintain authority over colonial Americans were the desires of enslavers intoxicated by power.[9] The conjoining of temperance and antislavery in Revolutionary rhetoric helped to make temperance reform particularly appealing to Northern free blacks, who formed some of the first temperance groups in the United States in the late eighteenth century. By the 1820s and 1830s temperance was central to the emergent black press and black convention movement of the period; and a generalized view of temperance as essential to black elevation dominated African American writings until the mid-1830s, when "temperance became viewed more narrowly, but more effectively, as a survival strategy and as an antislavery tactic." By the 1840s, Donald Yacovone observes, "temperance and abolitionism had become virtually synonymous."[10]

Fully aware of the overlapping concerns of these "synonymous" reforms, Frederick Douglass, soon after arriving in Ireland in October 1845 at the start of his great British tour, delivered a speech titled "Intemperance and Slavery" to a group of temperance advocates and sympathizers brought together by Father Theobald Mathew, otherwise known as the "Apostle of Temperance." Credited by historians with accumulating over six million temperance pledges in Ireland, across the Continent, and overseas, Father Mathew made Douglass one of the six million two days later during a special ceremony at Dublin. Though Douglass would eventually become disenchanted with Mathew, he had for years seen a close connection between antislavery and temperance reform; thus there is a certain appropriateness in his having taken the temperance pledge the same year as the publication of his *Narrative*. As he remarked in "Intemperance and Slavery," from the moment he escaped from bondage, "I set my voice against intemperance. I lectured against it, and talked against it, in the street, in the way-side, at the fire-side; wherever I went during the last seven years, my voice has been against intemperance." Douglass's initial temperance work must have been relatively informal — cajolings at meetings, asides during speeches, private counselings — for "Intemperance and Slavery" is his earliest surviving piece primarily devoted to temperance.[11]

Douglass begins the speech with a declaration of his victimization at the hands of the intemperate: "I was not a slave to intemperance, but a slave to my fellow-men." But rather than lamenting the plight of slaves governed by brutes intoxicated by their power over their "fellow-men," he abruptly shifts his focus to the free blacks, as he worries over their tendencies toward excessive drinking: "We have a large class of free people of color in America; that class has, through the influence of intemperance, done much to retard the progress of the anti-slavery movement — that is, they have furnished arguments to the oppressors for oppressing us." Yet just as it seems that Douglass is closing his eyes to the racism driving marginalized blacks to drink, he shifts his emphasis yet again, describing the "intemperate" actions of a white mob against free blacks attempting to advance the cause of temperance. He reports how twelve hundred black members of Philadelphia's Moyamensing Temperance Society, marching in the 1 August 1842 celebration of West Indies emancipation, were viciously attacked by "*an infuriated mob*" of Philadelphia's white citizenry. For Douglass, the lessons here are twofold: that African Americans, whether temperate or not, have to confront the realities of white racism, which itself can be viewed as a form of intemperance; and that whites sympathetic to the goals of black progress should open their temperance organizations to blacks. But by the conclusion of the speech he attempts to sidestep issues of race by resorting to a universalizing peroration that simultaneously implicates and absolves all parties concerned: "I believe, Mr. President, that if we could but make the world sober, we would have no slavery. *Mankind has been drunk.*" Though he refers to the need to get "the slaveholder sober for a moment" and to the role of "public opinion . . . to break the relation of master and slave," the large thrust of the speech is to charge not only white Americans or white Southerners or even actual slaveholders but *all* mankind with intemperance.[12] From this perspective, temperance, so it would seem, must take priority over antislavery, as temperance embraces antislavery or, to put it another way, becomes the necessary condition for the abolition of slavery.

Given this tight linkage between temperance and antislavery, it is not surprising that the Washingtonian movement of the 1840s was enthusiastically embraced by Frederick Douglass and other black temperance writers as an antislavery movement of sorts. Spawned by six casual drinkers who in the spring of 1840 ceremoniously took a pledge in a Baltimore tavern against the use of alcoholic beverages, by the mid-1840s the Washingtonians had tens of thousands of adherents who themselves had proffered the teetotaler pledge.[13] As their invocation of George Washington suggests, the Washingtonians took their inspiration from the nation's Revolutionary heritage of self-government. Meeting in groups to tell their life histories, the Washingtonians, with their sacralizing of the testimonies of formerly poor or "enslaved" individuals, offered the hopeful prospect of the "slaves" themselves bringing about their own emancipation. For example, in a report printed in an 1842 issue of Stephen Meyers's *Northern Star and Freeman's Advocate* that anticipated the use of similar emancipatory rhetoric in Douglass's *Narrative*, the New York State Temperance Society observed of the Washingtonian movement: "An unprecedented effort at self-reform has burst forth from the very bosoms of the wretched victims of this evil [intemperance]. . . . Those lost wretches themselves, from the depths of their own desperate debasement, have called up their manliness, and stood forth emancipated, disenthralled, the preachers of that temperance they had so long despised. It was like a resurrection from the grave; it was as if the tomb had spoken; no wonder that the voice of hope echoed over the land." Such "hope" was possible because the end of "slavery" was in sight. As T. S. Arthur reported in his fictional "bible" of the movement, *Six Nights with the Washingtonians* (1842), at Washingtonian meetings there were "men who had been slaves, some for a long series of years, to the most degrading vice. But now they stood up as free men, and there was scarcely a face, marred sadly as some were, that had not an expression of serious, manly determination and confidence." Former "slaves," they regularly assembled for their mutual benefit to tell their "simple unadorned histories of real life"; and in telling their authentic histories of "manly determination," they forged the bonds of fraternal community that would fend off "reenslavement." The group experience of listening as an "association" to speeches that "stirred the heart to the very depths" became the primal quasi-religious act that impelled formerly enslaved individuals to take the community's freedom-ensuring temperance pledge.[14]

In his March 1848 speech "Principles of Temperance Reform," Douglass reflected on the impact of Washingtonianism on the larger culture, focusing in particular on the importance of first-person testimonies to the movement: "A mightier and more thrilling eloquence is that which has come up from the dram-shop and gutter. The simple, straightforward, unvarnished narration of individual suffering—the graphic pictures of family distress and ruin—the painful exhibitions of shattered and broken constitutions—the powerful exposures of the subtle schemes and alluring charms of rum-vendors, have nearly all come from this class of persons; men who have seen, heard, and felt, the workings of the prison-house."[15] Substitute "slave owner" for "rum-vender" and "plantation" for "dram-shop and gutter" and the Washingtonian testimony, in Douglass's anatomy, sounds very much like a slave narrative. Douglass's 1848 celebration of the simplicity and authenticity of Washingtonian testimonies encourages us to read his 1845 *Narrative*—his own "unvarnished narration" of the "prison-house"—as deliberately working *both* in the Washingtonian and slave-narrative modes of testimonial discourse.

Garrison's account of Douglass's initial speech to the Nantucket antislavery meeting, in the preface to the *Narrative*, conveys a "Washingtonian" sense of the power of authentic testimony to reform and (re-)create community, as he describes Douglass in a way that parallels T. S. Arthur's descriptions of the poor, untutored former "slaves" stepping forth at Washingtonian meetings to offer their testimonies: "He came forward to the platform with a hesitancy and embarrassment. . . . After apologizing for his ignorance, and reminding the audience that slavery was a poor school for the human intellect and heart, he proceeded to narrate some of the facts in his own history as a slave, and in the course of his speech gave utterance to many noble thoughts and thrilling reflections." The speech, of course, galvanizes the antislavery meeting, as his later speeches would galvanize the antislavery community; the printed text— "entirely his own production"—attempts to perform the same cultural work on a larger scale.[16]

And yet how easy was it for the slaves to achieve "self-reform" and stand "forth emancipated"? Was enslavement in a plantation, like "enslavement" in a tavern, really an instance of the slaves' "own desperate debasement"? Similar questions about the appropriateness of Washingtonian discourse to the enslaved blacks' situation may be raised about Douglass's famous account in the *Narrative* of his "manly" resistance to slavery; for I think it is no small coincidence that he uses almost the same religiously and politically charged Washingtonian language of the New York State Temperance Society in describing his "emancipation" from the slave breaker Edward Covey: "This battle with Covey . . . rekindled the few expiring embers of freedom, and revived within me a sense of my own manhood. It recalled the departed self-confidence, and inspired me again with a determination to be free. . . . He only can understand the deep satisfaction which I experienced, who has himself repelled by force the bloody arm of slavery. I felt as I never felt before. It was a glorious resurrection, from the tomb of slavery, to the heaven of freedom."[17] Of course, Douglass has hardly achieved literal freedom; he remains enslaved for several more years. And indications exist that something more than manly resolution allows him to savor his resurrection: the murder of the resistant slave Denby earlier in the text demonstrates that, among other things, Douglass has benefited from providential good fortune as well. Arguably what Douglass is doing in the "resurrection" passage, with its emphasis on self-help, is addressing the free blacks, who, after all, would be the only U.S. blacks having ready access to *Narrative*. Attempting to persuade free blacks to take control of their lives (however much that is possible) by accusing them, through metaphor, of remaining slaves in body and spirit, Douglass makes use of rhetorical tactics similar to those of the Washingtonians, who likewise enjoined the poor and economically disadvantaged to liberate themselves from the "slavery" of drink in order to revitalize self and community.

In an 1848 lecture, "Colored People Must Command Respect," reprinted in the *North Star*, Douglass asserted what a number of black temperance advocates had been asserting since the early 1800s: "They ["Colored People"] must be temperance people, otherwise they may expect to remain in degradation."[18] This self-help (or Washingtonian) version of temperance as a summons to free blacks to use their "freedom" to uplift themselves and (by their example) their enslaved brethren predominated in the discussions of temperance in the *North Star*. As we have seen, coeditor Martin Delany had himself, during the 1830s and early 1840s, embraced temperance reform; and though Delany would eventually break with Douglass on a number of issues, he continued to share Douglass's belief in the worth of temperance to the free blacks. In one of his early "Western tour" letters to Douglass, printed in a March 1848 issue of the *North Star*, Delany proclaimed, "The Temperance cause is beginning to 'look up,' I having, by invitation, addressed the Pittsburgh Society of Washingtonians, on Monday evening last, in Temperance Hall." Later that year Douglass reprinted an article from the *Philadelphia Daily Republic* on a "Temperance Celebration in Philadelphia," which noted that "Dr. M. R. Delany made a brief and able speech, which was received by the audience with approbation." And in a letter to Douglass of 18 December 1848, printed in the 5 January 1849 *North Star*, Delany reported: "This evening, I addressed the Good Samaritan Division of the Sons of Temperance, in the Colored Methodist Church."[19]

Convinced of the importance of black temperance to the interrelated causes of antislavery and black elevation, Douglass published numerous items in the *North Star* emphasizing, as Delany emphasized in his "Western tour" dispatches, personal hygiene, thrift, and industry. In a January

1848 issue, for example, he printed a temperance squib in the "Miscellaneous" column: "A rumseller once visiting a victim of his murderous traffic on his death-bed, said to him: 'Do you remember me?' 'Yes,' said the dying man with a startling emphasis, 'I do remember you, and I remember your shop, where I formed the habit which has ruined me; and when I am dead, my beggared widow and fatherless children will remember you.'" Though the trafficking rum seller could be analogized to a slave trader or slave owner, in this way encouraging a reading of the sketch as protoprohibitionist, the main emphasis of the anecdote is on the responsibility of the individual to form good habits. As a sketch of 28 April 1848 pointed out, in the temporal mode of Hogarth and Arthur, but one drink could diminish the individual's ability to act "freely." The sketch, "The Young Man's Course," begins with the narrator observing the young man at a party choosing to take "a single glass of wine"; the sketch concludes, years later, with a final observation: "I saw him yet once more—he was pale, cold and motionless, and was carried by his friends to his last resting place. . . . His mother wept to think she had ever given being to such a child." In an article of 1 September 1848 titled "Disagreeable Breath," the anonymous author asked rhetorically: "What is more repulsive than a disagreeable breath? Nothing conceivable; yet this proceeds entirely from . . . careless negligence of persons to keep their teeth clean." An article printed two months later, "The Humanizing Influence of Cleanliness," advised that "a filthy, squalid, noxious dwelling . . . contributes to make its unfortunate inhabitants selfish, sensual, and regardless of the feelings of others; the constant indulgence of such passions renders them reckless and brutal."[20]

Surely the grime of the free blacks' dwelling places had much to do with the quality of residences available to them in racist urban centers, and as the *North Star*'s numerous articles attacking Southern enslavers and Northern racists made clear, Douglass hardly placed the entire burden of temperance on the shoulders of African Americans. In his famous lecture "Colorphobia," printed in a May 1849 issue, he described whites' racist responses to blacks as akin to temperance reformer "[John] Gough's description of 'delirium tremens.'" Moreover, as suggested in "Intemperance and Slavery," Douglass could be quite critical of white temperance organizations. His several articles on Father Mathew during the period moved from lauding him for obtaining one thousand temperance pledges in Brooklyn to pillorying him for disconnecting temperance from antislavery. In June 1850 Douglass printed an article in which he vilified the Sons of Temperance for excluding blacks from their ranks.[21] But even with these various attacks on institutional racism among white temperance advocates and organizations, Douglass found the space to print a number of conventional pieces on temperance. "The Sweetness of Home," an unattributed article that appeared in one of the final issues of the *North Star*, offered the following T. S. Arthur–like paean to domesticity: "The home of a temperate, industrious, honest man will be his greatest joy."[22]

The temperate home would continue to be celebrated in the pages of *Frederick Douglass' Paper* as a guarantor of (or prerequisite for) the productivity of black males in the marketplace. But a significant change in Douglass's attitude toward temperance occurred around the time he broke with Garrison's moral-suasion philosophy and began publishing the political-abolitionist *Frederick Douglass' Paper*: he embraced as a model for social reform the prohibitionary tactics of the Maine Law of 1851, which banned the sale and production of alcoholic beverages in the state. Douglass's promotion of such a law for New York State, in the numerous pieces he (re)printed on the issue in *Frederick Douglass' Paper*, evinced his revised approach to the politics of antislavery and antiliquor, as he came to place less of an emphasis on promoting moral suasion, or good habits, and more on promoting legislative action and intervention to achieve black elevation and emancipation. Douglass signaled his change from moral suasion to political interventionism in his decision to publish in 1851 and 1852 issues of his paper speeches by others who self-consciously articulated similar ideological transformations. In the issue of 27 November 1851, for example, he reprinted a sermon by temperance reformer George Cheever that, in calling for the spread of the Maine Law throughout the nation, spoke of "the hopelessness of doing anything under present circumstances with moral suasion" in attacking "corporate interests" and "the liquor traffic." Similarly, in an issue of May 1852 he reprinted a speech by Elizabeth Cady Stanton in support of the law, wherein she declared that she and her associates had learned, in their heretofore thwarted efforts to save man (and, hence, woman) "from subjugation to his mere animal nature," that "moral suasion will not do."[23]

In the context of the antislavery imperatives of Douglass's paper, Cheever's attack on the liquor trade and Stanton's attack on patriarchy could be taken as attacks as well on enslavers and the slave trade. For what linked all his articles and reprintings on antislavery and temperance was a focus on the dangers of succumbing to or being victimized by the appetites of the body. This focus was in accord with Gerrit Smith's 1854 speech to Congress in praise of the Maine Law, a speech that Douglass reprinted on the front page of his paper. In this speech, Smith referred to the "dramshop" as "a filthy, noisy hole where the slaves of appetite congregate." The image of the dramshop as the home of the "enslaved," a conflation that addressed Smith's commitment to temperance and anti-slavery, was consistent with Douglass's own writings of 1854 on temperance and antislavery. In a speech delivered in New York City in May 1854 and reprinted in his paper, Douglass proclaimed the Weld- and Smith-like sentiment that "a system which gives absolute power to one man over the body and soul of another man . . . is the parent of all manner of treachery and fraud. It is never satisfied, but becomes more rapacious with every new accession to its power." That "rapaciousness," imaged as a form of addiction, can culminate in the bodily violation (the rape) of those enslaved to masters who are themselves, in their endless pursuit of corporeal gratification, "slaves of appetite." Hence the need for laws that would forcibly curb such appetites. When the state legislature of New York passed a modified version of the Maine Law in 1855, Douglass devoted the entire front page of his paper to celebrating the triumph; for the next several months he maintained a regular section on efforts to enforce (and keep on the books) a bill that eventually would be repealed.[24]

Though I think it important to emphasize the legislative component of Douglass's post-1851 articles and reprintings on temperance, I would not want to obscure the fact that in Washingtonian fashion he persisted in stressing the importance of individual and group initiatives in overcoming slavery, whether to Southern masters or alcohol. This was especially true of his writings directed at Northern free blacks. Thus he continued to print in his paper sketches intended to demonstrate the restorative workings of "temperate" domesticity. In a sketch titled "A Horrible Picture of Intemperance," which appeared on the front page of an 1854 issue of *Frederick Douglass' Paper*, the anonymous author describes a (white) drunken man who, desperate for money to support his habit, locks his wife and baby outside their home while taking their last remaining pennies; the infant freezes to death. Several months after printing this piece, Douglass advised Canada's blacks to "leave the grog shops and taverns, and no longer stand idling at the corners of the streets, but go out into the world."[25]

Like Delany in *Condition*, then, and consistent with the two men's *North Star* writings, Douglass continued during this period to enjoin blacks to become "a business people."[26] But because Douglass, unlike Delany, remained committed to improving blacks' prospects within the national borders of the United States, it could be argued that his temperance politics—and the politics of the black temperance movement generally—may have helped to consolidate, rather than to challenge, the institutions, ideologies, and social practices that marginalized and enslaved African Americans. Teresa A. Goddu and Craig V. Smith and other more recent commentators on the "self-help" side of Douglass therefore lament what they regard as Douglass's "movement into white discourse, a movement which involves a . . . separation from his black roots." David Leverenz offers an equally condemnatory account of Douglass in the mid-1850s, indicting him for distancing himself from "lower-class black people," for embracing "white male culture," and for voicing an "unswerving advocacy of middle-class individualism and hard work."[27]

My specific disagreements with Goddu and Smith and with Leverenz will be developed more fully in the reading of *Bondage* that follows. I should say at the outset, though, that what I find troubling about both these analyses is how little self-consciousness or appropriative power they are willing to grant to Douglass.[28] In my reading of *Bondage*, I will be addressing the ways in which Douglass sought to use temperance discourse, which, given its centrality to several decades of black elevation efforts, can hardly be termed a "white discourse," to persuade his free black readers, contra Delany, to continue to struggle for their rights in the United States (as well as to suggest how that struggle might be waged). My sense is that Douglass's 1855 autobiography, informed as it is by a commitment to temperance values, also complicates and at times undermines those values, in large part because Douglass was aware that there *were* some fundamental incompatibilities between temperate self-help and the quest for revolutionary social change. An attempt to yoke together and in this way mutually energize these apparently divergent agendas, as in his "Fourth of July" speech on temperate revolutionism, is one of Douglass's large projects in *Bondage*.

Temperate Revolutionary

As its title suggests, *My Bondage and My Freedom* tells a story of liberation that, with its evocation of Exodus, means to underscore Douglass's representative identity as a kind of Moses to his people. William L. Andrews, in one of the most sensitive (and influential) readings of *Bondage*, observes that in "its tone, dominant metaphors, and structure, the . . . book represents a quiet but thorough revision of the significance of the life of Frederick Douglass," conveying as it does "the story of a black man's circuitous route toward black community." Central to Douglass's strategies of accentuating that circuitousness are his efforts to present the boy and young man of the narrative as very different from the accomplished public figure who tells his story.[29] Consider, for example, Douglass's account in *Bondage* of the significance of his move from Colonel Lloyd's plantation to the Aulds' Baltimore home: "I may be deemed superstitious and egotistical, in regarding this event as a special interposition of Divine Providence in my favor; but the thought is a part of my history, and I should be false to the earliest and most cherished sentiments of my soul, if I suppressed, or hesitated to avow that opinion, although it may be characterized as irrational by the wise, and ridiculous by the scoffer."[30] The 1845 version, in contrast, makes no mention of a "scoffer" and never explicitly qualifies any thought as being "a part of my history." Distancing himself from the self-consecrated leader of *Narrative* by imagining a "scoffer" in the crowd, even as he evokes the figure of Moses in *Bondage*'s title, Douglass presents himself as an acting subject in history — as the subject, in short, of an author. John Freccero argues that inherent in the most complex autobiographies is "the death of the self as character and the resurrection of the self as author."[31] Douglass calls attention to his authorial "resurrection" through the titles of *Bondage*'s opening three chapters: "The Author's Childhood," "The Author Removed from His First Home," and "The Author's Parentage." Underscoring right from the start the distance between author and subject, Douglass as a chronicler of self can proceed with a greater measure of irony and self-consciousness in putting his self-representation to his own particular uses.

Douglass's transformed sense of the rhetorical purpose of telling his life history (from fulfilling Garrison's moral-suasion agenda to encouraging his own agenda of achieving antislavery ends through black elevation and political action) is evident in his decision to replace the paternalistic letters from Garrison and Phillips that preface the *Narrative* with an editor's preface (consisting mostly of a letter that Douglass wrote to the publishing house's editor) and a substantial introduction by the noted black physician and abolitionist James McCune Smith. Smith was a particularly apt choice for the job of introducing *Bondage* to its free black readers, as he had written the report at the 1853 Rochester convention endorsing the creation of a national council for free blacks and had continued to work with Douglass in opposing black emigration. Around the same time he wrote the introduction to *Bondage*, Smith delivered a speech at the First Colored Presbyterian Church of New York City calling on blacks to elevate themselves in the United States primarily through "our own means" and in this way "maintain our citizenship and manhood in every relation — civil, religious, and social — throughout the land." [32] The argument implicit in his introduction is that Douglass's example, as limned in *Bondage*, can help blacks to further such a program. Thus he presents Douglass, in a Franklinian mode, as a "Representative American" (17) — an American who, through his initiative, hard work, and self-restraint, managed to raise himself "from the lowest condition in society to the highest" (9). [33] Accordingly, he champions him as a model for imitation: "I shall place this book in the hands of the only child spared me, bidding him to strive and emulate its noble example. You may do likewise" (23).

Smith's celebration of an African American as a "Representative American" may be taken as an act of ideological aggression that means to spotlight the gap between the nation's egalitarian ideals and white racist practices. Yet in *Bondage*'s prefatory material both Smith and Douglass, rather than chide white America for betraying its liberal ideology, echo the position of William Whipper and others committed to black uplift by saying that African Americans must do all they can to refute proslavery claims of their "natural" inferiority. In the editor's preface Douglass claims that his life history undermines white notions that blacks "are naturally, inferior; that they are so low in the scale of humanity, and so utterly stupid, that they are unconscious of their wrongs" (4). Though Smith subsequently laments the compulsion among some African Americans to pattern their lives so as to rebut and refute racist whites, he nevertheless maintains that to consolidate their place in U.S. society, blacks have to do just that: "The negro . . . must prove his title to all that is demanded for him" (9). Douglass himself states that his book has special relevance to the situation of "my afflicted people" (4); and there is an overall sense in the narrative that his ability to rise is central to what Smith terms his "special mission" (11) as a deliverer of his people. According to Smith, Douglass's "representative" life reveals "that the worst of our institutions, in its worst aspect, cannot keep down energy, truthfulness, and earnest struggle for the right" (23). The burden on blacks inspired by Douglass is to achieve a similar rise.

The prefatory messages on the significance of Douglass's life are a bit self-righteous and coercive, and all sorts of questions could be raised about the imitative behavior Smith and Douglass are urging upon African Americans—the same sorts of questions that I raised about Douglass's account in *Narrative* of his resistance to Covey. To what extent can the free and enslaved blacks be expected to follow Douglass's example? Does the fact of enslavement suggest a lack of "American" "energy, truthfulness, and earnest struggle for the right"? The large question of individual responsibility and action—the question of the text's Washingtonian dimension—remains a troubling crux of *Bondage*. Perhaps the best place to begin to explore the text's imitative politics of "self-restraint" is by looking at Douglass's discussion, sketchily put forth in *Narrative* and much more fully developed in *Bondage*, of the excessive drinking among plantation slaves that occurs annually between Christmas and New Year's Day.

That holiday period, Douglass reports in *Bondage* (drawing on his discussion in *Narrative*), "we regarded as our own, by the grace of our masters, and we, therefore used it, or abused it, as we pleased. . . . The sober, thinking, and industrious ones of our number, would employ themselves in manufacturing corn brooms, mats, horse collars, and baskets. . . . Another class spent their time in hunting opossums, coons, rabbits, and other game. But the majority spent the holidays in sports, ball playing, wrestling, boxing, running foot races, dancing, and drinking whisky; and this latter mode of spending the time was generally most agreeable to their masters" (154–55). The decision to use or abuse their "free" time, Douglass initially suggests, is a matter of free choice for the slaves; and there is a clear sense here that he honors the "sober, thinking, and industrious ones." Thus he presents the slaves not as a monolithic group but rather in terms of a moral-hierarchical "class" structure: at the top is the productive industrious class (whose labors nevertheless ultimately serve the ends of the slave plantation); one rung down is the hunting class (also productive, in that hunting provides the slaves with additional food); and at the very bottom is the gamester class, those who dissipate their time by seeking corporeal pleasure. Hence, running and dancing are put on the same continuum as intemperate drinking. At this point in the account, Douglass would appear to be directing his criticism at those slaves who regard intemperance as a form of ego-enhancing, conspicuous consumption. He pointedly remarks, "Not to be drunk during the holidays, was disgraceful; and he was esteemed a lazy and improvident man, who could not afford to drink whisky during Christmas" (155).

Henry Bibb, in his 1849 *Narrative of the Life and Adventures of Henry Bibb*, can seem similarly moralistic about the slaves' propensities toward drinking, presenting alcohol as the "lower" sort of slaves' substitute for religion: "Those who make no profession of religion, resort to the woods in large numbers on that day [the Sabbath] to gamble, fight, get drunk, and break the Sabbath." But though Bibb can seem harshly judgmental of the slaves, he clear-sightedly notes the role of the slave owners in tempting the slaves to drink in order to "get them wrestling, fighting, jumping, running foot races, and butting each other like sheep."[34] In his own account, Douglass abruptly shifts his focus from slave drinking as a matter of free choice (with the lower sort most likely to succumb) to slave drinking as the result of white manipulation. He thus subverts his initially moralistic stance — a stance more appropriate to the world outside the slave plantation — when he remarks, for example, on how the masters resort to "cunning tricks" to get the slaves drunk, including making bets on which slave "can drink more whisky than any other" (*Bondage*, p. 157). And while we might have supposed that Douglass meant at the outset of the discussion to suggest that he was one of the few "sober, thinking and industrious ones of our number," the fact remains, as he reveals near the end of his discussion, that when the slaves "were induced to drink, I [was] among the rest, and when the holidays were over, we all staggered up from our filth and wallowing, took a long breath, and went away to our various fields of work" (157).

As the "filth and wallowing" suggest, Douglass regards alcohol as having the capacity to make animals of men, thereby contributing to what he terms the "brutification" (152) of slavery. The masters deliberately proffer alcohol to their slaves, Henry Highland Garnet declared in an 1846 temperance address, because alcohol "stupefies the mind," thereby making it difficult for blacks to plan strategies of resistance.[35] Douglass similarly observes in *Bondage* that slaves "stretched out in brutal drunkenness, at once helpless and disgusting" (157), are the least likely to organize slave insurrections. The holidays in which uncontrolled drinking is encouraged therefore serve the ends of the masters by functioning as "safety valves" (156) of sorts, harmlessly releasing "the explosive elements inseparable from the human mind, when reduced to the condition of slavery" (156).[36] Moreover, Douglass contends, the excessive holiday drinking serves to convince the slaves that the "vicious and re-volting dissipation" resulting from intoxication was the result, and to a certain extent the moral equivalent, of "LIBERTY" (157). In this way, the masters cunningly manage "to disgust the slaves with their temporary freedom, and to make them as glad to return to their work, as they were to leave it" (157).

By dulling the mind, siphoning off revolutionary energies, and tar-nishing the merits of freedom, intemperance effectively (re)enslaves the slaves. As Douglass succinctly puts it in "Intemperance Viewed in Con-nection with Slavery," "This intemperance enslaves—this intemperance paralyses—this intemperance binds with bonds stronger than iron, and makes man the willing subject of its brutal control." But again we might ask whether Douglass has not lost sight, in this speech and in *Bondage*, of the central fact that slavery, not intemperance, enslaves. Although Douglass clearly states early in *Bondage* that "in the case of the slave, the miseries and hardships of his lot are imposed by others" (69), there remains a tension or conflict between his "prohibitionist" view that the slaves have little to no responsibility for their drinking, on the one hand, and his "Washingtonian" view that they participate in their enslavement, on the other. This is so even though Douglass's other writings indicate that he was well aware of the differences between intemperance and slavery and thus of the possible misuses of this metaphorical conflation. The initial lecture reprinted in *Bondage*'s appendix, "Reception Speech" (1846), signals just such an awareness: "It is common in this country to distinguish every bad thing by the name of slavery. . . . I do not wish for a moment to detract from the horror with which the evil of intemper-ance is contemplated—not at all. . . . But I am here to say that I think the term slavery is sometimes abused by identifying it with that which it is not."[37] And yet despite such a cautionary warning against rhetorical flaccidity, Douglass concludes his discussion of the slaves' intemperate holiday drinking in this way: "It was about as well to be a slave to *master*, as to be a slave to *rum* and *whisky*" (157). Does he really believe the literal truth of this statement, or does this have for him a figura-tive truth beyond its obvious factual limitations? If so, does he wish to imply that enslaved blacks, like the Washingtonians' "enslaved" drink-ers, could free themselves from slavery and rise to an elevated station in the United States should they only employ the *will* to do so?

To address some of the large questions of agency and authority raised by Douglass's contradictory account of the slaves' holiday drinking, we need to return to the beginning of *Bondage*, where temperance themes are implicitly linked to the problem of self-elevation in a slave society. And here we note another of the major changes Douglass made in his 1855 autobiography. Whereas *Narrative* begins with the personal voice of an author who draws in the reader by revealing the dark ironies attending the childhood of a slave, *Bondage*, in Douglass's effort to offer a larger picture of slavery as a system, begins with a more matter-of-fact delineation of the social scene. In the first paragraph Douglass describes Tuckahoe, of Maryland's Talbot County on the Eastern Shore, which is "remarkable for nothing that I know of more than for the worn-out, sandy, desert-like appearance of its soil, the general dilapidation of its farms and fences, the indigent and spiritless character of its inhabitants, and the prevalence of ague and fever" (27). Douglass refers in the second paragraph to the "ignorance, indolence, and poverty of its people" (27); and only in the third paragraph does he make it clear why he is even writing about such a forlorn place: "It was in this dull, flat, and unthrifty district . . . surrounded by a white population of the lowest order, indolent and drunken to a proverb, and among slaves, who seemed to ask, '*Oh, what's the use?*' every time they lifted a hoe, that I — without any fault of mine — was born, and spent the first years of my childhood" (27).

These opening three paragraphs of *Bondage* tell us much about Douglass's values, his view of the social consequences of slavery, and his sense of his own relationship to the world he is describing and the story he is telling. Clearly, the emphasis on the dilapidation, indigence, and indolence among Tuckahoe's blacks and whites conveys Douglass's basic allegiance to free-labor ideology. For Douglass, a particularly telling sign of the failure of slavery as a system was that it undermined, both at the top and at the bottom, incentives toward the kinds of work that supposedly built moral character. The wealthy plantation owners managed to avoid hard work because they possessed slaves — that was fairly obvious. But the focus of free-labor critique often went in the other direction: to assess the implications of the lack of social mobility for considerably less privileged whites. These poorer Southern whites, who, free-labor advocates argued, might have had the opportunity to rise in Northern society, remained locked in poverty because the availability of slave labor meant that there was little paid work for them to do. Hence the indolence of the poor whites threatened to be perpetual, with broad moral consequences for Southern society.[38]

Unlike the poor whites, who, Douglass suggests, must take some responsibility for their intemperate condition, Douglass presents himself as literally born into bondage and figuratively born into a slavery of "appetite"—in both cases "without any fault of mine." That sense of blamelessness would seem initially to extend to the other enslaved blacks as well, though Douglass's insistence on his own particular blamelessness does raise the question, as in his account of the slaves' holiday drinking, of his relationship to the world he is portraying. In contrast to the holiday drinking section, where he presents himself as one of many intemperate blacks, Douglass almost immediately attempts to place his own family outside the social pathology he describes in the opening chapter. Although most of the whites are drunk and lazy and most of the slaves are imbued with a sense of futility about the worth of their labor, Douglass's grandmother, "more provident than most of her neighbors in the preservation of seedling sweet potatoes" (28), embodies the virtues of the temperate free laborer. Refusing to see her success as the result of her "careful and thrifty" (28) labors, the slaves, with the exception of the young Frederick Douglass, fail to learn from her example. Douglass's difference (and distance) from the slave community is further underscored when he observes that his mother was "the *only* one of all the slaves and colored people in Tuckahoe" (42) who knew how to read. Shortly thereafter he notes the "ignorance" (53) of the slaves at Colonel Lloyd's in relation to his own will to knowledge: "I am persuaded that I could not have been dropped anywhere on the globe, where I could reap less, in the way of knowledge, from my immediate associates, than on this plantation" (53).[39]

As self-aggrandizing and anticommunal as these early passages sound, we need to remind ourselves that Douglass's initially dismissive notions of slave "ignorance" reflect the naïve pride of his eight-year-old self "in history." The young Douglass displays an equally naïve pride when he is sent off to Colonel Lloyd's massive plantation, despite his adult awareness that the forced separation from his mother "is in harmony with the grand aim of slavery, which, always and everywhere, is to reduce man to a level with the brute" (29). Like Franklin arriving in Philadelphia, Douglass marvels at the opportunities "for industry and enterprise" (50) awaiting him at Lloyd's. But it does not take the foolish Douglass long to realize that his arrival at the plantation is, in fact, akin to "the addition of a single pig to [Lloyd's] stock!" (51).

The resultant disillusionment leads Douglass to turn his attention to the operations of power on the plantation, focusing at first on the authority of the white masters. As powerful as the masters may appear, when they are viewed through the lens of the corporeal temperance discourse so central to *Bondage*, they can also be regarded, as Weld and others suggested, as "enslaved" to, because intoxicated by, their unlimited power to rule. Adopting this view, Douglass at times can seem sympathetic to individual slave owners. "It is not the fault of the slaveholder that he is cruel," Solomon Northup writes in *Twelve Years a Slave* (1853), "so much as it is the fault of the system under which he lives. He cannot withstand the influence of habit and associations that surround him."[40] Douglass likewise declares in *Bondage*, "The slaveholder, as well as the slave, is the victim of the slave system" (54). He elaborates on the issue of the enslavers' "victimization" in his first extended discussion of Captain Anthony's cruelties, talking of how Anthony, like all enslavers, committed "outrages, deep, dark, and nameless" and yet "was not by nature worse than other men. Had he been brought up in a free state, surrounded by the just restraints of a free society—restraints which are necessary to the freedom of all its members, alike and equally—Capt. Anthony might have been as humane a man . . . as many who now oppose the slave system" (54).

As these comments suggest, Douglass has clearly broken with Garrison's more religious reading of the slave masters as blasphemous for assuming godlike powers over other human beings, a break that inevitably makes *Bondage* less dependent on melodrama than is *Narrative* and one that points to the political consequences of Douglass's larger break with Garrison's politics of dis-Union. The insistence on Anthony's victimization by the system, which parallels Maine Law supporters' imaging of the drunken patriarch as the victim of the liquor trade, contains within it an ameliorative vision of the possibility of aiding "victims" both at the top and at the bottom through legislative acts of prohibition. From this perspective, the large problem facing the patriarch, like the large problem facing the slave during the holiday drinking period, is the ready availability of intoxicants (in the case of the masters, the intoxicants of power and alcohol), as the patriarch, lacking in "just restraints," becomes, like the intoxicated slave, something of a brute in the way he is governed by the dictates of his body.

Working with traditional republican images of aristocratic luxury, Douglass ingeniously underscores this corporeal reading of the problem of slavery by presenting the slave owners' "intemperance" in relation to the excessive production and consumption of food at the plantation—in relation, that is, to their appetite qua appetite. Chapter 7, "Life in the

Great House," begins with a stunning paragraph in which the dinner table itself—laden with, among other things, "fish, flesh, and fowl. . . . Chickens of all breeds; ducks, of all kinds" (70); "wines and brandies from France; teas of various flavor, from China; and rich, aromatic coffee from Java" (71)—seems a victim of the master's ravenous desire to consume: "The table groans under the heavy and blood-bought luxuries gathered with painstaking care. . . . Immense wealth, and its lavish expenditure, fill the great house with all that can please the eye, or tempt the taste. Here appetite, not food, is the great *desideratum*" (70). When appetite rules, then the freedom to consume without restraint is an illusory freedom, signifying the masters' subservience to their own bodies. Douglass's description of the slave owners' "pride and indolence" (71) therefore builds to a peroration worthy of the health reformer Sylvester Kellogg (or Thoreau) on the abominations of excess: "This profusion of luxury; this exemption from toil; this life of ease; this sea of plenty; aye, what of it all? Are the pearly gates of happiness and sweet content flung open to such suitors? *far from it*! . . . Food, to the indolent lounger, is poison, not sustenance. Lurking beneath all their dishes, are invisible spirits of evil, ready to feed the self-deluded gormandizers with aches, pains, fierce temper, uncontrolled passions, dyspepsia, rheumatism, lumbago and gout; and of these the Lloyds got their full share" (72). True to the Thoreauvian dimensions of this account, Douglass contrasts the unhealthful consumption of the masters with the more temperate consumption of the slave child: "He eats no candies; get no lumps of loaf sugar; always relishes his food" (32). As a result, the (male) slave child "is, for the most part of the first eight years of his life, a spirited, joyous, uproarious, and happy boy" (32).

But clearly Douglass is being ironic here, in that the "temperance" of the slave children is imposed on them by their masters. Moreover, he takes pains to note that blacks are not *naturally* more temperate than whites, nor are they any less likely, in an institutional setting that encourages people metaphorically to "feed" on those under their power, to escape the demands of appetite. Thus Douglass portrays not only the enslavers' cruelty but also the cruelties of figures like the black cook Aunt Kathy. Even the kindly and religious slave Uncle Isaac Copper whips the young Douglass when he fails to get the Lord's Prayer exactly right. As in Richard Henry Dana's *Two Years before the Mast* (1840) and Herman Melville's *White-Jacket* (1850), both of which drew on antislavery (and temperance) rhetoric, the whip figures as a sign of intemperance. "Everybody, in the south, wants the privilege of whipping somebody else" (50), Douglass writes. "The whip is all in all. . . . Slaves, as well as slaveholders, use it with an unsparing hand" (50).[41]

Of course, the slaves' appetite for domination is ultimately restrained, as the slave owners' appetite for domination was not, by their enslavement. Within his conceptual matrix of power and intemperance, Douglass therefore wants principally to show how the power to enslave intoxicates (and thereby degrades) the slave owners and their hirelings. In *Bondage*, those who are most disposed to use the whip, those who are most governed by appetite, are the overseers, the majority of whom are drunkards. The overseer Mr. Plummer, we are told, is "little better than a human brute; and, in addition to his general profligacy and repulsive coarseness, the creature was a miserable drunkard" (55). The cruel overseer Sevier seems, at his death, to be in the throes of the D.T.'s: "In the very last hours of his life, his ruling passion showed itself, and . . . when wrestling with death, he was uttering horrid oaths, and flourishing the cowskin, as though he was tearing the flesh off some helpless slave" (63). Colonel Anthony, likewise, seems perpetually to be experiencing drunken hallucinations: "Most of his leisure was spent in walking, cursing, and gesticulating, like one possessed by a demon" (55). Are these men brutish drunkards because of slavery or because brutishness is an essential aspect of their nature? Typically, when Douglass describes the overseers, as opposed to the actual owners, he seems to suggest the latter, his point being that within the slave system, those who are primarily driven by corporeal appetite will inevitably gravitate to the system's most brutish jobs. As he remarks on the overseer Gore, who kills Denby with "savage barbarity and freedom from moral restraint" (78): "Men, whose malign and brutal propensities predominate over their moral and intellectual endowments, shall, naturally, fall into those employments which promise the largest gratification to those predominating instincts or propensities" (77).[42]

Sexual gratification, Douglass suggests several times in *Bondage*, is perhaps "the largest gratification" available to the masters' and overseers' "instincts." In this respect, the whip can be taken as a metonymy for the phallus of the master or overseer, a sign of the ways in which sexual appetite (like alcohol) dominates, or imbrutes, the bodies of those who pride themselves on the illusion of their self-restraint and corporeal control.[43] Douglass, whose very existence speaks to the reality of rape on the plantation, observes that the slave owners, as "traffickers in human flesh" (43), have financial motivations for their licentiousness, insofar as their sexual predatoriness helps to increase their stock of human beings. But ultimately their predatory actions are presented less as the calculated efforts of men determined to increase their plantation's holdings than as manifestations of the appetite and power that "enslaves" the "fathers." Both the overseers Plummer and Sevier are described as having brutalized slave women; but the most famous (and most vividly related) scene of such cruelty occurs when Anthony viciously beats Douglass's Aunt Esther after she takes up with Ned Roberts. In this primal scene in which Douglass's possible father whips the partly unclothed Esther, Douglass, as John Carlos Rowe acutely observes, revises the biblical story of "Ham witnessing his father, Noah, naked and drunken in his tent," presenting us instead with a clothed tyrant governed by an "intoxicating" power to rape.[44] Douglass's demystifying description of the arbitrariness and cruelty of the master's supposedly biblically sanctioned authority leaves the slave owner nakedly exposed in all his brutishness.

And yet Douglass's childhood discovery of brute patriarchal domination is followed in the subsequent chapter with an account of a slave woman's active and seemingly successful resistance to patriarchal sexual violation — an incident that goes unmentioned in *Narrative*. He introduces the account with the bold, uplifting (and arguably naïve) assertion, "What man can make, man can unmake" (61). It is a naïve, and even annoying, statement because the "man" of the first clause, the master, has a different referent than the "man" of the second clause, the slave (woman); moreover, Douglass says nothing about the relative power of the maker and unmaker. In the context of having just represented Aunt Esther's cruel punishment, Douglass comes close to implying that she bears some responsibility for her sufferings. For in the subsequent scene he portrays the slave woman Nelly, with the help of her protesting children, facing down, or "unmaking," the authority of the vicious overseer Sevier through her use of self-defensive physical resistance. Although she absorbs some punishment, Douglass asserts that the beating will not be repeated because overseers and slave owners "prefer to whip those who are most easily whipped" (63). Taking control of her body, Nelly gains moral authority and power over those, like Sevier, "embruted" by their rage for domination. The lesson is clear: the "slave who has the courage to stand up for himself [*sic*] against the overseer, although he may have many hard stripes at the first, becomes, in the end, a freeman, even though he sustain the formal relation of a slave" (63). While Douglass's reflections on Nelly's resistance risk insulting those slaves who, for a variety of sensible reasons, choose not to offer active resistance, the self-help lesson does bring back into focus one of the large rhetorical aims of the autobiography—to encourage the nation's free blacks to work for their elevation in the United States—along with the concomitant contradiction: that Douglass's rhetoric of self-help, directed at free black readers, describes the lives of slaves.

With his emphasis on the primacy of the individual's will and desire, Douglass's use of self-help and temperance themes to represent blacks in bondage, even in the context of his larger "Maine Law" vision of the entrapments of system, can thus seem ungenerous and judgmental about those who "fail" to exert efforts as heroic as those of Nelly and Douglass to overcome their enslaved condition. Douglass momentarily conveys his awareness of the anticommunal bent of his self-help focus when he has the providential good fortune of being conveyed from Lloyd's Eastern Shore plantation to the Aulds' home in Baltimore. From the boat taking him to Baltimore, he looks back to the plantation, in part out of solidarity for "the daily suffering of others" (87). But the community-oriented Mosaic leader has yet to emerge. Such are the seductions of self-help (both in history and, arguably, in 1855) that Douglass presents himself as abruptly turning around to face the bow and spending "the remainder of the day in looking ahead" (87).

The young Douglass turns his back on the plantation slaves because he believes he has much to look ahead to. Baltimore is presented as a locale where the values associated with temperance and self-elevation—cleanliness and industry, for example—have a greater sway than at the Eastern Shore. As Lucretia Auld notes just before his departure, "The people there were very cleanly" (86). Inspired by Baltimore's promise and unfazed by Hugh Auld's famous interdiction on reading, Douglass begins his industrious pursuit of education and, through his resourceful schemes of imitation, heroically teaches himself to read and write. (The implicit suggestion here is that the free blacks could teach themselves in a much easier manner). But as on the slave plantation, Douglass soon finds evidence of unrestrained uses of power against Baltimore's slaves, most notoriously in the sadistic practices of one Mrs. Hamilton. Though Mrs. Hamilton is exceptionally cruel, Douglass suggests through his use of a temperance analogy that all the white citizens of Baltimore are complicitous in her actions: "The cruelty of Mrs. Hamilton is as justly charge-able to the upholders of the slave system, as drunkenness is chargeable on those who, by precept and example, or by indifference, uphold the drinking system" (95).

The temperance analogue helps to illuminate his own, less harrowing situation at the Aulds'. Consistent with a Stowe-inspired desire to dem-onstrate the possibilities of transracial sympathy to effect social change, he presents Sophia Auld, as he earlier presented Lucretia Auld, as a sympathetic and motherly friend. But like Mrs. Hamilton, Sophia Auld eventually becomes infected by "the fatal poison of irresponsible power" (92), for the slave is to the home in *Bondage* as alcohol is to the home in temperance writings: the catalyst of precipitous decline from domestic harmony to chaos. "When I went into their family," Douglass writes, "it was the abode of happiness and contentment" (97). But soon the husband tyrannizes over the wife, the wife tyrannizes over the slave, and domestic order disintegrates. To convey a sense of that disintegration, Douglass lit-eralizes the temperance analogy, underscoring the direct causal linkages between his entrance into the Aulds', Auld's drinking, and the master's increasingly noxious authoritarianism: "A change had taken place, both in Master Hugh, and in his once pious and affectionate wife. The influ-ence of brandy and bad company on him, and the influence of slavery and social isolation upon her, had wrought disastrously upon the characters of both" (115).

The interconnections between drinking, authoritarianism, and moral decline so central to *Bondage*'s antislavery politics are brought into their boldest relief when Douglass is abruptly returned to the plantation fol-lowing the death of his master Anthony. The patriarch's son, Andrew Anthony, Douglass says, "was distinguished for cruelty and intemper-ance" (110). Although the younger Anthony dies shortly after Douglass's return, the attitude toward labor of this "confirmed sot" (110) is emblem-atic of St. Michael's, where Douglass is sent to live with Thomas Auld. Like Tuckahoe of *Bondage*'s opening chapter, St. Michael's is clearly the home of the intemperate: "The place, as a whole, wore a dull, slovenly, enterprise-forsaken aspect" (116). In large part slavery bears responsi-bility for this state of affairs, but again drinking (the corporeal analogue) is foregrounded as the more immediate cause of the town's degenerate moral character. Speaking in the voice of an elite moral reformer, Doug-lass elaborates how the intemperate consumption of alcoholic beverages affected the character of the community: "This drinking habit, in an ignorant population, fostered coarseness, vulgarity and an indolent disregard for the social improvement of the place, so that it was admitted, by the few sober, thinking people who remained there, that St. Michael's had become a very *unsaintly*, as well as an unsightly place, before I went there to reside" (116).

Douglass's elitism carries over into his subsequent discussion of Thomas Auld, who is described as "strictly temperate; *perhaps*, from principle, but most likely, from interest" (120). Yet Douglass seems to disdain him not only because he hypocritically uses the facade of the religious temperance man to cloak his cruelties to the slaves but also because he is a parvenu among slave owners—someone who married into power but does not know how to wield it with the authority of, say, Colonel Lloyd. In Thomas Auld there is the mere "swagger of authority, but his rule lacked the vital element of consistency" (119). Thus he has to resort to shipping out his "unbroken" slaves to "the Negro Breaker" (128) Edward Covey, another Methodist convert, who is presented, especially in the 1855 telling, as a kind of animal. Covey speaks "in a sort of light growl, like a dog, when an attempt is made to take a bone from him" (131); like the other slave owners and overseers of "dramshop" St. Michael's, he is a person ruled by appetite and body, by "his passions, rather than his thoughts" (131).

Placed under the authority of such a brute, Douglass must finally consider the possibility of resorting to violent resistance—which is to say that, in his own person (and in his own terms), he must risk, as Nelly earlier risked, having his "thoughts" overwhelmed by his "passions." As numerous readers have recognized, Douglass's decision to rebel against Covey represents a climactic turning point both in the *Narrative* and *Bondage*. In the 1855 text in particular, the scenes with Covey also represent a critical moment of distinct tension between temperance and revolution—between two of the large (and seemingly opposed) ideological paradigms informing *Bondage* and much African American writing of the period. In his excellent reading of *Bondage*, Sundquist views Douglass's revolt against Covey as "bound very closely to the paradigm of progress implicit in the revolutionary tradition." Central to the achievement of such progress and eventual liberty, Sundquist argues, is the willingness to use violence when necessary to overcome violent oppressors. Nancy Bentley writes of the importance of violence in Douglass's 1855 text from a somewhat different, though complementary, perspective, arguing that because "the body and its capacity for force over others . . . are tokens of 'humanity' for men in antebellum culture," Douglass in his description of his battle with Covey underscores the ways in which his use of force helps him to assert his own humanity.[45] In my reading of temperance themes and motifs in *Bondage* thus far, I have been suggesting, against the grain of Sundquist's and Bentley's analyses, that Douglass tends to privilege mind over body, self-control over rage; thus he typically depicts white violence against blacks as an imbruting form of intemperance. Within this discursive context, Douglass's challenge in the Covey section is to find a way to present his recourse to revolutionary violence, the recourse of the oppressed, as involving something other than self-"brutification."

An urgency exists in this rhetorical and ideological work, for during the 1850s Douglass increasingly saw the need for blacks to use violence to oppose fugitive slave hunters and enslavers. In fact, he asserts in *Bondage* shortly before the Covey incident that slave violence could be regarded as a morally legitimate form of self-help in the Revolutionary tradition: "The morality of *free* society can have no application to *slave* society. Slaveholders have made it almost impossible for the slave to commit any crime. . . . If he steals, he takes his own; if he kills his master, he imitates only the heroes of the revolution" (119). This view of the slave's moral right to resistance is consistent with Garnet's position in *An Address to the Slaves of the United States of America* (which Douglass had voted to reject at the 1843 national Negro convention), and it is consistent with the resolution adopted by Douglass and his supporters at the 1853 Rochester convention, which invoked Jefferson to support the contention "THAT RESISTANCE TO TYRANTS IS OBEDIENCE TO GOD."[46] Echoing David Walker's *Appeal* in a speech of 1854 calling on blacks to "KILL OR BE KILLED," Douglass's presentation in *Bondage* of his own turn to violence points to a problem implicitly addressed in the *Appeal*: that acts of black violence and their narrative representations could reinforce white stereotypes of blacks as vicious savages. Walker enjoined his black readers: "You have to prove to the Americans and the world, that we are MEN, and not *brutes* as we have been represented, and by millions treated." Yet, for Walker, violent resistance, rather than submission, ultimately promised to explode that stereotype by demonstrating blacks' love of "LIBERTY!!!!!" In *Bondage*, Douglass basically agrees with Walker, though with some important rhetorical qualifications.[47]

These qualifications center on the issues of "embrutification" and "appetite" that are at the heart of Douglass's representational politics of temperate revolutionism. For Douglass, the central concern is this: How does one respond violently to intemperate force without becoming as intemperate and brutish as the brute one wishes to overcome? Similar questions are brought to focus in Josiah Henson's slave narratives. In a scene that is at the center of both the 1849 *The Life of Josiah Henson* and the 1858 *Truth Stranger than Fiction*, Henson describes himself, when he is tempted to kill his master, as undergoing a transformation "from a lively, and, I will say, a pleasant-tempered fellow, into a savage, morose, dangerous slave" with "an almost uncontrollable fury." As he raises his ax to kill his master, he suddenly experiences this piercing insight: "I was about to lose the fruit of all my efforts at self-improvement, the character I had acquired, and the peace of mind that had never deserted me." Therefore he resists the temptation and, in so doing, "recovered my self-control and serenity."[48]

Committed as he is to linking temperance ideals to "self-improvement," Douglass likewise presents his turn to violence as posing a threat to his "self-control and serenity"—as posing a threat to his humanity. He does so, in part, by developing an analogy between himself and the "unbroken oxen" (130) that Covey orders him to subdue. In the 1845 version of his resistance to Covey, the narrative moves seamlessly from the oxen's violent rebellion against Douglass's authority to Douglass's violent rebellion against Covey's authority, with the implication being that in withstanding Covey, he inevitably had to become like an ox. The 1855 account shows Douglass much more aware of the disturbing implications of his analogy of rebellious ox to rebellious slave and consequently much more intent on distinguishing himself from oxen motivated merely by beastly force.[49] Though he continues to work with the analogy in the section devoted to his violent opposition, he breaks up the account into several chapters in such a way as to diminish the analogy's explanatory force, and he makes the recalcitrant oxen less beastlike. To be sure, as in the *Narrative*, the oxen teach Douglass a lesson about the uses of violence. But in *Bondage* it is a singular lesson. Rather than brutishly repelling Douglass, they respond to Douglass's exertions with a measured self-defensive violence that he types as temperate: after their successful resistance they "moved off as soberly as though their behavior had been natural and exemplary" (131).

With their rebellion against Douglass's authority, the oxen emerge as temperate revolutionaries not unlike the American Revolutionaries described by Douglass in "Fourth of July." Accordingly, they serve as models of, indeed inspirations for, revolutionary action. Like the Revolutionaries who, in "Fourth of July," *approach* madness under the duress of British oppression, Douglass portrays himself, following the failure of Sandy's root to fend off Covey, as tempted to a mad, violent rebellion. "The fighting madness had come upon me," he writes, "and I found my strong fingers firmly attached to the throat of my cowardly tormentor" (149). But how "mad" is he when, as he relates, "every blow of his [Covey's] was parried, though I dealt no blows in turn. I was strictly on the *defensive*" (149). Though he is a bit more aggressive in taking on Covey's cousin Hughes, the fact remains that, like the American patriots and like Madison Washington in "The Heroic Slave"—who evinces his awareness of "the principles of 1776" in leading a slave revolt that had no unnecessary bloodshed—Douglass and the hired man Bill and the slave Caroline, who help him by *not* responding to Covey's orders, were simultaneously "in open rebellion" (151) against tyrannical authority and in relatively complete control of their minds and bodies.[50]

In his more militant account of an impending hemispheric slave insurrection in *Blake* (1859–62), Martin Delany similarly emphasizes the temperate revolutionism of the slaves' leader, Henry Blake, who refuses all offers of alcoholic beverages from white enslavers: "I don't drink, sir."[51] He refuses intoxicating beverages for the same reason that Douglass asserts that slaves should refuse liquor proffered by their masters: "It is the sober, thinking slave who is dangerous" (*Bondage*, p. 157). Such slaves are dangerous because they retain the moral ability to see the acts of enslavers like Covey for what they are—"the unjust and cruel aggressions of a tyrant" (151)—and the moral insight to see the relevance of America's revolutionary history to the slaves' own situation: "He ever lisps a syllable in commendation of the fathers of this republic, nor denounces any attempted oppression of himself, without inviting the knife to his own throat, and asserting the rights of rebellion for his own slaves" (165).

And yet, despite Douglass's braggadocio here, the black patriots of the 1855 autobiography, unlike those in *Blake*, never really come close to killing whites, even when they have them under their physical power (as Douglass eventually has Covey). "I had drawn blood from him [Covey]," Douglass remarks, "and, even without this satisfaction, I should have been victorious, because my aim had not been to injure him, but to prevent his injuring me" (151). Given Douglass's insistence on the enslaving power of appetite, there are good reasons for his emphasis on the relatively controlled nature of his resistance, beyond what Leverenz characterizes as Douglass's genteel desire to portray himself in *Bondage*, in contrast to the lower-class Covey, as "at a distance from his body and at a great distance from his anger." If anything, by foregrounding the issue of self-control in the 1855 version of his rebellion, Douglass appears *more* conscious of his body and more thoughtful about the uses to which he puts his anger. Bentley asserts that Douglass's " 'glorious resurrection' is not a triumph *over* the body but most emphatically *in* the body. Freedom is not a release from the bondage of mortal flesh but a reclaiming of its physical powers." But in portraying himself as resisting what Weld might have termed the intoxications of power, it seems to me that Douglass has it both ways: he triumphs in *and* over the body, thereby claiming his *freedom* from his own body's appetitive desire to inflict pain on an enslaver even as the rebellion itself (temporarily) frees him from the mastery of an enslaver attempting to inflict pain on him. As Sundquist neatly puts it, Douglass's "mastery of Covey" produces a "mastery of himself." [52] The end result of these double acts of mastery is "manly independence" (152).

Recent critics have conceptually linked Douglass's valorization of the "manly" to dominant patriarchal models of power. [53] But surely such a reading is anachronistic: in the face of unfathomable domination and degradation, Douglass in *Bondage* is celebrating the achievement of a self-mastery that promises to help him attain a fuller sense of his humanity. Thus he concludes this section not with yet another bold pronouncement of his manhood but with a pronouncement of his non-animalhood. His rebellion against Covey, he declares, signifies "the end of the brutification to which slavery had subjected me" (152). Instead of descending to the level of a brute to battle a brute, Douglass (with an eye on his free black readers) presents his resistance as an example of temperate revolutionism put into action, a self-help strategy that, in (Madison) Washingtonian fashion, will allow him (and others who are inspired by his example) to emerge from the "prison-house."

In a Washingtonian mode, then, Douglass, following this triumphal scene of personal liberation, places a new emphasis on the communitarian ideals of black fraternalism. This emphasis may have something to do with the problematic role played by Sandy in the rebellion. Though Douglass stigmatizes the "genuine African" (147) Sandy as ignorant and superstitious for his use of conjure and then later, in his account of the failed slave flight, asserts that Sandy (the possible betrayer) was not "quite free from slaveholding priestcraft" (168), he suggests in *Bondage*, more than in *Narrative*, Sandy's possible influence over the outcome of Douglass's battle with Covey. Initially adopting the persona of the conventional Christian, Douglass ridicules Sandy's offering of a magical root as "positively sinful" (147). But then in a fascinating reversal, Douglass presents him as somewhat "Western" in his psychological acumen and presents himself as somewhat "African" in his willingness to turn to magic in preparing to challenge Covey: "I saw in Sandy too deep an insight into human nature . . . not to have some respect for his advice; and perhaps, too, a slight gleam or shadow of his superstition had fallen upon me" (147–48). Having affected this reversal, Douglass can present his successful rebellion against Covey in fairly mysterious terms, thereby destabilizing the positivistic conception of manly self-help so central to his temperate revolutionism: "Whence came the daring spirit necessary to grapple with a man who, eight-and-forty hours before, could, with his slightest word have made me tremble like a leaf in a storm, I do not know" (149). What he does know is that, precisely because of his rebelliousness, he is suddenly viewed by whites in superstitious terms as having "*the devil in me*" (154). Like Sandy, he subsequently wants to share his "demonism" with his fellow slaves: "I did not fail to inspire others with the same feeling" (154).

Sandy thus must be given some credit for transforming the rather elitist Douglass of earlier sections of *Bondage*—the Douglass who, as he presents himself *in* history, was often distant from his fellow slaves on the plantation—into a more fraternally concerned and responsive participant in slave culture. The root episode also encourages a reconsideration of Douglass's ties to that culture. Though at the outset of *Bondage* Douglass can seem at a superior distance from the Africanisms of the slaves—their dialects, their folk beliefs—he does learn a great deal from them, for as he emphatically states, it was precisely their orally transmitted account of how blacks "were stolen from Africa" that "filled me with a burning hatred of slavery" (61).[54] Moreover, though critics have noted the problematic aspects of Douglass's remarks on his mother's resemblance to the male Egyptian head depicted in James Prichard's *Natural History of Man* (39), James McCune Smith reads Douglass's account of his mother's "deep black, glossy complexion" (38) and "native genius" (42) as an effort to show "that for his energy, perseverance, eloquence, invective, sagacity, and wide sympathy, he is indebted to his negro blood" (22).[55] In the Baltimore chapters, Douglass additionally points to the central role of the African American preacher "Uncle" Lawson in his spiritual and political education. Described as possibly "the original of Mrs. Stowe's christian hero" (115), Lawson talks of the "better world" (105) to come. But unlike Uncle Tom, Lawson, a leader in the black community, encourages the *active* pursuit of freedom "in the world" (106).

It is therefore not entirely inconsistent with earlier sections of the text that upon his removal to Freeland's plantation after the Covey incident, Douglass should emerge as a leader in genuine sympathy with his fellow slaves. This coming into his own as a black leader marks the major transformation, discovery, and, as it were, *argument* of the 1855 narrative. To some extent, as Andrews suggests, Douglass's emergence as a leader can occur only after he has moved "outside the social structure and ideational superstructure of the white gods." Describing Douglass as a trickster and subversive who "must become his own self-authorizing presence," Andrews thus links him to "the rebel hero of Martin R. Delany's revolutionary novel *Blake*."[56] But however "devilish" Douglass reveals himself in his plottings, he remains true to his rhetorical advocacy of temperance and American Revolutionism. For example, in an apparent narrative distortion of his prior history, Douglass describes himself at Freeland's as a model of temperate self-control. In an 1846 lecture he had talked about his predilection for drink at Freeland's: "I lived with a Mr. Freeland who used to give his slaves apple brandy. Some of the slaves were not able to drink their own share, but I was able to drink my own and theirs too. I took it because it made me feel like a great man."[57] In his account in *Bondage*, however, as in the earlier *Narrative*, he represents himself as a sober leader: he sets up a Sabbath and night school for approximately twenty-five of the slaves and over the next year develops the kinds of emotional bonds with his "brother slaves" (164) that are only implicit in the opening half of *Bondage*. "I never loved, esteemed, or confided in men, more than I did in these" (165), he writes. His love, along with his teachings on "the clear conception of rights" (162), culminate in a group escape plot, which, as with his rebellion against Covey, Douglass places in the heroic tradition of America's temperate Revolutionaries.

Images of sobriety and insobriety frame the chapter devoted to the 1836 escape plot. Douglass begins with a Franklinian act of self-examination: "Sober people look both ways at the beginning of the year, surveying the errors of the past, and providing against possible errors of the future" (166). The "unusual sobriety" (169) he has attained (or claims to have attained) provides him with a pronounced sense of autonomy, despite his enslaved status. Yet he allows that slavery continues to ravage him and his compatriots, in the way that alcohol conventionally ravaged its victims in Washingtonian accounts, by "greedily devouring our hard earnings and feeding . . . upon our flesh" (172). Invoking Patrick Henry to portray their intended flight as a Revolutionary action, Douglass, who in his "Fourth of July" address described Baltimore slave owners as "ever ready to drink . . . and to gamble," shows how literally true it is that the slaves are attempting to escape from intemperance: imprisoned after the escape plot fails, Douglass and his compatriots are subsequently inspected by slave traders, "whisky-bloated gamblers in human flesh" (182), "whose very breathing is of blasphemy and blood" (182).[58]

Masters and workers alike intemperately feed on his flesh and blood when Douglass, rather than being sold, is sent back to the Aulds' Baltimore home. In the graphic accounts of the violence inflicted on him by the white dockworkers, Douglass wants to show sympathetically that, like the slaves, underpaid workers are "robbed by the slave system, of the just results of [their] labor" (188). Most severely robbed, however, as Douglass makes clear through his own example, are the slaves. Although he develops his skills until he "command[s] the highest wages paid to journeymen calkers [sic] in Baltimore" (193), the bulk of those wages must go to Hugh Auld. Thus the question arises once again as to the worth of temperate industry in a slave society that seems to undermine all possibilities of self-control, a society wherein Douglass's "elevation" owes perhaps as much to luck (that he was sent to Baltimore, that he was not shot or sold for resisting Covey, and so on) as to self-help. Nevertheless, Douglass describes how he continues to improve his caulking skills and earning potential, how he attends the East Baltimore Mental Improvement Society, and how he begins to hone his debating techniques, thereby suggesting that there is a close, seemingly causal, connection between his hard work and eventual escape from slavery and rise to prominence in the North. (He says little about the people who help with his escape.) In this sense, Douglass, the temperate revolutionary, the model of self-help, seems on his own to *earn*, and hence *deserve*, his "LIFE AS A FREEMAN" (203).

Mastering the Body

The large question that needs to be taken up here is this: In Douglass's terms, as developed in *Bondage*, what are the benefits of life as a temperate freeman? Addressing this question is crucial to any consideration of Douglass's representative leadership as "an economic revolutionary in the best American tradition."[59] One large benefit seems to be the "freedom" to participate in the North's market economy. In this respect, Douglass's emphasis on the various barriers in the way of the slave's (and worker's) ability to prosper in a slave economy anticipates his celebration in *Bondage*'s relatively short final section, "Life as a Freeman," of market capitalism's ability to enable individuals to achieve their fullest human potential, however that might be defined. Central to his rhetorical strategies are his appeals to capitalism's potential as a force for freedom — whether as a stimulus to industry, as an outlet for the consuming desires of appetite, or as a restraint on unchecked domination. As I noted earlier, Douglass's apparently uncritical embrace of the North's market economy has troubled some recent readers. And yet, having just escaped from what proslavery writers idealized as a precapitalist, organic agrarianism, Douglass would hardly want to undermine liberal capitalist ideals (as opposed to practices, which he *does* critique), for such a move would work against his project of depicting the ways in which blacks' equal access to the free market economy could ultimately serve as a reformative — or even revolutionary — force in U.S. society.

Douglass's "positionality" in antebellum culture, then, which he thematizes in *Bondage* by developing a dialectic between being inside (as a participant) and outside (as an analytic chronicler) of the events he describes, is absolutely central to the narrative's moral and political vision. Arguing from a neopragmatic perspective, Giles Gunn reminds us of how differences in individuals' (or groups') cultural situations may contribute to differences in attitudes toward capitalism: "Clearly, . . . the rhetoric of market capitalism in the antebellum period and its association with the concept of political freedom meant one thing to the American slave, Frederick Douglass, and quite another to white slaveholders. . . . To Douglass, the ideological linkage between capitalism and liberty quickened his resolve to escape by enabling him for the first time to envisage what it might mean to lay claim to the rights of his own labor."[60] Like Benjamin Franklin, Douglass regarded temperance capitalism as serving the ends of freedom (and in this way he anticipated historian Thomas L. Haskell's arguments on the possible interrelationship between the rise of capitalism and the rise of antislavery). Viewing Douglass's advocacy of market capitalism in this context, we could regard *Bondage*, in Mary Louise Pratt's terms, as an "autoethnographic" text, a text that, in its effort to "find a point of entry" for blacks into the dominant culture, "involves partial collaboration with and appropriation of the idioms of the conqueror."[61]

But we might still ask whether Douglass's celebration of capitalism has to be so uncritical. Though he shows that racism continues to make life difficult in the North for free blacks, the emphasis of his portrayal of the "free" market remains on its ability to enable self-elevation. His New Bedford benefactor, the free black Nathan Johnson, for example, who in the South would be "regarded as a proper marketable commodity" (210), has in the North risen by virtue of his industry to economic, moral, and social prominence. Like Johnson, New Bedford's "laboring population" (210), white and black, lives more comfortably "than a majority of the slaveholders on the Eastern shore of Maryland" (210). Such a world of industry and self-elevation certainly seems worthy of praise, and Douglass goes on to celebrate the Northern economy in terms of the traditional temperance values of sobriety and cleanliness — the values of corporeal restraint that Max Weber and others have argued are central to the Protestant spirit of capitalism. Still, there is something chilling about Douglass's admiration for the mechanical tenor of life in the North; Leverenz has good reason to be disturbed by what he calls Douglass's "brave new world of large-scale organization and industrial power."[62] Consider, for example, Douglass's initial account of the industry he observes at New Bedford: "I saw industry without hustle, labor without noise, and heavy toil without the whip. . . . Everything went on as smoothly as the works of a well adjusted machine. . . . I found that everything was done here with a scrupulous regard to economy, both in regard to men and things" (211).

Despite the utilitarian accents of his rhetoric, however, "economy," as Douglass employs it here, with his suggestive underscoring of the symbiotic relationship between the accumulation of money and the physical expenditures of the body, reminds us of Thoreau's similar emphasis on the connections between the corporeal and the financial in the "Economy" chapter of *Walden* (1854). Given that such a symbiotic relationship simply does not exist in a slave economy, it makes good sense (as Gunn suggests) for Douglass to present his entrance into the North's "free labor" economy as presaging nothing less than an exhilarating new world of possibility and freedom. In such a world, where the ability to control one's own body equates (at least in the utopian view of things) with the ability to control one's own destiny, temperance takes on a whole new significance, becoming less an issue of power impinging from without (with the focus on the dangers of becoming a slave of a slave to appetite) than of power usurping from within (with the focus on the dangers of one-self becoming a slave to appetite). The process of learning how to be, in Douglass's terms, "my own master" (212) therefore requires paying careful attention to the problem of maintaining and regulating—of mastering—the body. Anticipating Booker T. Washington's obsession with the connections between worldly success and the private care of the body, Douglass marvels at the mechanical contrivances insuring the cleanliness of those who live in New Bedford: "In-door pumps, sinks, drains, self-shutting gates, washing machines, pounding barrels, were all new things, and told me that I was among a thoughtful and sensible people" (211).

Of course from Douglass's antislavery perspective, a commitment to the care of one's own body, along with a more general commitment to temperate self-regulation, seems hardly an enslaving of the body, but rather a liberation of it from the demands of others' appetites. Cleanliness is next to revolutionariness! The achievement of temperate self-control, as Douglass presents it, rather than mechanizing individuals or "enslaving" them to a capitalistic order's demands for self-mastery, provides a variety of newfound freedoms, including that of contractual relations with others, a freedom that encompasses the freedom *not* to make contractual relations with others. (Thus a central drama of the book's final chapters involves Douglass's breaking his ties with the Garrisonians to become the editor and publisher of his own newspaper.) Within Northern liberal capitalist culture, as Douglass presents it, the freedom enabled by "contractarian ideology" allows for the achievement of something *more* than contractual relations: it allows individuals (and groups) to explore and develop as fully as possible their sense of what it means to be human.[63] As C. B. Macpherson puts it, "The individual in market society *is* human as proprietor of his own person. However much he may wish it to be otherwise, his humanity does depend on his freedom from any but self-interested contractual relations with others."[64]

I want to suggest, then, that during the 1850s Douglass championed temperance capitalism not only as a social program of economic elevation for oppressed African Americans but also as a moral or spiritual agenda. As Sacvan Bercovitch remarks, Douglass's writings testify "to the *liberating* force of free enterprise ideology," as "those commercial catchwords —self-possession, contract society, upward mobility, free trade, open opportunity—were the key to [his] most private aspirations and most urgent social visions."[65] Viewed in this light, we may discern in *Bondage* Douglass's "private aspirations" for something like the transcendentalist idealism and self-culture of such "representative" men as Emerson or Thoreau, aspirations that his pragmatic capitalistic rhetoric threatens to obscure. For the temperance-capitalist Douglass, as for Thoreau, the possibility of achieving the fullest spiritual growth is centrally tied to ideals of mobility. In "Walking" (1862), for example, Thoreau refers to the "walker" as someone who is "free from all worldly engagements," and he expresses disbelief at those "who confine themselves to shops and offices the whole day for weeks and months, ay, and years almost together." From Thoreau's point of view, as he makes clear in *Walden* as well, such commitments to the exigencies of the market are themselves forms of slavery that, while elevating individuals economically, become a kind of ballast that keeps them from attaining a vastly more important spiritual elevation: "We hug the earth—how rarely we mount! Methinks we might elevate ourselves a little more. We might climb a tree, at least." Ironically troping (or "signifying") on capitalist programs of self-elevation, Thoreau uses the literalizing metaphor of elevation to equate physical with spiritual elevation. Hence he concludes the essay by invoking the sun: "One day the sun shall shine more brightly than ever he has done, shall perchance shine into our minds and hearts, and light up our whole lives with a great awakening light." When this glorious moment occurs, the walker will be "equally at home everywhere," though in a world, we should note, decidedly elsewhere: "Where he lives no fugitive slave laws are passed."[66]

In the real world of Frederick Douglass, however, fugitive slave laws are passed and enforced; there was not a black in antebellum America who could say that he or she felt "equally at home everywhere." Hence Douglass's pragmatic (and political) position on the importance of black elevation to antislavery. But the spiritual exists in *Bondage* as well, and crucially so. Early in the narrative he describes a ladder ascending to an "upper apartment" of his grandmother's "log hut, or cabin" (29). A source of fascination for the boy, the ladder could be taken as an allegorical figuring of the upward mobility that he will eventually pursue and achieve (and, by his representative example, encourage others to pursue and achieve), though the ascent he describes soon seems something more than a merely Franklinian ascent up the social-economic ladder: "This upper apartment was reached only by a ladder—but what in the world for climbing could be better than a ladder? To me, this ladder was really a high invention, and possessed a sort of charm as I played with delight upon the rounds of it" (29). Subverting any reification of capitalistic ascent as *the* demand of "nature," Douglass insists on the "inventedness" of the ladder and insists as well on the way the "ladder" serves ends — joyful and spiritual — other than merely to help the boy to attain the "upper apartment."[67] The pleasure lies in the enabling freedom of ascent — a self-created and self-creating freedom simultaneously corporeal and spiritual.

Images of "unrestrained mobility and unlimited freedom" are everywhere in *Bondage*.[68] As a slave child Douglass has the short-lived joy of running wild on the plantation with virtually no restrictions; in doing so he experiences what the older Douglass retrospectively regards as "the veriest freedom" (32). Desires for mobility are central to his famous apostrophe to the sailboats on Chesapeake Bay — "You are loosed from your moorings, and free; I am fast in my chains, and am a slave!" (136) — and the achievement of mobility is central to his life as a freeman. In New York he marvels that he is actually "walking amid the hurrying throng," having for the past "ten or fifteen years . . . been dragging a heavy chain with a huge block attached to it" (205). And, of course, during his travels to Great Britain he glories in the mobility accompanying his status as antislavery celebrity, as well as in the concomitant freedom from subjection to the enslaving appetites of others. Thus it is significant that Douglass's account of sailing from the United States to England includes mention of how he thwarts the efforts of passengers from Georgia and New Orleans, who, "under the inspiration of *slavery* and *brandy*" (224), wish to throw him overboard because they object to his (speaking) presence on board the ship. The Southerners' behavior makes clear why Douglass attends the World's Temperance Convention while in England.

For Douglass, as for Thoreau, temperance is a necessary condition for the apprehension of the spiritual. Spiritual desires inform Douglass's discussion of the slaves' songs, which testify to the "soul-crushing and death-dealing character of slavery" (65); and again and again Douglass speaks of his own spiritual needs. As Thoreau writes in *Walden*'s "Higher Laws" chapter of his "instinct toward a higher, or, as it is named, spiritual life," so Douglass writes of his wish to move from a condition of imbrutedness to one of integration with a "Higher Law than [the] master's will" (194).[69] He speaks most passionately of this desire shortly after his acquisition of literacy. In an extraordinary passage on his recent reading of emancipatory texts, Douglass describes his revitalized insights into "nature":

> My spirit was roused to eternal wakefulness. Liberty! the inestimable birthright of every man, had, for me, converted every object into an asserter of this great right. It was heard in every sound, and beheld in every object. It was ever present, to torment me with a sense of my wretched condition. The more beautiful and charming were the smiles of nature, the more horrible and desolate was my condition. I saw nothing without seeing it, and I heard nothing without hearing it. I do not exaggerate, when I say, that it looked from every star, smiled in every calm, breathed in every wind, and moved in every storm. (101)

Sensing "liberty" to be inhering in nature, Douglass develops in this passage, worthy of Wordsworth or Emerson, a picture of nature as an animistic, elusive otherness. As in Emerson's "Experience" (and Delany's romantic depiction of the Alleghenies in the final letter of his "Western tour"), an apprehension of nature's "charm" only accentuates an apprehension of his distance from that charm, and the desire to bridge that distance. *Bondage*, in this respect, charts a movement from alienation to integration (a much more hopeful trajectory than that charted by "Experience") that culminates in Douglass's achievement of a new mobility aided and informed by nature. The breathing "wind" of the above passage is thus echoed near the end of *Bondage* when he describes himself escaping from slavery "in a flying cloud or balloon, (pardon the figure,) driven by the wind" (205).

As the balloon image suggests, a logical direction in which to take Douglass's celebration of mobility and spirituality is in advocating flight from a corrupt United States. But Douglass ultimately works against unconstrained notions of flight and mobility, as he worked against Delany's emigration projects, by emphasizing, at the very point in *Bondage* when is he outside the United States, the antislavery work that remains to be done in his native country and his recognition of his responsibility to lead that work. His recognition of his leadership role as a freeman is staged in relation not to Delany (or Garnet or any other black) but to Garrison, whom he initially describes as "the Moses, raised up by God, to deliver his modern Israel from bondage" (216). Coming to see Garrison and his associates as paternalistic, misguided in their approach to antislavery, and not terribly concerned about the situation of the free blacks,

Douglass ultimately usurps Garrison's Mosaic status, emerging at the end of the book as a black Moses who is much more genuinely committed to the project of delivering "my people" (101) from bondage to freedom.

But the point that needs to be made here is that in assuming the burden and challenge of what he terms "my mission — under a gracious Providence" (247) to "labor in the future, as I have labored in the past, to promote the moral, social, religious, and intellectual elevation of the free colored people" (248), Douglass in his 1855 autobiography tells a highly sentimental story of his disinterested acceptance of the mantle of leadership. Such a story fails to attend to the fact that at the time of composition Douglass is attempting to recover and consolidate his status as the free blacks' preeminent (and representative) black leader. Andrews writes that *Bondage* "represents the most communally as well as self-conscious stage of Douglass's progressive autobiographical recreation of himself, for by 1855 he was not trying just to prove who he had been in the past . . . but who he wished to become in the future — a man with a community-affirming mission for the truly free black men and women among whom he could feel fully and finally at home."[70] What Andrews and other commentators neglect to note is that Douglass's presentation of his discovery of his communal mission works strategically to elide the presence of other blacks of the time, most notably Martin Delany, who had rather different conceptions of African Americans' "community-affirming mission" and of the leadership necessary to fulfill that mission. Though Douglass never mentions Delany by name in the text, he develops an implicit argument against his emigrationist agenda.

Thus, even as Douglass conveys his pleasure in his freedom and mobility in England, he underscores his antiemigrationist position by maintaining that, had he been concerned only about his own personal freedom, he "could have easily remained in England" (229) or even "gone to some other country" (230). Though tempted to do so, he resists on the high ground that, as he puts it, "I had a duty to perform — and that was, to labor and suffer with the oppressed in my native land" (229). As he elaborates, he believes that educated and accomplished blacks have a special obligation to remain in the United States, for it is these elites who can perform the double duty of countering negative stereotypes of blacks even as they inspire less accomplished free blacks to make efforts to better their situation. In addition to adducing the social-reform arguments central to black self-help rhetoric since the 1830s, Douglass also contends that blacks, particularly those who were once enslaved, develop special ties (or roots) to their "native land" that would make the sort of "transplantation" called for by Delany in *Condition* and "Political Destiny" traumatic and counterproductive. In effect, Douglass pulls rank on Delany, making it clear that because he (Douglass) was formerly a slave, he has access to blacks' land-oriented mentality in ways that never-enslaved free blacks would not. Douglass portrays Northerners as a rootless people whose very mobility, even as it enables spiritual development of a personal sort, cuts off possibilities of developing close connections to place: "The people of the north, and free people generally, I think, have less attachment to the places where they are born and brought up, than have the slaves. Their freedom to go and come, to be here and there, as they list, prevents any extravagant attachment to any one particular place" (110–11). For the slave (or former slave), on the other hand, "the idea of removal elsewhere, comes, generally, in the shape of a threat. . . . And hence he looks upon separation from his native place, with none of the enthusiasm which animates the bosoms of young freemen, when they contemplate a life in the far west, or in some distant country where they intend to rise to wealth and distinction" (111). By privileging the point of view of (former) slaves, Douglass portrays emigrationist programs of removal to "some distant country" as manifestations of a modernistic restlessness characteristic of those in selfish pursuit of status and gain.

Moreover, as Douglass argues in the "Life as a Freeman" section, a free black (like Delany) who has never been a slave has little understanding of the anxieties attending flight and mobility. "It is difficult for a freeman to enter into the feelings of . . . fugitives. He cannot see things in the same light with the slave" (207). At this point in the narrative Douglass goes to an extreme in positing that some fugitives, on reaching a free state, might decide to return to their masters rather than confront the "loneliness, apprehension, hunger and anxiety, which meets them on their first arrival in a free state" (207). The imagery Douglass deploys to describe his arrival in New York makes freedom seem anything but "free": "A free state around me, and a free earth under my feet!" (205), he glories, even as the phrase "around me" continues to suggest enclosure. He then remarks on how freedom can seem "like the quick blaze, beautiful at first, but which subsiding, leaves the building charred and desolate" (206). The point that Douglass is making here, which encapsulates his larger suspicion of unlimited mobility (or emigration), is that the escaped slave has achieved "freedom" not only "from slavery, but . . . from home, as well" (207). Central to Douglass's antiemigrationist position, then, is both a political position (similar to Delany's), that blacks have contributed to the development of the United States and thus have the *right* to call it home, and a psychosocial one, that enslaved blacks come to develop an attachment to place that, because it constitutes such a central part of their individual and group identity, neither can nor should be so easily dispensed with, as he felt Delany's emigration plan would require. Thus while Douglass sees all sorts of value in mobility, his antiemigrationism and quest for leadership compel him to make a case for its limits. Antislavery and antiracist work remains to be done in the United States, a nation that Douglass continues to regard as African Americans' rightful home. And so, even as he puts forth at the end of *Bondage*, in his paraphrasing of Psalms 68:31, a Christian-transcendental sense of blacks' spiritual potential as Africans — " 'Ethiopia shall yet reach forth her hand unto God' " (248) — he calls on African Americans to persist in their efforts to develop themselves spiritually and politically through programs of economic elevation in the United States.

But though *Bondage*'s moral-reform ideology works against emigrationism by implying that blacks, by following Douglass's representative example, can overcome what Douglass refers to as "the ten thousand discouragements . . . which beset their existence in this country" (247), he nonetheless presents a disturbing picture of the ways in which "intemperate" whites, by enslaving and degrading blacks, have created a separate black caste in the United States — "a nation within a nation." In this respect, when Douglass, over the course of the text, refers to "my afflicted people" (4), to "my people" (101), and, especially, to "the blood-written history of Africa, and her children, from whom we have descended" (247), he can sound a bit like Delany in assuming a oneness not among "the human family," as he did in his contemporaneous "The Claims of the Negro Ethnologically Considered," but among the African diaspora.[71] Whatever he might have intended by citing the paraphrased quote from Psalms at the end of *Bondage*, the Ethiopian messianism of the biblical passage implies a Pan-African sense of racial distinctiveness and community that raises questions about whether the project of black elevation should be so focused on enabling blacks' rise within the borders of the United States. At the same time, Douglass seems aware that in suggesting such a racialized view he may be ratifying the racial politics of Delany's "Political Destiny," which would ultimately make the "pure" black Delany, and not the mulatto Douglass, the possessor of the more appropriately representative identity as a black leader. James McCune

Smith's introductory assertion that the "Egyptians, like the Americans, were a *mixed race*, with some negro blood circling around the throne, as well as in the mudhovels" (23), together with Douglass's own account of his genealogy, work to affirm the appropriateness of the "mixed"-blood Douglass as a leader of his people. Still, by the end of the text, particularly with its Ethiopian messianic vision of Douglass as the leader who promises to bring about "the universal and unconditional emancipation of my entire race" (248), there are aspects of the temperate-revolutionary patriotism of Douglass's *Bondage* that anticipate the revolutionary Pan-Africanism of Delany's *Blake*.

On the evidence of Douglass's strained efforts to maintain his antiemigrationist position at the end of *Bondage* and the racial collectivism that punctuates the volume throughout, we could posit that Delany's emigrationist and racial views had more of an impact on Douglass than he would have been willing to allow. Delany's views on race, colonization, and emigration, as I will discuss in the next chapter, may have also had an impact on the post-1852 writings of Harriet Beecher Stowe, whose representation of George Harris's temperate revolutionism in *Uncle Tom's Cabin*, inspired by her reading of Douglass's *Narrative*, in all likelihood had an impact on Douglass's politics of temperate revolutionism. Douglass's *Bondage* and other writings, in turn, had an impact on Stowe's writings of the mid-1850s (and beyond), which may well have had an important influence on Delany's *Blake*. By the early 1860s, the evidence suggests, Delany revised his opinion of Stowe, for without any apparent irony on his part he used a Stowe poem, "Caste and Christ" (1853), as a running epigraph to the 1861–62 periodical printing of his novel. What changed his mind, I think, was the 1856 publication of Stowe's *Dred*, a novel that in its responsiveness to the black discourses of the time managed to appropriate, interrogate, and, at various points, champion black elevation, emigration, and revolutionism.

Chapter 4

Heap of Witness

The African
American
Presence in
Stowe's *Dred*

On the front page of the 1 February 1856 issue
of *Frederick Douglass' Paper*, Douglass ran an
anonymous review celebrating the publication of
Harriet Beecher Stowe's *The May Flower and
Miscellaneous Writings*. The reviewer declared,
"Whatever Mrs. Stowe writes, has a pure, genial,
strength-giving moral tone, which never becomes wearisome and in-
sipid, and never degenerates into mere cant." Three weeks later, Stowe
celebrated Douglass's *My Bondage and My Freedom* in the review essay
"Anti-Slavery Literature," which appeared in the *New York Independent*.
Douglass's *Bondage*, she maintained, represents a major advance over
the "rude form" of his *Narrative* and "will compare favorably in point of
style and execution with any work of the kind in our language. Douglass
has a natural genius for writing." Though Douglass was singled out for
special attention, Stowe in the course of her lengthy review also praised
the "vigor, shrewdness, and originality" of the autobiographies of Josiah
Henson, Henry Bibb, Lewis Clarke, and William Wells Brown. These "bi-
ographies of former slaves written by themselves," Stowe informed her
readers, allow "us to know how a human heart like our own felt and

thought and struggled, coming up in so strange and unnatural a state as that of slavery."[1]

Robert Stepto has discussed "the complex relationship between [*Uncle Tom's Cabin*] and the many Afro-American antislavery texts published in the late 1840s and 1850s," pointing out that Stowe took pains to seek "the forms of black testimony that could both counter and corroborate the white testimony she already had in hand." Stepto's sympathetic reading of Stowe's textual "conversations" with black writers, especially Bibb and Douglass, represents something of a minority report, as more recent critics have tended to emphasize Stowe's deleterious influence on the emergence of the African American novel, while downplaying the impact of black writing on her own fictional practices. In this interpretive schema, Stowe is presented as having created in *Uncle Tom's Cabin* a hegemonic racialist text whose colonizationist politics and literary stereotypes had to be revised and resisted by subsequent black writers. Viewed in this way, such a text as Douglass's *My Bondage and My Freedom*, despite the evidence of Douglass's admiration for Stowe's novel, could be taken as a revisionary "corrective" to *Uncle Tom's Cabin*. Eric Sundquist puts the case like this: "Douglass's rewriting of *Uncle Tom's Cabin* into the fabric of his own narrative traded on its power while at the same time reducing it to a set of impotent racialist generalizations."[2]

But as the "exchange" of reviews between Douglass and Stowe suggests, these writers, despite their break in late 1853 over the funding of Douglass's proposed black mechanics institute, continued to read, learn from, and admire each other. Sundquist's critical practice here cuts off the possibility of fully exploring the significance of their ongoing interracial conversation by, in effect, succumbing to the current disciplinary rage: disciplining Stowe for her patronizing and racist attitude toward blacks. How else to explain how a reader as astute as Sundquist can argue that "Stowe was willing to grant African Americans the language of sentiment, but she withheld the language of liberty." That language of liberty, of course, is regularly employed by George Harris and Cassy in *Uncle Tom's Cabin*, and it is virtually the *only* language granted to Dred and Milly in Stowe's "other" antislavery novel, *Dred: A Tale of the Great Dismal Swamp*, published in 1856, the year in which she argued for the continuing importance of attending to black voices and perspectives when addressing the problem of slavery.[3]

In her seminal essay "Unspeakable Things Unspoken: The Afro-American Presence in American Literature," Toni Morrison maintains that "the presence of Afro-American literature and the awareness of its culture" should inform our readings of white-authored texts, for "the presence of Afro-Americans has shaped the choices, the language, the structure—the meaning of so much American literature." As an example, Morrison remarks on how newly resonant "meanings" become available in the works of Melville when his writings are "scoured for this presence and the writerly strategies taken to address or deny it."[4] In the case of Stowe, however, not much "scouring" is required, for Stowe, most notably in *A Key to "Uncle Tom's Cabin"* (1853), regularly acknowledged the shaping impact of African American texts on the politics and representational strategies of her antislavery writings. In addition to discussing the influences of Douglass, Henson, J. W. C. Pennington, Solomon Northup, and many other African Americans on *Uncle Tom's Cabin*, Stowe revealed in *Key* that she saw herself as engaged in a continuing dialogue with important black writers of the period—writers whose influence, implicitly and explicitly, can also be discerned in *Dred*.[5]

Published four years after *Uncle Tom's Cabin*, *Dred* has become a missing text in Stowe's canon. Judged by many critics to be racist and a botch, an embarrassment to Stowe and her admirers, the overwhelming response to *Dred* has been simply to ignore it. This collective neglect is the true embarrassment, for it exposes contemporary critical practices as unwilling to deal with transformations in Stowe's complex and contradictory racial politics; as averse to attending to black influences on Stowe's texts, except when those influences "expose" her mendacity and blindness; and as reluctant to challenge essentialist notions of discrete black and white expressive traditions.[6] This chapter contests these current critical orthodoxies by resituating *Dred* in relation to contemporaneous African American debates on slavery and racism. I will discuss Stowe's remarkable responses not only to the high-profile debates between Douglass and Delany on colonization, emigration, and black elevation but also to some of the many other African American texts and people that she interacted with during the celebrity years of 1852–56. These encounters and exchanges had a major impact on the racial politics of *Dred*, a novel that, with its heroic portrayal of a prophetic black conspirator seeking to bring about the slaves' deliverance, can be regarded as an African American–inspired revision of *Uncle Tom's Cabin*. Indicative of the impact of Douglass and other African American reformers on her conception of black representative identity, Stowe presents the Mosaic Dred as a temperate revolutionary who "never tasted strong liquors in any form."[7]

In *Dred*, Stowe underscores the importance of considering black perspectives when writing about slavery: "We have been accustomed, even those of us who feel most, to look on arguments for and against the system of slavery with the eyes of those who are at ease. . . . We shall never have all the materials for an absolute truth on this subject, till we take into account, with our own views and reasonings, the views and reasonings of those who have bowed down to the yoke, and felt the iron enter into their souls."[8] Though Stowe, in her wish to convey the "absolute truth" of slavery, regularly attempted to incorporate into her antislavery writings the "views and reasonings" of former slaves (and other African Americans), I will allow the unsurprising: that she, like her contemporaries, could at times be utterly confused and contradictory on questions of racial identity. That said, as I hope to show in the first section of this chapter, Stowe's reading in African American texts and her interactions with African American personalities after the publication of *Uncle Tom's Cabin* had a dramatic effect on her racial politics. Attending to the African American presence in her 1856 novel helps us to see that *Dred* is a fundamentally different book from *Uncle Tom's Cabin* — a book that is far more engaged with blacks' perspectives on their situation in antebellum culture. Insofar as it explodes critical myths about her purported blindness to African American realities, *Dred* is critical to an understanding of Stowe's career.

Cross-Racial Revisions

More deeply and thoroughly than most other whites of the time, Stowe paid regard to what African Americans had to say about slavery.[9] Such attention led her regularly to revise her opinions on slavery and race. For this reason, I would argue, one risks considerable reductionism in attempting any sort of precise anatomy of Stowe's racial views. This is not to deny that Stowe worked with racialist categories throughout her writing career. But Stowe continually tested those categories and the politics to which racialist thought could give rise, and it is simply unfair to isolate a particular statement from a particular text as evidence for her hidebound racial views. Invariably, any statement conveys Stowe's ideas at a precise textual/historical moment, conditioned by the language and conceptualizations available to her at that time. It is frequently contradicted by other statements in the Stowe corpus, sometimes on the very same page. Rather than constituting some sort of coherent and programmatic worldview of racial difference, Stowe's ideas, when considered over time, come across as provisional, inconsistent, and contradictory, in large part because she was willing to situate her ideas in a dialogical context. A compelling instance of her willingness to share and modify her views may be discerned in her initial interactions with Frederick Douglass.

In *Key*, Stowe adduced Douglass's *Narrative* as a source that corroborated (and inspired) her depiction of George Harris's ability to sustain his "intelligent and active mind through all the squalid misery, degradation, and oppression of slavery." But in the midst of writing *Uncle Tom's Cabin* Stowe wanted more from Douglass than the published record of his 1845 autobiography, and on 9 July 1851 (to consider from a different perspective some of the material discussed in Chapter 2), she wrote him asking for information on the workings of cotton plantations. She explains herself as follows: "I have before me an able paper written by a Southern planter, in which the details and *modus operandi* are given from his point of sight. I am anxious to have something from another standpoint." That additional "standpoint," she suggests, will help make her picture of the cotton plantation "true to nature in its details." Clearly, for Stowe a central "detail" of any representation of southern plantations is an "authenticating" black perspective. Her desire to incorporate into her work blacks' "point of sight" is evident not only in her inquiry to Douglass but also in her revelation in the same letter that she has become a subscriber to his paper and has "read it with great interest." It is precisely her reading of Douglass's paper that has raised questions in her mind about his positions on two large issues — "the church and African colonization" — and as part of an effort to establish a dialogue with Douglass, she states her desire to change his views. She does so, however, with a full recognition that she addresses an intelligent individual who may well resist her ideas: "I would willingly, if I could, modify your views on both points." Although she has nothing specific to say about colonization, she does defend the antislavery work of her father, Lyman Beecher (a colonizationist), and of other ministers in her family, maintaining that the church has "the purest and most high-principled men and women of the country."[10]

Though Stowe, through George Harris, endorses Liberian colonization in *Uncle Tom's Cabin*, it is a tentative endorsement at best, for she uses George Harris's rationalizing remarks on God's deeper spiritual purpose in establishing the colony to expose the racism that underlies whites' commitment to the movement. And though critical of the proslavery ministers praised by Marie St. Clare, she reserves her greatest scorn for the hypocritical ministers of Northern churches who remain in silent complicity with proslavery practices. If Stowe in her 1851 letter set out to "correct" Douglass, the rhetoric of her novel suggests that Douglass, through the columns of his newspaper, "corrected" Stowe instead.

Given that Stowe in all probability continued to subscribe to Douglass's newspaper—hence her willingness to contribute in 1853 and 1854 to Julia Griffiths's fund-raising volumes, *Autographs for Freedom*—and given her ability to attend to black perspectives and modify her views accordingly, we may similarly posit that Delany's and Douglass's debate on *Uncle Tom's Cabin* in *Frederick Douglass' Paper* worked to "correct" Stowe's views on Liberian colonization. As I noted in Chapter 2, Stowe at around the same time of this epistolary debate sent a letter to the May 1853 meeting of the American and Foreign Anti-Slavery Society declaring that she was "not a Colonizationist."[11] Moreover, in *Key* she implicitly renounces colonizationism. In the final chapter of *Key*—"What Is to Be Done?"—she says nothing about colonization, arguing instead for abolition and black elevation. In the mode of the black uplift admonitions of Douglass and Delany, Stowe calls for an end to segregationist practices that hinder blacks' efforts to rise in the culture, proclaiming to her white readers in particular, "As far as in you lies, endeavor to secure for them [free and enslaved blacks], in every walk of life, the ordinary privileges of American citizens."[12] Committed to the principles espoused in *Key* on blacks' right to rise in the United States, during her 1853 tour of Great Britain Stowe recommended the proceedings of the 1853 Rochester Convention of Colored People to her supporters as evidence that the "colored people in this country are rapidly rising in every respect . . . [and] that the slanders against this unhappy race should be refuted."[13]

In 1855 Stowe wrote the introduction to the black abolitionist William C. Nell's *The Colored Patriots of the American Revolution*, which argued against colonization by insisting, as Douglass and Delany did, that blacks' heroic willingness to fight against the British in 1776 and 1812 should have earned them their U.S. citizenship. According to Stowe's introduction (which she directs toward the book's white readers), Nell's "collection of interesting incidents" promises to "redeem the character of the race from [the] misconception" that they are "deficient in energy and courage." Of course, by 1855 that "misconception" had a good deal to do with Stowe's valorization of Uncle Tom. Nell's book, then, oddly enough, may be read as an effort to revise Stowe's *Uncle Tom's Cabin* under the legitimating authority of Stowe herself. Like Delany, whose *Condition* he cites as an important precursor of his own book, Nell instructs his readers on the accomplishments of black scientists, soldiers, writers, musicians, teachers, and businesspeople, presenting various "colored patriots" as evidence of the immorality of slavery and racist practices in the United States. And he shares with Delany the view that African Americans should be able to "participate with other Americans in the duties of legislation." Where he departs from Delany is on the interrelated issues of emigration and black separatism, arguing that blacks should continue to pursue their rights of citizenship in the United States. As he remarks in the text's conclusion, which directs anger at "colonizationists and slaveholders," "Colored Americans should not be isolated." In her introduction, Stowe concurs with Nell's anticolonizationist and integrationist sentiments, calling African Americans "magnanimous" in fighting "for a nation which did not acknowledge them as citizens and equals." And, like Nell, she offers the hope that blacks' "white brothers in reading may remember, that generosity, courage and bravery, are of no particular race and complexion." [14]

Stowe expresses similar antiracist sentiments in an 1858 newspaper article "A Brilliant Success," which honors the achievements of three Haitian blacks who "have just carried off the three first prizes in Greek, Latin, and Rhetoric, in the old university of the Sorbonne in Paris." Though a post-*Dred* text, the article sheds retrospective light on Stowe's attitudes towards racialist and environmentalist thought during the 1850s. Asserting that "no race so abused, maltreated, and enslaved, could have developed faster than the African during the last fifty years," Stowe mocks the notion that blacks "are naturally inferior, incapable of the education and progress of the white races." As the achievements of the three Haitian students reveal, blacks have an "aptitude . . . for civilization and improvement," perhaps even greater than that of many whites. To make this argument, Stowe, at a key moment in the essay, turns against the racialist views of her culture, rendering "scientific" notions of environmentalism and racialism — the ideas she supposedly picked up from Alexander Kinmont's *Twelve Lectures on the Natural History of Man* (1839) — as mere metaphors for racism. Looking forward to the day when similar prizes will be awarded to U.S. blacks in U.S. universities, she remarks on the Parisian environment that helped to produce the Haitians' successes:

Is there not something in the fraternal spirit of France, its absolute and philosophic superiority to the prejudices of races, which may account for this result in Paris? The Africans as a race are exceedingly approbative. They are sensitive to kindness or unkindness. They need a warm, kindly atmosphere to grow in, as much as tropic plants. The pitiless frosts and pelting storms of scorn, ridicule, contempt, and obloquy which have fallen upon them could not have found a race more sensitive, more easily beaten back and withered.

While racialism has a role in Stowe's thinking—blacks are portrayed as more "sensitive" and in need of approval than whites—the colonizationists' environmentalist insistence on blacks' "natural" need for tropical climes is here turned on its head, as climate, or "atmosphere," is presented in terms of metaphors of social fairness and justice. By the end of the article Stowe seems to share in the outrage of more militant blacks at whites' failures to offer the proper "atmosphere" for growth in the United States, and so she concludes with an arch prediction of the possibility of black violence. Blacks, she warns, will soon "feel an electric thrill of pride and sympathy,—and in that day let oppressors tremble. They may have proofs of the capacity of the race far other than they desire." [15]

Although Stowe argued quite sympathetically for black men's intellectual capacities and right to resort to violence, and at times (as with Douglass) revised her views in response to theirs, her interactions with black women in the years immediately following the publication of *Uncle Tom's Cabin* have proven to be more problematic. Stowe's awkward exchanges with African American women may have resulted from an elitist and racist need to remain at a superior distance from black women, even as she tended to represent them as her spiritual superiors. Still, the fact of the inequity in cultural authority between Stowe and antebellum black women—and even Stowe's apparent condescension—need not be used to make her into a sort of antislavery parasite or the black women into her unwitting victims.

Consider, for example, Stowe's "exchanges" with Harriet Jacobs, who attempted to enlist Stowe in the project of telling her life story. Uneasy about approaching the famous author of *Uncle Tom's Cabin*, in late 1852 or early 1853 Jacobs had her friend Amy Post act as an intermediary, instructing her that "if Mrs Stowe would undertake it I should like to be with her a Month," during which time "I could give her some fine sketches for her pen on slavery." In subsequent letters her demands on Stowe were to increase, as she proposed, through Post, that Stowe should also take her daughter, Louisa, to England, because "Louisa would be a very good representative of a Southern slave." Karen Sánchez-Eppler terms Stowe's unwillingness to accommodate Jacobs's proposals an "insult": "In Stowe's response, both the representative slave girl and the representation of a slave girl are denied the integrity of individuation." We should note, however, that it was Jacobs herself who insisted on the daughter's representative status; that Stowe had never met Jacobs or her daughter (thus it would have been difficult for Stowe to have granted either of them full "individuation"); and that Stowe was traveling to England at the invitation of the New Ladies' Anti-Slavery Society (of Glasgow) and New Association for the Abolition of Slavery, which was paying for all her expenses (hence it would have been presumptuous of her to foist an additional expense onto the group).[16] Meanwhile, even as Stowe rejected Jacobs's proposals, she was considering writing up her life history for *Key* and thus sought to corroborate the facts by consulting with Jacobs's employer, Cornelia Willis. Perhaps Stowe assumed that if Jacobs had shared with her, a complete stranger, such details of her past as her self-defensive sexual liaison with Samuel Tredwell Sawyer, she would also have shared them with her beloved employer. But this was not the case, and as a result of Stowe's hurtful betrayal of her sexual history, Jacobs decided to hold on to her story. Joan D. Hedrick rightly asserts that Stowe's disclosure of Jacobs's past to Mrs. Willis was "an extreme example of insensitivity bred by class and skin privilege." But what Hedrick and others fail to note are Jacobs's mixed motives in her interactions with Stowe, as she wanted *both* a commercial success on the order of *Uncle Tom's Cabin* and respect for her privacy. These motives, as Michael Newbury has recently argued, were simply incompatible.[17]

Stowe had a more positive experience with Milly Edmondson, in part because Edmondson allowed Stowe free use of her story. Stowe's thirteen-page account in *Key* of Milly's efforts to liberate her family from slavery reveals both appealing and unappealing aspects of Stowe's attitude toward African American women, as she comes off as desirous of but not completely willing to let Milly tell her story from her own perspective. Stowe remarks on the narratorial powers of the illiterate but exemplary Christian Milly: "She had often a forcible and peculiarly beautiful manner of expressing herself, which impressed what she said strongly." It is mostly through Milly, then, that we learn of how the emancipatory rhetoric of the European revolutions of 1848 inspired seventy-seven slaves, including six of Milly's children, to try to escape from the *Pearl* when it docked in Washington in April 1848. At this key point in the storytelling, however, Stowe abruptly switches the point of view: "The incidents of the rest of the narrative will now be given as obtained from Mary and Emily Edmondson, by the lady in whose family they have been placed by the writer for an education." As a result, though Mary's and Emily's perspectives are presented as important sources for the subsequent narrative, we now have the mediating voice of a "lady" telling us of Milly's efforts to locate and free her children. Only at the end of the chapter does Milly's voice return, though now subsumed by Stowe's moralizing voice. Stowe proclaims that Milly, who urges her freed daughters to forgive their white enslavers, has "learned to solve the highest problem of Christian ethics, and to do what so few reformers can do,—hate the *sin*, but love the *sinner!*"[18]

Stowe presents in a similar light the figure of Sojourner Truth—the African American woman whose "presence" can be discerned most clearly in *Dred*. Stowe described her 1852 encounter with Truth in a sketch entitled "Sojourner Truth, the Libyan Sibyl," which appeared in the April 1863 *Atlantic* and was reprinted in the 1878 *Narrative of Sojourner Truth*. Jean Fagan Yellin writes of Stowe's portrayal of Truth: "Stowe's Libyan Sibyl is passive. She possesses knowledge but she cannot act on it; further, because her language cannot readily be understood, no one else can use her knowledge as the basis for effective action."[19] Such a reading, however, is confuted by even a cursory glance at Stowe's text, which begins with an account of an actively engaged Truth arriving at Stowe's house in request of an interview with the famous author of *Uncle Tom's Cabin*. From the outset, Truth, hardly nonplussed by Stowe's eminence, seems in control of the situation. Stowe describes her initial viewing of and conversation with Truth in this way:

She seemed perfectly self-possessed and at her ease; in fact, there was almost an unconscious superiority, not unmixed with a solemn twinkle of humor, in the odd, composed manner in which she looked down on me. Her whole air had at times a gloomy sort of drollery which impressed one strangely.

"So this is *you*?" she said.

"Yes," I answered.

"Well, honey, de Lord bless ye! I jes' thought I'd like to come an' have a look at ye. You's heerd o' me, I reckon?" she added.

"Yes, I think I have. You go about lecturing, do you not?"

"Yes, honey, that's what I do. The Lord has made me a sign unto this nation, an' I go round a-testifyin', an' showin' on 'em their sins agin my people."

So saying, she took a seat, and, stooping over and crossing her arms on her knees, she looked down on the floor, and appeared to fall into a sort of reverie.

From beginning to end, as I read this account, Truth remains in control of the situation, in part because she is so enigmatic (note, for example, her "solemn twinkle of humor," her "gloomy sort of drollery," and her lapsing into "a sort of reverie"). It is Truth who initiates and shapes the dialogue; it is Truth who "looks down" on Stowe with "an unconscious superiority"; it is Truth who is "perfectly self-possessed." Rather than deferring to Stowe, she aggressively seeks to ascertain whether Stowe knows who *she* is; and rather than deferring to Stowe's husband, she asserts her own qualifications to be a minister: "When I preaches, I has jest one text to preach from, an' I always preaches from this one. *My* text is 'WHEN I FOUND JESUS!'"[20]

Truth emerges in Stowe's account as a transcendent figure whose capacity to love the slaveholder links her to God. In addition to underscoring Truth's Christlike religiosity, Stowe also emphasizes her "spiritualistic" and curative capacities, as Truth helps to heal an invalid woman staying at the Stowes' house. Truth's apprehension of godhead and her ability to love her enemies are presented by Stowe as absolute forms of knowledge, knowledge that resonates, I would argue, precisely because of—rather than in spite of—Stowe's use of dialect to render Truth's speech. As Truth herself realized, whites took greater notice of her preachings when she theatricalized herself as an "African" illiterate whose perspective was radically different from that of the white middle class. As her more recent biographers remark, Truth, though capable of speaking more conventional English, "seemed to keep her speech considerably homely, ungrammatical, and in dialect because she found her audiences liked it that way. . . . In a sense she molded her public image around her illiteracy." Similarly, it could be argued that during her visit Truth "molded" herself for Stowe, not only deliberately speaking in dialect but also, in ways calculated to keep Stowe off balance, moving in and out of spiritualistic reveries. Truth thus must take some responsibility for encouraging Stowe to describe her "religious element" in terms of racialist stereotypes of the "wild" African.[21]

In a brilliant speculative analysis of the characterization of Nat Turner in Thomas Gray's 1831 "Confessions of Nat Turner," Sundquist likewise raises the possibility "that Turner himself had staged a performance for Gray and his audience, adopting the guise of religious madness in order to protect other slaves or potential plots, or simply to exercise his intelligence and imagination."[22] In doing so, Turner would have cunningly asserted an "authorship" role in Gray's text. Though Stowe's relation to Truth and other African Americans is quite different from Gray's relationship to Turner, Sundquist suggestively points to the ways in which an African American presence in white-authored texts can, at times, be an actively created presence.

We need to resist the paternalistic tendency of regarding blacks as always the "victims" of racialist representations. In my reading of *Dred*, I will be paying close attention to those moments in the text when Stowe's representations of black characters are indebted to black self-representations. Turner's "Confessions" is one of the texts that had a major impact on racial themes and characterizations in Stowe's novel, as attested by her reprinting of a large section of the "Confessions" in the novel's appendix. To some extent, then, we could argue that Turner had an "authorship" role in *Dred*. Stepto argues that Stowe took Turner as a subject for her second novel in response to Douglass's "The Heroic Slave," his revisionary celebration, in response to Stowe's Uncle Tom, of black revolutionary violence.[23] Thus *Dred* must be viewed, in part, as the result of Stowe's creative exchanges with Douglass (and, by extension, with Delany) on the question of black leadership in a slave culture. I will discuss several other such instances in which Stowe responds to black voices and perspectives that have themselves responded to her earlier writings. In this respect, one of the large aims of the reading of *Dred* that follows is to resituate Stowe's second novel amid the black rhetoric that helped to bring it into being.

Day of Vengeance

Despite its antislavery agenda, *Dred* seems oddly indebted to the plantation novel tradition inaugurated by John Pendleton Kennedy, beginning rather conventionally by focusing on the eighteen-year-old plantation belle, Nina Gordon, and her "crisis" of the moment: that she has accepted three marriage proposals from suitors. Because her parents are dead and her younger brother, Tom Gordon, has adopted "every low form of vice," Nina is expected to play a central role in watching over the slaves of her North Carolina plantation.[24] In view of this paternalism, it is not surprising that we are presented early on with such stock characters as the "mammy" Aunt Katy and the scheming stablehand Old Hundred.[25] But, unlike in Kennedy, we are also introduced to rather substantial and complex black characters who challenge white paternalistic models, and it quickly becomes clear that the frivolous Nina, who is pushing the plantation toward bankruptcy, remains "very much in the hands of those she professed to govern" (1:41). Supervising the plantation, for example, is a slave named Harry, described by one character as "a very clever quadroon servant" (1:24). Unbeknownst to Nina, Harry also happens to be her older half-brother. As in Douglass's *Narrative* and *Bondage*, William Wells Brown's *Clotel*, Jacobs's *Incidents*, and many other works by black writers, Stowe's account of the genealogical backgrounds of the Gordon family exposes the licentiousness of the patriarchal master and the tragic consequences for the children. Caught between his love for his wife, Lisette, the slave of a French Creole woman, and his love for Nina, Harry, in the manner of Douglass in his autobiographical narratives, declares his envy of those slaves who (supposedly) have never thought about their condition: "How often I've wished that I was a good, honest, black nigger, like Uncle Pomp! Then I should know what I was" (1:76).[26]

But how thoughtless and content are the novel's "good, honest" blacks? Appearing to fit Harry's description is Old Tiff, the male slave of an impoverished young woman, Sue Cripps, with distant connections to the "aristocratic" Peytons of Virginia. Introduced as he cares for Sue in a shabby room containing "some medicinal-looking packages, a turkey's wing, . . . some bundles of dry herbs" (1:97), Tiff in effect is presented as doctoring Sue through the art of conjure. Indeed, as Tiff speaks of God in this Africanized spiritual space, Sue experiences a vision of heaven just before she dies; unlike the more conventional white ministers introduced later in the novel, Tiff brings forth a genuine convert from his syncretic Afro-Christian preachings.[27] His subsequent decision to become the guardian of Sue's children, Fanny and Teddy, could be taken as a form of lackeyism, but it is more to the point, I think, to view his guardianship as a genuine act of love that transcends the bounds of race.

Tiff also transcends the bounds of gender, as throughout the novel Stowe emphasizes the ways in which he resembles "an old woman" (1:98). At times the "womanly" Tiff can seem similar to, and partly modeled on, Sojourner Truth. For example, in the course of teaching Fanny how to speak "proper" English, Tiff insists that his own use of dialect is a matter of free choice: "Old Tiff *knows* what good talk is. An't he heard de greatest ladies and gen'lemen in de land talk? But he don't want de trouble to talk dat ar way, 'cause he's a nigger! Tiff likes his own talk — it's good enough for Tiff" (1:278). As a self-theatricalized "nigger," Tiff, like Sojourner Truth, can retain a modicum of power in a racist culture by appearing knowable and unthreatening to whites, even as he mocks the notion of blood as a determinant of character by overinsisting on the importance of such connections when instructing the white children on their need for good speech: "It's in de blood; and what's in de blood must come out — ho! ho! ho!" (1:279). As will become clear when we see him interacting with the subversive slaves of the Dismal Swamp, any reading of Tiff that fails to take into account the knowledge contained in his elusive and mocking "ho! ho! ho!" is a partial and blinkered one.

When Tiff first arrives at Nina's to announce the death of Sue, the slave Aunt Milly admiringly refers to him as a "faithful old creature" (1:123). Milly, who emerges as a central character, herself initially appears to be the "good, honest" slave of the plantation novel. The "waiting-woman" (1:58) of Nina's selfish Aunt Nesbit, Milly is presented in spiritual terms as a woman waiting patiently for her day in heaven. There is also some suggestion that she is waiting to return to Africa. Wearing a brightly colored Madras turban about her head, exuding passions that "burned in her bosom with a tropical fervor" (1:60), the beautiful and "regal" Milly, the narrator remarks, would be in perfect harmony with "the gorgeous surroundings of African landscape" (1:59). Yet Milly has a history in the United States that links her with the slaves of Southern plantations. When younger, she had married a "mulatto man, on a plantation adjoining her owner's" (1:60–61) and had had a number of children who, one by one, were sold to distant plantations. Without sentimentalizing afflictions as somehow necessary for conversion, Stowe exalts Milly, as she exalted Milly Edmondson and Sojourner Truth, for a Christlike capacity for suffering, remarking on how most "souls" would be broken by such experiences: "where one soul is thus raised to higher piety, thousands are crushed in hopeless imbecility" (1:61).[28]

By moralizing on Milly's experiences, Stowe exerts her command over the character in these initial descriptions. But when Milly makes her next major appearance in the novel, she tells her own story to Nina and draws her own moral from it. In this sense Milly's narration speaks to and reveals key aspects of Stowe's interactions with Sojourner Truth (and other blacks of the period); for what emerges of interest here are not simply the details of Milly's story that correspond to Truth's but the reordering of power relations that such storytelling can bring about. Describing her angry response to her mistress's betrayal of her promise not to sell her youngest son, Alfred, into slavery, Milly tells of how she shook Miss Harriet by the shoulders and cursed her (as Truth similarly cursed her mistress for selling her youngest child). Unlike Truth, however, who resourcefully reclaimed her son, Milly relates a sadder story of how the self-educated Alfred was killed by the overseer he boldly sought to resist. This leads her, in a moment similar to that described by Truth, to demand that God take vengeance on her mistress. According to Milly, she walked into her mistress's room with Alfred's bullet-riddled jacket and declared: "*You* killed him; his blood be on you and your chil'en! O, Lord God in heaven, hear me, and *render unto her double!*" (1:219). The narrator describes the storytelling scene: "Nina drew in her breath hard, with an instinctive shudder. Milly had drawn herself up, in the vehemence of her narration, and sat leaning forward, her black eyes dilated, her strong arms clenched before her, and her powerful frame expanding and working with the violence of her emotion . . . like the figure of a black marble Nemesis in a trance of wrath. She sat so for a few minutes, and then her muscles relaxed, her eyes gradually softened; she looked tenderly, but solemnly, down on Nina" (1:219). Momentarily, Nina becomes a surrogate for Miss Harriet (whose name further suggests Stowe's implication in this scene). The slave's rage thus transcends the particularity of the past and, as Nina herself senses, focuses on the white auditor at hand. As a wrathful Nemesis, Milly embodies a full and righteous potential for violence, even as she maintains a "Christian" (temperate) self-command over her rage. For it is Milly, not Nina, who gets things back under control, as from the heights of her impassioned storytelling, "she looked tenderly, but solemnly, down on Nina." (Recall Stowe's description of the "perfectly self-possessed" Truth looking down on her.)

Milly's subsequent account of her conversion stands as one of the few genuinely Christian conversions of the novel. Several years before the composition of *Dred*, Truth described to Stowe how she had found Christ at "a Methodist meetin' somewhere in our parts." Milly describes a similar moment of conversion at a camp meeting, where her apprehension of Christ's suffering patience leads her to feel "a rush of love in my soul!" (1:221). Truth at her moment of conversion, as described by Stowe in 1863, spoke of "another rush of love through my soul, an' I cried out loud — 'Lord, Lord, I can love *even de white folks!*'"[29] Milly similarly declares at the moment of her conversion: "Lord, I ken love even de white folks!" (*Dred*, 1:221). In both cases, the ability to love suggests a hierarchical reordering that empowers black women, making them, however temporarily, into "masters" over and ultimately ministers to racist whites. Like Truth, who found that her curse on the mother of the man who sold her son seemed to have been answered by God the avenger (the woman's daughter was murdered by her new husband), so Milly finds that her curse is answered as well: Harriet's drunken son beats her and then dies when he accidentally shoots himself while loading a gun. In both cases, the seemingly divine retribution leads these black women to take pity on whites. As Milly explains, the grief of her mistress taught her that "we was sisters in Jesus" (1:222).

In telling her life history to a white auditor, Milly both represents and effects power reversals, with the implication being that proslavery idealizations of hierarchical relations on the plantation fail to speak to deeper realities of black rage and spirituality. This point is worth underscoring, for in the first third of the novel, despite the emphases of my discussion, black voices and perspectives remain subordinate to the narrator's focus on Nina's growing love for Edward Clayton, an antislavery reformer who owns a plantation where, with his sister Anne, he is "training" (1:42) slaves for their eventual freedom. But shortly after Milly narrates her life history, a new black voice and perspective is introduced into the novel that even more boldly challenges racial hierarchies. That perspective is in effect summoned forth by another manifestation of black rage. Furious at his half-brother Tom's sadistic efforts to purchase Lisette as his (sexual) slave, Harry declares to Nina, in the spirit of George Harris: "I hate your country! I hate your laws" (1:175). Though Nina (with Clayton's help) purchases Lisette, thereby providing her with some protection, Tom continues to assert his mastery over Harry, striking him in the face with a whip when he encounters him by the Dismal Swamp. At which point there emerges from the swamps a Herculean black man who, like Milly, wears a marker of his Africanity—a turban—but, unlike the Christlike Milly, also carries a knife, hatchet, and rifle. Harry's offhand response to the black's unnerving appearance is this: "O, it is you, then, Dred!" (1:241).

Harry's immediate recognition of "Dred," who before this relatively late moment has not even been mentioned in the text, can seem to enact a point of rupture in the novel, as readers will initially find themselves disoriented by their own lack of knowledge of the existence and motives of this swamp-dwelling black. Lacking such knowledge, readers are linked with the plantation whites. As Stowe remarks, "Harry, in common with many of the slaves on the Gordon plantation, knew perfectly well of the presence of Dred in the neighborhood, and had often seen and conversed with him. But neither he nor any of the rest of them ever betrayed before any white person the slightest knowledge of the fact" (1:258).[30] Alice C. Crozier has influentially argued that changes in "the style and direction of the novel occur quite abruptly halfway through with the sudden introduction of the wild pariah of the Great Dismal Swamp, Dred"; and she asserts that these changes were the direct result of Stowe's anguished response, in the midst of writing *Dred*, to the South Carolina congressman Preston Brooks's caning of Massachusetts's antislavery senator Charles Sumner on the floor of the Senate chambers. Yet the caning occurred in May 1856, only several months before publication of the novel. I want to suggest that what we experience with the introduction of Dred is less a transformation than a revelation: that Stowe, in a deliberately implicating fashion, has to this point encouraged a reading of blacks and the plantation (novel) that is partial and misleading, as she has left out of the picture the "presence" of black revolutionism. Her subsequent efforts to explore the "views and reasonings" (2:213) of black insurrectionaries represents a significant departure from the more acquiescent fundamentalism of *Uncle Tom's Cabin*.[31]

When Dred steps forth from the swamps to address Harry, Stowe describes him, to the point of obsession, in terms of his body: he is a "tall black man, of magnificent stature and proportions" (1:240), whose bulging muscles suggest "herculean strength" (1:240).[32] But Dred, we quickly learn, is more than just a body: he is the leader of the maroons of the Dismal Swamp. Rather than remaining in one place to develop "local attachments," as Stowe in *Uncle Tom's Cabin* suggests blacks prefer, Dred roams "the whole swampy belt of both the Carolinas, as well as that of Southern Virginia" (1:258). His roaming works literally to enlarge the maroon community: "Wherever he stopped, he formed a sort of retreat, where he received and harbored fugitives" (1:258). This community, Stowe proclaims, drawing on the same language she used to describe George Harris's revolutionism, should be regarded as a revolutionary community similar to that "which purchased for our fathers a national existence" (1:257). It is also similar to that which sought to bring republicanism to Europe: "What the mountains of Switzerland were to the persecuted Vaudois, this swampy belt has been to the American slave" (1:255).[33]

An immediate African American source for Stowe's revisionary thinking on black revolutionary violence would have been Nell's *The Colored Patriots of the American Revolution*, which, as mentioned, Stowe introduced in 1855. In addition to supplying lengthy commentary on black participants in the Revolutionary War and the War of 1812, Nell also provides sections on black provocateurs and conspirators such as Denmark Vesey, David Walker, Nat Turner, the "Virginia Maroons" of the Great Dismal Swamp, and Madison Washington. In a chapter on "The Virginia Maroons," Nell writes, "The Great Dismal Swamp, which lies near the Eastern shore of Virginia, and, commencing near Norfolk, stretches quite into North Carolina, contains a large colony of negroes, who originally obtained their freedom by the grace of God and their own determined energy, instead of the consent of their owners, or by the help of the Colonization Society." A consecrated group of revolutionaries, the colony has "endured from generation to generation," Nell proclaims, "and is likely to continue until slavery is abolished throughout the land."[34]

These are precisely the terms in which Stowe represents Dred and his accomplices, the heirs of Vesey and Turner. Temporarily taking leave of Dred to provide a historical account of the 1822 Denmark Vesey conspiracy in South Carolina, Stowe portrays Vesey and his accomplices as inspired by the Declaration of Independence to enact their own "patriotic" revolution against the slave masters' despotic authority. Stowe guilefully encourages her readers to project themselves into the perspectives of black revolutionaries by citing the white legal documents from Vesey's trial that so clearly fail to speak to the liberationist goals of his conspiracy. Offering as an example of the "considerable naïveté" of Vesey's "historians" (1:249) an assertion from the trial transcript that it

" 'is difficult to conceive *what motive he had to enter into such a plot,* unless it was . . . that Vesey had *several children who were slaves,* and that . . .
he wished he could see them free' " (1:249), Stowe expects us to discern on
our own that Vesey's familial motivations were self-evidently compelling
human motivations. In addition, she links the political and the familial
to the spiritual, pointing out that Vesey was inspired not only by the
Bible, the "book that has always been prolific of insurrectionary movements, under all systems of despotism" (1:250), but also, in Stowe's effort
at representing religious syncretism, by African religions. For among
Vesey's accomplices was Gullah Jack, who, according to official accounts,
was " 'regarded as a sorcerer, and, as such, feared by the natives of Africa,
who believe in witchcraft. . . . He was artful, cruel, bloody; his disposition, in short, was diabolical' " (1:251). What the white masters regard
as "diabolical" is ultimately represented by Stowe as central to the black
revolutionary consciousness that the historical Vesey and his compatriots bequeath to Stowe's fictional invention: his son Dred, a stand-in
for another "son," or ideological descendant, of Vesey—Nat Turner.[35]

In her account of Dred's "genealogical" inheritance of Vesey's revolutionism, Stowe emphasizes that political, familial, and spiritual goals, and
not simply "blood," guide Dred toward his own revolutionary action.[36]
Having learned magic, snake charming, and the use of second sight from
his African grandfather (2:6–7), Dred, at the age of ten, becomes "his
father's confidant" (1:254) in the conspiratorial plot. When the plot is
discovered, father and son "counterfeit alienation and dislike" (1:254)
so that Dred can carry on Vesey's work after he is executed by the state.
Sold from one plantation to the next, feared by overseers throughout
the region because of what they term "his desperate, unsubduable disposition" (1:254), Dred eventually kills an overseer: "In the scuffle that
ensued Dred struck him to the earth, a dead man, made his escape to
the swamps, and was never afterwards heard of in civilized life" (1:255).
Stowe describes how whites' terror at the knowledge of the existence of
this militant black and his ever-expanding swamp community comes to
act as "a considerable check on the otherwise absolute power of the overseer" (1:255). In this respect, she presents Dred and his community of
conspirators in the way Sundquist suggests we should regard Turner and
his community of conspirators—as successfully trading in the "power of
retributive terror."[37]

Experiencing states "of exaltation and trance" (2:5) reminiscent of
what Nat Turner declared himself as having experienced, Dred manages

to exist apart from what Stowe terms the "hot and positive light of our modern materialism" (2:5). In his prophetic language in particular, Dred can seem, as Nell describes Turner, overwhelmed by his "communion with the spirit."[38] When he demands of Harry, for example, "How long wilt thou cast in thy lot with the oppressors of Israel?" (1:241), we sense that Dred is as responsive to biblical language as the Christly saints Uncle Tom and Little Eva. Unlike the saints of *Uncle Tom's Cabin*, however, he responds less to the image of Christ in the New Testament than to the wrathful Old Testament prophets. Absorbed in the hope and promise that he has been chosen by God to be the prophetic avenger whose leadership will bring about the deliverance of his people, Dred spends much of his time "in a kind of dream" (1:256). Drawing on Nat Turner's description in the "Confessions" of his own spirituality, Stowe tells of how Dred "would fast and pray for days; and then voices would seem to speak to him, and strange hieroglyphics would be written upon the leaves" (1:257).

In a racialist account of blacks' capacities to achieve such a spiritualistic state—to become, in effect, God's mediums—Stowe reports that blacks "are said by mesmerists to possess, in the fullest degree, that peculiar temperament which fits them for the evolution of mesmeric phenomena; and hence the existence among them, to this day, of men and women who are supposed to have peculiar magical powers" (2:6–7). In *Key*, Stowe similarly asserts that blacks possess "a nervous organization peculiarly susceptible and impressible" for mesmeric experimentation, and she links Africans' beliefs in " 'fetish and obi,' in 'the evil eye,' and other singular influences" to such constitutional proclivities.[39] Stowe's interest in blacks' spiritualistic character would have had sources in her culture's interest, indeed implication, in African religions. As Lynn Wardley brilliantly argues, the reformist spiritualism of the 1840s and 1850s, so central to *Uncle Tom's Cabin*, "resonated with West African religious beliefs." According to historians of antebellum slave religion, the syncretic linking of traditional African religious beliefs in "spirit possession and mediumship" to Christian notions of the Holy Spirit contributed to what can be called the "Africanization" of American Christianity—one of *Dred*'s main subjects.[40]

Viewing Dred in this cultural context, particularly given that Stowe emphasizes the roles of his African grandfather and the sorcerer Gullah Jack in forming his religious and political sensibility, helps us to see that Stowe means to represent Dred's Afro-Christianity as a legitimately revolutionary antislavery perspective. Nowhere is this more apparent than in the climactic camp meeting at the midpoint of the novel. Presenting the meeting, with its occasionally wild outbursts of enthusiastic energies and spiritual visions, as an ironic signifier of the Africanization of white Southerners' Christianity, Stowe makes Dred into the true minister of the meeting.[41] Journeying to the campgrounds after witnessing the death in the swamps of a fugitive slave and after apprehending, as if "in a somnambulic dream" (1:294), God's command to "'be a sign unto this evil nation!'" (1:295), Dred from out of the darkness interrupts the sermon of the corrupt slaveholder Father Bonnie to speak himself on judgment, wrath, and vengeance. As he preaches with the sort of devotional energy that Clayton links to the African's "tropical lineage and blood" (1:299), and that the narrator links to Dred's "savage familiarity with nature" (1:321), Stowe keeps the point of view fixed on the whites, who can barely make sense of what Dred is saying and cannot even see him. Yet the auditors are stirred by his impassioned declarations, fearing that they may have come under the judgment of a genuine prophet "strangely commissioned to announce coming misfortunes" (1:321).

James M. Cox argues that Dred's "linguistic identity as an Old Testament prophet promising an apocalypse is directly at odds with Mrs. Stowe's New Testament commitment to abject humility as *the* Christian virtue."[42] But this powerful scene presses us to ask how committed Stowe was to such an unchanging vision or, perhaps more to the point, just how univocal was her Christ. William L. Andrews observes that "Black Christianity in the South assimilated the self-sacrificial Jesus with the idea of Moses as a communal deliverer in order to reconcile 'spiritual freedom' and 'earthly deliverance.'" Significantly, several years before the publication of *Dred*, Stowe presented a similar merging of Moses and Christ in her poem "Caste and Christ," which portrays Christ as the deliverer and lover of "the dusky stranger":

> By Myself, the Lord of Ages,
> I have sown to right the wrong,
> I have pledged my work, unbroken,
> For the weak against the strong.[43]

Appearing in the same volume of *Autographs for Freedom* as Douglass's "The Heroic Slave," "Caste and Christ" could be read as Stowe's response to African Americans who had criticized Uncle Tom for his passivity. Similarly, in *Dred*, Stowe radically revised, or enlarged on, her sense of Christ's character to create in Dred a sympathetic (and representative) picture of a black Christlike avenger—a fact not lost on one of Stowe's most vociferous critics of the Christlike (and representative) Uncle Tom, Martin Delany, who, as I noted above, used excerpts from "Caste and Christ" as running epigraphs to the chapters from *Blake* published serially in the *Weekly Anglo-African*. That Dred has both the potential and moral warrant to enact a well-deserved vengeance on white enslavers emerges as the haunting possibility—and promise—of the remainder of the novel.

Soon after delivering his "sermon" on God's eventual righting of wrongs, Dred "plunged into the thickets, and was gone" (1:329). He is simultaneously "gone" and ubiquitous, for it is difficult not to read all subsequent events of the novel in relation to our knowledge of Dred's lurking presence. From this perspective, Clayton's and Nina's efforts to obtain legal redress for Milly, shot in the arm by a drunken employer to whom she had hired herself out, seem naïve, particularly as they imagine themselves as coming to the aid of a helpless, childlike woman. Much more aware of the power dynamic central to slavery is Clayton's father, the chief justice of the North Carolina Supreme Court, who, despite his personal "feelings" (2:99), overturns the jury decision in Milly's favor with a clear statement of the legal principles upholding slavery: "THE POWER OF THE MASTER MUST BE ABSOLUTE, TO RENDER THE SUBMISSION OF THE SLAVE PERFECT" (2:103).[44] In response to his father's ruling, the idealistic Clayton resigns from the legal profession, even as he paternalistically chooses to retain over his slaves the "legal relation of owner simply as a means of protecting my servants from the cruelties of the law" (2:108). But Clayton is not the only key character in attendance at the court; the mulatto slave Harry Gordon also witnesses the ruling. As observed by the uncomprehending younger Clayton, Harry responds with a visceral and politicized anger that seems of a piece with Dred's: "His face became pale, his brow clouded, and . . . a fierce and peculiar expression flashed from his dark-blue eye" (2:105).[45]

With the depiction of Harry's rage, "THE CLOUD BURSTS" (2:111), as Stowe titles the subsequent chapter. A cholera epidemic strikes the region, and Stowe, through her biblical references, makes connections between the fatal disease and the biblical judgment of vengeance—" 'The pestilence that walketh in darkness' " (2:111)—that such a plague could be taken to represent. In William Wells Brown's *Clotel* (1853), a novel that may well be "present" in *Dred* (Stowe met Brown in England the year he published his novel), a similar connection between fever and vengeance is developed through the portrayal of the militant black leader Picquilo. Described as "a bold, turbulent spirit . . . [who] from revenge imbrued his hands in the blood of all the whites he could meet," Picquilo, like Dred, lurks in the Dismal Swamp and is introduced into the novel at the time of the cholera epidemic of the early 1830s—the time of Nat Turner's rebellion. Stowe too insists on the link between cholera and Turner's brand of revolutionism, having Dred remark when he learns about the coming of the cholera epidemic: "Nat Turner—they killed him; but the fear of him almost drove them to set free their slaves! . . . A little more fear, and they would have done it" (2:89).[46]

And yet despite Dred's hopes, Nina, who succumbs to cholera several hundred pages before the end of the novel, fails to free her slaves, thereby leaving them vulnerable to the "uncontrolled power of a man like Tom Gordon" (2:138). But given the presence of Dred and his compatriots in the swamps and the rage of the slaves at white oppressors, how vulnerable are they? Apparently not as vulnerable as Nina and Clayton fear, for when Tom, in attempting to take possession of Harry, strikes the resistant slave with a "gutta-percha cane" (2:145) of the sort Preston Brooks used to strike Charles Sumner, Harry, unlike Sumner, in Stowe's rewriting of the incident, violently returns Tom's blow and then escapes with his wife, Lisette, to Dred's revolutionary community in the swamps. Surprisingly, Tiff too joins Dred's community. Faced with the prospect of coming under the control of the drunken Cripps and his new wife, an alcoholic prostitute, Tiff has a vision in which God instructs him to take the white children under his charge to the temperate haven of the swamps: "Bress de Lord, dere an't no whiskey here!" (2:166).[47] As it turns out, even Tiff has links with Dred; for Stowe cunningly reveals that in the past Dred "had occasion to go to [Tiff] more than once to beg supplies for fugitives in the swamps, or to get some errand performed which he could not himself venture abroad to attend to. Like others of his race, Tiff, on all such subjects, was so habitually and unfathomably secret, that the children, who knew him most intimately, had never received even a suggestion from him of the existence of any such person" (2:170). That about five hundred pages into the novel the reader has likewise "never received even a suggestion" of Tiff's knowledge of and connection to Dred works once again to implicate readers with the ignorant white masters of the Carolinas.

When we next meet Tiff he is "hoeing in the sweet-potato patch" (2:214), along with Harry and Lisette, as part of Dred's alcohol-free community.

From within this domestic community of temperate revolutionaries, Harry initiates a letter exchange with Clayton that simultaneously marks the growth of his "black" political consciousness and puts on display the possibilities of black-white exchange. Informing Clayton that he has been reading widely in American Revolutionary history, Harry poses the question that was raised earlier in the novel by Dred's "father" Denmark Vesey (and in Douglass's 1852 "What to the Slave is the Fourth of July?"): "If it were proper for your fathers to fight and shed blood for the oppression that came upon them, why is n't [sic] it right for us?" (2:201). Harry also asks after his sister, who had recently been captured by Tom Gordon. In response, Clayton conveys the tragic news that, while in a slave prison in Alexandria, Cora Gordon had killed her two children. She did so, she confided to Clayton, who conveys her words in his letter to Harry, "because I loved them!" (2:206). Though Clayton sympathetically responds to Cora's arguments, to the point that race seemingly vanishes as an issue—he remarks that he saw Nina Gordon in Cora Gordon's face—Clayton's advice to the swamp-dwelling Harry is to continue to be patient, as militancy "would only embitter the white race against them [blacks], and destroy that sympathy which many are beginning to feel for their oppressed condition" (2:210). And yet, even as he offers this advice, Clayton concedes that his exchanges with Harry have provided him with a black "standpoint" that ultimately undercuts such advice, allowing that if he were in Harry's situation, "I feel that I might not have patience to consider any of these things" (2:211). The fact that he has come to recognize the limits of one of Stowe's privileged values in *Uncle Tom's Cabin*—patience—works to implicate Stowe herself in this "conversation."

That patience (and sympathy) have their limits is further revealed in Stowe's subsequent representation of the breakdown of the white Southern community presided over by the intemperate, power-driven Tom Gordon. As presented in the post–Nina Gordon chapters of the novel, in a fulfillment of Lyman Beecher's darkest nightmares about the social consequences of intemperance, this community consists of "mobs composed of the dregs of creation."[48] After leading a mob attack on the antislavery minister Dickson (and his wife), the inebriated Tom uses his gutta-percha cane to strike Clayton, as he struck Harry, "in the vicinity of the swamp" (2:270). In doing so, Stowe sardonically notes, Tom "proved his eligibility for Congress" (2:271). At the same time, Clayton, in resisting Tom, proves his eligibility for the swamps. Rescued by Harry and Dred, who breaks Tom's arm in the exchange, the unconscious Clayton is carried off to be nursed within the maroon community. His arrival serves as Clayton's baptismal moment, as it were, into a black revolutionary perspective. Over the course of several interviews with Dred, whom he self-protectively regards "as a psychological study" (2:291), Clayton begins to approach an understanding of African American revolutionism, eventually concluding "that nothing but the removal of some of these minds from the oppressions which were goading them could prevent a development of bloody insurrection" (2:302).

Through Clayton, Stowe therefore suggests near the end of the novel her own sense that there are "goads" to black insurrection. As for the morality of acting on those "goads," Stowe addresses the issue through an ongoing "debate" between Milly and Dred, a debate that is informed by a notable exchange that took place between Sojourner Truth and Douglass in 1852.[49] Stowe writes of the exchange in her 1863 article on Truth: "Douglass had been describing the wrongs of the black race, and as he proceeded, he grew more and more excited, and finally ended up saying that they had no hope of justice from the whites, no possible hope except in their own right arms. It must come to blood; they must fight for themselves and redeem themselves, or it would never be done." Truth's withering, silencing response, according to Stowe, was this: "Frederick, *is God Dead?*"[50] In the wake of the Emancipation Proclamation, Stowe wanted to emphasize that, contrary to Douglass's expectations, whites did come to the aid of blacks in what she (and Truth) increasingly came to view as a holy war of millennial redemption. But in *Dred*, written before the war began, Stowe writes out of a cultural moment of greater uncertainty about the uses of, or need for, black violence. Though she positions her Truth character in the camp of Christian patience and forgiveness, her alliance with Milly (Truth) is not all that firm, and she allows Dred (an "excited" Douglass) equal place and stature in articulating a rationale for slave insurrectionism.

The debate between Milly and Dred is initiated in the novel's first volume when Harry meets Dred in the swamps after being struck by Tom Gordon. Though he tries to resist Dred's call for militant action, Harry feels his pull, and exclaims, "I will not be a slave!" (1:243). Milly then arrives on the scene to articulate an alternative position based on the virtue of Christian forgiveness, seemingly triumphing when Harry returns to the plantation and Dred returns alone to the swamps. The debate is resumed in the novel's second volume precisely at that moment when Harry appears to have become a full participant in Dred's maroon community. Awaiting the return of their compatriot Hark (named after one of Nat Turner's coconspirators), the fugitives seem on the verge of taking some sort of violent action against slave owners. Congregated around a campfire, the men "clasp their hands in a circle, and join in a solemn oath never to betray each other" (2:224). Each member then steps forward to tell his story; all their voices are honored within the circle. The meeting resembles the African ring ceremonies that, as historian Sterling Stuckey observes, honored ancestors at burials and thereby ritually linked successive generations. Stowe points to the linkages among generations (and black male leaders) by noting that Dred reads from "the Bible of Denmark Vesey" (2:214). And it soon becomes clear that the ceremony has been functioning as a burial ceremony of sorts, for news arrives that Hark has been tortured and killed by Tom Gordon. Dred's response is to invoke covenantal typology by echoing Laban's swearing of a promise of fellowship to Jacob—"*Jegar Sahadutha!*" (2:229), or "heap of witness" (2:298), as Stowe later translates the phrase from Genesis 31:46–47— and to call for a "day of vengeance" (2:233) in which blacks simply kill as many whites as possible.[51] Whereupon Milly enters the scene, singing of Christ as a peaceful, loving Lamb.

Milly's entrance at this particular moment thus brings to focus the ongoing debate between Dred and Milly on the proper course of black action to combat slavery. The critical consensus is that Milly, in articulating a pacifist religiosity similar to that informing *Uncle Tom's Cabin*, wins the debate, both in terms of theology and action, as Dred ultimately fails to launch a successful rebellion. As one critic asserts, Milly "persuades him [Dred] to at least postpone his plans."[52] But how persuasive is she? And to what extent does Stowe privilege her position? Milly, because of her own victimization at the hands of enslavers, can claim that she has "been whar you be" (2:233). She urges Dred and his associates, in terms that even Clayton comes to regard as limited, that they should strive to be like Christ in their patient suffering; they should await "de new covenant" (2:233). Dred's response can seem to suggest capitulation to her vision: "Woman, thy prayers have prevailed for this time! . . . The hour is not yet come!" (2:234). But the fact is that just *prior* to Milly's arrival Dred had already decided to wait, announcing to the group from within his trancelike state that though he now perceives only "silence in heaven" (2:232), "when the Lord saith unto us, Smite, then will we smite!" (2:232).[53] We should also note that Stowe herself, in the spirit of "Caste and Christ," challenges Milly's appropriation of Christly Lamb imagery as a signifier of nonviolence, for shortly after Dred declares his intention of postponing vengeful action, the narrator declares that "the wrath of the LAMB" (2:276) can be "a strong attribute of the highest natures; for he who is destitute of the element of moral indignation is effeminate and tame" (2:275).

Dred's desires to "smite," therefore, along with his claims to leadership, retain a privileged place in the novel, not even to be annulled by Milly's Christlike insistence on patience. What prevents Dred from putting his desires into action, in addition to his apprehension of God's silence at this particular moment, is what prevented other slaves from leading successful rebellions: the state's brutal legal and policing authority. Additionally, Stowe makes Dred's heroism a cause of his "fall," for it is precisely his brave decision to venture out on his own to spy on Tom's drunken crew that leads to his death. Returning to the group bleeding from a wound in his breast, Dred is himself described in Christlike spiritual terms, with the implication being that his imminent death has every promise of being as redemptive and sacred as Eva's and Tom's in *Uncle Tom's Cabin*. Even with respect to Nina's death, I would argue that the two chapters on Dred's death constitute the sacred space of the novel.[54] Stowe describes Dred's "majestic and mournful" (2:299) dying hours: "It was evident to the little circle that He who is mightier than the kings of earth was there" (2:295). Stowe has not simply "killed off" Dred or otherwise aligned herself with Milly. She has instead figured a glorious, redemptive, fraternal death in the "hush harbor" of the swamps. A historian of slave religion remarks on how in "the secrecy of the quarters or the seclusion of the brush arbors ('hush harbors') the slaves made Christianity truly their own." At the Afro-Christian burial of Dred, Stowe insinuates herself into this sacred community by echoing in her narrative commentary Dred's earlier appeal to "*Jegar Sahadutha*," thus making herself into a covenanted "witness" (2:298). What needs to be addressed here, in light of this sacred witnessing, is the large question that Stowe raised in *Key*: "What Is to Be Done?"[55]

The Work of Justice

Clayton's answer to this question is, as I have said, to insist on the importance of educating and emancipating the "four hundred odd" (1:27) slaves of his plantation. His reformism, Crozier asserts, "assumes an extremely patronizing attitude toward the slaves."[56] But, as we have seen, Douglass, Delany, and other free blacks concerned about the elevation of the slaves could also be patronizing in their insistence on the slaves' need for the sort of education that would help them prosper in bourgeois society. In assuming that he knows what is best for the former slaves, however, Clayton can seem somewhat smug, in large part because this white reformer, until his arrival in the swamps, possesses such a limited knowledge of black perspectives. And yet Stowe appears to be sympathetic to his reformist project, especially as put into practice by his sister Anne Clayton, whose program of black elevation through education, industry, and hygiene (similar to Douglass's own temperance emphases in the New Bedford sections of *Narrative* and *Bondage*) is presented unironically as a sensible way of preparing former slaves for freedom.[57] Nevertheless, as Anne herself had earlier confided to Nina, the education project is hopeless as long as Southern whites refuse to offer their support. It is only near the end of the novel, when Edward returns from the swamps to confront the social anarchy unleashed by Tom Gordon, that he reaches a similar conclusion. His friend Russel assesses the situation after a mob burns down the black schoolhouse on the Claytons' plantation, concluding that Anne and Edward have one of two options with their slaves: "You must either send them to Liberia, or to the Northern States" (2:323). They choose to do neither.

It is simply mistaken, then, to say that "Stowe again wrote favorably of colonization in her novel *Dred*."[58] Rather than arguing for colonization, Stowe, like Delany, Mary Ann Shadd Cary, and many other black abolitionists, shows the advantages of black emigration to Canada. In Sarah J. Hale's colonizationist antislavery novel *Liberia; or, Mr. Peyton's Experiments* (1853), the noble Mr. Peyton, before taking his emancipated slaves to Liberia, "experiments" with Canadian emigration only to find, according to Hale, that the blacks hate the cold climate and thus produce but a "little collection of hovels and wretched tenements that was dignified with the name of the village."[59] Anne and Edward achieve quite different results when they take their liberated slaves to Canada. Using funds secured from selling their plantation to purchase a "valuable tract of land" in western Canada, the Claytons help to establish a black township that, with its integrated schools and thriving farms, quickly becomes "one of the richest and finest [towns] in the region" (2:330). Stowe informs her readers in a footnote that the community's success mirrors the success "of the Elgin settlement, founded [in 1849] by Mr. King, a gentleman who removed and settled his slaves in the south of Canada" (2:331). Located just south of Chatham, Ontario, where Martin Delany emigrated the year of *Dred*'s publication, the Elgin community emerged during the 1850s as one of the most successful black communities in Canada. Though paternalism was undoubtedly central to the Presbyterian minister King's modus operandi, his overall goal was to empower the black participants by allowing them voting and property rights.[60] In her portrayal of the Claytons' Canadian community, Stowe takes care to underscore the central place of its blacks: Harry emerges as one of the principal leaders; Dred's former associate Hannibal, "instead of slaying men, is great in felling trees" (2:331); and Jim, Tom Gordon's former slave, has become an industrious farmer. That said, Clayton never seems to renounce his "superintending" role.

It is crucial to note, however, that Stowe presents the Claytons' emigration project as but one of several possibilities for the novel's black characters. Although Russel asserts that Clayton must either "send" the blacks of his plantation to the North or to Liberia, Stowe describes blacks who are not sent but rather make their escape, on their own terms, to New York. They do so in such a way as to suggest that Stowe may have been revising Douglass's 1853 "The Heroic Slave," his revision of *Uncle Tom's Cabin*, to place a greater emphasis on ideals of black fraternity and community. In "The Heroic Slave," the black rebel Madison Washington tells the white abolitionists Mr. and Mrs. Listwell of his escape to "the dismal swamps," where he lived a solitary existence for five years until his whereabouts were inadvertently revealed by a black lumberer to whom he had given a dollar to purchase food.[61] In *Dred*, Stowe portrays black lumberers who, following the death of Dred, enable the escape of slaves, for all along, Stowe writes, the lumberers had linked themselves to Dred's subversive group, providing them with "secret supplies" and even "attend[ing] some of Dred's midnight meetings" (2:303). Rather than calling attention to the maroons' presence, the lumberers hide them on a ship to Norfolk, the first of several stopping points on their way North.

Significantly, Dred's compatriots are not the only slaves who make their way North. Milly too decides to escape; she proves to be not so acquiescent and patient after all. Her pretext for escaping is that such an action would benefit her grandchild Tomtit; without Tomtit, Stowe writes, Milly would have remained "patiently in the condition wherein she was called, and bearing injustice and oppression as a means of spiritual improvement" (2:304). By linking Milly to a grandchild whose odd name evokes the titular hero of her first novel, Stowe, in a major revision of *Uncle Tom's Cabin*, rescues Milly from what the novel increasingly suggests would have been a pointless martyrdom at the hands of Southern enslavers; she rescues her from the fate of Uncle Tom. Consistent with *Dred*'s revisionary project, Stowe, through her account of Milly's social-reform work in New York City, provides a stateside rewriting of Topsy's African missionary work that conveys her post-1852 conviction that the free blacks did have an important role to play in the United States. Through the representative identity of Milly, Stowe also provides a gendered vision, one that looks forward to that of Anna Julia Cooper, of the ways in which the seemingly modest ameliorative efforts of black women reformers contribute to the cross-racial cultural work of uplifting the nation. After the passage of several years Clayton arrives in New York to find that Milly lives "in a neat little tenement in one of the outer streets of New York, surrounded by about a dozen children, among whom were blacks, whites, and foreigners. These she had rescued from utter destitution in the streets, and was giving to them all the attention and affection of a mother" (2:333). Surprised by the inclusive nature of Milly's reformism, Clayton remarks, "I see you have black and white here" (2:333). In response Milly affirms the integrationist ideals central to the antislavery reformism of Nell and Douglass: "I don't make no distinctions of color, — I don't believe in them. White chil'en, when they 'haves themselves, is jest as good as black, and I loves 'em jest as well" (2:334). The humor here and the concomitant biting social point are conveyed through Milly's "black"-centered rhetoric that has her affirming the equality of the races by insisting that whites can one day be as good as blacks.[62]

Milly's Sojourner Truth–like ability to love whites, despite what we have seen of Tom Gordon and his drunken minions, is shared by Tiff to the very end of the novel. Like Milly, he has decided to escape to the North with the beloved white children under his charge. At first he and the children live with Milly and her grandson in "a humble tenement" (2:329); eventually a distant aunt bequeaths to the children the Peyton fortune, and they move on to better things. In the novel's concluding chapter, Tiff attends Fanny's wedding to George Russel (the son of Clayton's friend) and in effect renounces the absurd notions of Peyton superiority that have seemingly played such a large role in guiding his actions: "When all's said and done, it's de man dat's de thing, after all; 'cause a gal can't marry all de generations back" (2:336). Yet in the novel's final paragraph, the motherly Tiff pridefully remarks on Fanny's baby that it is "de very sperit of de Peytons" (2:337). Tiff here is nothing less than ridiculous, as even he has come to realize, but his love for Fanny and pride in her family can be regarded as a sign of his strength (he acts upon, rather than is embarrassed by, the "inappropriateness" of his love). With her images of Tiff's and especially Milly's transracial love, Stowe concludes the novel with a more hopeful picture than critics have generally recognized of blacks successfully finding a place in and having an impact on Northeast culture.

But the novel doesn't end with the final paragraph; it offers at least one more answer to the question, "What Is to Be Done?" For immediately following the depiction of Tiff comes a three-part appendix, the first section of which presents "a few extracts" from Thomas Gray's "Nat Turner's Confessions" (2:338) (the other two sections discuss slavery in legal and ecclesiastical contexts). Actually, Stowe reprints virtually all of the "Confessions," with a couple of key exceptions. She cuts most of Gray's negative comments on Turner; she cuts Gray's political moralizing; and, most crucial, she cuts Gray's reassurances to his Southern readers that "fortunate for society, the hand of retributive justice has overtaken them [Turner and his accomplices]; and not one that was known to be concerned has escaped." [63] By leaving open the possibility that some of Nat Turner's retributive accomplices may still be at large, Stowe rhetorically participates in the political terror inspired by the prophetic tradition of the black heroic deliverer as embodied both by Turner and her fictional creation Dred. Further, by noting in her prefatory comments to the "Confessions" that one of Turner's "principal conspirators in this affair was named Dred" (*Dred*, 2:338), Stowe presents violent rebellion as a logical, perhaps even sacred, response to slavery that will be passed along by blacks from generation to generation until slavery is abolished. Sympathetic to and aligned with the prophetic Nat Turner, the ultimate African American presence in the novel, Stowe in *Dred* anticipates, promotes, and helps to supply the terms for understanding the bloodshed of the Civil War.

In the "Confessions," Turner envisions "the Holy Ghost" as a compatriot rebel after he views "drops of blood on the corn . . . [and] then found on the leaves in the woods hieroglyphic characters and numbers, with the forms of men in different attitudes, portrayed in blood" (in *Dred*, 2:342). In "The New Year" (1865), published in the *Atlantic* several months before Lee's surrender, Stowe similarly links Nat Turner to a God who chastens oppressors: "The prophetic visions of Nat Turner, who saw the leaves drop blood and the land darkened, have been fulfilled. The work of justice which he predicted is being executed to the uttermost."[64] Douglass too invoked Turner and other slave revolutionaries in his famous 1863 broadside calling on the free blacks to enlist in the Union army: "Remember Denmark Vesey of Charleston; remember Nathaniel Turner of Southampton; remember Shilds Gree and Copeland, who followed John Brown, and fell as glorious martyrs for the cause of the slave. Remember that in a contest with oppression, the Almighty has no attribute which can take sides with oppressors."[65] During the Civil War, Douglass and Stowe shared a sense of the teleological significance, as it were, of Turner's rebellion. Implicit in their typological linking of Turner to the Civil War was a desire to view him within a national-millennial framework.

Though Delany would eventually embrace the Union cause, he was much more inclined during the late 1850s and early 1860s to understand black violence in the larger context of blacks' history in the Americas. Somewhat surprisingly, in the chapter on Dred's funeral in the swamps, Stowe expresses a vision of black violence similar to Delany's. Attempting to implicate in the scene's grief those who may continue to distance themselves from a black militant, Stowe instructs the reader that had Dred (or, by implication, Vesey or Turner) been more fully known and successful, he might have been "celebrated in mournful sonnet by the deepest thinking poet of the age" (2:299). In the 1853 *Autographs for Freedom*, to which Stowe contributed "Caste and Christ," the black writer William Allen, in the course of celebrating the black Cuban poet-rebel Placido, compares him to Toussaint L'Ouverture by adducing several lines of William Wordsworth's "mournful" sonnet "To Toussaint L'Ouverture" (1803). During the funeral scene, Stowe likewise compares Dred to Toussaint by quoting six lines from the sonnet, thereby implicitly linking Dred to Placido and other Caribbean rebels. Earlier, Clayton's friend Russel had remarked on the Southern slave power: "They are going to annex Cuba and the Sandwich Islands, and the Lord knows what and have a great and splendid slaveholding empire" (2:243). The connections among Toussaint, Placido, and the contemporary debate on Cuban annexation, oblique as these several references may seem, suggest that Stowe views her eponymous hero in a surprisingly broad literary, historical, and political context.[66] In *Blake*, Delany takes these intersecting contexts and concerns as one of the central subjects of his own novel about a prophetic (and representative) black conspiratorial leader.

Chapter 5
The Redemption of His Race
Creating Pan-African
Community in Delany's
Blake

Martin Delany's *Blake; or, The Huts of America* (1859–62) may be read as an effort on his part, comparable with Douglass's in *My Bondage and My Freedom*, to define, fashion, and celebrate his representative identity as a Mosaic black leader. But how coherent is that self-representation? The evidence suggests that the novel, first published in book form in 1970, emerged from multiple contexts and addressed Delany's sometimes competing interests and concerns.[1] Eric J. Sundquist and Jean Fagan Yellin hypothesize, for example, that Delany began *Blake* in 1852 or 1853 as a revisionary response to *Uncle Tom's Cabin*. Perhaps the early chapters on plantation blacks were drafted shortly after Delany read sections of Stowe's novel, but references later in part 1 to the condition of blacks in Canada, where Delany moved in 1856, would suggest that Delany did his main work on *Blake* sometime between 1856 and 1859. Taking these years as the novel's primary compositional period would allow us to read *Blake* as a response, both critical and admiring, not just to *Uncle Tom's Cabin* but also to *Dred*. Delany's decision to use Stowe's poem "Caste and Christ" as a running epigraph to all the published chapters in the 1861–

62 serialization of *Blake* could thus be taken as an act of homage to, or even (I sentimentally surmise) forgiveness of, the writer he had vilified in 1853. Like Stowe in *Dred*, Delany in *Blake* portrays a black conspirator who conceives of his plottings in relation to the prophetic conspiratorial tradition of Denmark Vesey and Nat Turner; and Delany conceives of the problem of slavery, just as Stowe presents Clayton's friend Russel conceiving of it, in the larger context of U.S. expansionistic interests in Cuba. Notably, when Delany moved to Canada he settled in Chatham, Canada West, in close proximity to William King's Elgin community (the model for Clayton's black community); and by 1859 he had become friendly with King—the model, so the historians William Pease and Jane Pease argue, for Clayton himself.[2]

Viewed as a text written for the most part between 1856 and 1859, *Blake*, a novel of black revolutionism, could also be read in relation to Delany's anger and despair at the Dred Scott decision of 1857. For Delany, the Dred Scott case (mentioned in part 2 of *Blake*) once again revealed, as had the Crosswait case of 1848 and the Compromise of 1850, the ways in which the law helped to sustain and legitimate the Southern slave power. In the wake of Dred Scott, Delany and other blacks, including Douglass, renewed their calls for violent black resistance to slavery; and in May 1858 Delany chaired a convention in Chatham that enthusiastically supported John Brown's mission to organize the slaves' resistance. Approximately six months later, Delany presented a manuscript of *Blake* to Thomas Hamilton, editor of the *Anglo-African Magazine*, a New York monthly. Chapters 1–23 and 29–31 in the Miller edition would appear in the January–July 1859 issues of this magazine. In prefatory remarks to the three chapters of the novel published in the January 1859 issue, Hamilton told his readers that, among other things, Delany's novel portrayed a black's desire to take revenge on whites "through a deep laid secret organization," describing the novel as having two parts and eighty chapters, while maintaining that he printed just three chapters (which later became chapters 29–31) because "they were the only ones the author would permit us to copy." Writing to Garrison in February 1859, Delany urged him to read the three chapters in the hope that he might recommend the completed novel ("written in Parts 2, pp. about 550") to book publishers. Assuring Garrison that "its course of publication in the Magazine, is not to interfere with its publication in book form whenever I can obtain a publisher," Delany confessed his desire to "make a penny by it."[3] The fact that Hamilton in the February issue began to print the novel in its entirety, starting with chapter 1, would suggest that Delany, around the time he wrote to Garrison, was despairing at the hope of finding a commercial publisher for a novel of black insurrectionism.

Delany wanted to "make a penny" by his novel in order to finance his Niger Exploring Expedition of 1859–60, which sought to establish an African American colony in West Africa in the Yoruba region near Lagos. Rather than joining John Brown at Harpers Ferry, Delany departed for Africa in July 1859 and several months later signed a treaty with the *Alake* (king) of Abeokuta that provided him with the land he needed to establish his colony. Delany subsequently toured Great Britain in search of financial support for his project, returning to Canada early in 1861 to recruit black emigrants. Later that year he offered a complete manuscript of *Blake* to Thomas Hamilton for publication in the *Weekly Anglo-African*; the novel ran serially in the paper from 23 November 1861 to (in all probability) late May 1862.[4]

But was this the same novel Delany gave Hamilton in late 1858? It is difficult to say, despite the fact that there are only small differences between the twenty-five chapters Hamilton published in 1859 and republished in 1861. The numerous "authenticating" footnotes on Africa in the novel's second part, however, suggest that Delany had reconceived aspects of the novel during 1861 to bring it more into accord with his hopes to "regenerate" Africa. But Delany's African regeneration plans came under considerable pressure from the course of contemporary events. Not only was Delany's treaty with the Alake annulled in mid-1861, but Hamilton began serializing the novel at a time when many African Americans, including the editor himself, regarded the Civil War as an opportunity for blacks to secure their rights to citizenship in the United States. The last extant chapter of the novel, chapter 74, appeared in an April 1862 issue of the paper. Because Hamilton wrote in *Anglo-African Magazine* in 1859 that the novel had eighty chapters, critics have assumed that the final six chapters appeared in May 1862 issues of the paper, which have yet to be found, if they in fact exist.

Given the novel's multiple and conflicting sources, purposes, and audiences, and also its truncated ending, we need to be wary of efforts to develop a "coherent" formalist reading of it. This is not to deny that large motifs hold the novel together, such as its global perspective on slavery and its Pan-African thematics. But I would suggest that just as important as these deliberatively developed motifs are the desires that work to hold together and define Delany's career, particularly, as one critic puts it, his quest "to be a Moses for his people." In thinking himself a kind of Moses, similar to the "consecrated" figure of Douglass's *Narrative* and the deliverer of *Bondage*, Delany, like Douglass, tapped into the black nationalist and messianic implications of the Moses analogy, devoting himself, like the eponymous leader of *Blake*, to "the redemption of his race."[5] Delany's vision of the crucial role that could be played by an intelligent, "full-blooded" black leader (like himself) in *creating* a Pan-African community in the Americas (and beyond) is the central subject of this chapter. To assess the novel's autobiographical and political implications, I will be reading *Blake* in relation to Delany's ongoing debates with Douglass, his interactions with John Brown, his interest in Cuba, his efforts at African "regeneration," and his participation in the Civil War. I take Delany's 1868 first-person account of his purported interview with Lincoln as his ultimate effort to consecrate himself the redeemer of his race. As we shall see, by the end of the Civil War, Delany paradoxically was presenting Pan-Africanism as a form of, indeed as central to, blacks' U.S. Americanization. The path from Delany's 1854 Cleveland emigration convention to his commission as the first black major in the U.S. Army has a number of surprising turns, all of which bear on Delany's sometimes contradictory representations of black leadership and Pan-African community in *Blake*. Let us begin, then, with Delany's seemingly incongruous decision, in light of the Central and South America emigrationist mandate of "Political Destiny of the Colored Race on the American Continent," to "emigrate" to Canada.

Redeeming Africa

"We are pleased to state to our readers, the arrival of our esteemed and talented friend, Dr. M. R. Delany, of Pittsburgh, Pa., in this town, yesterday morning, who intends making this his home." So the editors of the *Provincial Freeman*, a Canadian black newspaper, welcomed Delany and his family to Chatham, Canada West, in February 1856.[6] From within the embrace of his adopted Canadian community, Delany continued to pose a challenge to Douglass's antiemigrationist position and to his reputation as *the* representative black leader. Two months after Isaac Shadd announced that Delany would join the paper's "force of efficient contributors" and only a week after Mary Ann Shadd voiced her approval of Delany's call for an 1856 emigration convention in Cleveland (which

Delany, because of an illness, ultimately was unable to attend), Delany delivered a scathing indictment of Douglass in the 12 July 1856 *Provincial Freeman*. What precipitated the attack, ironically, was Douglass's editorial in a June 1856 issue of *Frederick Douglass' Paper* praising the black communities of Canada. In his response to Douglass, "What Does It Mean?," Delany expresses his fury at what he regards as Douglass's self-serving admission that he has come to look at Canada's blacks " 'with a friendly eye,' " noting that Douglass for years has "denounced the Emigration movement, designating all those concerned with propagating the sentiments as being Colonizationists." Now that Douglass and his "adherents" see some value in Canada's black emigrant communities, Delany mockingly states, "surely Emigration must be safe." And yet the hypocrisy of what Delany describes as Douglass's "subtle attempt at commending Emigrationists" cannot be concealed, for behind the facade lurks "a monster the construction of whose deformity, will alarm and dismay those heretofore delighted in the exhibitions of the performer." Feigning gratitude nonetheless for the hypocrite's recognition of the Chatham community, Delany proclaims, "For this we are very thankful, and bow uncovered with obsequious reverence!"[7]

Venting his anger at Douglass for condescending to Canadian blacks, while at the same time insisting on their independence, their significant accomplishments in encouraging black elevation, and their links to blacks unconnected with Douglass, Delany would seem to be setting forth similar truths about his own status in relation to Douglass. Delany's emotionally charged and rhetorically excessive "What Can It Mean?" could thus be read as an attempt to liberate himself from the evaluative gaze of African Americans' "representative" leader. That he should continue to be driven by such a strong desire to undermine Douglass suggests how difficult it was for Delany to conceive of himself as operating apart from his former coeditor.

Even when Delany decided two years later to consider working with John Brown, he found himself implicated with Douglass, who had his own relationship with the rebel. Though still far apart on the issue of black emigration, Douglass and Delany, on the evidence of their interactions with John Brown, would seem to have been in agreement after the Dred Scott ruling on the worth of entertaining the possibility of a slave insurrection in the United States.[8] Early in 1858, a little more than a year after his notorious raid at Pottawatomie, Kansas, Brown arrived at Douglass's Rochester home, where he wrote a "Provisional Constitution and

Ordinances for the People of the United States," which he hoped would be adopted following a rebellion of the slaves. In addition to drafting the "Constitution" while at Douglass's, Brown also wrote letters describing his insurrectionary plans to a number of black leaders, including Delany. Brown met with Henry Highland Garnet in Philadelphia in March 1858, and approximately two weeks after that he returned to Douglass's home, where he spent the night before crossing the border into Canada. There he met with Delany and obtained his promise to attend a secret convention to be held in Chatham in May. Douglass was invited to the meeting but failed to attend, perhaps because he had become skeptical about Brown's chances for leading a successful slave revolt but more likely, I think, because of the company he would have had to keep.[9]

The meeting took place on 8 May 1858 in a black schoolhouse. Twelve whites and thirty-four blacks attended; William C. Munroe served as the presiding officer and Delany as chairman. According to the Canadian black Osborne P. Anderson, who published a book about Harpers Ferry in 1861, John Brown, "ANOTHER MOSES," talked at the meeting of the "progressive" nature of revolutionary violence against slavery. Though Anderson does not reveal the specifics of what was discussed at Chatham, he quotes from the "minutes" that "Mr. Delany and others spoke in favor of the project and the plan, and both were agreed to by general consent." Hints of what the participants agreed to may be gleaned from the "Journal of the Provisional Constitution Held on Saturday, May 8th, 1858," which contains the "Provisional Constitution and Ordinances for the People of the United States" and rather sketchy minutes of the discussions of the forty-eight adopted articles. Most heatedly debated by the group was Article 46, which states as follows: "The foregoing articles shall not be construed so as in any way to encourage the overthrow of any State Government or of the General Government of the United States, and look to no dissolution of the Union, but simply to amend and repeal. And our Flag shall be the same that our Fathers fought under in the Revolution." According to the minutes, Delany argued to keep this article in place, and it was eventually adopted with but one negative vote. Article 46 thus placed the conspiratorial plans of the group within the historical and ideological frame of the "patriotic" American Revolution.[10]

Following this enthusiastic meeting, Brown departed from Chatham to take up the more laborious task of fund-raising and recruitment. When Brown became ill several months later, Delany wrote to his white associate J. H. Kagi, reasserting his commitment to the cause: "I have been anxiously looking and expecting to see something of Uncle's movements in the papers, but as yet have seen nothing. . . . All are in good spirits here, hoping and waiting the 'Good time coming.' " Though Delany may well have been hopeful for Brown's enterprise, there was something disingenuous about his letter, for he had recently committed himself to a different cause: establishing an African American colony in Africa. No clear indication exists as to why Delany abandoned Brown, though it is tempting to speculate that he simply was unwilling to serve under a white "Moses." Brown would liberate but, Delany may have wondered, would he regenerate? Increasingly convinced that there was an intimate connection between "the Moral, Social, and Political Elevation of Ourselves, and the Regeneration of Africa," Delany solicited Henry Ward Beecher for funds on 17 June 1858, two months before he wrote Kagi, so that he could to travel to Africa and "negociate with the natives for Territory or land" and thus help to establish "an Enlightened and Christian nationality in the midst of these tractable and docile people." [11] In August 1858 in Chatham, Delany hosted the third National Emigration Convention, where his primary goal was to obtain support for such a project.

In the account of the 1858 Chatham emigration convention in his 1861 *Official Report of the Niger Valley Exploring Party*, Delany, in a blatant effort at historical revisionism, stated that support for his African emigration project would *not* have contradicted the mandate of the 1854 Cleveland emigration convention, despite the fact that the convention went on record *against* African emigration. He now disclosed that "Secret Sessions" were held at the 1854 convention, wherein the delegates made "Africa, with its rich, inexhaustible productions, and great facilities for checking the abominable Slave Trade, its most important point of dependence." [12] As Delany elaborated in *Official Report*, he expected that the development of Africa as a commercial power would convince whites throughout the world of blacks' capabilities as producers and thus would pose a significant ideological challenge to the premises upholding U.S. slavery. Nevertheless, the delegates at the 1858 Chatham convention remained lukewarm to Delany's Africa project, withholding funding, though the General Board did grant him the authority to establish a Niger Valley Exploring Party.

Delany thus had to pursue financial support elsewhere, and he eventually found himself implicated, financially and otherwise, with Henry Highland Garnet's African Civilization Society, an organization of blacks and whites with links to the American Colonization Society. Douglass, who had once remarked, "Thank God, the alternative is not quite so desperate as that we must be slaves here, or go to the pestilential shores of Africa," attacked Garnet's African Civilization Society in an article in the February 1859 issue of *Douglass' Monthly* on the grounds that it was a colonizationist society. Douglass's hostility helped to bring Delany and Garnet together as opponents of Douglass.[13] Further linking Delany to the African Civilization Society were the actions of Robert Campbell, Delany's Jamaican-born colleague on the Niger Valley Exploring Party, who in 1859, without Delany's approval, successfully solicited funds from the African Civilization Society and the American Colonization Society. Making his own effort to obtain funds, Delany in April of that year assured Boston colonizationists that he would tour Liberia while in Africa. Floyd Miller neatly sums up Delany's paradoxical commitments as he boarded the bark *Mendi* on 24 May 1859 to begin his exploring expedition: "Now totally isolated from the emigration movement he had sustained during most of the decade, and aided by the very colonizationists he had earlier ridiculed and assailed, Delany set off for the west coast of Africa in search of a hospitable home for the Black Nationality he wished to create."[14]

Delany spent nine months in Africa, arriving in West Africa in July 1859 and departing in March 1860. At his first stop in Liberia, he was welcomed by former president Roberts, whom he had once termed "a fawning servilian to the negro-hating Colonizationists."[15] Writing in the *Liberian Herald* on the occasion of Delany's visit, Edward Blyden rightly referred to Delany as "this great antagonist to the American Colonization Society." Nonetheless, in what was ultimately a celebratory article, Blyden went on to describe how hundreds came to view "this great man" when he delivered two lectures in Monrovia on the "Political Condition and Destiny of the African Race." In the lectures, as transcribed by Blyden, Delany "advocated the emigration of the six hundred thousand free colored men of the North, to Africa, where they may join the one hundred and sixty millions of their degraded brethren, assist to elevate them, and . . . from such a nationality the reflex influence upon America must be felt and must be powerful, in behalf of the slaves."[16]

Delany here sounds very much like Alexander Crummell, who, from a more pronounced religious perspective, similarly hoped to see Africa regenerated and redeemed under the "civilizing" auspices of (Protestant) Christianity and commercial development. During his Liberian tour Delany met with Crummell, whose well-known essay "The Relations and Duties of Free Colored Men in America to Africa" was written in response to what he termed his "two pleasant interviews with Mr. Campbell and Dr. Delany." In "Relations and Duties" Crummell called for the influx of "large amounts of capital from moneyed men of America," "not less than 50,000 *civilized men*," and, of course, "evangelization" to regenerate the continent. Such regeneration, Crummell hopefully affirmed, would bring together even such perpetually feuding personages as Douglass and Delany: "On *this* platform, Douglass and Delany can stand beside the foremost citizens and merchants of Liberia."[17]

In "What Africa Now Requires," the closing chapter of *Official Report*, Delany offered similar sentiments about the millennial possibilities of African regeneration (though he did not go so far as to imagine himself in a harmonious relationship with Douglass). Asserting that "Christianity certainly is the most advanced civilization that man ever attained to," Delany, without noting the obvious irony that slavery exists in the "Christian" United States, underscored the need for developing in Africa an "enlightened Christian civilization" as a way of ending the slave trade. He suggested that Africa could "become regenerated" and at the same time help put an end to slavery in the United States by producing cotton in quantities large enough to undercut the Southern slaveholders' market share in Europe. Blacks' success in such an enterprise "in their own-loved native Africa," Delany proclaimed, would serve "to enrich themselves, and regenerate their race."[18] These hopes and plans for regeneration were central to Delany's and Campbell's negotiations with the Alake of Abeokuta in December 1859.

Meeting up with Campbell in Abeokuta, Delany began his negotiations with the Alake for land of the Egba people that could be used to establish a colony of African American emigrants. But Delany was negotiating for title to land with a group of people who worked with conceptions of property ownership radically different from his own. Miller explains: "Since the kinship group owned the land on behalf of themselves and their future descendants, neither the king, chief, nor any other individual could alienate the land." Despite these problems, Delany went ahead in forging the treaty—a treaty that had an important antecedent in the plan appended to his 1852 *Condition*, "A Project for an Expedition of Adventure, to the Eastern Coast of Africa." As Delany elucidated in that plan, which he claimed to have written in the 1830s, he regarded Africa as in effect already alienated from the native Africans precisely because of their lack of commercial expertise. Thus, in the same colonizing spirit in which he urged blacks to emigrate to Central and South America, he encouraged "a limited number of known, worthy" African Americans to journey to Africa to develop lands that he claimed were only tangentially connected to the actual people who lived there: "The land is ours — there it lies with inexhaustible resources; let us go and possess it." These "enlightened freemen," Delany explained, by building a transcontinental railroad for the transport of precious metals, would enable Africa to "rise up a nation, to whom all the world must pay commercial tribute."[19]

Similar elitist notions guided his 1859 treaty with the Alake. According to the articles, those of the "African race in America" who came to Abeokuta would administer their own laws and would have an autonomous relation to the Egba people. In return for this autonomy, Delany promised that the emigrants would "bring with them, as an equivalent for the privileges above accorded, Intelligence, Education, a Knowledge of the Arts and Sciences, Agriculture, and other Mechanical and Industrial Occupations." The fantasy implicitly informing Delany's vision, which, as Basil Davidson observes, imagined the construction of a black nation-state "on entirely non-African lines," was that he would emerge as the principal leader of a "regenerated" and "redeemed" Africa. His well-known remark at the end of his *Official Report* — "*Africa for the African race, and black men to rule them*" — while perhaps intended as a black nationalist rejection of white colonialism, spoke to those desires. For when Delany asserted that "by black men I mean, men of African descent who claim an identity with the race," he both tapped into the mystical Pan-Africanism of Psalms 68:31 and underscored the distinctions between "degraded" native-born Africans and those "select and intelligent [African Americans] of high moral and religious character," who, he suggested, could make even greater claims of descent from Africa's heroic past — the biblical and classical past he had celebrated in his 1853 *Origin and Objects of Ancient Freemasonry*.[20] To the latter were granted the rights of governance.

Several months after the successful negotiation of this treaty, Delany departed for England, arriving in May 1860 for what would be an enormously successful seven-month tour. Delany's tour nearly overlapped with the tours of Douglass and Harriet Beecher Stowe. Suspected of having conspired with John Brown, whom he praised in the November 1859 *Douglass' Monthly* for having "attacked slavery with the weapons precisely adapted to bring it to the death," Douglass fled to England later that month, returning to the United States in March 1860 on learning of the death of his daughter Annie. Shortly before departing from

England in June 1860, Stowe too wrote a piece celebrating Brown as "a witness slain in the great cause which is shaking Hungary, Austria, Italy, France."[21] Meanwhile, the man who had collaborated with Brown in Chatham in 1858 remained intent on pursuing financial support for his Niger project.

In his quest for funds, Delany addressed numerous antislavery and manufacturing groups during the spring and summer of 1860. In lectures in London, Glasgow, and elsewhere, Delany spoke not only of the money white capitalists could make on their investments in his Niger colony but also of his authoritative knowledge, as a black, of Africans' desires for the "regenerative" forces of commerce and Christianity that would help to lift them from their "degradation." As a result of his insistence on his "authentic" connection to Africa, Delany, as one historian remarks, became "courted for his color." His establishment of the African Aid Society, an alternative to the white-led African Civilization Society, further contributed to his emerging prominence in British antislavery circles.[22]

But no event during Delany's British tour did more to develop his celebrity as a representative black leader than his participation in the International Statistical Congress in London in July 1860. At the opening session of the congress, a gathering of the leading scientists of the day, Lord Henry Peter Brougham pointedly introduced Delany to the assembled scientists. The *Manchester Weekly Advertiser* described the scene:

> Lord Brougham, seeing Mr. Dallas, the American minister, present said: I hope my friend Mr. Dallas will forgive me reminding him that there is a negro gentleman present, a member of the congress. (Loud and vociferous cheering) After the cheering had subsided, Mr. Dallas made no sign; but the negro in question, who we understood to be a Dr. Delany, rose amid the cheers and said: I pray your Royal Highness will allow me to thank his lordship, who is always a most unflinching friend of the negro, for the observation he has made, and I assure your Royal Highness and his lordship that I also am a man. This unexpected incident elicited a round of cheering very extraordinary for an assemblage of sedate statisticians.

The delegate from the United States, Judge Augustus Longstreet of South Carolina, protested Brougham's comments by walking out of the congress; George M. Dallas, the American minister to Britain, remained to observe what he regarded as the humiliating spectacle of Delany becoming the center of attention. Over the course of the congress, Delany addressed the delegates on how best to control the spread of cholera, on his African project, and on his overall appreciation of the congress, remarking that the delegates' spontaneous cheers at his introduction were "intended as an expression of sympathy for the race to which he belonged, who, though they had undergone for ages the process of degeneration, he was glad to think were now being fast regenerated."[23]

In "Dallas and Delany," a column in the September 1860 *Douglass' Monthly*, Douglass wrote favorably of Delany's participation at the congress. For Douglass, the incident underscored the basic irony that "DELANY, in Washington, is a *thing*; DELANY, in London, is a *man*." But in building to this humanistic point about the objectification resulting from slavery's legal codes, Douglass, in his account of the incident, places a special emphasis on the role of Delany's blackness. He describes Delany's response to Lord Brougham's introduction of him as a "negro" in this way: "DELANY, determined that the nail should hold fast, rose, with all his blackness, right up, as quick and as graceful as an African lion, and received the curious gaze of the scientific world. It was complete. Sermons in stones are nothing to this. Never was there a more telling rebuke to the pride, prejudice and hypocrisy of a nation." Significantly, Douglass keeps Delany silent in his account, preferring to let his dark skin and animal-like Africanness do the work of argumentation. As a result, there is something demeaning in Douglass's celebration. Delany, however, apparently responded positively to the column, for he had Rollin reprint most of it in her 1868 *Life and Public Services of Martin R. Delany*, where Douglass at this particular legitimating moment in the text is referred to as Delany's "friend."[24] From Delany's perspective, the incident at the congress would have underscored the politics of representative identity so central to his African project and British tour: his notion that the most effective way to convince whites of blacks' potential was to present them with a racially "pure" black of great accomplishment—a black about whom it would have been impossible to credit "white" blood for achievements, as was not the case with Douglass.

Buoyed by the moral and financial support he obtained in Great Britain, Delany sailed from Liverpool in December 1860 and by early 1861 was working with Reverend William King of the Elgin settlement to put his emigration plans into operation. Under pressure from Anglican missionaries and the British Foreign Office, however, the Alake renounced the treaty early in 1861. Undeterred, Delany worked to recruit what King in a lecture to the African Aid Society referred to as "experienced, intelligent, practical Christian [black] men" for African emigration.[25] King, who viewed the Yoruba colony as an extension of his evangelical work at Elgin, had managed to sign up nearly forty blacks for the emigration project. But with the outbreak of the Civil War and the Alake's renunciation of the treaty, only two or three families remained interested.

In response to the diminishment of interest, Delany merged his organization with the formerly colonizationist African Civilization Society. Throughout 1861, when he published *Official Report*, and well into 1862 he continued to argue forcefully for African emigration. In a January 1861 letter to James Holly, for example, he proclaimed, "My duty and destiny are in Africa," and in a letter to the *Weekly Anglo-African*, printed in the 5 October 1861 issue, he again asserted that "my destiny is fixed in Africa, where my family and myself, by God's providence, will soon be happily situated." In an open letter to the *Weekly Anglo-African*, printed in the issue of 25 January 1862, Delany responded to the question of whether he had abandoned his Africa project with an unequivocal denial: "I simply answer, — not at all, nor never will."[26]

Delany held firm in his support for his projected African colony in part because he believed in its importance. But it seems equally clear that his continuing support, in the face of vastly changing realities, was an effort to retain the status of representative African American leader that he had consolidated in the final months of his British tour. In an effort to shore up his leadership position, he wrote an open letter to Dr. James McCune Smith, printed in the 11 January 1862 *Weekly Anglo-African*, calling for the convening of "a great Council of the leading men among us" to "determine on a settled policy as a rule of action, by which we should be guided." But it was Delany, not the antiemigrationists, who would have profited from such a policy statement, as antiemigrationism had become the mainstream position by 1862. With the advent of the Civil War, Douglass announced his break with the Haitian emigration movement in the May 1861 issue of *Douglass' Monthly* and with that issue began to run an American eagle and flag on the masthead. Similarly, as I noted at the outset, Thomas Hamilton, the publisher and editor of the *Weekly Anglo-African*, embraced the Civil War as a war of emancipation. By printing in his *Weekly* pieces by Smith and others encouraging U.S. blacks to enlist in the Union army, Hamilton inevitably made Delany appear out of step. Given Delany's emigrationist politics, it is a remarkable fact of African American literary history that *Blake* should have been published in Hamilton's antiemigrationist paper.[27]

In publishing *Blake*, Hamilton, who genuinely admired Delany, primarily sought to use the novel to boost the paper's sagging circulation. In his 5 October 1861 announcement of the forthcoming full serialization of the novel, he puffed *Blake* as "stand[ing] without a rival, not even excepting the world wide known 'Uncle Tom's Cabin,'" and he concluded with this plea: "We would suggest, that with [*Blake*'s] commencement, our friends make a special effort to obtain the subscriptions of their neighbors, that they may be furnished with all the early chapters, of which we do not intend to keep a large supply." This announcement appeared only a week after the paper printed a condescendingly favorable review of Delany's *Official Report of the Niger Valley Exploring Party* (published, surprisingly, by Hamilton himself), in which the anonymous reviewer remarked that "the interesting little *brochure* before us" possesses "the power to withdraw our strained attention from eager watching for every rumor or breath from the seat of war." Hamilton in all probability regarded *Blake* as an anachronistic historical novel that performed a similar diversionary function.[28]

Yet the novel, I will argue, can be viewed both as an allegorical account of Delany's quest for leadership and community, circa 1852–59, and as an engaged response to and intervention in events of 1859–62 (even if he did not rewrite a word of the 1859 manuscript, which seems unlikely, given the post-1859 footnotes on Africa). Hence Delany's desire for its full publication in 1861–62. Whatever Hamilton may have thought about *Blake*, Delany saw it as making a vital intervention in what he regarded as the unresolved debate on blacks' place in the United States. Unconvinced at the time of the novel's serialization that even with a Union victory blacks would become part of the nation's "ruling element," Delany presents in *Blake* a Pan-African vision of black nationalism that means to combat and expose the limits of the U.S. nationalism espoused by blacks aligned with Douglass. Ranging throughout the Americas and even to Africa, Delany's heroic surrogate Blake attempts to restore to blacks degraded by white racist practices a sense of their glorious potential as a unified people. Delany's complex representation of the pragmatically innovative means and utopian ends of such a black nationalist program in the Americas will be the main focus of my discussion.

Redeeming the Americas

As suggested by its full title, *Blake; or, The Huts of America: A Tale of the Mississippi Valley, the Southern United States, and Cuba*, Delany's novel aspires to provide an uncommonly broad view of the problem of slavery in the Americas.[29] His sense of the interrelationships among various sites in the Americas is adumbrated in the novel's opening chapter, which depicts Northerners and Southerners, Americans and Cubans, meeting in Baltimore to discuss their plans to make over the Baltimore clipper *Merchantman* into a slaver. Though *Blake* can seem lacking in formal unity in the manner of a picaresque novel, that clipper and its group of owners work to hold the novel together. Blake is the slave of the investor from Mississippi, Stephen Franks; Blake's wife will be sold to the Cuban investor, Captain Juan Garcia; Blake will make his way to Cuba with another of the investors, Captain Richard Paul; and in part 2 of the novel he will journey to Africa on the refitted ship with Paul and two other investors (U.S. and Cuban) at the helm.

Crucial as the ship is to the novel's global perspective on slavery, there is another aspect that also works to hold the novel together: its portrayal of the heroic black leader Henry Blake, who may be regarded as a surrogate for Delany himself.[30] The novel builds to a coronation of Blake's leadership role, and it is with this autobiographically charged scene, which brings into focus key aspects of Delany's thematics of Pan-African community and representative identity, that I want to begin my reading of the novel.

In a culminating series of chapters first printed in the 1862 *Anglo-African Magazine*, Blake, at secret Grand Council meetings at the Havana home of the wealthy mulatto Madame Cordora, assumes the mantle of "Commander in Chief of the Army of Emancipation" before his adulating admirers.[31] The meetings ritually celebrate what has been clear from the opening chapters of the novel: that Blake, "the Leader of the Army of Emancipation and originator of the scheme to redeem them from slavery and an almost helpless degradation" (251), has a messianic, Moses-like ability to get blacks "intelligently united" (252) against their oppressors.

At Blake's side during the meetings is the great Cuban poet Placido, whose speeches and poems further validate Blake's leadership position. But when Placido recites a poem on the providential destiny of "Ethiopia's sons" (260), Madame Cordora pointedly queries, "Are not some of us left out in the supplication, as I am sure, although identified together, we are not all Ethiopians[?]" (260). (Of course, they are not all "sons" either.) In a historically anachronistic moment that serves to sanctify Blake's (and implicitly Delany's) claims to black leadership, the mulatto Placido, who was in fact executed by Cuban authorities in 1844 for allegedly conspiring against the state, explains to Madame Cordora that the best way for blacks to demonstrate their equality with whites is to elevate "the descendants of Africa of unmixed blood" (260). Given the existence of racism among even antislavery whites, the spectacle of racially "pure" black leaders, such as Blake, would serve the rhetorical purpose of persuading "white men" to offer their "respect" (261) to blacks. Perhaps a figure for Douglass, who here *capitulates* to blackness as a superior source of leadership, Placido explains (echoing the similar argument set forth by Delany in *Condition*): "The instant that an equality of the blacks with the whites is admitted, we [mulattos] being the descendants of the two, must be acknowledged the equals of both" (261).[32] As the approving Blake looks on from the majesty of his leadership position, Placido, now echoing the "civilizationist" stance of Delany's 1861 *Official Report*, extends his argument to suggest the need for black leaders to help in "regenerating" Africa (261). Though Placido's concern for African regeneration may seem irrelevant to the blacks' impending insurrection in Cuba, he asserts that, from a political/rhetorical perspective, racially pure *and* mixed-blood blacks are all "implied in the term [Ethiopian], and cannot exist without it" (260).

"Africa," as Madame Cordora comes to realize, is the signifying term of black community, and it is precisely the Ethiopianism articulated by Placido and embodied by Blake that promises to forge a community from the "promiscuous mingling . . . of every complexion of his [African] race" (249). This historical, biological, and spiritual sense of racial unity and wholeness is central to the novel's Pan-Africanism. Wilson Moses writes (rather critically) that nineteenth-century Pan-African nationalists sought "to unite the entire black racial family, assuming that the entire race has a collective destiny and message for humanity comparable to that of a nation."[33] Yet in the context of the practice of slavery in the Americas, the rhetorical and spiritual Pan-African nationalism espoused at Madame Cordora's makes pragmatic sense as a way of mobilizing blacks for united oppositional action. Cordora's embrace of her "blackness" should thus be viewed in not only mystical but also political terms as a sign of her solidarity with the oppressed.

In this culminating scene, then, Blake and Placido join hands in insisting on the importance of having intelligent, "civilized," "pure-blood" blacks in the leadership position of a hierarchically conceived "African" collectivity. There is a close connection between the collectivist, elitist Pan-African politics expressed near the conclusion of the novel and the politics informing the presentation in part 1 of Blake's efforts to set in motion a slave conspiracy in the United States. Delany remarks early in the novel on the challenges facing Blake in his U.S. endeavors: "Light, of necessity, had to be imparted to the darkened region of the obscure intellects of the slaves, to arouse them from their benighted condition to one of moral responsibility" (101). As is true of the culminating scene in Cuba, this passage suggests that in the United States, precisely because the slaves are so "benighted," a pressing need exists for an intelligent black to lead the slaves from slavery to freedom. Underscoring this point is the stanza from Stowe's poem "Caste and Christ" that Delany uses as an epigraph to the novel's first part: "By myself, the Lord of Ages, / I have sworn to right the wrong, / I have pledged my word, unbroken, / For the weak against the strong." In the poem, these words represent the voice of Christ as he embraces "thou dark and weary stranger," a black man, perhaps a slave, "bowed with toil, with mind benighted." [34] Wrenched from its poetic context, the stanza guides the reader to regard Blake, somewhat in the spirit of Stowe's *Dred*, as a prophetic redeemer, a black Moses *and* a black Christ, who will be attempting to liberate the "weak" from the "strong."

Blake's uniquely heroic and intelligent character, his potential to bring about "the redemption of his race" (199), is clear from the opening chapters of the novel, as Delany emphasizes just how different he is from the other slaves on Colonel Franks's Mississippi plantation. In a revisionary parody of the opening chapters of *Uncle Tom's Cabin*, Delany portrays Mammy Judy overhearing Mr. Franks telling his wife that he has sold her "beloved" (6) slave Maggie (Blake's wife) to the Northerner Judge Ballard. In *Uncle Tom's Cabin*, Eliza, on learning of her son's sale, flees with Harry, while Uncle Tom ruefully accepts his own sale as the will of God. In *Blake*, Delany portrays the slaves as pathetically turning to the religion of their oppressors. Informing her daughter of her imminent fate, Mammy Judy advises, "Look to de Laud, my chile!" (9). When her father, Daddy Joe, returns to find that Maggie has been sent to Baltimore and separated from her son, he too prays: "Laud, dy will be done!" (12). In his 1849 "Domestic Economy" essays, Delany urged blacks to resist resorting to prayer when "a physical, or temporal end" is desired; and, of course, he attacked *Uncle Tom's Cabin* for its advocacy of prayer over action.[35] Near the end of *Blake*, in the scene at Madame Cordora's, Blake asserts as one of the insurrectionary group's pragmatic creeds that "no religion but that which brings us liberty will we know; no God but He who owns us as his children will we serve" (258). In other words, religion should serve black people, not the other way around. Like Stowe's own revolutionary black hero, Dred, Blake attempts to teach this lesson to the "benighted" slaves from the moment of his introduction into the novel.

Introduced as "Henry Holland," the name he was given when remanded into slavery, Blake is so enraged at the sale of his wife that Mammy worries for the state of his soul.[36] She urges him to "put yeh trus' in de Laud" (15). Blake, "the intelligent slave" (16) who, unlike the other slaves of the plantation, does not speak in dialect, asserts his readiness to act: "I have waited long enough on heavenly promises; I'll wait no longer" (16). But though he seems to be renouncing religion, it is his visionary insight into (not rejection of) a scriptural phrase that provides him with the germ of his insurrectionary plot.

In *Condition* Delany writes about blacks' religiosity: "They carry it too far. Their hope is largely developed, and consequently, they usually stand still—hope in God, and really expect Him to do that for them, which it is necessary they should do themselves."[37] Ironically, the phrase "stand still," regularly adduced by proslavery preachers to encourage slave obedience, has its sources in the emancipatory moment in Exodus when Moses at the Red Sea convinces the fleeing Israelites not to return to slavery but rather "to stand still, and see the salvation of the Lord" (Exodus 14:13). Parroting the words of the preachers, without having any insight into their typological significance, Daddy Joe urges Blake to "'stan still an' see de salbation'" (21). When Blake responds that he will "'stand still' no longer" (21), he appears suddenly to envision how these scriptural words speak to the possibility of black insurrectionary action under his Moses-like leadership. Rather than explaining to Daddy Joe and Mammy Judy what he apprehends, however, he simply intones, in the manner of Christ (2 Corinthians 6:2), "'Now is the accepted time, today is the day of salvation'" (29). Only later, when he has more fully formulated his plan, does he reveal to several of his coconspirators that his insight into Exodus 14:13 has been the key to it all—that his idea for a slave conspiracy came to him when he realized that "the slave-holding preacher's advice to the black man is appropriate, 'Stand still and see the salvation'" (38).

As soon becomes clear, Blake's ingenious (and elitist) conspiratorial plan is to organize a slave insurrection by word of mouth, with the particularly intelligent slaves entrusted to spread the word. (Given Douglass's and other black abolitionists' insistence on the importance of literacy to slave liberation, it is noteworthy that Blake's conspiracy depends on oral forms of communication.) Blake explains his plan to his followers Charles and Andy soon after escaping from Franks's plantation: "All you have to do, is to find one good man or woman — I dont [sic] care which, so that they prove to be the right person — on a single plantation, and hold a seclusion and impart the secret to them, and make them the organizers for their own plantation, and they in like manner impart it to some other next to them, and so on. In this way it will spread like smallpox among them" (41). Though he never reveals his "secret," his war song suggests the nature of the plot: "Insurrection shall be my theme! / ... One simultaneous war cry / Shall burst upon the midnight air!" (44). At an agreed on time and date, the slaves shall rise in unison to kill the masters.[38]

In effect, Blake has taken it on himself to spread the "germs" of insurrection by creating a sort of black Masonic network in the slave South, with himself as grand master. Several aspects of Delany's presentation of black Freemasonry in his 1853 *Origin and Objects of Ancient Freemasonry* are especially relevant to the presentation of Blake as a Moses-like leader in part 1 of the novel. In *Origin and Objects of Ancient Freemasonry* Delany describes Moses as a fugitive slave who obtained "all his wisdom and ability" in Egypt, "a colony of Ethiopia." An "African" and a fugitive slave, Moses, like "the wise men of Egypt and Ethiopia," recognized that wisdom must be "handed down only through the priesthood to the recipients of their favors." As Delany goes on to explain, it is the leader's job to inculcate among the enslaved "a manly determination to be free." In doing so, the leader performs a religious function, teaching the principal tenet of Delany's black Freemasonry (and of the transcendentalism of the time): "MAN THE LIKENESS OF GOD." Delany sums up his vision of black leadership as presented in *Origin and Objects of Ancient Freemasonry*: "What can be more God-like than this, to . . . give man a proper sense of his own importance, and consequently his duty to his fellows, by which alone, he fulfills the high mission for which he is sent on his temporary pilgrimage."[39]

That Blake may be regarded as a Mosaic leader on a "high mission" is made clear when he affirms (or discovers) his religiosity just after "christening" his travels by killing his first overseer. Following the killing, he journeys into "the wilderness, determining to renew his faith and dependence upon Divine aid, . . . [and] he opened his heart to God, as a tenement of the Holy Spirit" (69). His crossing of the Red River into Louisiana soon after his wilderness experience thus evokes the scriptural parallel of the crossing of the Red Sea, which had already been evoked in his allusion to Exodus 14:13. That parallel is reinforced when Blake explicitly compares himself to Moses: "Could I but climb where Moses stood, / And view the landscape o'er" (69). It is only after this interlude, with his "faith . . . now fully established" (70), that Blake begins to spread his liberationist message.[40]

Unlike Dred, who similarly kills an overseer before proceeding to the "wilderness" of the Dismal Swamp, Blake assumes a much greater mobility in Southern slave culture. Rather than roaming within the confines of the swamps, he travels from plantation to plantation (and even to an American Indian camp in Arkansas). Sundquist writes that Delany's intent in detailing Blake's travels is to show the "sources in African American slave culture of a readiness for organized political resistance that can be called into action by proper black leadership."[41] But this is to romanticize the extent to which Blake (Delany) links himself with slave culture. If anything, Delany believes, as the American Indian chief Culver notes as well (86), that the degradations of slavery have virtually obliterated black sources of resistance and that there is therefore an especially crucial need for a "boss" (41) who can mobilize even "the most stupid among the slaves" (39). To be sure, Mammy Judy, Daddy Joe, and their friends on Franks's plantation eventually adopt Blake's rebellious plan and help him to escape. But so rare are Blake's encounters with intelligent and resistant blacks that when he finally meets a slave on a Texas plantation exhibiting both intelligence and a fierce desire for liberty, he is nearly beside himself with happiness: he "fell upon Sampson's neck with tears of joy in meeting unexpectedly one of his race so intelligent in that region of the country" (85).

While embracing Sampson, Blake offers only token recognition of Sampson's wife, described as "a neat, intelligent, handsome little woman" (83). It should be noted in this regard, in what may be taken as a further influence of Delany's Masonic fraternalism, that although Blake early on affirms his desire to work with male and female leaders, he mostly seeks out black males for assistance in organizing his plot. After interviewing a woman on a Louisiana plantation, for example, he states, "I must see your husband a little, then go" (73). At the next plantation he asks the young woman he interviews, "Is there among your men, a real clever good trusty man?" (78). Significantly, when Blake first learns that something dreadful had happened to Maggie, he concludes that this could mean only one thing—that she has had sexual relations with her master: "My God! Has she disgraced herself?" (15). Here and elsewhere it can seem that Blake believes black women slaves' one large task is to remain sexually inviolate. Delany writes in *Condition*: "No people are ever elevated above the condition of their *females*; hence, the condition of the *mother* determines the condition of the child."[42] In *Blake* the male's plot is predicated on the importance of elevating the female—that is, freeing her from the deprecations of her male owner—as a way of elevating the race. Hence, in the novel, women for the most part (though not entirely) are presented as the grateful beneficiaries of, rather than full participants in, the unfolding conspiracy.

Because he encounters so few Sampsons on his travels, Blake, even as he spreads the word of his plot, advises the slaves to wait before taking action. Incongruously, he encourages them first to lift themselves from what he terms "their benighted condition" (101). He remains vague, however, as to how this should be done, beyond suggesting that the slaves need to conceive of themselves as free *before* taking insurrectionary action. Yet in New Orleans, Blake finds a number of slaves responsive to his plan and ready to act, and in a scene that looks forward to the meeting at Madame Cordora's in part 2 of the novel (and perhaps draws on Delany's Chatham meeting with John Brown), he secretly convenes with fifteen black leaders of nearby plantations "for the portentious [sic] purpose of a final decision on the hour to strike the first blow" (102). Though they evidently wish to proceed with the insurrection posthaste, Blake discerns that someone in the group is intoxicated and abruptly calls everything off. He then pontificates on blacks' limitations: "You are not yet ready for a strike. . . . You have barely taken the first step in the matter" (105). As if to demonstrate the truth of Blake's contentions, a drunken black subsequently betrays the plan by yelling "Insurrection! Death to every white!" (106). The result of this intemperate display is a reactionary white reign of terror that works further to destroy blacks' "self-respect and manhood" (108).

This lack of "self-respect and manhood" among U.S. blacks is one of the large themes of the novel's first part. In an effort to underscore the full extent of blacks' degraded status, Delany, as he earlier did in the *North Star*, satirizes those mulattoes who, ashamed of their blackness, view their white blood as a sign of their superiority. In South Carolina, Blake is snubbed by members of the "Brown Society," a mulatto group that, according to the narrator, was "created by the influence of the whites, for the purpose of preventing pure-blooded Negroes from entering the social circle" (109). Though the scene could be read as an attack on any sort of racialist pride, Delany emphasizes the "miserable stupidity and ignorance" (110) of those blacks who reject their "African" or "Ethiopian" blood.[43]

Delany's damning portrayal of self-loathing mulattoes thus makes highly curious and problematic his equally critical portrayal of the revolutionary "pure-blood" blacks that Blake encounters in the Dismal Swamp. The narrator describes the scene: "In this fearful abode for years of some of Virginia and North Carolina's boldest black rebels, the names of Nat Turner, Denmark Veezie [*sic*], and General Gabriel were held by them in sacred reverence. . . . With delight they recounted the many exploits of whom they conceived to be the greatest men who ever lived. . . , some of the narrators claiming to have been patriots in the American Revolution" (113). In presenting the blacks of the swamp as a Revolutionary community, Delany aligns himself with W. C. Nell, Stowe, and other antislavery writers. And yet, in the spirit of the "civilizationist" goals of his plan to "redeem" Africa from its "benighted" condition, Delany keeps his hero Blake at a distance from "African" revolutionaries who are presented as somewhat ignorant in preferring conjure to action. Just as Sandy's offering of a root to Douglass to fend off Covey is described as a "superstition . . . very common among the more ignorant slaves," so Delany criticizes as a hindrance to significant action the conjurer Gamby Gholar's offering to Blake of "a forked breastbone of a small bird, which . . . he called 'the charm bone of a treefrog'" (113). Delany suggests as well that the conjurors are self-interested liars whose overriding concern is less for the blacks' liberation than for maintaining their power over credulous slaves.[44] And yet as critical as he is of the conjurors, he ultimately portrays them as smart enough to recognize Blake as a leader more worthy, and implicitly more in the tradition of Gabriel Prosser, Vesey, and Turner, than themselves. The scene in the Dismal Swamp therefore culminates in a coronation scene, anticipating the more momentous one at Madame Cordora's, in which the conjurors anoint Blake their "Head" (115).

The emphasis of the final chapters of part 1 is on Blake's role as "Head" in leading the relatively ignorant slaves of Franks's plantation to Canada. As if talking to children, Blake explains to the fugitive slaves how to find the North Star and use a compass. When Blake uses the word "intermediate" as part of his explanation, Mammy Judy laments, "'E gone into big talk g'in! Sho!" (133), whereupon he patiently (pedantically) explains, "Intermediate means between, mammy" (134).[45] In addition to teaching the slaves the basics of astronomy and the English language, Blake, in the closing chapters of the novel's first part, also attempts to instruct them on the moral exigency and benefits of using violence against the masters. Though Andy and Charles fulminate against the enslavers, with Charles going so far as to assert that "ole Frank's head would be nothin' for me to chop off" (127–28), they admit that they would be unable to perform such a deed. In an effort to "redeem" these slaves, whom he regards as lacking in both courage and political consciousness, Blake boasts to them that while on his tour he had killed whites, and he thanks God for giving him the opportunity to act. Quoting from Garnet's 1843 "Address to the Slaves," Blake instructs his followers, " 'Rather to die as freemen, than live as slaves!' " (128).[46]

Despite his bold rhetoric, Blake and the formerly enslaved blacks eventually escape by exhibiting a "temperate revolutionism." Unlike the drunken New Orleans black who betrayed the plot, Blake and his compatriots remain in control of their bodies and eventually "elevate" themselves to Canada. When offered alcohol in Indiana, Blake speaks for the group in asserting, "We don't drink, sir" (144). As in Douglass's *Bondage*, the intemperate in *Blake* are the enslavers and their racist sympathizers, who are presented as literally and metaphorically intoxicated. After drunken whites incarcerate the blacks in a tavern's stables, Blake finds a butcher knife and cuts them free while the whites "revelled with intoxication" (150). In a scene that reverses the terms of the holiday drinking scenes of Douglass's and other slave narratives, Blake then forces the white sentinel to drink himself into a stupor before leading the fugitive slaves to Canada.

But theirs is a tentative, limited freedom. Though Blake has enough money to buy fifty acres for Mammy Judy, Daddy Joe, his son, and others, and though several of the black fugitives joyously take advantage of their newfound opportunity to marry, we have reached simply the halfway point of the novel. Delany thus works against the typological figuring in *Uncle Tom's Cabin* of Canada as heaven, presenting a more critical reading of the northern nation, based on having resided in Chatham, as a place where "privileges were denied [blacks] which are common to the slave in every Southern state—[such as] the right of going into the gallery of a public building" (153). More important, at the midpoint of the novel there is a sense that Blake's larger mission remains unfulfilled. Not only does Blake have the personal desire to free his wife from slavery in Cuba, but his larger project of uniting and empowering blacks is still to be accomplished. Part 1 ends, then, with Blake making his plans to journey to Cuba in quest of both his wife and what I term his Masonic, Pan-African vision of a regenerated and redeemed black community. As suggested by the series of Blake's border crossings—from the United States to Canada, back to the United States, and then on to Cuba—the black community has no fixed boundaries, though its "political destiny" would appear to be in "America."

With Blake's arrival in Cuba at the opening of part 2, Delany makes explicit the interconnections between the United States and Cuba that had been implicit in the relationship between U.S. and Cuban businesspeople/enslavers in the novel's first chapter. Everywhere Blake travels in his effort "to witness all that he could pertaining to Cuban slavery" (169), he views U.S. influences in Cuba, with the corollary implication, given the centrality of Cuba to the slave trade, that he had viewed Cuban influences everywhere he had traveled in the United States. Direct discussion of these interrelationships is mostly avoided in the novel's first part, with the important exception of a revealing conversation between the Northerner Judge Ballard and the callous Mississippi enslaver Major Armsted. During a visit to the South, Ballard declares that "Cuba must cease to be a Spanish colony, and become American territory" (62), and he goes on to complain of the close physical contact he observed between Cuba's white masters and black slaves during a recent tour of the island, declaring that he refused to smoke cigars proffered by "black fingers" (62). Mocking Ballard's fastidiousness, Armsted points out that Cuba's blacks, in the very process of making Ballard's treasured cigars, "frequently in closing up the wrapper, . . . draw it through their lips to give it tenacity" (63). Armsted's striking image of Cuban slaves "smoking" the cigars of the masters figures the possibility of a violent reversal of power relations between the races. As is clear throughout the novel, the specter of black revolutionism haunts the imaginations of white Southerners and Northerners alike and helps to give rise to desires, like Ballard's, to make Cuba "American."

Blake's insurrectionary plotting occurs in this context of racial anxiety and imperialistic desire, and in limning the connection between whites' racial fears and will to power in the novel's second part, Delany means to intervene in contemporaneous debates on U.S. expansionism and slavery. For the Judge Ballard–like belief that, as Russel prophesied in Stowe's *Dred*, the United States would soon "annex Cuba" was shared by many in the United States during the antebellum period. In an 1849 issue of the *North Star*, Delany warned that "there is a deep-concerned scheme for the annexation of Cuba to the United States," and two years later Douglass observed that "our voracious eagle is whetting his talons for the capture of Cuba."[47] Northern businesspeople craved sugar-rich Cuba for its natural resources, while Southern proslavery advocates wanted to make Cuba part of an expanding slave empire. Both of these groups supported the efforts of the anti-Spanish, proslavery Cuban filibusterer Narciso López, who led three separate military expeditions against Cuba before being captured and executed in 1851.[48] In 1854 President Franklin Pierce, in quest of a national consensus in favor of the Kansas-Nebraska bill, renounced filibusterism. Yet he continued to pursue diplomatic efforts to purchase Cuba from Spain, charging his foreign ministers to articulate a statement of his policy. The result was the notorious Ostend Report of October 1854, a summa of "Africanization" fears and a crucial discursive context for Delany's representation of Blake's Pan-African revolutionism.

Presented in the form of a letter to Secretary of State William L. Marcy, the Ostend Report, signed by James Buchanan, J. Y. Mason, and Pierre Soulé, asserted that "Cuba belongs naturally to that great family of States of which the Union is the Providential Nursery." In fact, the ministers stated, oblivious to the perspectives of Afro-Cubans, the two nations "look upon each other as if they were one people and had but one destiny." The ministers therefore proposed offering Spain over $100 million for the island nation. The report could have ended there, but the ministers went on to proclaim that should Spain refuse to sell, the United States had the right, "by every law human and Divine," to take Cuba from Spain, "if we possess the power; and this upon the very same principle that would justify an individual in tearing down the burning house of his neighbor, if there were no other means of preventing the flames from destroying his own home." That "burning house," as the ministers made clear in their concluding paragraphs, was the specter of a large-scale black rebellion against the Creole and Peninsular powers. Fearing that Spanish "liberalization" policies could bring about the "Africaniza-tion" of Cuba—the emergence of a black republic "almost in sight of our shores," as the Louisiana state legislature warned in 1854—the ministers declared: "We should . . . be recreant to our duty, be unworthy of our gallant forefathers, and commit base treason against our posterity, should we permit Cuba to be Africanized and become a second St. Domingo, with all its attendant horrors to the white race, and suffer the flames to extend to our neighboring shores, seriously to endanger or actually to consume the fair fabric of our Union."[49]

With its patriotic appeals and fearful imagery of racial conflagration, the Ostend Report only further stoked desires among proslavery spokes-people to pursue Cuban annexation. But because of continued anti-slavery resistance in the North, that pursuit had to be developed through unofficial channels. Talked out of his filibustering plans by Pierce, General John A. Quitman, a former governor of Mississippi and an admirer of López, threw his support to the notorious William Walker, eventually joining with him in his successful invasion of Nicaragua in 1855. Delany, in "Political Aspect of the Colored People of the United States" (1855), referred to the "despicable puerile attempt by the buccaneer Walker, to overthrow the government of Lower California and Nicaragua." But what at first might have seemed "puerile" eventually took on a more insidi-ous cast, as Walker hoped to use his base in Nicaragua to invade Cuba and create a federation of five Central American republics with himself as military leader. Using rhetoric similar to that deployed by Delany to advance his African project, Walker, as he explained in his 1860 *The War in Nicaragua*, sought to import "an American element into Nicara-guan society" to "regenerate Central America." To this end, he relegal-ized slavery there. President Buchanan's decision to extend a "paternal hand to General Walker, and his band of Filibusters and Pirates who have invaded and effected a lodgment in Nicaragua," Frederick Doug-lass asserted soon after Buchanan recognized Walker's government, re-vealed "the foreign policy of a slave power." Concerned about Walker's designs on Cuba, Spain joined with Costa Rica in 1857 to overthrow Walker, and at around the same time, Buchanan renewed U.S. efforts to acquire Cuba. In the March 1859 *Douglass' Monthly*, Douglass again de-cried Buchanan's imperialistic machinations: "Surely this talk about the acquisition of Cuba, is nothing other than a talk about stealing Cuba."[50]

In the context of debate in the United States on Cuba, which, historian Robert May argues, remained "a central, if not the central, issue in American politics" during 1859 and 1860, Blake's revolutionary conspiracy, particularly as it unfolds in part 2 of the novel, can be regarded as a pragmatically conceived defense of blacks' rights to become part of the "ruling element" in Cuba and throughout the Americas.[51] Inspired as much by William Walker as John Brown, Delany has his black revolutionary hero attempt to fight off white annexation through black "annexation" and oppose white filibusterism through black filibusterism, all to bring about precisely what the authors of the Ostend Report so feared: a revolutionary transformation of Cuba that would "endanger" the white power structure in the Americas.

Yet we might ask the same questions about Blake's revolutionary project that we asked about Delany's Central and South American emigration plans of the mid-1850s: What is the relationship of the indigenous peoples to the emerging black nation(s) that Blake hopes to bring forth? Or, to put things another way, what makes Blake in Cuba less of a filibusterer — or less of an imperialist — than Walker in Nicaragua? In his 1860 *War in Nicaragua* Walker finesses the question of imperialism when he asserts that his decision to reintroduce slavery into Nicaragua was "in the fullest sense of the word, the act of the sovereignty of Nicaragua."[52] Eliding issues of race, Walker breaks down the distinction between his own will and that of the Nicaraguan people by figuring himself as the corporeal and spiritual embodiment of the nation.

In *Blake*, Delany somewhat differently attempts to resolve the problem of imperialism inherent in Blake's building of a black nation by connecting the revolutionary hero to the region through his personal history and black body. In doing so, Delany more explicitly brings to the center of the novel the problem of conjoining race and nation that had interested him since the 1852 publication of *Condition*. For if we read *Blake* in relation to Delany's political hopes and actions of the mid- to late 1850s, we can view the novel as an effort to revise his 1852 and 1854 emigrationist texts by linking black nationhood not to some mystical notion of blacks' Manifest Destiny in the Americas but instead to the fact of blacks' historical ties to the region, thereby imaginatively implicating himself, through his heroic surrogate, in the history of Cuba, the Caribbean, and Africa. It is crucial to note in this respect that soon after Blake helps his wife purchase her freedom, he journeys to the Havana residence of Placido, Cuba's renowned mulatto poet, where he reveals to Maggie and Placido (and the reader) that he is in fact Placido's long-missing cousin Carolus

Henrico Blacus.[53] Not only that, Blake makes the even larger claim that "I am *the* lost boy of Cuba" (193; emphasis mine). What is it that makes Blake not simply another foreign intruder but the embodiment of Cuba? Oddly enough, it is the fact of his implication in mastery.

Critics have yet to take the full measure of Blake's problematic family history and the relationship of that history to the novel's political vision. As initially recounted by Placido, Blake, elliptically referred to in part 1 as "educated in the West Indies, and decoyed away when young" (17), is in fact "the son of a wealthy black tobacco, cigar, and snuff manufacturer, who left school and went to sea" (193). In light of the earlier discussion between Ballard and Armsted on Cuban cigar making, it seems reasonable to conclude, then, that Blake is the son of a man who has been dependent on slave labor. Though Delany doesn't explicitly address this aspect of the father's past, he does make clear that it is precisely because of Blake's status as a native-born member of Cuba's black elite that he has the right to think of himself as "the lost boy of Cuba." In the account of Blake's family past, which is withheld for nearly two-thirds of the novel, Delany also suggests that because Blake (like Delany) was not raised a slave, his enslavement is particularly "unfair" and arbitrary. After participating in the African slave trade with the crew of what he initially believed was a Spanish man-of-war, Blake, as he recounts to Placido, protested to the captain when he found the ship stopping at Key West instead of going directly to Cuba and was immediately sold to "one Colonel Franks, of Mississippi. . . . He seized me under loud and solemn protest" (194). Given that Blake had not offered "loud and solemn protest" at the African slave trade itself, it would appear that his education on slavery begins only after his own enslavement. Viewed in this way, his "fall" into slavery was a fortunate one, especially for the slaves he now seeks to liberate and elevate through revolutionary action.[54]

What I want to take up here is the role played by Placido in validating Blake's status as exemplary black revolutionary leader. The poet's validating role is significant because many African Americans of the 1840s and 1850s regarded Placido as *the* exemplary black revolutionary leader of the time. He achieved this reputation soon after he was executed in 1844 by Cuba's governmental authorities for supposedly being one of the leaders of what came to be known as the conspiracy of La Escalera—a conspiracy of slaves, free blacks, Creoles, and "foreigners" to overthrow white Spanish rule. In a speech of 1848 Garnet proclaimed that Placido was "a true Poet, and of course a Patriot. His noble soul was moved with pity as he saw his fellow men in chains. Born to feel, and to act, he made a bold attempt to effect a revolution, and failing in it, he fell a martyr to his principles." Delany himself, in his 1852 *Condition*, apotheosized "the nobel mulatto, PLACIDO, the gentleman, scholar, poet, and intended chief Engineer of the Army of Liberty and Freedom in Cuba," asserting that Cuba's blacks "only want intelligent leaders of their own color, when they are ready, at any moment to charge to the conflict—to liberty or death."[55]

Of course, in *Blake* Delany presents his eponymous hero, unlike Placido, as an intelligent leader who is also blacks' "own color." In his characterization of the relationship between the "mulatto" Placido and the "black" Blake, Delany both honors and undermines Placido's status as black hero, ultimately installing in his place the heroic Blake. As I noted earlier, it seems clear that something similar to the racial dynamic troubling Delany's relationship with Douglass is enacted in Delany's portrayal of Placido, for the narrator in rather hostile fashion repeatedly refers to Placido's "yellow" (193) skin. (In *Bondage* Freeland's mother calls Douglass a *"yellow devil."*) As mentioned, at the climactic meeting at Madame Cordora's it is Placido himself who maintains that the most effective leader of a black revolution would have to be a "pure-blooded" black. Resurrected from the grave in a novel that, like William Wells Brown's *Clotel*, anachronistically conflates historical periods, making black memory the essential register of history, Placido is used most audaciously by Delany to legitimate Blake's leadership when he portrays Placido reading a poem at the celebration of Blake's ascension to leadership. The seven-stanza poem calling for the slaves to fight "for Justice, Liberty, or death!" (196) first appeared in somewhat different form at the end of Delany's 1849 *North Star* essay "Annexation of Cuba." By attributing to Placido his own poetry, Delany makes him into a kind of ventriloquist's dummy who both summons and authorizes Delany's vision of himself as the quintessential black deliverer.[56]

Placido plays a less obvious legitimating role when he escorts Blake and Maggie to the home of Blake's father (who is never apprised that Blake is his son). For the light it casts on Delany's elite politics of black male leadership, the final paragraph of the two-paragraph chapter on Placido, Blake, and Maggie is worth quoting in full:

Here everything around was strange to Maggie, who found herself transferred from wretchedness as a slave on the hacienda of Emanuel Garcia, to that of the happiness of a lady in the elegant mansion of one of the wealthiest and most refined black merchants in the West Indies. Everything was kindness and affection, and but for the thought of the absence of her husband for a time, she would have been the happiest of women. But now she had reconciled herself to his course, for since meeting with the poet, she was satisfied that he was not alone in the important scheme for the redemption of his race. (199)

At this point, with much of the plot still to unfold, Maggie virtually drops out of the novel. This does not mean that women will have no place in Blake's plotting, for Delany eventually portrays a black African woman fully up to the task of revolution. The role Maggie plays at this particular moment, I would suggest, is of a surrogate for the reader, in the sense that her reconciliation to Blake's "grand design upon Cuba" (191) can be taken as Delany's effort to guide a resistant reader to a similar reconciliation. What is noteworthy is how Maggie's reconciliation comes about: through her recognition of Blake's family ties to "one of the wealthiest and most refined black merchants in the West Indies" and through her recognition that the great Placido, equally aristocratic, embraces the plan.

That plan, as soon becomes clear, has Africa at its center; the 1861–62 periodical printing of the novel thus speaks to Delany's own personal investment in Africa circa 1858–62, conveying a much more sympathetic relationship to Africanness than the 1859 periodical printing of the novel's first part (and even the 1861 *Official Report*). Soon after Blake's arrival in Cuba, for example, he links himself with a slave family whose history embodies the geopolitics of the slave trade. Kidnapped from Africa ten years earlier, the Oba family, renamed Grande by their Cuban enslavers, "proved to be native African, having learned English on the coast, French Creole at New Orleans, and Spanish at Cuba" (172).[57] In contrast to the novel's first part, where Blake mocks the use of conjure by the "African" revolutionaries of the Dismal Swamp, he now embraces the African religious practices of the Obas to the point that, after bloodhounds pass their hut, he requests information from them on the art of conjure (173).

A similar desire to tap into African sources of black resistance motivates Blake's plan, which he reveals to the approving Placido, to join an African slaver and foment a mutinous rebellion. Hoping that such a rebellion would enable him and his revolutionary black compatriots to obtain a vessel laden with munitions with which they could "make a strike"

(198) on Cuba, Blake signs on as a sailing master with the Spanish slaver *Vulture*, the refitted U.S.-Cuban *Merchantman* of the novel's first chapter. By setting the proposed mutiny on this specific ship, Delany participates in a symbolic "mutinous" undoing of the slave power, punningly setting the stage for Africa's "native Krumen" (198) to overthrow white crewmen. The comedy of the crossing to Africa centers on the Cuban and U.S. captains' efforts to make sense of the blacks' increasingly obvious subversive activities. As in Melville's theatricalized slave rebellion in "Benito Cereno," the blacks aboard the *Vulture*, under the directorship of Blake, "acted well their part" (205), expressing their hostility toward the whites by chanting parodic versions of Cuban and U.S. national anthems while appearing to be "merry when they work" (208).[58]

In the chapters set in Africa, Delany, in the notes and in the text, incorporates some of his own African experiences of 1859–60.[59] For example, his Stowe-like account of the decision of "the great factor, a noted Portuguese, Ludo Draco" (211) to renounce the slave trade may have been inspired by a story he heard during his visit; Delany remarks in a footnote that the opposition to the slave trade of Draco's wife, Zorina, "a handsome native African" (212), is similar to that "exhibited by the sister of the native wife of a once-noted slave trader on the Coast, whom the writer met in Africa — a very respectable, intelligent, Christian young woman" (212). Even more resistant to the slave trade is Draco's daughter Angelina, home from a Lisbon convent, who rebels against her father when, incredibly enough, she realizes for the first time that he is a slave trader: in the manner of Little Eva she begins to die of grief after hearing the wails of the slaves aboard the *Vulture*. In his note on Angelina, who "spring[s] up in the bed" (220) when her father promises to renounce the slave trade (though not before selling eighteen hundred slaves to the owners of the *Vulture*), Delany refers to the "young mulatto daughter of a slave trader on the coast [who] peremptorily refused to leave her people and go with him to Portugal to finish an education" (215).

With his emphasis on the moral and social efficacy of Zorina's and Angelina's "respectable, intelligent, Christian" characters, Delany displays a consistency with his African project, which saw education and Christian morals as central to a regenerative, hierarchically conceived, and "civilized" black nationalism. In the horrific accounts of the middle passage that follow, Delany continues to honor such values, showing how those who are most responsive to Blake's mutinous plot are the African "elites" to be found among the slaves. He focuses his attention on two slaves in particular, one female and one male. The first, Abyssa, a cloth vendor from Soudan, who "had been converted to Christianity" (224), immediately recognizes Blake as a compatriot: "She saw that he was a civilized man, and desired that he should observe her. The look was reciprocated, and as he passed close by where she sat, to get a better observation of her, he startled as his ears caught the whisper in good English — / 'Arm of the Lord, awake!'" (224). The second, Mendi (the name of the ship Delany took to Africa and of the African blacks who rebelled on the *Amistad*), is a "native chief" (239), who, unlike the "mere slave," the narrator remarks, was "a powerful accession to their forces" (239).

Evidence of Mendi's leadership capacity becomes clear when, soon after the *Vulture* evades a British ship by dumping into the sea over six hundred dead and dying Africans, he convinces the remaining blacks in the hold to rebel. In an apocalyptic moment that points to the possible influence of Stowe's *Dred* on Delany's conception of prophetic black revolutionism, the American midshipman Spencer views Mendi, as lightening illuminates the hold, with his "face upturned to Heaven, falling upon his knees with hands extended in supplication to Jehovah, with great piercing eyes sparkling from under the heavy black brow, . . . a sight which struck terror to the heart of the young American" (234). As is true for Dred, Mendi's "storm of silent vengeance" (235) is typologically imaged as Jehovah-like wrath. And as is also true for *Dred*, the promise of large-scale black revolt remains unfulfilled. Impelled by the storm to protect their investment (and their lives), the white officers put an end to the incipient mutiny by securing the hatches until the *Vulture* returns safely to Cuba.

Through all the mutinous action, Blake, "strangely passive to occurring events below" (236), assumes a spectatorial role appropriate more to an evaluator of talent than a fellow revolutionary. The "strangely passive" relation to events he exhibits during the return from Africa in many respects comes to characterize his relation to plot in part 2 of the novel. Portraying Blake as watching more than doing, Delany may be giving expression to his own fears, similar to Douglass's, that uncontrolled revolutionism could erupt as a form of intemperance. Such intemperate revolutionism, as Blake himself insists when rejecting insurrectionist actions in New Orleans, would do little to bring about blacks' elevation. James Holly, in his 1857 book on the revolution in San Domingue, *A Vindica-*

tion of the Capacity of the Negro Race for Self-Government, and Civilized Progress, argued that it was the "judicious self-control" of the revolutionary blacks under the leadership of Toussaint and Dessalines that ensured Haiti's subsequent emergence as a civilized black nation with "thrifty commercial trade." Consistent with his own commitment to what Holly terms "a *strong, powerful, enlightened, and progressive negro nationality, equal to the demands of the nineteenth century*," Delany presents Blake as less interested in fomenting an immediate revolution than in finding leaders who can help him to develop in Cuba what Delany hoped to develop in Africa: a "progressive negro nationality." [60] It is significant, then, that the immediate result of Blake's African trip is not a John Brown–like guerrilla action but the acquisition of leaders like Mendi and Abyssa.

Delany stresses the centrality of leadership to the liberation of the black masses when Placido announces upon Blake's return from Africa that he has been chosen "General-in-Chief of the army of the emancipation of the oppressed men and women of Cuba!" (241). Placido pedagogically elaborates the broad principles of the group's commitment to uplift:

> You must remember that there's a great difference between Franks' slaves and General Blake and wife. As the former, you were irresponsible, the latter responsible; that was a life of trouble and sorrow, this of care and pleasure. One shuns adventure, the other seeks it; the slaves feel an issue, and the freeman makes it. A slave must have somebody to care for him; a freeman must care for himself and others. The position of a man carries his wife with him; so when he is degraded, she is also, because she cannot rise above his level; but when he is elevated, so is she also; hence, the wife of Henry the slave was Maggie the slave; but the wife of Mr. Henry Blake will be Mrs. Maggie Blake; and the wife of General Blake will be Mrs. General Blake. What objections have you to this, cousin? (242)

Paul Gilroy remarks that Delany saw a "necessary relationship between nationality, citizenship, and masculinity." [61] But what needs to be emphasized about this particular speech as much as the gender subordination that is being enforced on Maggie (though not on *all* women) is Delany's underscoring of the connection between black elevation and black revolution. As in Delany's *North Star* writings and Douglass's *Bondage*, there is a strong suggestion that bondage and freedom are states of mind as well as actual material and social conditions. Slaves are irresponsible, freemen are responsible; slaves are dependent, freeman are independent.

Like Blake in New Orleans, then, Placido is warning that a black revolution would fail if it should occur *before* blacks attain the consciousness of freemen.

The challenge facing Blake and the revolutionary leaders is to mobilize and channel collective energies toward the interrelated goals of black liberation and elevation. They do so, as Sundquist brilliantly demonstrates, by participating in festivals that ironize and invert the ongoing national festivals of the Spanish authorities.[62] Hence Blake assumes his position as general-in-chief on the occasion of "the celebration of the nativity of the Infanta Isabella, by a grand national fete at the palace of the Captain General" (240); hence the Afro-Cubans and their allies take a "general holiday" (244) at the time of the Spanish nationalistic festivities at Moro Castle. As the free blacks stream into Havana for their holiday, in what seems to be a rehearsal for revolution, a new sense of unity exists among them. The narrator proclaims: "Never before had the African race been so united as on that occasion, the free Negroes and mixed free people being in unison and sympathy with each other" (245).

In a footnote to his account of the holiday, Delany writes, "The term 'African race' includes the mixed as well as the pure bloods" (247). And in many ways it includes more than that, for the narrator describes at this festive gala day the emergence of a strikingly inclusive, pan-ethnic "racial" unity among the "masses of the Negroes, mulattoes and quadroons, Indians and even Chinamen" (245). In "Political Destiny," Delany declared that "the great issue, sooner or later, upon which must be disputed the world's destiny, will be a question of black and white, and every individual will be called upon for his identity with one or the other." Working against essentialist or "romantic" notions of race, Delany suggests at the end of *Blake*, as he suggests in the earlier attacks on the "Brown Societies," that "blackness" is as much a matter of politics as biology.[63]

Nevertheless, the large emphasis of the description of the festivals in the novel's closing chapters is to suggest the ways in which they serve simultaneously utopian and pragmatic ends in helping to create from within the "webbed network" of the "black Atlantic world" a Pan-African collectivity that both challenges the dominant slave powers and promises to elevate oppressed *black* peoples throughout the world.[64] In this respect, important similarities exist between the seemingly quite different projects of Blake's insurrectionism and Delany's African regeneration project. As becomes clear at the coronation of Blake's leadership at Madame Cordora's, the goal of Blake's plotting, similar to the goal of Delany's Niger plan, is to "redeem" oppressed blacks from their "almost helpless degradation" (251). Blake's conspiracy, like Delany's proposed African community, is to be guided by intelligent and charismatic black leaders committed to a liberationist Christianity; Blake's envisioned black community, like Delany's, would emerge as a global commercial power. As Blake and his cohorts move closer to putting their insurrectionist plan into effect, Delany suggests another link between his own African project and Blake's plotting: both would lead to the recovery of land "intended" for blacks. In Africa, where colonial rule usurped lands from the natives, Delany's vision of rightful ownership was highly problematic, for as I have noted, Delany's plan called for African American emigrants to "reclaim" Africa for (and from) its "degraded" native blacks. Delany's view of land and nation is just as problematic in *Blake*, despite the fact that he presents Blake as a native Cuban, for by the end of the novel Delany espouses the providential notions set forth in *Condition* and "Political Destiny": that blacks' destiny lies in the Americas, a notion that, while posing a significant challenge to U.S. Manifest Destiny, shares its colonizing and imperialistic assumptions.

In the second-to-last chapter in which Blake appears, Delany elaborates on the providential Pan-African vision guiding Blake's insurrectionist plottings in Cuba. According to Blake and his coconspirators, the impending insurrection can be justified "on the fundamental basis of original priority . . . that the western world had been originally peopled and possessed by the Indians—a colored race—and a part of the continent in Central America by a pure black race. This they urged gave them an indisputable right with every admixture of blood, to an equal, if not superior, claim to an inheritance of the Western Hemisphere" (287). Grouping the "Indians" with blacks as a unified "colored race" allows Blake and his compatriots to ignore the distinctive claims of the native inhabitants, thereby enabling an untroubled assertion of "black" Manifest Destiny in the Western Hemisphere. Blake and his group make their strongest claims on the southern regions of the hemisphere, arguing in racialist terms that the "colored races . . . were by nature adapted to the tropical regions of this part of the world" (287). By contrast, the whites of the region (like those of Africa), in addition to not being racially suited for survival in the tropics, "were there by intrusion, idle consumers subsisting by imposition" (287).

Such assertions of racial destiny and rights, as I have said, make the mulatto Madame Cordora uneasy about the actual inclusiveness of Blake's politics, about whether his notions of blackness are really meant to serve the political ends of creating a diasporic collectivity among all shades and classes of oppressed peoples. Recalling Delany's inclusive definition of the "African race" as those of "mixed as well as the pure bloods" who are "in unison and sympathy with each other," I would suggest that the novel ends up having it both ways (as novels often will), pragmatically insisting on the value of a pan-ethnic community of the oppressed, on the one hand, while mystically imagining the glorious advent of a racialized black community, on the other. That mystical sense of black community, which could be understood in relation to Delany's Freemasonry and his typological reading of Exodus, is underscored when Blake asserts to Madame Cordora the Ethiopianism of Psalms 68:31, which Delany also quotes in his *Official Report* (and Douglass quotes at the end of *Bondage*), that " 'Ethiopia shall yet stretch forth her hands unto God; Princes shall come out of Egypt' " (285). Such a passage could be read as the ultimate legitimation of Blake's (Delany's) Moses-like status as redemptive black leader.

Yet when all is said and done, Blake's goals by the end of the novel seem relatively limited, particularly as elaborated in chapter 70, the last chapter of the novel in which he actually appears (the extant version has 74 chapters). On the day of Special Indulgence, another holiday giving festive license to the blacks, Blake declares apocalyptically: "I am for war—war upon the whites" (290). But he then offers religious and political qualifications of his martial desires. In what seems to contradict the attitude toward religion that he has been preaching throughout—that blacks must act on their own in the physical world—Blake, as is consistent with the need for providential intervention implicit in his original watchcry of "Stand still and see the salvation," takes on the guise of Stowe's Dred in wanting an authorizing sign from God before unleashing violence. In the midst of a group prayer, he declares, "We are more and more sensible that without thy divine aid, we can do nothing" (292).

Blake's second qualification is even more striking, to the point of nearly undermining the entire rationale of his secret plotting. He again asserts his desire for war, but this time he brings Spain into the equation: "I now declare war against our oppressors, provided Spain does not redress our grievances!" (292). Astonishingly, the possibility of insurrection is put into the hands of the colonial power. But what could Spain possibly do to address blacks' grievances, and why does Blake offer this last olive branch to the oppressors? The answer, I think, lies in the way Delany revises the 1844 conspiracy of La Escalera through the lens of the "Africanization" scare and filibustering of the 1850s.

The conspiracy that came to be named after the tool of torture employed by the Spanish rulers—a ladder on which suspects were bound and tortured—had its origins in November 1843, when a slave rebellion occurred on a plantation in Matanzas. Captain-General Leopoldo O'Donnell used fears about possible slave conspiracies to crack down not only on the slaves but also on what he regarded as the threatening network of slaves, free blacks, Creoles, and foreigners who were plotting to wrest power from Spain.[65] In *Blake*, conspiratorial fears arise among the Spanish when a female slave reveals to government authorities the existence of an impending plot in which "all at once at de same time, each [black] is to seize a white and slaughter 'im" (271). While the revelation of the plot exacerbates the concerns of Lady Alcora, who has a nightmare of "being in the interior of Africa surrounded entirely by Negroes" (266), Captain-General Alcora works strenuously to have all accounts of impending black insurrection contradicted, for he realizes that it is in the interests of Matanzas's "American party" (298) to stoke fears of black insurrectionism as a way of deflecting attention away from U.S. plottings to acquire Cuba. Regarding the greatest threat to Cuba as coming from proslavery U.S. annexationists, Alcora refuses to act against the blacks, thus increasing fears among U.S. and Creole slaveholders that the "Africanization" of the island is in progress. The conspiratorial fears that so seize the white imagination thus owe as much to the politics of Alcora as to the plottings of Blake.

As noted, fears of the Africanization of Cuba were especially pronounced in the United States during the 1850s and contributed to increased efforts to purchase or invade the island.[66] In the final chapters of the novel, Delany portrays the captain-general's suspicions of U.S. annexationists and filibusters as exactly on the mark, as the focus shifts from Blake's impending conspiracy to an apparent conspiracy among U.S. whites to foment reactionary moves by the government against blacks (304). Because increasing conflicts between the Spanish authorities and blacks would make Cuba especially vulnerable to a filibustering invasion, the captain-general declares martial law not against plotting blacks but against what he somewhat naïvely regards as the more threatening U.S. whites. To make clear just how crucial the 1850s context is to his representation of Alcora's position here, Delany takes note of the 1851 "execution of Lopez on the garrote with many of his followers" (306). In certain respects, then, Delany, by imposing the 1850s political context on La Escalera, links himself more closely to Spain than to the slaveholding Creoles or, certainly, the U.S. annexationists. Such a linkage would imply that perhaps what his surrogate Blake most wants from Spain is that it allow blacks, through emancipation and social reforms, to become (as Blake's father once had been) part of Cuba's ruling element; he wants precisely the "Africanizing" liberalizations that U.S. annexationists feared would lead to black revolutionism but that he regards as crucial to efforts to fend off U.S. annexation.

Yet the prospect of black revolution on the island remains very real. Delany suggests as much by supplying near the end of the extant novel, as Melville supplied in the deposition near the end of "Benito Cereno," a white account of black revolutionism that, because of the blindness at the center of the account, demands of the reader a greater ability to see. According to the journalist, whose 1849 report (the narrator states) has been lifted from a U.S. periodical, the annual celebration on the sixth of January of King's Day, "El Dia de los Reyes" (299)—an occasion in which blacks are allowed publicly to "assemble according to their tribes" (299), put on the "Congo Dance" (299), "use their own language and their own songs" (301), and honor their tribal kings—performs at least two key functions for the Spanish authorities: it allows them to "threaten" the Creoles and Americans with the prospect of "Africanization," and it also provides them with a safety valve for the release of blacks' revolutionary energies. The Spanish Captain-General Roncall extends the festivities for three days in light of López's known plans for a filibustering invasion. (The novel thus collapses 1844, 1849, and 1851 with the 1850s generally.) What King's Day reveals to the reporter is how terrifying it would be if the blacks should be emancipated as part of a liberalization movement, though he concludes his account by scoffing at the possibility that blacks could be their own agents of liberation: "It would be easy on King's Day for the Negroes to free themselves, or at least to make the streets of Havana run with blood, if they only knew their power; Heaven be praised that they do not" (301).[67]

What the journalist of course fails to see is that King's Day, with its syncretic festivities and ritual inversions, signals the imminent irruption of a conspiratorial black revolution of the sort that Blake seems to have been setting in motion over the course of the novel. But just as Blake keeps his distance from the mutinous outbreak aboard the *Vulture*, so he keeps his distance from the various festive inversions at the novel's close. Instead Delany foregrounds the important role played by the militant black revolutionary Gofer Gondolier, the knife-toting palace caterer suspected by the captain-general of wanting to "establish a Negro government" (270). When confronted by two Irish patrols, it is Gofer, not Placido and Blake, who strikes them down (275). When Ambrosina Cordora, the daughter of Madame Cordora (Montego), is brutally assaulted by a white man who tears off her clothes and publicly whips her, it is Gondolier and Montego who seek immediate revenge. And it is Gondolier, not Blake, who offers the biblically vengeful, David Walker–like final words of the extant novel: "Woe be unto those devils of whites, I say!" (313).

In his 1849 *North Star* writings on Cuba, Delany looks forward to "that eventual moment, which as certain as the heavens must and will come, when the oppressed and bondmen of every origin, grade and hue under the despotism of the white race, shall determine to strike the fateful blow and remove the yoke from every neck." He imagines the possibility of a "day of deliverance" in the Americas: a "simultaneous rebellion of all the slaves in the Southern States, and throughout that island [Cuba]." In 1853 Douglass similarly imagines the possibility of a black nationalist uprising among the slaves of the Americas, warning that "Americans should remember that there are already on this Continent, and in the adjacent islands, all of 12,370,000 negroes, who only wait for the life-giving and organizing power of intelligence to mould them into one body and into a powerful nation." At the end of the novel, presumably because of Blake's marshaling offstage "intelligence," the time for such Pan-African revolutionism appears to be at hand.[68]

Redeeming the Nation

For many readers, Gondolier's expression of black rage against white oppressors seems an appropriate ending to *Blake*, as it keeps in perpetual suspension the threat of black insurrection, making the creation of white paranoia itself the potent end product of Blake's plotting.[69] Thus, despite the fact that the reputedly eighty-chapter novel ends with chapter 74, the novel can be said to have achieved a satisfying sense of completion with its vision of united blacks poised for insurrectionary violence against white enslavers. Yet it may well have been the case that rather than keeping in suspension the possibility of a bloody war between the races, or even representing its outbreak, Delany actually ended the novel with a series of relatively nonviolent scenes that enabled Blake to emerge at the helm of a regenerated society in which blackness is seen not as an exclusive or essential good but as equally worthy (or unworthy) as whiteness. The ascent to leadership of a "pure-blooded" black, as Blake and Placido suggest at the coronation scene at Madame Cordora's, would serve as a daily refutation of whites' racist beliefs in black inferiority. Occurring in such close proximity to the United States, Blake's ascent would therefore provide U.S. whites with an image not of black homicidal fury but of responsible black leadership. The hopeful suggestion of such a possible ending, then, would have been that the elevation of Delany's heroic surrogate would contribute to the emancipation and elevation of blacks in the United States.

My counterintuitive speculation about the possible existence of such an ending to *Blake* has been prompted in part by Delany's conception of his politics of blackness and nationhood circa 1863–68 as articulated in Frances Rollin's 1868 *Life and Public Services of Martin R. Delany*. Central to the portrayal of Delany's representative identity in Rollin's text is the depiction of his relationship to Douglass, who continued to play a critical role in Delany's efforts to conceive of blacks' place in the United States. Before considering Delany's perspective on Douglass during the early 1860s and its possible implications for imagining a "patriotic" ending to *Blake*, I want first to consider Douglass's perspective on Delany during this time.

Though in 1859 Douglass attacked Garnet's and Delany's respective African emigration plans as simply the latest form of black colonization — efforts by black and white racists to remove U.S. blacks from their rightful place in the nation to the "pestilential shores of Africa" — Douglass's suspicions in 1860 and early 1861 of what he termed the "pro-slavery truckling" of Lincoln eventually led him to regard emigration to Haiti as "highly advantageous to many families, and of much service to the Haytian Republic." So disturbed was Douglass by Lincoln's 1860 inaugural address, which he took as an announcement of "complete loyalty to slavery in the slave States," that in the May 1861 *Douglass' Monthly* he announced his plans to travel to Haiti so that he might "experience the feeling of being under a Government which has been administered by a race denounced as mentally and morally incapable of self government." But in the midst of the announcement he declared an abrupt change of plans, describing the outbreak of the Civil War as having "made a tremendous revolution in all things pertaining to the possible future of the colored people of the United States." Like Thomas Hamilton, he very quickly came to view the Civil War as a war of emancipation. As he remarked in July 1861, "To fight against slaveholders without fighting against slavery, is but a half-hearted business, and paralyzes the hands engaged in it."[70]

Douglass argued from late 1861 until the end of the war that the Union's best hope for victory against the slaveholders was to enlist blacks into the military so that they themselves could do battle against those who sought their "perpetual enslavement."[71] But even as he called for black participation in the war, Lincoln was exploring the possibility of colonizing blacks to the tropics of Central and South America. Sensing that colonization lay behind the administration's plans, Douglass in the January 1862 issue of his monthly answered the question of "What Shall Be Done with the Slaves If Emancipated?" with a series of rhetorical questions meant to insist on blacks' rights to U.S. citizenship: "But would you let them all stay here? — Why not? What better is *here* than *there*? Will they occupy much more room as freemen than as slaves?" But as it became increasingly clear that Lincoln regarded "there" as better than "here," Douglass began regularly to attack Lincoln for betraying the promise of the Civil War. Writing in response to Lincoln's putative remarks that colonization was "the duty and the interest of the colored people," Douglass proclaimed: "Illogical and unfair as Mr. Lincoln's statements are, they are nevertheless quite in keeping with his whole course from the beginning of his administration up to this day. . . . Mr. Lincoln is quite a genuine representative of American prejudice and negro hatred."[72]

As Douglass would have known full well, Lincoln's colonization plan of 1862 bore some similarity to Delany's emigration plan of 1854. That it did was hardly coincidental, for it is a grand irony of U.S. political history that the House committee impaneled to explore the possibility of black colonization appended as a supporting document to its July 1862 *Report of the Select Committee on Emancipation and Colonization* Delany's address to the Cleveland emigration convention, "The Political Destiny of the Colored Race on the American Continent." The congressional report, which in the manner of Douglass equated Delany's voluntaristic emigrationist program with forced colonizationism, called for the appropriation of $20 million to help settle emancipated slaves outside the borders of the United States.[73] To oppose this colonizationist mandate, Douglass had to challenge the leadership of its black progenitors, particularly Delany, who now championed black emigration not to Central and South America but to Africa. And he would once again have to address the relation of Africa to African Americans. That is precisely what he did in July and August 1862 issues of *Douglass' Monthly*, in essays on Alexander Crummell and Martin Delany.

In his review of Crummell's *The Future of Africa*, Douglass conveyed his concerns that the book may "stir up a general African spirit among the colored people of the United States" by seeming to validate "the old offensive assumption of colonizationists, that the black man is doomed to unalterable degradation in the United States." Published as Lincoln sought to remove blacks from the United States, Crummell's book, Douglass feared, could give quarter to the enemy by equating voluntary emigration with forcible colonization. But what Douglass most objected to was Crummell's contention that the future of the race was in Africa. In the strongest possible terms Douglass maintained that talented U.S. blacks could devote themselves to Africa by remaining in the United States to fight for the cause of African Americans: "No intelligent born American black man, is under the necessity of crossing the ocean to prove his devotion to the people of Africa. He can if he will, do that a little nearer home, and with as high advantage to the world, as if he were to fix his habitation in the very centre of Africa." [74]

Douglass expressed similar objections to Delany's 1862 speeches to blacks urging them to fulfill their "African" identity by emigrating to Africa. In an essay on Delany's lectures in Rochester, printed one month after his review of Crummell, Douglass despairs that the "most fashionable churches of this city were flung open to [Delany], and the most intelligent audiences assembled to hear him." In providing Delany with a platform for his African emigration program, Douglass maintains, Rochester's blacks only further encouraged racist colonizationists, for the "black man however shunned and detested when his face is turned towards America, becomes at once an object of interest and regard when his face and his steps are turned towards Africa." As he had in the past, Douglass contests Delany's racialist valorization of "the pure black uncorrupted by Caucasian blood," and as in his account of Delany's participation in the International Statistical Congress, he takes advantage of Delany's trumpeting of his own blackness to suggest that a back-to-Africa program is appropriate mainly for Delany. He thus concludes his account of Delany in this way: "He himself, is one of the very best arguments that Africa has to offer. Fine looking, broad chested, full of life and energy, shining like polished black Italian marble, and possessing a voice which when exerted to its full capacity might cause a whole troop of African Tigers to stand and tremble, he is just the man for the great mission of African civilization to which he is devoting his life and powers."[75] Douglass's celebration of Delany as a black African and not as a black American archly performs a rhetorical act of "colonization" or "emigration" that rids the nation of a leader whose politics Douglass deems harmful to the cause of black elevation in the United States.

Two months after this column appeared in *Douglass' Monthly*, Delany sent Douglass a friendly letter on the need for blacks to represent their own interests, signing it, "For self-regeneration and the redemption of Africa, I am dear sir, most sincerely your old friend and co-laborer, M. R. DELANY." But however much Delany was committed to the "regeneration and the redemption of Africa," within six months he became as ardent as Douglass in his embrace of the Civil War. Just before Delany's conversion to the war effort in early 1863, Douglass began recruiting free blacks to fight in the newly formed Fifty-fourth Massachusetts Volunteers. Delany soon joined the effort, and in March of that year his son Toussaint L'Ouverture Delany signed up for duty in the Fifty-fourth, along with two of Douglass's sons. It was only after Toussaint survived the regiment's bloody attack on Fort Wagner in July 1863 that Delany seemed to have completely committed himself to the war against the South. He applied for the post of surgeon in black regiments, contracted with the state of Connecticut to recruit troops for its black divisions, and, in a letter of December 1863 to Secretary of War Edwin Stanton, volunteered "to recruit Colored Troops in any of the Southern or sceded [sic] states."[76]

But what was the relationship of Delany's support for the Civil War to his African regeneration project, his vision of Pan-African insurrectionism in *Blake*, his interactions with Douglass, and his ongoing efforts to fashion himself as the representative black leader of the period? Delany suggestively pointed to the significance of these interrelationships in the account of his life he provided Frances Rollin in the fall and winter of 1867–68 for her *Life and Public Services of Martin R. Delany*.

At the time he shared his life history with Rollin, Delany was an officer at the Freedmen's Bureau in South Carolina. Wishing to present himself as a model U.S. citizen, Delany has virtually nothing to say about his meetings with John Brown, his insurrectionary novel *Blake*, or his Niger project (in a single sentence, he refers to "his expedition into Central Africa"). What appears in the biography instead, in the account of Delany circa 1859–63, is a complete misrepresentation of the facts — a misrepresentation that nonetheless suggests how Delany made sense of them in the wake of having committed himself to the war effort in 1863. Rollin writes of Delany's response when news of "the secession of South Carolina reached Great Britain": "With almost prophetic vision he saw the great work apportioned for his race in the impending struggle. Therefore he turned his thoughts homeward to prepare himself for his portion of it." The "great work apportioned for his race," in Rollin's telling, turns out not to have been promoting African emigration, which Delany in fact continued to do during 1861 and 1862, but rather, like Douglass, to have been encouraging Northerners to regard the Civil War as a war of emancipation. Instead of urging blacks to journey to Africa or even to support a limited project of selective emigration, as Douglass had suggested was the intent of Delany's 1862 Rochester lectures, Delany, according to Rollin, was in fact attempting to make money for the Union side by selling his Africa book, *Official Report*, to "the most refined and influential of society."[77]

More important, Rollin maintains that Delany lectured on Africa during 1861–2 because he believed that was the best way to bring "forward the claims of his race to the war." In this conception of things, the more *African* African Americans regard themselves as being, the less degraded they will feel, the more respect they will gain from whites, and the greater the possibility of their U.S. *Americanization*. It is noteworthy in this regard that in Rollin's book Delany for the first time publicly offers his family genealogy as traced back to Africa. Delany's purposes in offering this genealogy have regularly been misinterpreted as a sign of his continuing commitment to a back-to-Africa program. But in claiming to be able to trace his family lineage to "native Africans — on the father's side, pure Golah, on the mother's Mandingo" — and in further asserting that his father's father was a "chieftain" and his mother's father was "an African prince" who was "heir to the kingdom which was then the most powerful of Central Africa," Delany wants to suggest not that he should return to Africa but that he is a sort of John Adams natural aristocrat who rightly belongs in a leadership role in the United States. Near the end of the war, Lincoln himself ratified Delany's claims to leadership by commissioning him the first black major in the Union army.[78]

Douglass had wanted a similar commission. In July 1863 he met with Lincoln to call for equal treatment of blacks in the army, and he was led to believe, both by Lincoln and Stanton, that he would soon be named an officer. So buoyed was he by his meeting that, as William S. McFeely notes, he suspended the publication of *Douglass' Monthly* because he expected to receive orders "to take up his commission as the first black officer in the United States Army." But the offer never came, perhaps (as Benjamin Quarles and McFeely speculate) because Lincoln thought it best to move slowly on a commission that risked racial polarization. One year later Douglass again met with Lincoln, this time to propose a plan of having Northern blacks infiltrate behind Southern lines and encourage slave flight and rebellion. As Douglass's subsequent letter to Lincoln of 29 August 1864 suggests, he expected to be named the "General ag[en]t" to help carry out the plan.[79] Again, an offer never came. Instead, when Lincoln was at last prepared to commission the first black major in February 1865, he chose Delany.

In the Rollin biography, Delany attempts to show why he was the obvious choice for this commission. In a stunning act of historical revisionism (and distortion) that trumps Douglass's "colonizing" Africanization of his "co-laborer," Delany presents himself as *the* African American who was most responsible for convincing Douglass to support the Civil War as a war of emancipation. Delany tells of how in 1862 he visited Douglass in Rochester to make the case for the war and Lincoln, saying that before leaving he "had the satisfaction of hearing Mr. Douglass express himself more favorably editorially in his able journal." Because of "this change of opinion in my great-hearted friend," Delany states, there came in 1863 "a special official request for Mr. Douglass to visit Washington." According to Rollin, a grateful Douglass developed an even greater admiration for his former coeditor and friend, to the point that when "an accomplished European lady" attacked Delany for his support of Lincoln, Douglass came to his defense, proclaiming, "Madam, you do not know the gentleman with whom you are conversing; if there be one man among us to whose opinion I would yield on the subject of government generally, that man is the gentleman now before you." In *Life and Public Services of Martin R. Delany*, it is that "gentleman," not Douglass, who first develops a plan to infiltrate Southern lines with black troops. Rollin tells of how Delany presented "his plans to his always noble-hearted friend, Frederick Douglass, [who] gave [Delany] encouragement, adding that he was no soldier himself."[80] And she writes that it was Delany, not Douglass, who, during a private meeting with Lincoln, proposed the specifics of how to carry out such a mission.

In an account that would have to be dismissed as fiction were there not the "corroborating" fact that (as Rollin notes) Lincoln wrote to Stanton of his admiration for Delany shortly before Delany received his commission as major, Rollin includes in her book Delany's testimony, in his "own language," of his "PRIVATE COUNCIL AT WASHINGTON" with Abraham Lincoln. According to Delany, he told Lincoln he sought council with him not to ask for any special favors but to "propose something to you, which I think will be beneficial to the nation in this critical hour of her peril." He then reveals his plan to end the war:

> I propose, sir, an army of blacks, commanded entirely by black officers, except such whites as may volunteer to serve; this army to penetrate through the heart of the South, and make conquests, with the banner of Emancipation unfurled, proclaiming freedom as they go, sustaining and protecting it by arming the emancipated, taking them as fresh troops, and leaving a few veterans among the new freedmen, when occasion requires, keeping this banner unfurled until every slave is free, according to the letter of your proclamation. I would also take from those already in the service all that are competent for commission officers, and establish at once in the South a camp of instructions. By this we could have in about three months an army of forty thousand blacks in motion, the presence of which anywhere would itself be a power irresistible. You should have an army of blacks, President Lincoln, commanded entirely by blacks, the sight of which is required to give confidence to the slaves, and retain them to the Union, stop foreign intervention, and speedily bring the war to a close.

According to the Rollin/Delany text, Lincoln exultantly proclaims in response: "This . . . is the very thing I have been looking and hoping for; but nobody offered it. I have thought it over and over again. I have talked about it; I hoped and prayed for it. . . . When I issued my Emancipation Proclamation, I had this thing in contemplation." As Delany and Rollin would have it, it took Martin Delany to bring to fruition Lincoln's emancipatory vision. Delany's fashioning of his representative identity as black leader, which I have been arguing centrally informs both *Blake* and his African regeneration project, is at last simultaneously fulfilled and consecrated when, as if inspired, Lincoln, "suddenly turning" toward Delany, beseeches him (and not Douglass), "Will you take command?"[81]

From Rollin's perspective, it is precisely Lincoln's recognition that Delany (and not Douglass) is the proper person to take command that promises at last to bring about black elevation in the United States.

In a letter included in Rollin's biography, Lincoln refers to Delany as "this most extraordinary and intelligent black man," thereby suggesting the importance of both talent and race in his decision to commission Delany a major. Delany's acceptance of the commission allows him finally to reclaim in the United States what Rollin refers to as his "lost and *regal* [African] inheritance"; ironically, in Rollin's account it is precisely Delany's princely Africanness that legitimates his U.S. Americanness.[82]

Rollin underscores this point by concluding her biography with an assessment that once again plays off the mulatto Douglass against the racialized "identity" of Delany, declaring approvingly that "few, if any, . . . have so entirely consecrated themselves to the idea of race as [Delany's] career shows. His religion, his writings, every step in life, is based upon this idea. His creed begins and ends with it — that the colored race can only obtain their true status as men, by relying on their identity. . . . This he claims as the foundation of his manhood. Upon this point, Mr. Frederick Douglass once wittily remarked, 'Delany stands so straight that he leans a little backward.'" Delany's willingness to "lean a little backward," so Rollin avers, "has triumphantly demonstrated negro capability for greatness in every sphere wherein he has acted." The example of Delany's inspired leadership, she states, echoing the goals so central to his African project, to his heroic surrogate Blake, to his Reconstruction work in South Carolina, indeed, to his entire career, shall inspire blacks to begin "their onward march towards that higher civilization."[83] Whereas *Blake*'s Masonic and Pan-African vision would seem to conceive of a black diasporic community that confutes the very idea of the bordered nation, the suggestion in Rollin, which no doubt echoes Delany's own perspective on the promise of Reconstruction, is that if blacks wish to "stand still and see the salvation," they should do so, under the aegis of the black major, in the United States. At least that is how things stood with Delany in 1868.

Epilogue

True Patriotism/
True Stability

 In his 1881 *Life and Times of Frederick Douglass,* Douglass provided his own narrative account of his interviews with Lincoln. Douglass may have been less fanciful than Delany in the ways in which he figured himself in relation to Lincoln. Nevertheless, there are striking similarities between Douglass's and Delany's storytelling, in large part because they both wished to link themselves, as deliverers of the race, to the historical figure who came to be seen by antislavery blacks and whites alike as an American Moses. At his "first interview with this great man," in August 1863, Douglass is greeted cordially by Lincoln: "'I know who you are, Mr. Douglass. . . . Sit down, I am glad to see you.'" By the end of the interview, Douglass has successfully made the case for the fairer treatment of black troops and is promised a commission. At his second interview, this time arranged by Lincoln in August 1864, Douglass is asked for his ideas on "the means most desirable . . . to induce the slaves in the rebel states to come within the federal lines." He proposes something like what Delany claimed he proposed, to organize a group "of colored men, whose business should be somewhat after the original plan of John

Brown, to go into the rebel states, beyond the lines of our armies, and carry the news of emancipation, and urge the slaves to come within our boundaries." During the course of the interview, an absorbed Lincoln refuses to cut off the discussion in order to meet with Governor Buckingham of Connecticut. Although Douglass confesses that his inclusion of this incident "may savor a little of vanity on my part," Lincoln's choice of Douglass over a white governor becomes the focus (and main point) of the account, as it serves to ratify Douglass's representative identity as black leader. As Douglass remarks on Lincoln's interest in his opinions, "I am quite sure that the main thing which gave me consideration with him was my well-known relation to the colored people of the Republic."[1] Though at other places in *Life and Times* Douglass presents himself as transcending the bounds of race, his point here is to show that Lincoln, in dealing in equitable fashion with him, reveals himself as prepared to deal in equitable fashion with all African Americans. For Douglass, their exchanges incarnate the very promise of Reconstruction.

The relation of Delany and Douglass to African Americans and "America" has, of course, been one of the central subjects of this book. Typically, critics have viewed Douglass as the figure who was more willing to interact with white culture, Delany as the figure more resistant. Douglass's putative assimilationism has been attacked by some, but W. E. B. Du Bois offers a strong reading of Douglass, particularly after the Civil War, as desiring what could be termed a contradiction (or oxymoron): "assimilation *through* self-assertion." Du Bois presents this desire as consistent with "the ideals of [Douglass's] early manhood." As for the putatively self-assertive, black separatist Delany, Wilson Moses remarks that after the emancipation of the slaves, "Delany revealed the assimilationist and integrationist aspirations always basic to his personality." In interesting ways, Du Bois and Moses suggest a reversal of the conventional binary understanding of Delany and Douglass that points to what could be viewed as inconsistencies in their positions. In the late 1840s, the *North Star*'s coeditors, seemingly anticipating the charge of inconsistency, asserted in separate statements the large principles undergirding their politics and writings. Delany, in an issue of 1848, proclaimed that guiding his commitment to black elevation was "True Patriotism" — an "uncompromising hostility to that which interferes with [man's] divine God-given rights" — a patriotism that, in a racist nation, would inevitably make him seem out of step, perhaps even a "felon and outlaw." Douglass concurred on the risks of undertaking antiracist and antislavery reforms, and in an 1849 issue of the *North Star* he announced his commitment to (in)consistency: "The only truly consistent man is he who will, for the sake of being right today, contradict what he said wrong yesterday. . . . True stability consists not in being of the same opinion now as formerly, but in a fixed principle of honesty, ever urging us to the adoption or rejection of that which may seem to us true or false at the ever-present now."[2]

Responding to the contingencies of the "ever-present now," Delany and Douglass could at times enmesh themselves in contradictions, as they periodically revised their self-representations, political positions, and strategies for black elevation, often in response to each other. In crucial ways, Delany and Douglass were never more "consistent" than when engaged with each other, as their competitive interactions helped bring to focus issues of race and nation central to their representative ambitions. As a black who overcame slavery, Douglass privileged models of self-possessive individualism and thus appropriated the Franklinian model of individual/national uplift as a source of his leadership. Distrustful of what he regarded as Douglass's concessions to white racist culture, Delany privileged his black skin as a sign of his historical links to the leadership tradition inherent in Freemasonry's glorious origins in classical Africa. But this schematic model of their respective attitudes toward representative leadership is not meant to suggest that Douglass was unconcerned with racial identity or that Delany was oblivious to U.S. nationalism. In this concluding section, I want briefly (and sketchily) to trace their respective careers after the Civil War, focusing on several key moments when each man's politics and self-conception were brought into relief in response to his contending other.

In "True Patriotism," Delany predicted that "contempt and neglect" would be the patriot's rewards for honest labors, and to some extent he anticipated his own fate in the United States. Immediately following the war, however, the still quite eminent Major Delany was appointed a subassistant commissioner in the Freedmen's Bureau in Beaufort, South Carolina, where he emerged as one of the most zealous African American proponents of Reconstruction. Initially the white officers at the bureau suspected Delany of being a "thorough hater of the white race," but in an "inconsistent" reversal of the insurrectionary Pan-African politics of *Blake*, he soon proved his mettle by taking on the responsibility of ferreting out possible conspiracies among South Carolina's blacks. In response to rumors that the "negroes of Port Royal Island had matured an insurrection, to take place on Christmas night" of 1865, Delany made "a requisition for a detachment of the 21st United States Colored Troops" and preemptively led them on Port Royal on Christmas Eve. Though he found that the conspiracy existed mainly in the minds of what Rollin terms "insurrection-haunted whites," it may well have been (as in *Blake*) that the creation of anxiety among whites was precisely what the blacks had in mind in the first place. If so, Delany had become the victim of the kind of plotting he had explored so perceptively in his novel.[3]

Despite being at a hierarchical remove from the blacks of the region, Delany regarded black leadership as a form of racial solidarity that promised to improve the lot of the freed people. Convinced that possibilities for black elevation in the United States were never better than right after the Civil War, Delany in 1865 developed a plan for "a domestic triple alliance," in effect "a copartnership" among Northern capital, Southern white landowners, and black labor, with "the net profits being equally shared between the three." Central to the implementation of the plan over the next several years was his managerial leadership. Despite being a subassistant commissioner, Delany placed himself at the center of all negotiations between white capital and black labor, emerging (much to the displeasure of most whites and many blacks) as a "boss" of the region. Delany wrote the contracts for his district, made sure that all black laborers renounced alcoholic beverages before going to work, and even set up his own police force. In a report submitted from the Freedmen's Bureau, Delany stated: "On the Plantations throughout my Bureau District, I have adopted police regulations. On each place the best man selected by the people, is appointed by me as Head man or Chief of Police, with authority to choose four assistants. . . . He is to report all his doings once a month to Head Quarters." Even Delany's sympathetic biographer Ullman remarks that in overseeing relations among capitalists, planters, and freedmen, Delany could be "downright dictatorial."[4]

In contrast to Delany, Douglass appears more consistent and egalitarian in his commitment to Reconstruction, as he tended to argue for Americans' need to transcend racial differences by blending into a "composite nationality." Prepared to elide issues of race from the national ideology of self-making, Douglass became implicated in what was arguably a misguided strategy. For the elision of race went hand in hand with racism. As representative self-made African American, Douglass was cynically embraced by the Republican party as an African American who both embodied and transcended race. Such a strategy allowed the Republicans to make symbolic gestures toward blacks by gesturing toward Douglass. Though Douglass was not unaware of how he was being used, he had come to believe that African Americans' hopes for elevation were inextricably linked to the party that fought against slavery, and so he attempted to rise to the challenge of the representative identity the Republican party confirmed upon his person, accepting such positions as assistant secretary to the commission of inquiry to Santo Domingo (1871) and president of the ill-fated Freedmen's Bank (1874). He viewed these commissions as hopeful signs that the days of racism (and race) were over in the United States.[5]

His optimism fueled his patriotic nationalism. As a result of his work in Santo Domingo, for example, Douglass came to support the movement to annex what is now called the Dominican Republic. Putting nationalism above race, he argued in a speech of 1873 for a humane and enlightened imperialism: "It may, indeed, be important to know what Santo Domingo can do for us; but it is vastly more important to know what we can do, and ought to do, for Santo Domingo." According to Douglass, "a large majority of the people of that island" supported annexation, and they hoped for annexation (Douglass implies) for the same reason that blacks hoped to be part of the United States: "They want Saxon and Protestant civilization." And so Douglass enjoined his auditors, "Let us lift them up to our high standard of nationality."[6] For Douglass in this particular speech, nationality eclipsed race, or to put it another way, "Saxon and Protestant civilization" became emblematic of race.

In short, around the time of the passage of the Fifteenth Amendment, Delany and Douglass had charted out career paths that risked implicating them in contradictions and inconsistencies. Douglass emerged as the representative African American in the North who, for the most part, was a spokesman for the Republicans' project of uplifting the nation. Accordingly, nation more than race became the primary focus of his lectures, as he merged race and nation in the figure of his own uplifted body. Delany, on the other hand, can seem retrospectively the more ingenious improviser. His suspicions of whites led him resourcefully to seek unconventional ways of empowering himself and African Americans. At the Freedmen's Bureau he managed to take control of constituencies that otherwise controlled blacks—Northern capitalists and Southern landowners—and in doing so helped numerous freed people find jobs. At the same time, he never lost sight of the fact that blacks were enormously disadvantaged in the United States, despite the Reconstructionist rhetoric that argued otherwise, and even as he was working at the Freedmen's

Bureau, he encouraged some blacks to emigrate to Liberia under the aegis of the American Colonization Society.[7]

If Douglass can be viewed as a U.S. nationalist whose racial thinking surfaced at times of stress or dissonance, Delany can be viewed as a racial thinker whose U.S. nationalism expressed itself at moments of hopefulness (such as when he was telling his life history to Frances Rollin in 1867–68). The two men seemed particularly hopeful (and of a piece) in 1870, for in the spring of that year the Fifteenth Amendment, granting African American men the right to vote, had become the law of the land. Douglass joyfully proclaimed on the significance of the amendment: "It means that color is no longer to be a calamity; that race is to be no longer a crime; and that liberty is to be the right of all." Delany too was buoyed by the amendment's adoption, and he joined with Douglass in becoming a contributor to the *New National Era*. Established in Washington, D.C., shortly before the passage of the Fifteenth Amendment, the paper, edited at first by J. Sella Martin and eventually by Douglass, sought to instruct blacks on their rights and duties as citizens in the "new era" of Reconstruction. As Douglass remarked in the inaugural issue of 27 January 1870: "The time has come for the colored men of the country to assume the duties and responsibilities of their own existence." In an effort to champion these goals, Delany submitted four essays to the paper on the duties and responsibilities of black citizenship.[8]

One year later, however, in August 1871, Delany sent a letter to Douglass, now editor in chief of the *New National Era*, suggestive of their sharp differences on race, nation, and Reconstruction. This was not the first time that Delany had criticized Douglass after the Civil War, for in February 1866 he had written an open letter, reprinted in several newspapers, chastising "the noble Douglass" and other blacks for calling on President Johnson at the White House to demand that he change his policies toward blacks. Like Harriet Beecher Stowe, who thought it would be best for the nation if blacks gradually became part of the national polity, Delany urged Douglass and the other blacks in the delegation not to "misjudge the president, but believe, as I do, that he means to do right; that his intentions are good." Declaring in nationalist terms that "we are one in interest and destiny in America," Delany concluded his letter with advice to the black leaders that strikingly revised his use of Exodus in *Blake*: "In the cause of our country you and I have done, and still are doing, our part, and a great and just nation will not be unmindful of it. God is just. Stand still and see his salvation." The following year, in a letter to Henry

Highland Garnet printed in the *New York Tribune* and other papers, Delany similarly spoke out against the "nonsense" of nominating a black vice president, declaring, "Let colored men be satisfied to take things like other men, in their natural course and time."[9] By 1871, however, he was no longer satisfied, and he focused his ire (and hopes) on Douglass.

Delany begins his 1871 letter to Douglass with a cordial reference to their meeting in Rochester ten years earlier "to discuss and reconcile ourselves to President Lincoln's war policy." He then offers a history lesson on what has happened since then, commenting on how at the end of the Civil War the blacks of the South were at a distinct disadvantage because they required political leaders sympathetic to their position but instead got Northern white racists who "sought by that guile and deception, known only to demagogues, under the acceptable appellations of Yankee, Republican, and Radical, to intrude themselves into the confidence of the blacks, and place themselves at their head as leaders." Convinced that the Republican party has been taking blacks' support for granted, Delany states that he had abandoned his gradualist position of the mid-1860s to demand an immediate place for worthy blacks in the government's power structure. His emphasis on the need to place blacks of distinct accomplishment in leadership positions is in line with his elitist politics of black elevation and regeneration of the past thirty years or so. What is new in his letter is his "affirmative action" demand that "colored people" have governmental positions "in proportional relation to their population in the U.S." Remaining true to the politics of "blood" in "Political Destiny" and *Blake*, Delany makes it clear that he has something very specific in mind when he refers to black leaders: "pure black men," or what he calls "the real Negro." Asserting that white racist Republicans seek to divide the black community against itself by refusing to appoint any but "mixed bloods" to government positions, Delany implicitly suggests that Douglass has obtained his recent appointment on the Santo Domingo commission because he is a mulatto. Delany states, "It is a fact most noticeable in executive appointments of colored men; there are none of pure black men, the pure negro race, but all have been more carefully selected from those having an admixture of white blood."[10]

To remedy the situation, Delany proposes a quota system based on blood and proportionality. He explains:

The entire population of the African race [in the United States] is about five millions; one-eighth of the whole American people. According to the ratio of population, they are entitled to thirty-two (32) representatives in Congress, and a corresponding ratio of official appointments. Allowing one and a half million to be mixed blood, leaves three and a half millions of pure-blooded blacks. These, by the foregoing estimate, are entitled to about twenty-six (26) representatives, with their ratio of Federal offices. And yet these three and a half millions of people, with their political claims, have been persistently neglected and almost ignored, by both general and State governments (except in cases of incompetent blacks for mere political purposes, to conciliate the ignorant blacks), while their more favored brethren of mixed blood have received all the places of honor, profit, and trust, intended to represent the race.

Declaring that he himself is "no candidate nor aspirant for office," Delany concludes his letter with an audacious plea to Douglass, "in the name of a common race," to join him in the project of developing such a racial quota system that, whatever Delany's claims about his desires for office, would work against Douglass and for Delany.[11]

In response, Douglass cordially praises Delany "for the elaborate letter with which you have honored me," and he applauds his "boldness, candor, and manly independence." But quickly he moves to the defense of the Republican party. While agreeing with Delany that some of the freedmen could have been the victims of demagogues, Douglass underscores the progress that Southern blacks have made. And he implicitly uses this defense of Southern blacks' economic and educational progress to attack Delany. Referring to "the colored people of South Carolina," Douglass declares: "It does not seem to me that their degeneracy is so complete as you describe it to be. Were you not M. R. Delany, I should say that the man who wrote thus of the manners of the colored people of South Carolina had taken his place with the old planters. You certainly cannot be among those of the South who prefer the lash-inspired manners of the past. . . . All that old-fashioned *How-do-Aunty?* and *Sarvent massa* manners is out of joint with our times." That sort of behavior may be "out of joint," but as Douglass probably knew, Delany, in his efforts to forward his "domestic triple alliance," *had* made demands for subserviency and obedience that, in certain respects, aligned him with the "old planters."[12]

As for the more central issue of race, while Douglass proclaims a willingness to join Delany in denouncing mulatto societies and notions of "brown" superiority, he ridicules his proposal for racial quotas. He points out that "the present Republican administration" has recently appointed two clerks "who are without doubt as dark as even Mr. Delany would require." But rather than questioning Delany on the rather difficult issue of how to make distinctions between the "pure" black and the mulatto, and rather than challenging Delany's notion of the "real" black, Douglass addresses the problems he sees as inherent in any race-based quota system:

> As a matter of arithmetic your figures are faultless. The mulattoes, on a solid census basis, ought to have so many offices, the blacks so many, and other classes and nationalities should have offices according to their respective numbers. The idea is equal and admirable in theory; but does it not already seem to you a little absurd as a matter of practice? . . . According to the census, the colored people of the country constitute one-eighth of the whole American people. Upon your statistical principle, the colored people of the United States ought, therefore, not only to hold one-eighth of all offices in the country, but they should own one-eighth of all the property, and pay one-eighth of all the taxes of the country. Equal in numbers, they should, of course, be equal in everything else. They should constitute one-eighth of the poets, statesmen, scholars, authors, and philosophers of the country. . . . The Negro should edit just one-eighth of all the books written and printed in the United States; and, in a word, be one-eighth in everything. Now, my old friend, there is no man in the United States who knows better than you do that equality of numbers has nothing to do with equality of attainments.

Appealing to Delany's elitism, Douglass, through his reductio ad absurdum, attempts to make clear that if he has moved up higher in the political hierarchy than Delany, that may well tell the story of their relative attainments. Though rejecting Delany's proposals, Douglass concludes his letter with an (ironic) offer of fellowship: "Let me assure you of my cordial co-operation with you in all well-directed efforts to elevate and improve our race."[13]

That fellowship never developed. Disillusioned by the Republicans' policies, Delany in 1874 broke with South Carolina's Republican party and accepted the nomination for lieutenant governor of the Democrat-led Independent Republicans. In an October issue of the *New National Era*, Douglass printed a piece warning that if Delany and his running mate were to win the election, there would ensue "the inevitable destruction of Republicanism." Though his ticket lost the 1874 election, two years later

Delany supported the Democratic candidate for governor, Wade Hampton. His endorsement of Hampton was printed on the front page of the *Charleston News and Courier*. As Delany explained, he decided to embrace the party of the Confederacy because he believed the Democrats offered the best hope "to bring about *a union of the two races, white and black*, (by black I mean all colored people,) *in one common interest in the State*, with all the rights and privileges of each inviolable and sacredly respected." Reviled by many of South's Carolina's blacks, who heckled and even shot at Delany while he stumped for Hampton, Delany was awarded a judgeship when the Democrat won the election. But Delany's hopes for the Democratic party in South Carolina were never realized, and by the late 1870s, he was arguing that "blacks" and "whites" belonged apart. In response to the 1877 withdrawal of federal troops from the Southern states and the emergence of the Jim Crow laws that would lead to the "separate but equal" principles of *Plessy v. Ferguson*, Delany developed a reactive "separate but more than equal" perspective that once again envisioned blacks achieving their destiny by emigrating from the United States. In the midst of the black exodus movement from the South of the late 1870s, Delany urged blacks to consider voluntary emigration to Liberia.[14]

In 1873 Douglass referred to efforts by the American Colonization Society (ACS) to encourage Liberian emigration as indicative of the society's "diabolical" belief "that the black man has no right here as a freeman." By the late 1870s Delany had come to believe that the ACS was responding responsibly and hopefully to the dire situation of the freed people in the South. Delany was not alone in taking a despairing view of the situation of blacks in the South, for with the return of racist black codes, Southern blacks began to depart en masse for what was believed to be a more hospitable environment in the North and Midwest. Douglass viewed the movement as somewhat akin to "emigration." In 1879 he declared that "Exodusters" have done more harm to "business and enterprise by schemes of emigration than from any other cause." And he declared in his 1881 *Life and Times* that Exodus typology was simply inapplicable to post–Civil War America: "Exodus is a medicine, not food; it is for disease, not health; it is not to be taken from choice, but from necessity." Delany, on the other hand, encouraged the black "exodus," both to the North and to Africa, as a way of demonstrating to Southern whites just how dependent they were on black labor. In 1878 he became a member of the board of directors of the Liberian Exodus Joint Stock Steam

Ship Company, he negotiated with Liberian officials for land for emigrants from Georgia and South Carolina, and he acted as a public spokesperson for the company. The ACS's ship, the *Azor*, which left Charleston in the spring of 1878, was forced to land at Sierra Leone and returned to South Carolina in considerable debt. By 1879 the debts amounted to over four thousand dollars, and Delany, who was named chairman of the Committee on Finance, attempted to raise the money, but eventually the ship was sold at auction at a considerable loss. Though this particular plan failed, Delany clung to the hope that he could obtain a federal appointment that would help to finance his emigration to Africa, which he referred to in 1880 as "the field of my destined labor."[15]

The idea of "destiny" informs his *Principia of Ethnology* (1879), a compelling and disturbing statement of Delany's late 1870s thinking on the origin and characteristics of races. Read out of context, the short book presents absolutist notions of racial difference that can seem quite noxious. Read in the context of the failure of Reconstruction, *Principia* is one of Delany's most moving efforts to argue for black pride and to make sense of the failure of his efforts to achieve black elevation in the United States. That failure, Delany argues, was providential, for as he elaborates in his treatise, he has come to believe that God's plan for the "Progress of Civilization" requires that each race should pursue its own "destiny" apart from other races. As Delany tells the story, God, concerned that "the Human Race" was not progressing as quickly as possible, chose to create three races from Noah's sons, all of whom "differed in complexion." The "yellow" Shem went to Asia, the "swarthy" Ham to Africa, and the "white" Japheth to Europe. They "emigrated" because it was God's "design" to fix "in the people a desire to be separated by reason of race affinity." As in *Origin and Objects of Ancient Freemasonry*, Delany wants to show that God has a "prophetic destiny" for the followers and descendants of Ham, and much of *Principia* celebrates the ancient civilizations of Ethiopia and Egypt.[16] The burden on black people in the present day, Delany argues, is to recover that greatness.

Thus, in a radical departure from Douglass's calls for Americans to transcend race, Delany urges blacks (and whites) to embrace race as the *ne plus ultra* of individual and group identity. The book concludes, then, with a radical critique of miscegenation as a blasphemous act that depletes the purity of the races and has harmful effects for the progress of humanity in general. Delany explains, "We place on record the fact, that the races as such, especially white and black, are indestructible; that *miscegenation* as popularly understood—the running out of two races, or several, into a *new race*—cannot take place." Delany's utopian vision, then, as expressed in 1879, is of racial purity achieved by black emigration to Africa: "There is no doubt but that the time will come when there will be but the three original sterling races as grand divisions of people on the face of the whole earth, with their natural complexions of yellow, black and white." This is a vision that both counters and contributes to contemporaneous white efforts to impose a color line, though his intention here is not to argue for black disfranchisement but rather for the connection between the regeneration of Africa and the empowerment of the black diaspora. Accordingly, he concludes the text by invoking the Ethiopianism of Psalms 68:31.[17]

Delany's argument against racial intermarriage, oddly enough, can seem to pose a proleptic challenge to Douglass's 1884 marriage to his former secretary, the white woman Helen Pitts, approximately a year and a half after the death of his first wife, Anna Douglass, an illiterate black woman. In his writings of the period, Douglass attempted to transcend color by eliminating color (something that Delany had argued in *Principia* was an impossibility), contending that "God almighty made but one race." As opposed to Delany's call for blacks to achieve their destiny in Africa, Douglass continued to argue for blacks' destiny in the United States, declaring in a speech of 1883, "Assimilation and not isolation is our true policy and our natural destiny." One year later he championed intermarriage as an assimilationist program that promised to make racial distinctions in the United States a thing of the past. "I adopt the theory," he stated to an interviewer shortly after marrying Helen Pitts, "that in time the varieties of races will be blended into one."[18]

But though Douglass could seem starkly opposed to Delany on intermarriage and "miscegenation," the pressures brought to bear on him by his marriage to a white woman and his own increasing concerns about the failure of Reconstruction led him to become more of a racial thinker in the final years of his life. Concerned about the harmful affects of white "race pride," Douglass by the late 1880s was regularly affirming his black identity. Though he never encouraged emigrationism, he celebrated Egypt, as he had in his 1854 "Claims of the Negro," as a black nation that should be central to African Americans' racial pride. He explained in the 1892 edition of *Life and Times* that he traveled to Egypt in 1887 with his wife Helen in the "hope to turn my visit to some account in combating American prejudice against the darker colored races of mankind, and at the same time to raise colored people somewhat in their own estimation and thus stimulate them to higher endeavors." In the final years of his life he sounded most like Delany in rejecting notions of racial "blending" and affirming the need for exemplary black leadership. In an address on Haiti at the 1893 World's Columbia Exposition, Douglass pridefully referred to Haiti as "the only self-made Black Republic in the world" and thus as an inspiration to black peoples of the United States: "The people of Haiti, by reason of ancestral identity, are more interesting to the colored people of the United States than to all others, for the Negro, like the Jew, can never part with his identity and race." That same year he remarked that he wished the famous scientist Benjamin Banneker had been "entirely black" so that his intelligence would not be credited to his white blood (with the rhetorical implication being that Douglass himself wished to be "entirely black"). As a critic of white racism in the 1880s and 1890s, Douglass had come to share a good deal with Delany, perhaps in response to the assimilationism and accommodationism of the new star on the horizon: Booker T. Washington. Nonetheless, in his last great public speech, "Lessons of the Hour" (1894), Douglass denounced an overwrought attention to Africa and to collective emigration, proclaiming: "All this native land talk is nonsense. The native land of the American negro is America."[19]

A final scene: On New Year's Day of 1883, approximately forty black leaders gathered at Freund's restaurant in Washington, D.C., to celebrate the twentieth anniversary of the Emancipation Proclamation. Indicative of the representative status Douglass had achieved by this time, the banquet was also in honor of Douglass's achievements. Delany, still in search of a government appointment to fund his emigration to Africa, was among the invited guests. In his remarks at the dinner, Douglass proclaimed to the group: "You have given me to-night every reason to be proud of my career and my company," though he allowed, "I have not the vanity to suppose that the gentlemen who have invited me here, meant by this entertainment to approve everything which I have said and done, written and spoken, during more than forty years of my public life." In fact, he noted, perhaps gazing upon Delany, "there are some here from whom I have been compelled by irresistible conviction to differ widely, and to state that difference in a manner as pronounced and striking as I could possibly command." Having testified to his own integrity, Douglass then affirmed the principles that, he maintained, have guided his work for black elevation in the United States: "Nothing has occurred within these twenty years which has dimmed my hopes or caused me to doubt that the emancipated people of this country will avail themselves of their opportunities, and by enterprise, industry, invention, discovery and manly character vindicate the confidence of their friends and put to silence and to shame the gloomy predictions of all their enemies." Following the speech, most of the guests offered toasts to the future of African Americans in the United States. Delany, however, urged his compatriots to join him in a countertoast to the linked destinies of the blacks of America and Martin Delany: "The Republic of Liberia."[20]

The hopeful assimilationist, the African dreamer: Douglass and Delany were in character at this Emancipation Proclamation celebration. From the time of their break in 1849, the former coeditors were never *more* in character than when they were debating each other, thinking of each other, or speaking in the same room. We continue to think of Delany and Douglass in the terms in which they defined themselves at this dinner — in the terms, that is to say, in which they defined themselves against each other in their pursuit of the status of representative African American leader. But like other moments in their histories that I have spotlighted, this dinner is a single moment in history that fails to convey the full complexity of their social and political visions, their deviations from their best-known public stances, their creative elaborations in their writings, and their dynamic impact on the culture. The consistency and the promise of Delany's "true patriotism" and Douglass's "true stability" lie in the differences that mask the likenesses.

Notes

ABBREVIATIONS USED IN THE NOTES

BAP   *The Black Abolitionist Papers*, 5 vols., ed. C. Peter Ripley et al. (Chapel Hill:
         University of North Carolina Press, 1985–92)
FDP   *Frederick Douglass' Paper*
NS   *North Star*
Papers   *The Frederick Douglass Papers*, ser. 1, *Speeches, Debates, and Interviews*,
         5 vols., ed. John W. Blassingame et al. (New Haven: Yale University Press,
         1979–92)
Rollin   Frank A. Rollin [Frances A. Rollin], *Life and Public Services of Martin R.
         Delany* (1868; rpt., Boston: Lee and Shephard, 1883), in *Two Biographies by
         African American Women*, ed. William L. Andrews (New York: Oxford
         University Press, 1991)
Writings *The Life and Writings of Frederick Douglass*, 5 vols., ed. Philip S. Foner
         (New York: International Publishers, 1950)

INTRODUCTION

1. Anna Julia Cooper, "Womanhood a Vital Element in the Regeneration and Progress of a Race," in *A Voice from the South*, ed. Mary Helen Washington (1892; rpt., New York: Oxford University Press, 1988), pp. 31, 30. The speech was delivered at the Protestant Episcopal Church in Washington, D.C.

2. Nell Irvin Painter remarks that Delany at his death in 1885 "remained virtually forgotten until his resurrection three-quarters of a century later as the father of black nationalism and the epitome of proud blackness" ("Martin R. Delany: Elitism and Black Nationalism," in *Black Leaders of the Nineteenth Century*, ed. Leon Litwack and August Meier [Urbana: University of Illinois Press, 1988], p. 149). That vision of Delany informs Victor Ullman's standard biography, *Martin R. Delany: The Beginnings of Black Nationalism* (Boston: Beacon, 1971).

3. Paul Gilroy, *The Black Atlantic: Modernity and Double Consciousness* (Cambridge: Harvard University Press, 1993), p. 20.

4. At this writing, Delany is not represented in the Harper, Heath, Norton, Prentice-Hall, or Macmillan anthologies of American literature. Symptomatic of the neglect of Delany, he is not mentioned even in two of the more important recent collections of essays on black literature and culture: Geneviève Fabre and Robert O'Meally, eds., *History and Memory in African-American Culture* (New York: Oxford University Press, 1994); and Werner Sollors and Maria Diedrich, eds., *The Black Columbiad: Defining Moments in African American Literature and Culture* (Cambridge: Harvard University Press, 1994).

5. Deborah E. McDowell, "In the First Place: Making Frederick Douglass and the Afro-American Narrative Tradition," in *Critical Essays on Frederick Douglass*, ed. William L. Andrews (Boston: G. K. Hall, 1991), p. 208. Henry Louis Gates Jr. argues

that Douglass "was Representative Man because he was Rhetorical Man, black master of the verbal arts. Douglass is our clearest example of the will to power as the will to write" (*Figures in Black: Words, Signs, and the "Racial" Self* [New York: Oxford University Press, 1987], p. 108).

6. Wilson J. Moses, "Where Honor Is Due: Frederick Douglass as Representative Black Man," *Prospects* 17 (1992): 181–82. On Douglass's aspirations to representativeness, see also James Olney, "The Founding Fathers—Frederick Douglass and Booker T. Washington," in *Slavery and the Literary Imagination*, ed. Deborah E. McDowell and Arnold Rampersad (Baltimore: Johns Hopkins University Press, 1989), pp. 1–24; Rafia Zafar, "Franklinian Douglass: The Afro-American as Representative Man," in *Frederick Douglass: New Literary and Historical Essays*, ed. Eric J. Sundquist (Cambridge: Cambridge University Press, 1990), pp. 141–65; and Henry Louis Gates Jr., "A Dangerous Literacy: The Legacy of Frederick Douglass," *New York Times Book Review*, 28 May 1995, pp. 3, 16. For a superb short discussion of Douglass as an African American leader, see Waldo E. Martin Jr., "Frederick Douglass: Humanist as Race Leader," in *Black Leaders of the Nineteenth Century*, ed. Litwack and Meier, pp. 59–84. On ambition to representativeness, see Mitchell Robert Breitwieser, *Cotton Mather and Benjamin Franklin: The Price of Representative Personality* (New York: Cambridge University Press, 1984), chap. 1.

7. See Benjamin Quarles, *Frederick Douglass* (Washington, D.C.: Associated Publishers, 1948). Though Douglass debated Samuel Ward, Henry Highland Garnet, and Martin Delany, among others, on a number of central issues of the time, William S. McFeely, in his otherwise excellent *Frederick Douglass* (New York: W. W. Norton, 1991), has nothing to say about Ward and devotes less than ten pages to Garnet and Delany.

8. Ralph Waldo Emerson, *Representative Men: Seven Lectures* (1850), in *Ralph Waldo Emerson: Essays and Lectures*, ed. Joel Porte (New York: Library of America, 1983), pp. 615, 627.

9. Emerson, *Representative Men*, p. 628; Harold Cruse, *The Crisis of the Negro Intellectual* (New York: William Morrow, 1967), p. 6; Sterling Stuckey, ed., *The Ideological Origins of Black Nationalism* (Boston: Beacon, 1972), pp. 27, 6, 1. Wilson Jeremiah Moses also argues against reductive binarisms: "There was no clear-cut distinction between black nationalism and assimilation. Black chauvinists, like Delany, were dedicated to Christianizing and 'civilizing' the African continent and actively solicited the support of whites to accomplish this goal. Avowed integrationists, like Douglass, were willing to participate actively in all-black institutions, and defended their right to do so" (*The Golden Age of Black Nationalism, 1850–1925* [Hamden, Conn.: Archon, 1978], p. 45).

10. Rollin, p. 19; Frederick Douglass, "Dr. M. R. Delany," *Douglass' Monthly*, August 1862, p. 595; Rollin, p. 18.

Frances Anne Rollin met Delany in 1867 when she journeyed from Philadelphia to South Carolina to teach the freed people. The twenty-year-old black schoolteacher was so impressed with Major Delany's work at the South Carolina Freedmen's Bureau that she decided to write his biography, which was published in 1868. Because the biography is based on Rollin's conversations with Delany, I've found it a useful (though at times unreliable) "autobiographical" source. For a good discussion of Rollin, see William L. Andrews's introduction, xxxiii–xliii.

11. Frederick Douglass, "Slavery Exists under the Eaves of the American Church" (1846),

in *Papers*, 1:471; Douglass, "A Nation in the Midst of a Nation" (1853), in *Papers*, 2:437; Douglass, "Dr. M. R. Delany," p. 595. Douglass was not the only African American leader who responded negatively to Delany's publicizing of his "pure-blooded" blackness. See William Wells Brown's comments on Delany in "The Colored People of Canada" (1861), in *BAP*, 2:472–73; and Bishop Daniel Alexander Payne, *Recollections of Seventy Years* (1888; rpt., New York: Arno, 1968), p. 160.

12. M. R. Delany, *The Origin and Objects of Ancient Freemasonry; Its Introduction into the United States, and Legitimacy among Colored Men: A Treatise Delivered before St. Cyprian Lodge, No. 13, June 24th, A.D. 1853 — A.L. 5853* (1853; rpt., Xenia: Ohio, 1904), p. 10; Frederick Douglass, "What Are the Colored People Doing for Themselves?" (1848), in *Writings*, 1:316. On the origin of the St. Cyprian Lodge, see Leonard P. Curry, *The Free Black in Urban America, 1800–1850: The Shadow of the Dream* (Chicago: University of Chicago Press, 1981), p. 210. For Delany's 1847 funeral oration for a fellow member, see M. R. Delany, *Eulogy on the Life and Character of the Rev. Fayette Davis* (Pittsburgh: Benjamin Franklin Peterson, 1847). (According to the title page, Delany's *Eulogy* was "published by request of the St. Cyprian Lodge, No. 13.") On Delany's interest in Masonry after the Civil War, see Ullman, *Martin R. Delany*, p. 459. Delany's *Origin and Objects of Ancient Freemasonry* was privately reprinted by Delany's son Anthony Dumas Delany, who was himself a Mason. The St. Cyprian Lodge was an outgrowth of Prince Hall Masonry, which was founded in 1784 in Boston and which was primarily devoted to black uplift and antislavery, providing a refuge, sounding board, and elite sense of community for its black members. See Loretta J. Williams, *Black Freemasonry and Middle-Class Realities* (Columbia: University of Missouri Press, 1980); and Carla L. Peterson, *"Doers of the Word": African-America Women Speakers and Writers in the North (1830–1880)* (New York: Oxford University Press, 1995), pp. 170–71.

13. Delany, *Origin and Objects of Ancient Freemasonry*, pp. 16, 22.

14. Delany, *Origin and Objects of Ancient Freemasonry*, pp. 40, 37, 40. In *Middle-Class Blacks in a White Society: Prince Hall Freemasonry in America* (Berkeley: University of California Press, 1975), William A. Muraskin, without even referring to Delany's Masonry pamphlet, asserts that Delany as a Mason sought to "out Anglo-Saxon the Anglo-Saxon" (80). Given the centrality of Africa to Delany's pamphlet, this is a serious misreading of Delany's position. Clearly, Delany was contesting the tendency among eighteenth- and nineteenth-century racists and proslavery writers to image Egypt as "essentially and originally 'white'" (Martin Bernal, *Black Athena: The Afroasiatic Roots of Classical Civilization* [New Brunswick: Rutgers University Press, 1987], 1:188). Debate on the African sources of European culture continues to have a central place in debates on U.S. cultural origins and character. See Mary R. Lefkowitz and Guy MacLean Rogers, eds., *Black Athena Revisited* (Chapel Hill: University of North Carolina Press, 1996); and Mary R. Lefkowitz, *Not out of Africa: How "Afrocentrism" Became an Excuse to Teach Myth as History* (New York: Basic, 1996).

15. Delany, *Origin and Objects of Ancient Freemasonry*, pp. 16, 35, 16, 39, 17, 21. An important precursor of Delany's *Origin and Objects of Ancient Freemasonry* is David Walker's *Appeal* (1829), in which he proclaims that it was among "the Egyptians, [who] were Africans or colored people, such as we are," that "learning originated, and was carried thence into Greece" (*Walker's Appeal, with a Brief Sketch of His Life. By Henry Highland Garnet. And Also Garnet's "Address to the Slaves of the United States*

of America" [New York: J. H. Tobitt, 1848], pp. 18, 30). For a provocative discussion of the ideological uses of Africa in nineteenth- and twentieth-century writing, see Kwame Anthony Appiah, *In My Father's House: Africa in the Philosophy of Culture* (New York: Oxford University Press, 1992).

16. Gilroy, *Black Atlantic*, p. 59; Frederick Douglass, "The Douglass Institute: An Address Delivered in Baltimore, Maryland, on 29 September 1865," in *Papers*, 4:93. Peter F. Walker makes an unconvincing case for what he calls Douglass's "hopeless secret desire to be white," in *Moral Choices: Memory, Desire, and Imagination in Nineteenth-Century American Abolition* (Baton Rouge: Louisiana State University Press, 1978), p. 247; see also pp. 209–61. Allison Davis too pays obsessive attention to Douglass's attraction to white leaders and culture; see *Leadership, Love, and Aggression* (New York: Harcourt Brace Jovanovich, 1983), pp. 15–101.

17. Frederick Douglass, "The Claims of the Negro Ethnologically Considered: An Address Delivered in Hudson, Ohio, on 12 July 1854," in *Papers*, 2:505, 506, 502, 519, 517, 508.

18. Douglass, "Claims of the Negro," pp. 520, 525, 520, 510, 511.

19. Delany, *Origin and Objects of Ancient Freemasonry*, p. 40; Douglass, "Claims of the Negro," pp. 522, 523; Douglass, "The Douglass Institute," p. 93. Though he addressed an audience of nearly three thousand and his speech was widely hailed in newspapers throughout the Midwest and North, Douglass, when looking back on "Claims of the Negro," termed it "a very defective production"; see his *Life and Times of Frederick Douglass, Written by Himself: His Early Life as a Slave, His Escape from Bondage, and His Complete History* (1881) (1892; rpt., New York: Collier, 1962), p. 374.

20. Douglass, "Claims of the Negro," pp. 505–6, 525. Delany would make similar assertions in *The Condition, Elevation, Emigration, and Destiny of the Colored People of the United States* (1852; rpt., New York: Arno, 1969), arguing for the "CLAIMS OF COLORED MEN AS CITIZENS OF THE UNITED STATES" (5). But by the end of the text he states that it is the responsibility of educated blacks to leave the United States in order to claim their destiny in an "America" that is something other than the United States.

21. Frederick Douglass, *Narrative of the Life of Frederick Douglass, an American Slave: Written by Himself*, ed. Houston A. Baker Jr. (New York: Penguin, 1982), p. 159. Like Christ, Douglass takes up a "severe cross" (151), and in a Jeremiadic mode he asks, "Will not a righteous God visit for these things?" (93). Informing the text is his conviction that "divine Providence [interposes] in my favor" (75). In his preface, William Lloyd Garrison asserts in visionary fashion that Douglass is "consecrated . . . to the great work of breaking the rod of the oppressor, and letting the oppressed go free!" (34). William L. Andrews perceives Douglass in the *Narrative* primarily as a black Jeremiah; see *To Tell a Free Story: The First Century of Afro-American Autobiography, 1760–1865* (Urbana: University of Illinois Press, 1986), esp. p. 126. This seems to me an accurate way of figuring Douglass's relationship to the white community. My interest is in Douglass's relationship to African Americans as well. Mosaic imagery has a more significant place in Douglass's 1855 *My Bondage and My Freedom*. On black Jeremiahs and messiahs, see David Howard-Pitney, *The Afro-American Jeremiad: Appeals for Justice in America* (Philadelphia: Temple University Press, 1990),

esp. pp. 12, 17–52; and Wilson Jeremiah Moses, *Black Messiahs and Uncle Toms: Social and Literary Manipulations of a Religious Myth*, rev. ed. (University Park: Pennsylvania State University Press, 1993).

On Maria Stewart's appropriations of Exodus, see Peterson, *"Doers of the Word,"* chap. 3. Benjamin Quarles writes that Harriet Tubman "felt that Divine Providence had willed her freedom and that a guardian angel accompanied her, particularly on her missions of deliverance. . . . When she was referred to as Moses, she did not demur" ("Harriet Tubman's Unlikely Leadership," in *Black Leaders of the Nineteenth Century*, ed. Litwack and Meier, p. 45).

22. Cooper, "Womanhood a Vital Element," p. 31.

23. Robyn Wiegman, *American Anatomies: Theorizing Race and Gender* (Durham: Duke University Press, 1995), p. 71, and see also chap. 2; *NS*, 3 December 1847, p. 1; Gilroy, *Black Atlantic*, p. 26. On Douglass and feminist reform, see the excellent collection of primary texts in *Frederick Douglass on Women's Rights*, ed. Philip S. Foner (1976; rpt., New York: Da Capo, 1992); and Waldo E. Martin Jr., *The Mind of Frederick Douglass* (Chapel Hill: University of North Carolina Press, 1984), chap. 6. We learn from the transcript of Delany's 1854 emigration convention, *Proceedings of the National Convention of Colored People; Held at Cleveland, Ohio, on Thursday, Friday, and Saturday, the 24th, 25th, and 26th of August, 1854* (Pittsburgh: A. A. Anderson, 1854), that women had a significant role in the convention. For example, four of the seven participants on the "Finance Committee" were women (9). On African American women writers and speakers of the period, see Frances Smith Foster, *Written by Herself: Literary Production by African American Women, 1746–1892* (Bloomington: Indiana University Press, 1993); and Peterson, *"Doers of the Word."* On the emancipatory implications of challenges to antebellum culture from "within" conventional (patriarchal) discourses, see Maggie Sale, "Critiques from Within: Antebellum Projects of Resistance," *American Literature* 64 (1992): 695–718. Also useful is Jean Matthews, "Race, Sex, and the Dimensions of Liberty in Antebellum America," *Journal of the Early Republic* 6 (1986): 275–91; and Lydia Liu, "The Female Body and Nationalist Discourse: *The Field of Life and Death* Revisited," in *Scattered Hegemonies: Postmodernity and Transnational Feminist Practices*, ed. Inderpal Grewal and Caren Kaplan (Minneapolis: University of Minnesota Press, 1994), pp. 37–62.

24. Donald E. Pease, "National Identities, Postmodern Artifacts, and Postnational Narratives," in *National Identities and Post-American Narratives*, ed. Pease (Durham: Duke University Press, 1994), p. 3; Russ Castronovo, *Fathering the Nation: American Genealogies of Slavery and Freedom* (Berkeley: University of California Press, 1995), p. 6; Homi K. Bhabha, "DissemiNation: Time, Narrative, and the Margins of the Modern Nation," in *Nation and Narration*, ed. Bhabha (London: Routledge, 1990), p. 300. See also Benedict Anderson, *Imagined Communities: Reflections on the Origin and Spread of Nationalism* (London: Verso, 1983); Khachig Tölölyan, "The Nation-State and Its Others: In Lieu of a Preface," *Diaspora* 1 (1991): 3–7; Paul Giles, "Reconstructing American Studies: Transnational Paradoxes, Comparative Perspectives," *Journal of American Studies* 29 (1994): 335–58; Priscilla Wald, *Constituting Americans: Cultural Anxiety and Narrative Form* (Durham: Duke University Press, 1995); and Betsy Erkilla, "Ethnicity, Literary Theory, and the Grounds of Resistance," *American Quarterly* 47 (1995): 563–94.

1. *Writings*, 1:256; *Papers*, 1:lxi. Garrison promised Douglass a fairly lucrative regular column in the *National Anti-Slavery Standard* if he would relinquish his plan to establish a black newspaper.

2. William Lloyd Garrison to Helen E. Garrison, [13] August 1847, *The Letters of William Lloyd Garrison: No Union with Slave-Holders, 1841–1849*, ed. William M. Merrill (Cambridge: Harvard University Press, 1973), 3:509; Dorothy Sterling, *The Making of an Afro-American: Martin Robison Delany, 1812–1885* (Garden City, N.Y.: Doubleday, 1971), p. 96; Garrison to Helen E. Garrison, 16 August 1847, *Letters of William Lloyd Garrison*, 3:510–11. For texts of Douglass's speeches in Norristown and Philadelphia, see *Papers*, 2:84–93.

3. Douglass to Sidney Howard Gay, letter of September 1847, *National Anti-Slavery Standard*, 9 September 1847, rpt. in *Writings*, 1:263; Benjamin Quarles, *Frederick Douglass* (Washington, D.C.: Associated Publishers, 1948), p. 81; Garrison to Helen E. Garrison, 20 October 1847, *Letters of William Lloyd Garrison*, 3:532–33 (Garrison was already angry at Douglass for having returned to Rochester while he remained in Cleveland with a serious illness).

4. Delany to Douglass, letter of 14 January 1848, *NS*, 28 January 1848, p. 2. On the *North Star*, see Quarles, *Frederick Douglass*, pp. 80–98.

5. Rollin, p. 68; Nathan Irvin Huggins, *Slave and Citizen: The Life of Frederick Douglass* (Boston: Little, Brown, 1980), p. 45; William S. McFeely, *Frederick Douglass* (New York: W. W. Norton, 1991), p. 152. In his excellent *Frederick Douglass*, Quarles writes of the "dissolution of the dual editorship after a six months' trial. After June 1848, the paper was under Douglass's exclusive control" (84). Quarles cites Rollin (68) as his source for the 1848 date; but Rollin had given the correct date of June 1849. The mistaken June 1848 date (or a duration of six months, as opposed to eighteen months) is repeated in *Writings*, ed. Foner, 1:92; Huggins, *Slave and Citizen*, p. 45; and the reprint of Douglass's *My Bondage and My Freedom* edited by William L. Andrews (Urbana: University of Illinois Press, 1987), p. 241 n.

6. A substantial portion of Delany's "Western tour" letters may be found in *"Stand Still and See the Salvation": A Martin R. Delany Reader*, ed. Robert S. Levine (Chapel Hill: University of North Carolina Press, forthcoming).

7. In 1849 two key essays began the process of canonizing the slave narrative as the distinctive contribution of African Americans to American literature. See Ephraim Peabody, "Narratives of Fugitive Slaves," *Christian Examiner*, July–Sept. 1849, rpt. in *The Slave's Narrative*, ed. Charles T. Davis and Henry Louis Gates Jr. (New York: Oxford University Press, 1985), pp. 19–28; and Theodore Parker, "The American Scholar," in *Centenary Edition of Theodore Parker's Writings*, ed. George Willis Cooke (Boston: American Unitarian Association, 1907), vol. 8, esp. p. 37. Peabody's and Parker's views on the importance of African American slave narratives were anticipated in Margaret Fuller's 1845 review of Douglass's *Narrative*, rpt. in *Critical Essays on Frederick Douglass*, ed. William L. Andrews (Boston: G. K. Hall, 1991), pp. 21–24.

8. Douglass to J. D. Carr, letter of 1 November 1847, in *Writings*, 1:279; Delany to Douglass, letter of 4 June 1848, *NS*, 16 June 1848, p. 2.

9. *Minutes and Proceedings of the First Annual Convention of the People of Colour, Held by Adjournments in the City of Philadelphia* (1831), rpt. in *Minutes of the Proceedings*

of the *National Negro Conventions, 1830–1864,* ed. Howard Holman Bell (New York: Arno, 1969), p. 5.

10. Samuel Cornish's editorials are reprinted in *BAP*, 3:217, 219, 216, 229. (*Colored American* was published in New York City.) Similar sentiments were expressed in the inaugural 16 March 1827 issue of Samuel Cornish's and John B. Russwurm's *Freedom's Journal,* the first African American newspaper. The editors declared that their paper was "devoted to the dissemination of useful knowledge among our brethren, and to their moral and religious improvement." And they added: "We wish to plead our own cause. Too long have others spoken for us" (in *A Documentary History of the Negro People in the United States,* ed. Herbert Aptheker [New York: Citadel, 1951], 1:82). On the importance of the black press to free blacks' efforts to create community and challenge racism, see Martin E. Dann, *The Black Press, 1827–1890: The Quest for National Identity* (New York: G. P. Putnam's, 1971); Penelope L. Bullock, *The Afro-American Periodical Press, 1838–1909* (Baton Rouge: Louisiana State University Press, 1981); Frankie Hutton, *The Early Black Press in America, 1827 to 1860* (Westport, Conn.: Greenwood, 1993); and Carla L. Peterson, *"Doers of the Word": African-American Women Speakers and Writers in the North (1830–1880)* (New York: Oxford University Press, 1995), esp. p. 11.

11. As Carla Peterson observes, "African-American writers constructed a productive discourse generated from within the community that borrows the vocabulary and categories of the dominant discourse only to dislocate them from their privileged position of authority" (*"Doers of the Word,"* p. 14). On black elevation see the introduction to *BAP*, vol. 3; Frederick Cooper, "Elevating the Race: The Social Thought of Black Leaders, 1827–1850," *American Quarterly* 24 (1972): 604–25; Jane H. Pease and William H. Pease, *They Who Would Be Free: Blacks' Search for Freedom, 1830–1861* (New York: Atheneum, 1974); and Ira Berlin, "The Structure of the Free Negro Caste in the Antebellum United States," *Journal of Social History* 9 (1976): 297–318. See also Kevin K. Gaines's excellent *Uplifting the Race: Black Leadership, Politics, and Culture in the Twentieth Century* (Chapel Hill: University of North Carolina Press, 1996).

12. Sterling Stuckey, *Slave Culture: Nationalist Theory and the Foundations of Black America* (New York: Oxford University Press, 1987), p. 121; *Walker's Appeal, with a Brief Sketch of His Life. By Henry Highland Garnet. And Also Garnet's "Address to the Slaves of the United States of America"* (New York: J. H. Tobitt, 1848), p. 43; Henry Highland Garnet, "The Past and the Present Condition and the Destiny of the Colored Race" (1848), cited in Cooper, "Elevating the Race," 609. As Stuckey points out, in attacking restricted land ownership and various monopolistic practices, Garnet's lecture also set forth a decidedly "anticapitalistic ethic" (*Slave Culture,* p. 168). On the Jeremiadic strategies of Walker and other writers of the period, particularly Maria Stewart, see Peterson, *"Doers of the Word,"* esp. chap. 3. However assimilationist Walker's and Garnet's injunctions may seem, it was ultimately the case that their appropriations of conventional notions of uplift contributed to the development of a black nationalist consciousness that "emphasized the need for black people to rely primarily on themselves in vital areas of life — economic, political, religious, and intellectual — in order to effect their liberation" (Sterling Stuckey, introduction to *The Ideological Origins of Black Nationalism,* ed. Stuckey [Boston: Beacon, 1972], p. 1).

13. *Minutes of the Fifth Annual Convention for the Improvement of the Free People of Colour in the United States, Held by Adjournments, in the Wesley Church, Philadelphia* (Philadelphia: Gibbons, 1835), p. 26. Stuckey argues that Whipper's integrationist reformist discourse announces "the surrender of blacks in America to prevailing standards and power relationships and thus the uncontested triumph of Anglo-Saxon values" (*Slave Culture*, p. 211). And yet for Whipper (as for Douglass), there was something radical about blacks demanding a place in the dominant institutions of a nation committed to segregationist practices and something defeatist about a "retreat" into all-black institutions.

14. Augustine [Lewis Woodson], *Colored American*, 14 March 1840, rpt. in *BAP*, 3:324; "Ten Letters by Augustine," in *Ideological Origins*, ed. Stuckey, p. 136. In several of his letters Woodson suggested that blacks might consider leaving not only U.S. cities but the United States itself. On Woodson's emigrationism, see Floyd J. Miller, "'The Father of Black Nationalism': Another Contender," *Civil War History* 17 (1971): esp. 316–17; and Miller, *The Search for a Black Nationality: Black Emigration and Colonization, 1787–1863* (Urbana: University of Illinois Press, 1975), esp. pp. 94–104.

15. Sterling, *The Making of an Afro-American*, p. 55. On Delany in Pittsburgh, see also Victor Ullman, *Martin R. Delany: The Beginnings of Black Nationalism* (Boston: Beacon, 1971), pp. 20–76. The 1830 Pittsburgh census listed 473 blacks; see Ann Greenwood Wilmoth, "Pittsburgh and the Blacks: A Short History, 1780–1875" (Ph.D. diss., Pennsylvania State University, 1975), p. 8. See also Laurence Glasco, "Double Burden: The Black Experience in Pittsburgh," in *City at the Point: Essays on the Social History of Pittsburgh* (Pittsburgh: University of Pittsburgh Press, 1989), pp. 69–110. Howard Holman Bell notes that at least three meetings of the auxiliary branch of the American Moral Reform Society were held in Pittsburgh, with Woodson and Delany participating as "officers and managers" (*A Survey of the Negro Convention Movement, 1830–1861* [1953; rpt., New York: Arno, 1969], p. 47). On Delany's southwest tour of 1839, see Rollin, pp. 46–47.

16. "Proceedings of the State Convention of the Colored Freemen of Pennsylvania, Held in Pittsburgh, on the 23d, 24th, and 25th of August, 1841, for the Purpose of Considering Their Condition, and the Means of Its Improvement," rpt. in *Proceedings of the Black State Conventions, 1840–1865*, ed. Philip S. Foner and George E. Walker (Philadelphia: Temple University Press, 1979), 1:107, 114, 110.

17. "Prospectus of *The Mystery*," *Mystery*, 16 December 1845, p. 4. (This issue of the *Mystery*, the only extant copy of Delany's paper, is available at the Carnegie Library of Pittsburgh.) See also Mike Sanja's useful "*The Mystery* of Martin Delany," *Carnegie Magazine*, July/August 1990, pp. 36–40. Disappointed by Delany's marriage to a mulatto, Ullman refers to the marriage as "strange" (*Martin R. Delany*, p. 45). Delany asserted his racial pride in the marriage, however, by naming his seven children after great black men and women (for example Toussaint L'Ouverture, born 1846, and Charles Lenox Remond, born 1850).

18. Martin Delany, "Not Fair," rpt. in the *Liberator*, 20 October 1843, p. 166.

19. Cited in Ullman, *Martin R. Delany*, p. 61; *Mystery*, 16 December 1845, p. 1. Delany's 1845 motto was influenced by Garnet's similar use of Byron's *Childe Harold's Pilgrimage* in his 1843 "Address to the Slaves."

20. Frederick Douglass, *Narrative of the Life of an American Slave, Written by Himself*

(1845), ed. David W. Blight (Boston: Bedford Books, 1993), p. 61. On Douglass and New Bedford, see McFeely, *Frederick Douglass*, pp. 74–90.

21. Douglass, "American Prejudice against Color: An Address Delivered in Cork, Ireland, 23 October 1845," in *Papers*, 1:68, 69. Though less militant in his rhetoric than Delany, the fact is that, as reported in several issues of the 1843 *Liberator*, when Douglass, Charles L. Remond, and William A. White were assaulted by a racist mob in Pendleton, Indiana, Douglass resorted to violence both to resist the attackers and to inflict injury, using a piece of lumber to club his assailants (see McFeely, *Frederick Douglass*, pp. 109–10).

22. *Minutes of the National Convention of Colored Citizens: Held at Buffalo, on the 15th, 16th, 17th, 18th, and 19th of August, 1843. For the Purpose of Considering Their Moral and Political Condition as American Citizens* (New York: Piercy and Reed, 1843), pp. 13, 17, 5.

23. *Minutes of the National Convention of Colored Citizens*, pp. 13, 17, 5, 28; *Proceedings of the National Convention of Colored People and Their Friends, Held in Troy, N.Y. on the 6th, 7th, 8th, and 9th October, 1847* (Troy, N.Y.: J. C. Kneeland, 1847), pp. 6, 7, 19; *Report of the Proceedings of the Colored National Convention, Held at Cleveland, Ohio, on Wednesday, September 6, 1848* (Rochester: John Dick, 1848), p. 16. On the crucial role of newspapers in creating "imagined political community" (15), see Benedict Anderson, *Imagined Communities: Reflections on the Origin and Spread of Nationalism* (London: Verso, 1983).

24. Miller, *Black Nationality*, p. 115.

25. Frederick Douglass, "Our Paper and Its Prospects," *NS*, 3 December 1847, p. 2; and Douglass, "Colored Newspapers," *NS*, 7 January 1848, p. 2. Quarles estimates that in 1848 white subscribers outnumbered black subscribers by five to one (*Frederick Douglass*, p. 89).

26. Douglass, "Our Paper and Its Prospects," p. 2.

27. *NS*, 21 January 1848, p. 2; Frederick Douglass, "To Our Oppressed Countrymen," *NS*, 3 December 1847, 2.

28. Delany to Douglass, 14 January 1848; Frederick Douglass, "Our Movements," *NS*, 7 January 1848, p. 2; Delany to Douglass, letter of 6 February 1848, *NS*, 18 February 1848, p. 2; Delany to Douglass, letter of 22 March 1848, *NS*, 7 April 1848, p. 2. Douglass wrote in a squib printed in a March 1848 issue of the *NS*: "Mr. Delany is on a tour Westward, to promote the circulation of the paper, consequently we anticipate a large accession to our subscription list through his efforts in that region" (*NS*, 31 March 1848, p. 2). To be sure, Delany would try his best to gain new subscribers for the *North Star*. As he wrote Douglass in late January 1848: "I hope soon to be on my Western tour, and wish you to say to our Western friends, that they may all be prepared for subscription" (Delany to Douglass, letter of 28 January 1848, *NS*, 11 February 1848, p. 2). In two private letters to Delany, Douglass further underscored the importance of his subscription efforts. "Do all you can for us in Pittsburgh," he wrote Delany in a letter of 12 January 1848. "Our list does not yet reach more than seven hundred subscribers, and our expenses are all of fifty five dollars per week. Send on subscribers and money." And in a letter of 19 January 1848, Douglass wrote Delany: "Everything will depend on our getting subscribers." For both letters, see the Library of Congress's microfilm series "The Papers of Frederick Douglass," reel 1, Frederick Douglass Collection.

29. William W. Stowe, "Conventions and Voices in Margaret Fuller's Travel Writing," *American Literature* 63 (1991): 243. During the 1840s some of the best-selling books of the time were book-length collections of travel letters that first appeared in newspapers and journals. A short list of such books would include Lydia Maria Child, *Letters from New York* (1844), J. Bayard Taylor, *Views A-Foot; or, Europe Seen with Knapsack and Staff* (1846), and Caroline Kirkland, *Holidays Abroad; or, Europe from the West* (1848). Ahmed M. Metwalli remarks, "All kinds of books of travel, a large number of which were mere hasty collections of unedited letters or article serials, sold by the tens of thousands" ("Americans Abroad: The Popular Art of Travel Writing in the Nineteenth Century," in *America: Exploration and Travel*, ed. Steven E. Kagle [Bowling Green, Ohio: Bowling Green State University Press, 1979], p. 69).

Douglass's letters from Europe for the *Liberator* and other abolitionist journals, as well as his earlier letters from his antislavery tours, clearly anticipated (and established a model) for Delany's letters to the *North Star*, as did the letters of other blacks who acted as lecturers and correspondents for antislavery newspapers. The *Colored American*, for example, printed a series of letters from Charles B. Ray, who was described by editor Samuel Cornish as " 'Traveling Agent,' for the Colored American" (*Colored American*, 24 June 1837, p. 3). From the early 1830s on, Nathaniel Paul and Charles Remond similarly sent dispatches to the *Liberator* on their antislavery tours. On African American travel writing see William L. Andrews, *To Tell a Free Story: The First Century of Afro-American Autobiography, 1760–1865* (Urbana: University of Illinois Press, 1986), esp. pp. 170–73; and Peterson, *"Doers of the Word,"* chap. 4. Of course, slave narratives themselves could be read as black challenges and revisions of the period's popular travel narratives. For a fascinating discussion, see Richard Hardack, "Water Pollution and Motion Sickness: Rites of Passage in Nineteenth-Century Slave and Travel Narratives," *ESQ* 41 (1995): 1–40.

30. The editors of Margaret Fuller's European letters remark on "the new eclectic genre represented by the dispatches . . . [which] wander far outside the boundaries of conventional travel writing and take on the qualities of the history, the sermon, the political manifesto, the historical romance, and especially the diary" (see Fuller, *"These Sad but Glorious Days": Dispatches from Europe, 1846–1850*, eds. Larry J. Reynolds and Susan Belasco Smith [New Haven: Yale University Press, 1991], p. 8). Delany, Douglass, and many other black leaders of the period regarded the European revolutions as presaging revolutionary social change in the United States. As Henry Highland Garnet wrote in the 19 January 1848 *North Star*: "This age is a revolutionary age. . . , revolution after revolution will undoubtedly take place until all men are placed upon equality" (2). In a *New York Tribune* dispatch of the same month, Fuller similarly made explicit the connection between the revolutionary moment and antislavery: "I listen to the same arguments against the emancipation of Italy, that are used against the emancipation of our blacks. . . . I find the cause of tyranny and wrong everywhere the same—and lo! my Country the darkest offender" (1 January 1848, rpt. in *"These Sad but Glorious Days,"* p. 165). See also Frederick Douglass, "The 1848 Revolution in France," *NS*, 12 May 1848, rpt. in *Papers*, 2:116–17. For a good discussion of (white) American writers' responses to the European revolutions, see Larry J. Reynolds, *European Revolutions and the American Literary Renaissance* (New Haven: Yale University Press, 1988).

31. Delany to Douglass, 14 January 1848, p. 2.

32. Delany to Douglass, 6 February 1848, p. 2; Delany to Douglass, letter of 25 January 1848, *NS*, 11 February 1848, p. 2. For examples of Douglass's writings in the *NS* on similar topics, see "Henry Clay," in the issue of 28 January 1848, and "War with Mexico," in the issue of 25 February 1848. On race and the Mexican War, see Reginald Horsman, *Race and Manifest Destiny: The Origins of American Racial Anglo-Saxonism* (Cambridge: Harvard University Press, 1981), pp. 208–48.

33. Delany to Douglass, 6 February 1848, p. 2. For fuller elaborations of Delany's views on the appropriate use of physical means, see his "Domestic Economy," *NS*, 13 April 1849, p. 2. In a letter to Douglass of 25 January 1849, Mary Ann Shadd similarly criticized the black clergy for its submissiveness (*NS*, 23 March 1849 p. 2). For Delany on Shadd, see Delany to Douglass, letter of 16 January 1849, *NS*, 16 February 1849, p. 2.

34. Delany to Douglass, letter of 27 March 1848, *NS*, 14 April 1848, p. 2; Delany to Douglass, letter of 7 May 1848, *NS*, 26 May 1848, p. 2.

35. Delany to Douglass, 28 January 1848, p. 2; *Proceedings of the National Convention of Colored People . . . Held in Troy*, p. 23; Nell Irvin Painter, "Martin R. Delany: Elitism and Black Nationalism," in *Black Leaders of the Nineteenth Century*, ed. Leon Litwack and August Meier (Urbana: University of Illinois Press, 1988), p. 152. Cyril E. Griffiths notes that "Delany believed that Afro-American entrepreneurship was a vital aspect of self-determination, and he looked for evidence of it wherever he traveled" (*The African Dream: Martin R. Delany and the Emergence of Pan-African Thought* [University Park: Pennsylvania State University Press, 1975], p. 8).

36. Delany to Douglass, 27 March 1848, p. 2; Delany to Douglass, letter of 15 April 1848, *NS*, 28 April 1848, p. 2; Delany to Douglass, letter of 20 April 1848, *NS*, 12 May 1848, p. 2; Delany to Douglass, letter of 18 June 1848, *NS*, 7 July 1848, p. 2.

37. *Walker's Appeal*, p. 45; Delany to Douglass, letter of 20 May 1848, *NS*, 9 June 1848, p. 2.

38. Delany to Douglass, letter of 18 November 1848, *NS*, 1 December 1848, p. 2; Delany to Douglass, 15 April 1848, p. 2; Delany to Douglass, 7 May 1848, p. 2; Delany to Douglass, 18 November 1848, p. 2; Delany to Douglass, letter of 30 November 1848, *NS*, 15 December 1848, p. 2. On Cincinnati, see Delany to Douglass, 4 June 1848, p. 2.

39. Delany to Douglass, letter of 15 April 1848, p. 2. Douglass similarly wrote, "The white man is only superior to the black man, when he outstrips him in the race of improvement; and the black man is only inferior, when he proves himself incapable of doing just what is done by his white brother" ("Colored Newspapers," p. 2).

40. Delany to Douglass, 4 June 1848, p. 2.

41. On the nationalistic cultural work performed by the figure of Jeremiah, see Sacvan Bercovitch, *The American Jeremiad* (Madison: University of Wisconsin Press, 1978).

42. Douglass feared—as did Whipper—that even the existence of black churches would reinforce white racists' efforts to legitimate "every other institution founded on complexion" and thus perpetuate blacks' marginalization ("Colored Churches—No. III," *NS*, 10 March 1848, p. 2). Douglass also opposed segregated schools. See "Editorial Correspondence," *NS*, 7 April 1848, rpt. in *Writings*, 1:302–3. Floyd Miller points to similarities and differences between the coeditors at this time: "Although Frederick Douglass was similarly blending self-help with racial solidarity, few blacks were as attracted as Delany was to the belief that 'None can properly represent us but ourselves.' In sum, personal self-help led inexorably to racial self-sufficiency and, by implication, racial solidarity" (*Black Nationality*, p. 122).

43. Delany to Douglass, 15 April 1848, p. 2; Delany to Douglass, 4 June 1848, p. 2. Delany elaborates at greater length on Cincinnati's blacks in his two-part essay "Colored Citizens of Cincinnati," *NS*, 15 June 1849, p. 2, and *NS*, 6 July 1849, p. 3.

44. Frederick Douglass, "What Are the Colored People Doing for Themselves?," *NS*, 14 July 1848, p. 2. In a letter to Douglass, Delany similarly complains about blacks' lack of initiative during a revolutionary age: "What a reflection for the colored people of this country, that while the oppressed of France, Denmark, Sweden, Wallachie, Tunis, and even Bohemia, as well as several other places, have demanded a restitution of wrongs, demanded liberty and had it conceded, we are comparatively standing fast, not yet having made the first stride towards it" (*NS*, 5 January 1849, p. 3). On the "American 1848," see Michael Paul Rogin, *Subversive Genealogy: The Politics and Art of Herman Melville* (New York: Alfred A. Knopf, 1983), chap. 4. For a good discussion of Douglass's commitment to black self-help, see August Meier, "Frederick Douglass' Vision for America: A Case Study in Nineteenth-Century Negro Protest" (1967), rpt. in *Frederick Douglass*, ed. Benjamin Quarles (Englewood Cliffs, N.J.: Prentice-Hall, 1968), pp. 143–64. See also Frederick Douglass, "Self-Help" (1849), in *Papers*, 2:167–70.

45. Delany to Douglass, 20 April 1848, p. 2. For a discussion of the psychological implications of such repeated harassment, see M. R. Delany, "American Civilization — Treatment of the Colored People of the U. States," *NS*, 30 March 1849, p. 2.

46. Delany to Douglass, letter of 1 July 1848, *NS*, 14 July 1848, pp. 2–3. (The letter's date is given incorrectly in the *North Star* as "June 1st, 1848.")

47. Eric Lott, " 'The Seeming Counterfeit': Racial Politics and Early Blackface Minstrelsy," *American Quarterly* 43 (1991): 226, 247; Lott, "Love and Theft: The Racial Unconscious of Blackface Minstrelsy," *Representations* 39 (1992): 29; Delany to Douglass, 1 July 1848, p. 3.

48. Delany to Douglass, 1 July 1848, p. 3.

49. Lawrence Buell, *Literary Transcendentalism: Style and Vision in the American Renaissance* (Ithaca: Cornell University Press, 1973), p. 197.

50. Delany to Douglass, 15 April 1848, p. 2. In his letter to Douglass of 4 February 1848, printed in *NS*, 11 February 1848, Delany writes, "I omitted to mention in my former correspondence, that the cause of my long silence was owing to an indisposition in my family" (2). That Delany should have been moved to such an emotional pitch by the performance of a white girl suggests that, as would be the case with Douglass's response to Stowe, he can entertain the possibility of transracial emotional engagements.

51. Delany to Douglass, 20 May 1848, pp. 2–3. On Margaret Garner's killing of her child, a crucial source of Toni Morrison's *Beloved*, see Gerder Lerner, ed., *Black Women in White America: A Documentary History* (New York: Vintage, 1973), pp. 60–63.

52. Delany to Douglass, 20 May 1848, pp. 2–3.

53. Martin R. Delany, "Political Destiny of the Colored Race on the American Continent" (1854), in Rollin, p. 327.

54. Delany to Douglass, letter of 14 July 1848, *NS*, 28 July 1848, p. 2. Such was his anger at McLean that, so Delany reported to his biographer, he actively worked to make sure that McLean, thought to be a viable candidate for the presidency or vice presidency of the Free Soil Party, did not get either nomination (see Rollin, pp. 62–63). Delany further explores blacks' vulnerability before the law in his June 1848 obser-

vations on the dire situation of the approximately five hundred slaves freed by the Virginian John Randolph at his death in 1833. Denied by Randolph's legal executors the money and Ohio lands bequeathed them by Randolph himself, the former slaves became the easy marks of swindlers and price gougers in Milton, Ohio. In the course of his letter on Randolph's former slaves, he praised the white woman Lucy Coates for running a school at the settlement. This moment is one of several in the letters when Delany praises white abolitionists for their antiracist efforts. On John Randolph and the fate of his freed slaves, see William H. Pease and Jane H. Pease, *Black Utopia: Negro Communal Experiments in America* (Madison: State Historical Society of Wisconsin, 1963), pp. 26–27.

55. Delany to Douglass, 14 July 1848, p. 2. Delany concludes his letter genially with the hope that he will meet up with Douglass in Rochester the following week to celebrate the anniversary of emancipation in the West Indies.

56. Delany to Douglass, letter of 24 February 1849, *NS*, 9 March 1849, p. 3. For his thoughts on the election of Taylor, see M. R. Delany, "The End Is Not Yet," *NS*, 1 December 1848, p. 2. By beginning and ending his "Western tour" in Pittsburgh, Delany, whether deliberately or not, stays true to the generic conventions of the "tour" narrative. As Charles L. Batten Jr. explains, in the eighteenth century in particular, to call a travel account a "tour," as opposed to, say, "travels," "journey," or "voyage," was to convey something specific: "*tour* almost always narrates a trip during which the traveler completes a circuit, returning to the point from which he originally departed" (*Pleasurable Instruction: Form and Convention in Eighteenth-Century Travel Literature* [Berkeley: University of California Press, 1978], p. 38).

57. Delany to Douglass, 24 February 1849, p. 3.

58. Bruce Greenfield, *Narrating Discovery: The Romantic Explorer in American Literature, 1790–1865* (New York: Columbia University Press, 1992), pp. 158, 163.

59. Delany to Douglass, 24 February 1849, p. 3. For Delany's two-part essay on "Colored Citizens of Pittsburgh," see *NS*, issues of 6 July 1849, p. 3, and 13 July 1849, p. 3.

60. Frederick Douglass, "The North Star," *NS*, 29 June 1849, p. 2.

61. Wilson J. Moses, for example, writes of Douglass's collaboration with Delany on the *North Star*, "When in 1848, over the objections of Garrison, Douglass founded his newspaper, *The North Star*, it was with Delany as coeditor, but Douglass soon fell out with Delany over a number of issues, most important among them being the issue of black pride." Moses argues that "Douglass considered Delany a racial chauvinist and an extremist," but surely that more accurately describes his attitude in the 1850s and does little to help us understand their break in mid-1849. See Moses, "Where Honor Is Due: Frederick Douglass as Representative Black Man," *Prospects* 17 (1992): 183. The break between the coeditors, I want to emphasize, occurred in an entirely civil fashion, with Douglass continuing to speak well of Delany and with Delany even urging blacks, in an open letter printed in the 5 October 1849 issue, "to rally around the *North Star*" (Delany to M. H. Burnham, "Establishment of a Paper for the State by the Colored People of Ohio, &c.," *NS*, 5 October 1849, p. 3). Douglass *was* unhappy with Delany's abilities as a subscription agent. In a letter of 28 April 1848 to Julia Griffiths requesting additional funds, Douglass remarked that he was having difficulty meeting the *North Star*'s operating expenses "on account of the small assistance in getting subscribers rendered me by my Dear Friend Delany" (rpt. in *Writings*, 1:306).

62. Delany to "Star," letter of 25 September 1848, *NS*, 6 October 1848, p. 2.

63. Delany to Mr. Dick, *NS*, 11 August 1848, p. 2; Frederick Douglass, "In the Lecturing Field Again," *NS*, 26 August 1848, p. 2; and Douglass, "Colored National Convention at Cleveland," *NS*, 15 September 1848, p. 2.

64. "The Call," *NS*, 14 July 1848, p. 2.

65. "Proceedings of the Colored Convention, Held at Cleveland, Ohio, Sept. 6, 1848," *NS*, 29 September 1848, p. 1.

66. In fact, nearly two months after the publication of the Cleveland "Proceedings" in the *North Star*, Douglass printed a letter from Delany to W. H. Day, the recording secretary of the convention, in which he complained that "you have not reported me correctly": "I observed, in the course of my remarks before the Convention, that 'rather than *willingly* submit to, and, with any degree of allowance, *tolerate* and *encourage*, on the part of my own family, such as menial pursuits, I would prefer to receive a telegraph dispatch,' &c." (M. R. Delany, "To W. H. Day, Esq.," *NS*, 17 November 1848, p. 2). The words in italics suggest Delany's basic agreement with Douglass's qualifications on his resolution; the use of "&c." allows Delany to elide the overheated language that some delegates found offensive.

67. "Proceedings," p. 1. For Delany's comments on military science, see Sterling, *The Making of an Afro-American*, p. 111.

68. Frederick Douglass, "An Address to the Colored People of the United States," in *Report of the Proceedings of the Colored National Convention* (Rochester: John Dick, 1848), pp. 18, 20, 19.

69. *NS*, 15 September 1848, p. 2; Delany to M. H. Burnham, "Establishment of a Paper," p. 3. On Douglass and Ward, see *NS*, 4 May 1849; and on Douglass and Garnet, see *NS*, issues of 26 January 1849, 2 March 1849, 22 June 1849, 27 July 1849, and esp. 17 August 1849. See also Aptheker, *Documentary History of the Negro People*, 1:288–90; Stuckey, *Slave Culture*, chap 3; and Joel Schor, *Henry Highland Garnet: A Voice of Black Radicalism in the Nineteenth Century* (Westport, Conn.: Greenwood, 1977), pp. 103–7.

70. Ullman, *Martin R. Delany*, p. 111.

71. Douglass's 30 May 1850 attack on Ward in the supplement to the *North Star* is cited in *Writings*, 1:96.

72. Delany to Samuel R. Ward, letter of 13 June 1850, *NS*, 27 June 1850, p. 2. In his 1855 autobiography, Samuel Ringgold Ward had only this to say about Douglass: "Mr. Douglass, as an orator, is winning for himself and his people not only fame, but, what is far better, the power of great and varied usefulness" (*Autobiography of a Fugitive Negro: His Anti-Slavery Labours in the United States, Canada, and England* [London: John Snow, 1855], p. 96).

73. Delany to Douglass, 4 June 1848, p. 2.

74. Delany to Ward, 13 June 1850, p. 2. (Arthur Gorgëy, a commander of the Hungarian republican army, chose to surrender to Russia when he believed the cause was lost, forcing Kossuth to resign.)

75. *NS*, 27 June 1850, p. 2; Delany to Douglass, letter of 1 July 1850, *NS*, 11 July 1850, p. 2.

76. Delany to Lewis Woodson, letter of 12 October 1850, *NS*, 24 October 1850, p. 2. The letter is co-signed by J. B. Vashon and P. Blackston. On Douglass and Woodson, see Miller, *Black Nationality*, p. 104.

77. Delany to Douglass, letter of 24 July 1848, *NS*, 4 August 1848, p. 3.

1. Harriet Beecher Stowe, *Uncle Tom's Cabin; or, Life among the Lowly*, ed. Elizabeth Ammons (New York: W. W. Norton, 1994), pp. 374, 375. Founded in 1816, the American Colonization Society (ACS) sought to encourage free blacks to emigrate to the colony of Liberia. Central to the society's beliefs was the notion that whites and blacks could not live together in the United States. Stowe's father, Lyman Beecher, was a prominent supporter of the ACS.

2. Stowe, *Uncle Tom's Cabin*, pp. 375, 386, 387, 388. For a different reading of the novel's cataloguing of free blacks in the final pages, see Gillian Brown, *Domestic Individualism: Imagining Self in Nineteenth-Century America* (Berkeley: University of California Press, 1990), pp. 58–59.

3. Richard Yarborough, "Strategies of Black Characterization in *Uncle Tom's Cabin* and the Early Afro-American Novel," in *New Essays on "Uncle Tom's Cabin,"* ed. Eric J. Sundquist (New York: Cambridge University Press, 1986), p. 68. For a useful overview of African American debate on *Uncle Tom's Cabin*, see Marva Banks, "*Uncle Tom's Cabin* and Antebellum Black Response," in *Readers in History: Nineteenth-Century American Literature and the Contexts of Response*, ed. James L. Machor (Baltimore: Johns Hopkins University Press, 1993), pp. 209–27. Banks overstates blacks' resistance to the novel, arguing that the majority of blacks at midcentury regarded *Uncle Tom's Cabin* as "a curse that encouraged continuation of the doctrine of white supremacy in America" (225). The positive response of Douglass and his many associates to Stowe's novel belies this generalization; see, for example, the discussion below of the 1853 Rochester convention. On the response of modern African American critics to *Uncle Tom's Cabin*, see Thomas F. Gossett, *"Uncle Tom's Cabin" and American Culture* (Dallas: Southern Methodist University Press, 1985), pp. 388–96. Surely the most influential attack on the novel by an African American writer has been James Baldwin's "Everybody's Protest Novel" (1949), which excoriates Stowe for her "self-righteous, virtuous sentimentality" (rpt. in *Critical Essays on Harriet Beecher Stowe*, ed. Elizabeth Ammons [Boston: G. K. Hall, 1980], p. 92).

4. Floyd J. Miller, *The Search for a Black Nationality: Black Emigration and Colonization, 1787–1863* (Urbana: University of Illinois Press, 1975), p. 271; Frederick Douglass, "A Nation in the Midst of a Nation: An Address Delivered in New York, New York, on 11 May 1853," in *Papers*, 2:427; Martin Robison Delany, *The Condition, Elevation, Emigration, and Destiny of the Colored People of the United States* (1852; rpt., New York: Arno, 1969), p. 12.

5. Offering an interpretation of the end to the *North Star* coeditorship that is consistent with this binarism (and representative of critical commentary on the matter), Nell Irvin Painter argues that the break resulted from their "growing philosophical divergence . . . for Douglass welcomed the support of white abolitionists while Delany criticized them for racial prejudice and preferred that blacks help themselves" ("Martin R. Delany: Elitism and Black Nationalism," in *Black Leaders of the Nineteenth Century*, ed. Leon Litwack and August Meier [Urbana: University of Illinois Press, 1988], p. 153). Sterling Stuckey argues that "a cardinal tenet of nineteenth-century black nationalism" was that blacks should be willing to take "assistance from whites" (*The Ideological Origins of Black Nationalism*, ed. Stuckey [Boston: Beacon,

1972], p. 11). On these terms, both Douglass and Delany were in the mainstream of black nationalist thought circa 1849–52.

6. Avery founded the Allegheny Institute and Mission Church (renamed Avery College at his death in 1858). According to Delany, the white Avery was inspired by Delany to help Pittsburgh's blacks. As Rollin relates from her conversations with Delany, "After reading his [Delany's] editorial [in the *Mystery*] on the social requirements of the colored people, it is said that Rev. Charles Avery determined to do something tangible for them" (50). On Delany and Avery, see also Ann Greenwood Wilmoth, "Pittsburgh and the Blacks: A Short History, 1780–1875" (Ph.D. diss., Pennsylvania State University, 1975), pp. 27–29. According to Wilmoth, ten white doctors and three white ministers wrote in support of Delany's application to medical school (19).

7. Cited in Victor Ullman, *Martin R. Delany: The Beginnings of Black Nationalism* (Boston: Beacon, 1971), p. 112; Miller, *Black Nationality*, p. 124; Dorothy Sterling, *The Making of an Afro-American: Martin Robison Delany, 1812–1885* (Garden City, N.J.: Doubleday, 1971), p. 130. While the students nobly proclaimed that "we have no objection to the education and elevation of blacks," they nonetheless did not want educated at Harvard those "whose company we would not keep in the streets, and whose Society and associates we could not tolerate in our houses" (Sterling, *The Making of an Afro-American*, pp. 130–31). See also Philip Cash, "Pride, Prejudice, and Politics" (1980), in *Blacks at Harvard: A Documentary History of African-American Experience at Harvard and Radcliffe*, ed. Werner Sollors, Caldwell Titcomb, and Thomas A. Underwood (New York: New York University Press, 1993), pp. 22–31.

8. Though its name evokes the ominous confusions and racial uncertainties of Melville's "Benito Cereno," Greytown got its name in 1848 when the British seized the port city by the San Juan River, San Juan del Norte, and renamed it in honor of Sir Charles Grey, the British governor of Jamaica. Having established a presence in Nicaragua on the grounds that they were offering a "protectorate" to the indigenous Miskito Indians of Nicaragua's eastern Mosquito Coast, the British occupiers hoped to capitalize on the gold fever of 1848 to develop a profitable isthmian route to California. Despite the Clayton-Bulwer Treaty of 1850, with Great Britain and the United States agreeing that "neither will ever . . . occupy, or fortify, or colonize, or assume or exercise any dominion over Nicaragua, Costa Rica, the Mosquito Coast, or any part of Central America," San Juan del Norte remained a contested site between U.S. and British interests. Cornelius Vanderbilt acquired shipping rights there from the Nicaragua government, and throughout the 1850s U.S. military forces supported his efforts to extend his hold on the region in the face of British resistance and, eventually, William Walker's filibustering campaigns. In July 1854 the U.S. minister to Nicaragua, wounded by a tossed bottle when he came to the defense of an American captain, ordered U.S. naval ships to bombard San Juan del Norte. The firebombing completely destroyed the town. On the Clayton-Bulwer Treaty, see Mary Wilhemine Williams, *Anglo-American Isthmian Diplomacy: 1815–1915* (1916; rpt., New York: Russell and Russell, 1965), p. 97. On the United States and Great Britain in Nicaragua, see also Craig L. Dozier, *Nicaragua's Mosquito Shore: The Years of British and American Presence* (Tuscaloosa: University of Alabama Press, 1985); and Charles H. Brown, *Agents of Manifest Destiny: The Lives and Times of the Filibusters* (Chapel Hill: University of North Carolina Press, 1980), pt. 3.

9. Rollin, p. 80. In keeping with the nature of the election, Delany confided to Rollin that he thought it best to bring to Greytown "his own *council of state*" (80). I have been unable to corroborate Delany's claim that he was elected Greytown's civil governor. What emerged in Greytown around this time was a predominately Creole governing body that, in alliance with the British, remained in conflict with the United States.

10. See Rollin, p. 81. Painter argues that the book's origins lie in Delany's "objecting to Stowe's paternalism and to her use of colonization to solve the race problem" ("Martin R. Delany," p. 154).

11. The fullest account of the debate on emigration may be found in Miller, *Black Nationality*. See also Hollis R. Lynch, "Pan-Negro Nationalism in the New World, before 1862" (1966), rpt. in *The Making of Black America: Essays in Negro Life and History*, ed. August Meier and Elliott Rudwick (New York: Atheneum, 1971), 1:42–65; and Stuckey, *Ideological Origins of Black Nationalism*.

12. Delany, *Condition, Elevation, Emigration, and Destiny of the Colored People*, p. 1. Hereinafter, all page references to this edition (cited as *Condition*) will be given parenthetically in the text.

13. Robert M. Kahn, "The Political Ideology of Martin Delany," *Journal of Black Studies* 14 (1984): 425. My discussion of *Condition* is indebted to Kahn's excellent essay. For key African American texts on blacks' contributions to the United States, see William C. Nell, *The Services of Colored Americans in the Wars of 1776 and 1812* (Boston: Prentiss and Sawyer, 1851); and William Wells Brown, *The Black Man, His Antecedents, His Genius, and His Achievements* (New York: Thomas Hamilton, 1863). Delany's racial egalitarianism does not extend fully to Native Americans, who are described as less hardy than the transplanted Africans (hence the European colonizers' decision to enslave Africans and not Native Americans [*Condition*, 21–22]). On antebellum "scientific" racialism see William Stanton, *The Leopard's Spots: Scientific Attitudes toward Race in America, 1815–1859* (Chicago: University of Chicago Press, 1960); George M. Fredrickson, *The Black Image in the White Mind: The Debate on Afro-American Character and Destiny, 1817–1914* (New York: Harper Torchbook, 1972), esp. pp. 71–96; and Reginald Horsman, *Race and Manifest Destiny: The Origins of American Racial Anglo-Saxonism* (Cambridge: Harvard University Press, 1981), p. 134.

14. Wilson Jeremiah Moses argues that "black nationalism in the nineteenth century was much concerned with preserving Anglo-American values and transmitting them, in modified form, to the black community" (*The Golden Age of Black Nationalism, 1850–1925* [1978; rpt., New York: Oxford University Press, 1988], p. 11). Though Moses may be overstating the case (Delany might argue that "Anglo-American" values owe a good deal to "African" values), I think that Delany's attraction to such values had much to do with the conflicts I am describing in his oppositional rhetoric.

15. For a useful discussion of the ways in which Delany's emigrationism draws on "the diaspora concept" central to "Jewish experiences of dispersal," see Paul Gilroy, *The Black Atlantic: Modernity and Double Consciousness* (Cambridge: Harvard University Press, 1993), p. 23.

16. During 1850–51, efforts among Central American states to confederate into a Union called Representación Nacional failed when Guatemala defeated the unionists in a battle of 1851.

17. Gilroy, *Black Atlantic*, p. 23; Henry Highland Garnet, "The Past and the Present Condition and the Destiny of the Colored Race" (1848), rpt. in Earl Ofari, *"Let Your Motto Be Resistance": The Life and Thought of Henry Highland Garnet* (Boston: Beacon, 1972), pp. 179, 182, 180; Frederick Douglass, "The Destiny of Colored Americans" (1849), in *Writings*, 1:417. Soon after presenting his speech on the "destiny of the colored race," published in Troy in 1848, Garnet would be advocating selective emigration. But though he declared in a piece printed in the 26 January 1849 *North Star* that "I am in favor of colonization in any part of the United States, Mexico or California, or in the West Indies, or Africa, wherever it promises freedom and enfranchisement" (2), Garnet's main commitment at that time remained to blacks' "enfranchisement in this land of our birth" (*NS*, 2 March 1849, p. 2). In 1838, Delany's mentor Lewis Woodson had proposed Canada and the British West Indies as possible sites for African American emigration. By 1850, however, he had decided that black emigration was a mistake. See Floyd J. Miller, " 'The Father of Black Nationalism': Another Contender," *Civil War History* 17 (1971): 316–17.

18. Like Hawthorne in *The House of the Seven Gables* (1851), Delany suggests that the solution to the problem of generational transmission lies in transplantation. As he explains, in language that seems equally relevant to Hawthorne's Pyncheons and Chanticleer: "A continuance in any position becomes what is termed 'Second Nature;' it begets an *adaptation* and *reconciliation* of *mind* to such condition. It changes the whole physiological condition of the system, and adapts man and woman to a higher or lower sphere in the pursuits of life" (*Condition*, 206).

19. See Howard Holman Bell, *A Survey of the Negro Convention Movement, 1830–1861* (1953; rpt., New York: Arno, 1969), p. 134. Miller speculates that Delany refused during the 1851–52 period to commit himself to particular emigrationist movements because he wished "to maintain an independent and dominant role in any nationalist-emigrationist movement which might develop" (*Black Nationality*, p. 125). This seems to me a partial explanation for Delany's hesitancy, as it fails to note how conflicted Delany was in *Condition* between his Central and South American utopian emigrationism, on the one hand, and his hopes for social amelioration in the United States, on the other. The proceedings of what Douglass termed the "Great Anti-Colonization Meeting" appeared on the front page of the 29 April 1852 issue of *FDP*.

20. *Pennsylvania Freeman*, 29 April 1852, p. 70; *Pennsylvania Freeman*, 6 May 1852, p. 74.

21. *Liberator*, 7 May 1852, p. 74; *Liberator*, 21 May 1852, p. 83.

22. Delany to Douglass, letter of 10 July 1852, *FDP*, 23 July 1852, p. 3. A week earlier, Douglass had alerted his readers to the forthcoming publication of Delany's letter in a notice that mocked Delany's search for a black nation: "M. R. DELANY shall appear next week, and his order shall be attended to. We had missed our old friend, and was about making inquiries for him of a person now residing in Central America! Our readers will be glad to know that at last accounts Mr. Delany was on his way to Pittsburgh; and as far as we know, 'en route' to nowhere else" (*FDP*, 16 July 1852, p. 2).

23. Frederick Douglass, "Do Not Send Back the Fugitive" (1850), in *Papers*, 2:248; Douglass, "Resistance to Blood-Houndism" (1851), in *Papers*, 2:276–77.

24. Douglass to Gerrit Smith, letter of 21 January 1851, in *Writings*, 2:149–50. Douglass informed Smith in a letter of 30 March 1849, "My money is all gone" (*Writings*,

1:370). In the late 1840s Smith donated 140,000 acres of mostly uncultivated land in upstate New York to approximately 3,000 black beneficiaries (including Douglass). Though Douglass would swing back and forth between support for the Free Soil and Liberty parties, he showed great allegiance to Smith and was delighted when he won a congressional seat in the elections of 1852. On Douglass and Smith, see John R. McKivigan, "The Frederick Douglass–Gerrit Smith Friendship and Political Abolitionism in the 1850s," in *Frederick Douglass: New Literary and Historical Essays*, ed. Eric J. Sundquist (Cambridge: Cambridge University Press, 1990), pp. 205–32. See also Ralph Volney Harlow, *Gerrit Smith: Philanthropist and Reformer* (New York: Henry Holt, 1939), pp. 237–58.

25. Douglass publicly broke with Garrison in his May 1851 speech to the American Anti-Slavery Society in Syracuse (*Papers*, 2:331–37). See also David W. Blight, *Frederick Douglass' Civil War: Keeping Faith in Jubilee* (Baton Rouge: Louisiana State University Press, 1989), p. 33; and Benjamin Quarles, *Frederick Douglass* (Washington, D.C.: Associated Publishers, 1948), p. 75.

26. Quarles, *Frederick Douglass*, p. 83. On Douglass as a journalist, see ibid., pp. 80–98; and Shelly Fisher Fishkin and Carla L. Peterson, " 'We Hold These Truths to Be Self-Evident': The Rhetoric of Frederick Douglass's Journalism," in *Frederick Douglass: New Literary and Historical Essays*, ed. Sundquist, pp. 166–88.

27. *FDP*, 8 April 1852, p. 2. On the responses of black and white abolitionists to *Uncle Tom's Cabin*, see Gossett, *"Uncle Tom's Cabin" and American Culture*, pp. 168–78.

28. Stowe, *Uncle Tom's Cabin*, p. xiii; Jane Tompkins, *Sensational Designs: The Cultural Work of American Fiction, 1790–1860* (New York: Oxford University Press, 1985), pp. xi–xix.

29. Waldo E. Martin Jr., *The Mind of Frederick Douglass* (Chapel Hill: University of North Carolina Press, 1984), p. 96; William G. Allen to Douglass, 6 May 1852, *FDP*, 20 May 1852, p. 3. Similar hesitations about Tom's passivity would be voiced two more times in *FDP*; see the issues of 17 June 1853, p. 1, and 22 December 1854, p. 3.

30. William J. Wilson, "From Our Brooklyn Correspondent," *FDP*, 17 June 1852, p. 3. In a letter to Douglass printed in the 11 March 1853 *FDP*, Wilson elaborated further on his concerns about blacks surrendering literary authority to whites (2).

31. *FDP*, 13 August 1852, p. 1; *FDP*, 24 December 1852, p. 1; *FDP*, 13 May 1853, p. 3. On *Uncle Tom's Cabin* abroad, see also *FDP*, 8 October 1852, p. 1; *FDP*, 21 January 1853, p. 2; *FDP*, 11 March 1853, p. 1; *FDP*, 26 August 1853, p. 2; and *FDP*, 17 November 1854, p. 3.

32. Douglass thus found the space to print two reviews of W. L. G. Smith's *Life at the South; or, "Uncle Tom's Cabin" As It Is* (1852), among other novelistic proslavery "responses" to *Uncle Tom's Cabin*. As he (or Julia Griffiths) comments on Smith's effort, "To enter the lists in competition with Mrs. Stowe and be defeated, is no disgrace; but . . . we really feel it is a disparagement of the genius of the accomplished authoress before named, to connect, in any way, the mention of her almost perfect work with the trash before us" (*FDP*, 13 August 1852, p. 2). For examples of reviews of other such responses to *Uncle Tom's Cabin*, see *FDP*, 15 October 1852, p. 1; and *FDP*, 21 January 1853, p. 4.

Convinced both of the social uses of the novel and of Stowe's humanitarianism, Douglass, in addition to printing articles on the novel's cultural influence, also

sprinkled the pages of his paper with treacly *Uncle Tom's Cabin* poems and worship-
ful profiles of Stowe. Here is a sample stanza from Mary H. Collier's "Eva's Parting":

> And father, when I'm sleeping,
> In my quiet grave so green,
> And my soul the Lord is keeping
> In the world of bliss unseen;
> You will give the boon of Freedom
> To the old and faithful friend,
> Who has borne me on his bosom,
> Where the white magnolias bend.

See *FDP*, 13 August 1852, p. 4. See also A. N. Cole's "Lines to the Lowly, Written
upon Reading *Uncle Tom's Cabin*," *FDP*, 10 September 1852, p. 4. For Frances Ellen
Watkins Harper's more complex poems on *Uncle Tom's Cabin* in *Frederick Douglass'
Paper*, see "Eliza Harris" (23 December 1853, p. 3), "To Harriet Beecher Stowe"
(3 February 1854, p. 4), and "Eva's Farewell" (31 March 1854, p. 3). For a sample
hagiographic profile, see "Some Account of Mrs. Beecher's Family, by an Alabama
Man," *FDP*, 17 December 1852, p. 1.

33. *FDP*, 21 January 1853, p. 3; Frederick Douglass, "Graham vs. Uncle Tom," *FDP*,
    4 March 1853, p. 1.

34. Stowe to Douglass, 9 June 1851, *Life and Letters of Harriet Beecher Stowe*, ed. Annie
    Fields (Boston: Houghton, Mifflin, 1897), p. 134. On Stowe and Parker, see the fol-
    lowing issues of *FDP*: 29 October 1852, p. 3; 5 November 1852, p. 1; and 12 November
    1852, p. 1. Parker objected to Stowe's remarks in chapter 12 of *Uncle Tom's Cabin* on
    his preaching.

35. Frederick Douglass, "A Day and A Night in 'Uncle Tom's Cabin,'" *FDP*, 14 March
    1853, in *Writings*, 2:228, 227; *FDP*, 15 April 1853, p. 2. Douglass's education plans,
    like Delany's in *Condition*, included black women. As he writes in the 10 Febru-
    ary 1854 *FDP*, he feels it is important to provide "for the female sex, methods and
    means of enjoying an independent and honorable livelihood" (rpt. in *Frederick Doug-
    lass on Women's Rights*, ed. Philip S. Foner [1976; rpt., New York: Da Capo, 1992],
    p. 18).

36. Douglass to Stowe, letter of 8 March 1853, in *Writings*, 2:235; *FDP*, 6 May 1853, p. 2.
    As historians have recently noted, there emerged in mid-nineteenth-century America
    an increasing socioeconomic gap between those engaged in manual and nonmanual
    labor. That said, "upper mechanics," the sort of skilled laborers Douglass would have
    liked his mechanics institute to produce, were generally viewed as having achieved
    middle-class status. See Stuart M. Blumin, *The Emergence of the Middle Class: Social
    Experience in the American City, 1760–1900* (New York: Cambridge University Press,
    1989); and Jonathan A. Glickstein, *Concepts of Free Labor in Antebellum American
    Culture* (New Haven: Yale University Press, 1991).

37. For a somewhat different reading of Delany's debate with Douglass on Stowe's novel,
    see Yarborough, "Strategies of Black Characterization," pp. 71–72.

38. Delany to Douglass, letter of 20 March 1853, *FDP*, 1 April 1853, p. 2. Is Delany pun-
    ning on "deference"? Or did Douglass perhaps allow this typo in order to underscore
    Delany's *difference* from Stowe?

39. Frederick Douglass, "What Are the Colored People Doing for Themselves?," *NS*, 14 July 1848, p. 1; *Papers*, 2:169; Douglass, "Self-Elevation — Rev. S. R. Ward," *FDP*, 13 April 1855, p. 1; Douglass, "Remarks," *FDP*, 1 April 1853, p. 2.

40. Douglass, "Remarks," p. 2.

41. Delany to Douglass, letter of 15 April 1853, *FDP*, 29 April 1853, p. 3; Martin R. Delany, "Domestic Economy," *NS*, 13 April 1849, p. 2; Delany to Douglass, 15 April 1853, p. 3.

42. Delany to Douglass, letter of 18 April 1853, *FDP*, 6 May 1853, p. 3. Marva Banks takes this anecdote as unambiguous evidence of Stowe's colonizationist position: "Stowe's suggestion to the peddler *proves* that her endorsement of Liberia as an alternative homeland for American blacks extended beyond mere fictional license" (*"Uncle Tom's Cabin* and Antebellum Black Response," p. 225; emphasis mine).

43. Delany to Douglass, letter of 13 April 1853, *FDP*, 22 April 1853, p. 3; Delany to Douglass, 6 May 1853, p. 3. Douglass himself had criticized Greenfield for her willingness to perform before all-white crowds (*FDP*, 8 April 1853, p. 2).

44. Robert Purvis to Oliver Johnson, letter of 24 April 1852, *Pennsylvania Freeman*, 29 April 1852, rpt. in *BAP*, 4:124; *FDP*, 6 May 1853, p. 3. In his sympathetic review in the 26 March 1852 *Liberator*, Garrison had also expressed reservations about Stowe's apparent support for African colonization.

45. Delany to Douglass, 6 May 1853, p. 3. For Delany's views on Liberia and Haiti, see, for example, Delany to Douglass, letter of 21 January 1848, *NS*, 4 February 1848: "Liberia, the creature of Colonization, as you have seen, has declared her independence, (for which I commend her, that is, provided she is determined to exist without a *master* and *overseer*,) and for this, she is lauded to the skies as an evidence of the capacity of the colored man for self-government. The proud little Republic of Hayti has for the last fifty years fully demonstrated this truth; yet our *quasi* philanthropists are so *far*-sighted that this fact is too near and apparent to come within the reach of their vision" (2). See also Delany to Douglass, letter of 19 February 1848, *NS*, 3 March 1848, p. 2; Martin R. Delany, "Liberia," *NS*, 2 March 1849, p. 2; and Delany, *Condition*, pp. 169–71.

46. Frederick Douglass, "Henry Clay and Colonization Cant, Sophistry, and Falsehood" (1851), in *Papers*, 2:322, 325. As he argued at an 1851 meeting of the Liberty party: "Why should we not stay here? . . . *We* leveled your forests, *our hands* removed the stumps from your fields, and raised the first crops and brought the first produce to your tables" ("The Free Negro's Place Is in America," in *Papers*, 2:340). See also Douglass's anticolonizationist statements in his May 1851 speech at the meeting of the American Anti-Slavery Society in Syracuse (*Papers*, 2:331). William G. Allen noted in his letter printed in the 20 May 1852 issue of *FDP*: "I have but one regret, with regard to the book, and that is, that the chapter favoring colonization was ever written. I do not, however, apprehend so much harm from it, as some others seem to anticipate" (3). See also the letter of the black minister C. C. Foote in *FDP*, 22 April 1853, p. 2. The matter of Stowe and colonization was addressed at the meeting of the American and Foreign Anti-Slavery Society, the proceedings of which Douglass reprinted in the 27 May 1852 issue of his paper. After a general discussion of colonization, James McCune Smith asserted about *Uncle Tom's Cabin*, "I am thankful for the sunlight without finding fault with its spots" (*FDP*, 27 May 1852, p. 2). For a

later criticism of Stowe's novel as colonizationist, see the letter of George Downing in *FDP*, 10 May 1854, p. 2.

47. *FDP*, 6 May 1853, p. 2. (Note that Douglass, aware of the incendiary nature of Delany's charges, places his response on the page before Delany's letter.) For a discussion of resemblances between Delany's emigrationism and Stowe's colonizationism, see Moses, *Golden Age of Black Nationalism*, esp. pp. 27–45; and Wilson Jeremiah Moses, *Black Messiahs and Uncle Toms: Social and Literary Manipulations of a Religious Myth*, rev. ed. (University Park: Pennsylvania State University Press, 1993), pp. 49–66.

48. Douglass to Stowe, 8 March 1853, 2:233; *FDP*, 6 May 1853, p. 2; Gossett, *"Uncle Tom's Cabin" and American Culture*, p. 294. Benjamin Quarles is more skeptical of Stowe's recanting (*Black Abolitionists* [New York: Oxford University Press, 1969], p. 221).

49. Frederick Douglass, "The Heroic Slave," rpt. in *Frederick Douglass: The Narrative and Selected Writings*, ed. Michael Meyer (New York: Modern Library, 1984), p. 303. The novella appeared in the March 1853 issues of *FDP*. Subsequent parenthetical page references are to the more readily available Modern Library edition. On American Revolutionary ideology in the novella, see Eric J. Sundquist, "Frederick Douglass: Literacy and Paternalism," *Raritan* 6 (1986): 108–24. For backgrounds to the historical slave rebellion, see Howard Jones, "The Peculiar Institution and National Honor: The Case of the *Creole* Slave Revolt," *Civil War History* 21 (1975): 28–50.

The phrase "black, but comely" has its sources in the Song of Solomon (1:5). In his review of Delany's *Condition*, Garrison referred to Delany as " 'black and comely' " (*Liberator*, 7 May 1852, p. 74).

50. See Robert B. Stepto, "Sharing the Thunder: The Literary Exchanges of Harriet Beecher Stowe, Henry Bibb, and Frederick Douglass," in *New Essays on "Uncle Tom's Cabin,"* ed. Sundquist, pp. 135–53. The best close reading of Douglass's novella is Stepto, "Storytelling in Early Afro-American Fiction: Frederick Douglass' 'The Heroic Slave,' " *Georgia Review* 36 (1982): 355–68. See also Raymond Hedin, "Probable Readers, Possible Stories: The Limits of Nineteenth-Century Black Narrative," in *Readers in History*, ed. Machor, esp. p. 188; and P. Gabrielle Foreman, "Sentimental Abolition in Douglass's Decade: Revision, Erotic Conversion, and the Politics of Witnessing in 'The Heroic Slave' and *My Bondage and My Freedom*," in *Criticism and the Color Line: Desegregating American Literary Studies*, ed. Henry B. Wonham (New Brunswick: Rutgers University Press, 1996), pp. 191–204.

51. See esp. William L. Andrews, "The Novelization of Voice in Early African American Narrative," *PMLA* 105 (1990): 27–28; and Richard Yarborough, "Race, Violence, and Manhood: The Masculine Ideal in Frederick Douglass's 'The Heroic Slave,' " in *Frederick Douglass: New Literary and Historical Essays*, ed. Sundquist, pp. 178–79.

52. Yarborough, "Race, Violence, and Manhood," pp. 178–79. On politics and gender in the novella, see also Maggie Sale, "Frederick Douglass and the *Creole* Rebellion," *Arizona Quarterly* 51 (1995): 25–60.

53. See Henry Louis Gates Jr., *Figures in Black: Words, Signs, and the "Racial" Self* (New York: Oxford University Press, 1987), p. 107.

54. I would agree with Yarborough that Douglass's emphasis on Washington's manly individualism is troubling. The other slaves play but a small role in the rebellion, and women slaves, such as Washington's wife, disappear from the novella ("Race, Violence, and Manhood," pp. 176–77). See also Robyn Wiegman, *American Anatomies: Theorizing Race and Gender* (Durham: Duke University Press, 1995), pp. 71–78.

55. Frederick Douglass, "The National League," *NS*, 26 October 1849, in *Writings*, 1:410; Douglass to Gerrit Smith, letter of 21 January 1851, cited in Bell, *Negro Convention Movement*, p. 138.

56. Delany to Douglass, 20 March 1853, p. 2; Frederick Douglass, "A National Convention of the Colored People," *FDP*, 8 April 1853, p. 2; *FDP*, 6 May 1853, p. 2.

57. Frederick Douglass, "Call for a Colored National Convention," *FDP*, 20 May 1853, p. 3 (Douglass repeated the call, with Delany's name still included on the list of supporters, in the issue of 27 May 1853); Delany to Douglass, letter of 30 May 1853, *FDP*, 17 June 1853, p. 2.

58. *Proceedings of the Colored National Convention, Held in Rochester, July 6th, 7th, and 8th, 1853* (Rochester: Frederick Douglass, 1853), pp. 18, 40, 37, 7, 25, 17, 40.

59. Ibid., pp. 4, 36, 37, 40.

60. Douglass's conflict with Garrison flared in 1853 after Garrison insinuated in the 18 November 1853 *Liberator* that Douglass was involved with Julia Griffiths. Several months earlier Douglass criticized blacks associated with Garrison, including William Wells Brown and William C. Nell (the initial publisher of the *North Star*). In the 9 December 1853 issue of *FDP*, Douglass printed several articles published in the *Liberator* attacking him and then offered a long response. Garrison responded to that article in the *Liberator*, 16 December 1853. On Douglass and Garrison in 1853 and 1854, see Quarles, *Frederick Douglass*, pp. 75–79, 105–6.

61. Stowe to Garrison, 19 December 1853, *Life and Letters of Harriet Beecher Stowe*, p. 214; Frederick Douglass, "The Industrial College," *FDP*, 20 January 1854, p. 3. (Stowe had written the December 1853 letter to defend Douglass against Garrison's charge that he was an "apostate" from the cause. She demanded of Garrison: "Is there but one true anti-slavery church and all others infidels? Who shall declare what it is?" [*Life and Letters of Harriet Beecher Stowe*, pp. 214–15]).

62. Quarles, *Frederick Douglass*, p. 131. Though Stowe's 1853 letter to Garrison suggests her support for Douglass's project, in an undated letter to Wendell Phillips she expressed her anger at being pressured to be Douglass's major (single) sponsor, stating that if blacks want an industrial school "why dont [sic] they *have* one — many men among the colored people are richer than I am — & better able to help such an object — Will they *ever* learn to walk?" (cited in Joan D. Hedrick, *Harriet Beecher Stowe: A Life* [New York: Oxford University Press, 1994], p. 247).

63. Frederick Douglass, "The Significance of Emancipation in the West Indies," *FDP*, 7 August 1857, p. 1. In his newspaper in 1854 Douglass printed a series of ten articles by Stowe, "Shadows on the Hebrew Mountains"; extracts from and a positive review of Stowe's *Sunny Memories of Foreign Lands*; and her major essay "An Appeal to the Women of the Free States of America." That same year Stowe contributed, as she had in 1853, a piece for Julia Griffiths's *Autographs for Freedom*, a fund-raising volume for *Frederick Douglass' Paper*. See Harriet Beecher Stowe, "The Two Altars; or, Two Pictures in One," in *Autographs for Freedom*, ed. Julia Griffiths (1853; rpt., Mmemosyne Publishing, 1969), pp. 127–47; and Stowe, "A Day Spent at Playford Hall," in *Autographs for Freedom*, ed. Julia Griffiths (Rochester: Wanzer, Beardsley, 1854), pp. 277–303.

In 1855 Douglass proclaimed, "One flash from the heart-supplied intellect of Harriet Beecher Stowe could light a million camp fires in front of the embattled hosts of Slavery, which, not all the waters of the Mississippi, mingled as they are, with blood, could extinguish" ("The Anti-Slavery Movement," in *Papers*, 3:47). Yet later that year relations between Douglass and Stowe grew more tense. In a letter to Douglass of 24 November 1855, Stowe complained about a remark he had made about her in print and demanded "some definite explanation respecting it." Stowe's letter is available on the Library of Congress's microfilm series, "The Papers of Frederick Douglass," reel 3, Frederick Douglass Collection. My thanks to E. Bruce Kirkham for supplying me with a transcript from his edition-in-progress of Stowe's letters. I have not been able to determine the cause of her displeasure with Douglass.

64. Frederick Douglass, *Life and Times of Frederick Douglass, Written by Himself: His Early Life as a Slave, His Escape from Bondage, and His Complete History* (1881) (1892; rpt., New York: Collier, 1962), pp. 282, 291. In 1882 Douglass attended a celebration of Stowe's seventy-first birthday.

65. Martin R. Delany, "Call for a National Emigration Convention of Colored Men," *FDP*, 26 August 1853, p. 3. Douglass would reprint the call several more times in *FDP*.

66. Frederick Douglass, "The Emigration Convention," *FDP*, 26 August 1853, p. 2; *FDP*, 28 Oct 1853, p. 2; *FDP*, 7 November 1853, p. 3. Douglass also printed a letter from John Jones of Chicago attacking "our misguided friends, Delany, Webb & Co." (*FDP*, 18 November 1853, p. 3). For an early instance of Douglass's practice of attacking Delany by printing critical letters by others, see Johnson Woodlin to Douglass, letter of 17 April 1853, *FDP*, 6 May 1853, p. 3. Douglass's view of Delany as divisive has been reproduced in some of the historical scholarship sympathetic to Douglass. See, for example, Jane H. Pease and William H. Pease, *They Who Would Be Free: Blacks' Search for Freedom, 1830–1861* (New York: Atheneum, 1974), pp. 261–65.

67. Delany to Douglass, letter of 7 November 1853, *FDP*, 18 November 1853, p. 1; Delany to Douglass, letter of 22 November 1853, *FDP*, 2 December 1853, p. 3; Frederick Douglass, "M. R. Delany," *FDP*, 13 January 1854, p. 2 (in this column Douglass discusses Delany's letter to the *Aliened American*, which is not extant).

68. James T. Holly, "In Memoriam," *A.M.E. Church Review* 3 (1886): 120. Sterling similarly remarks, "The Emigration Convention was Martin Delany's show from beginning to end" (*The Making of an Afro-American*, p. 154). Interestingly, nearly one-third of those attending were women, and Delany's own wife, from whom he was frequently separated, was there as well. For information on the Cleveland convention, I am indebted to Miller, *Black Nationality*, pp. 144–49.

69. *Proceedings of the National Emigration Convention of Colored People; Held at Cleveland, Ohio, on Thursday, Friday, and Saturday, the 24th, 25th, and 26th of August, 1854* (Pittsburgh: A. A. Anderson, 1854), pp. 6, 26, 20.

70. Ibid., p. 26.

71. *Proceedings of the National Emigration Convention*, p. 12; Miller, *Black Nationality*, p. 149; Martin R. Delany, "Political Destiny of the Colored Race on the American Continent," in Rollin, pp. 329, 336. "Political Destiny" was first published in *Proceedings of the National Emigration Convention*; I have chosen to use the more accessible Oxford University Press reprinting. The text is also in Stuckey, *Ideological Origins of Black Nationalism*, pp. 195–236.

72. Delany, "Political Destiny," p. 327; *Proceedings of the National Emigration Convention*, p. 24; Delany, "Political Destiny," pp. 335, 334, 338, 352, 353, 354. Stuckey remarks on Delany's knowledge of Central and South America, "Not only did he not understand, for example, the state of Brazilian race relations, but his informa-

tion regarding the number of black people in Latin America was far from accurate" (*Ideological Origins*, p. 24). As was the case with *Condition*, Delany's emigrationism in "Political Destiny" projected utopian desires on the resistant realities of Central and South America.

73. Barbara J. Fields, "Ideology and Race in American History," in *Region, Race, and Reconstruction: Essays in Honor of C. Van Woodward*, ed. J. Morgan Kousser and James M. McPherson (New York: Oxford University Press, 1982), p. 162.

74. On similarities between what he terms "black chauvinism" and Stowe's romantic racialism, see Moses, *The Golden Age of Black Nationalism*, pp. 24–28. For the most part, Moses can seem quite unsympathetic to Delany, arguing (unfairly, I think) that he indulged in "breast-beating chauvinism" (41) and that he failed "to question racial stereotypes" (46). My reading of Delany emphasizes the local contextual factors — white racist practices, Douglass's editorial control of *FDP*—that led him to view racial chauvinism as an appropriate rhetorical means to marshal black support for his emigration program. For a provocative discussion of the progressive uses of racialist stereotyping, see Arthur Riss, "Racial Essentialism and Family Values in *Uncle Tom's Cabin*," *American Quarterly* 46 (1994): 513–44. On Stowe's romantic racialist belief that blacks were natural Christians, see Fredrickson, *Black Image in the White Mind*, pp. 97–129.

75. Delany, "Political Destiny," p. 335.

76. M. R. Delany, *The Origin and Objects of Ancient Freemasonry; Its Introduction into the United States, and Legitimacy among Colored Men: A Treatise Delivered before St. Cyprian Lodge, No. 13, June 24th, A.D. 1853—A.L. 5853* (1853; rpt., Xenia, Ohio, 1904), p. 22; Delany, "Political Destiny," p. 338.

77. *Proceedings of the National Emigration Convention*, pp. 12, 28.

78. Frederick Douglass, "Colored Emigration Convention," *FDP*, 8 September 1854, p. 2; G. B. Vashon, "The Late Cleveland Convention," *FDP*, 17 November 1854, p. 3. Vashon had helped Delany edit the *Mystery* during the mid-1840s, and in the *North Star* Delany had celebrated his legal achievements. See, for example, Delany to Douglass, 21 January 1848, p. 2.

79. Douglass, "Our Plan for Making Kansas a Free State," *FDP*, 15 September 1854, rpt. in *Writings*, 2:312.

80. B. D. J. to Douglass, letter of 7 November 1853, *FDP*, 18 November 1853, p. 3; Waldo E. Martin Jr., "Frederick Douglass: Humanist as Race Leader," in *Black Leaders of the Nineteenth Century*, ed. Litwack and Meier, p. 71.

CHAPTER THREE

1. Frederick Douglass, "Slavery, Freedom, and the Kansas-Nebraska Act" (1854), in *Papers*, 2:557. In the same speech, Douglass optimistically asserts, "I have no fear for the ultimate triumph of free principles in this country" (*Papers*, 2:558–59). David W. Blight argues that Douglass's optimism during the mid-1850s rested, "in part, on the romantic notion that black people possessed a kind of natural hopefulness forged by necessity under bondage" (*Frederick Douglass' Civil War: Keeping Faith in Jubilee* [Baton Rouge: Louisiana State University Press, 1989], p. 4).

2. Eric J. Sundquist, *To Wake the Nations: Race in the Making of American Literature*

(Cambridge: Harvard University Press, 1993), p. 89; John Ernest, *Resistance and Reformation in Nineteenth-Century African-American Literature: Brown, Wilson, Jacobs, Delany, Douglass, and Harper* (Jackson: University Press of Mississippi, 1995), p. 150. There are signs of a renewed critical interest in *My Bondage and My Freedom*. Notable readings include Thomas De Pietro, "Vision and Revision in the Autobiographies of Frederick Douglass," *CLA Journal* 26 (1983): 384–96; William L. Andrews, "The 1850s: The First Afro-American Literary Renaissance," in *Literary Romanticism in America*, ed. Andrews (Baton Rouge: Louisiana State University Press, 1981), pp. 38–60; Andrews, *To Tell a Free Story: The First Century of Afro-American Autobiography, 1760–1865* (Urbana: University of Illinois Press, 1986), pp. 214–39, 280–91; Andrews, introduction to *My Bondage and My Freedom*, by Frederick Douglass (Urbana: University of Illinois Press, 1987), pp. xi–xxviii; Sundquist, *To Wake the Nations*, chap. 1; Stephanie A. Smith, "Heart Attacks: Frederick Douglass's Strategic Sentimentality," *Criticism* 34 (1992): 193–216; and Priscilla Wald, *Constituting Americans: Cultural Anxiety and Narrative Form* (Durham: Duke University Press, 1995), chap. 1. For a provocative analysis of the reasons why some abolitionists and Americanists have preferred Douglass's *Narrative of the Life of Frederick Douglass, an American Slave* to *Bondage*, see Wilson J. Moses, "Dark Forests and Barbarian Vigor: Paradox, Conflict, and Africanity in Black Writing before 1914," *American Literary History* 1 (1989): 637–55, esp. 637–42.

3. Frederick Douglass, "What to the Slave Is the Fourth of July?: An Address Delivered in Rochester, New York, on 5 July 1852," in *Papers*, 2:371, 362. On antebellum blacks' invocations of American Revolutionary ideals, see Eric J. Sundquist, "Slavery, Revolution, and the American Renaissance," in *The American Renaissance Reconsidered: Selected Papers from the English Institute, 1982–83*, ed. Walter Benn Michaels and Donald E. Pease (Baltimore: Johns Hopkins University Press, 1985), pp. 1–33. For a fascinating discussion of Douglass's appropriation of Revolutionary rhetoric as a hybridized form of "discursive passing" (195), see Russ Castronovo, *Fathering the Nation: American Genealogies of Slavery and Freedom* (Berkeley: University of California Press, 1995), pp. 194–99.

4. *Walker's Appeal, with a Brief Sketch of His Life. By Henry Highland Garnet. And Also Garnet's "Address to the Slaves of the United States of America"* (New York: J. H. Tobitt, 1848), pp. 84, 27, 37, 95, 96; William Wells Brown, *St. Domingo: Its Revolution and Its Patriots. A Lecture, Delivered before the Metropolitan Athenaeum, London, May 16, and at St. Thomas' Church, Philadelphia, December 20, 1854* (Boston: Bela Marsh, 1855), p. 38; Martin R. Delany, *Blake; or, The Huts of America*, ed. Floyd J. Miller (Boston: Beacon, 1970), p. 113; Douglass, "What to the Slave Is the Fourth of July?," pp. 364, 383. For a useful discussion of blacks' hesitations in expressing anger in their fictional writings, see Raymond Hedin, "The Structuring of Emotion in Black American Fiction," *Novel* 16 (1982): 35–54.

5. Douglass, "What to the Slave Is the Fourth of July?," pp. 362, 365, 360. Near the beginning of the speech he states that the American Revolution is to Americans "what the Passover was to the emancipated people of God" (360).

6. Andrews, *To Tell a Free Story*, p. 239.

7. Theodore Weld, *American Slavery as It Is: Testimony of a Thousand Witnesses* (New York: American Anti-Slavery Society, 1839), pp. 115, 116, 132. For a discussion of the place of temperance in Garrison's antislavery career, see R. Jackson Wilson, *Figures*

of Speech: American Writers and the Literary Marketplace, from Benjamin Franklin to Emily Dickinson (New York: Alfred A. Knopf, 1989), pp. 117–58. On abolitionists' emphasis on the temptations of power, see Ronald G. Walters, The Antislavery Appeal: American Abolitionism after 1830 (Baltimore: Johns Hopkins University Press, 1976), p. 71. As a historian of antebellum temperance reform observes, central to the liberationist agenda of the movement was the belief that "to be free, it was necessary to curb appetites, to subordinate passions to reason, to control animalistic impulses through the development of moral ideals" (W. J. Rorabaugh, The Alcoholic Republic: An American Tradition [New York: Oxford University Press, 1979], p. 200).

8. Samuel Cornish, "Responsibility of Colored People in the Free States," in BAP, 3:219–20; "Proceedings of the State Convention of the Colored Freemen of Pennsylvania, Held in Pittsburgh, on the 23d, 24th, and 25th of August, 1841, for the Purpose of Considering Their Condition, and the Means of Its Improvement," rpt. in Proceedings of the Black State Conventions, 1840–1865, ed. Philip S. Foner and George E. Walker (Philadelphia: Temple University Press, 1979), 1:109; Northern Star and Freeman's Advocate 1 (1842): 18. See also William Whipper's important temperance address, delivered before the Colored Temperance Society of Philadelphia on 8 January 1834 and printed in the June and July 1834 issues of the Liberator, in BAP, 3:119–31. On Delany's interest in temperance in the 1830s, see Victor Ullman, Martin R. Delany: The Beginnings of Black Nationalism (Boston: Beacon, 1971), pp. 25–30; Dorothy Sterling, The Making of an Afro-American: Martin Robison Delany, 1812–1885 (Garden City, N.Y.: Doubleday, 1971), pp. 42–43; and Rollin, pp. 24, 42–44.

9. Anthony Benezet, for example, in a pamphlet revealingly titled Serious Considerations on Several Important Subjects; viz. on War and Its Inconsistency with the Gospel, Observations on Slavery, and Remarks on the Nature and Bad Effects of Spirituous Liquors (Philadelphia: Joseph Crukshank, 1778), warned his readers of the dangers of succumbing to "passions of fallen animal nature" such as "the lust of dominion." That "lust," Benezet argued, was evidenced both in British tyranny over the colonists and in enslavers' "uncontrollable power over their fellow-men." In both cases, Benezet warned, "the lust of dominion" brought about a loss of self-control not unlike that which resulted from drinking alcoholic beverages (6, 10, 27, 41). As Rorabaugh observes, Benezet and other antialcohol crusaders presented liberty "in a new light, not as man's freedom to drink unlimited quantities of alcohol but as a man's freedom to be his own master, with the attendant responsibility to exercise self-control, moderation, and reason" (Alcoholic Republic, p. 37). On Franklin, see Drew R. McCoy, "Benjamin Franklin's Vision of a Republican Economy for America," William and Mary Quarterly, 3d ser., 35 (1978): 605–28; and T. H. Breen, " 'Baubles of Britain': The American and Consumer Revolutions of the Eighteenth Century," Past and Present, no. 119 (May 1988): 73–104.

10. Donald Yacovone, "The Transformation of the Black Temperance Movement, 1827–1854: An Interpretation," Journal of the Early Republic 8 (1988): 285, 290. On black temperance see also Benjamin Quarles, Black Abolitionists (New York: Oxford University Press, 1969), pp. 91–100; Frederick Cooper, "Elevating the Race: The Social Thought of Black Leaders, 1827–50," American Quarterly 24 (1972): 604–25; Jane H. Pease and William H. Pease, They Who Would Be Free: Blacks' Search for Freedom, 1830–1861 (New York: Atheneum, 1974), pp. 56–57, 124–26; and Denise Herd, "Ambiguity in Black Drinking Norms: An Ethnohistorical Interpretation," in The

American Experience with Alcohol: Contrasting Cultural Perspectives, ed. Linda A. Bennett and Genevieve M. Ames (New York: Plenum, 1985), pp. 149–70.

11. Frederick Douglass, "Intemperance and Slavery: An Address Delivered in Cork, Ireland, on 20 October 1845," in Papers, 1:56. The speech survives as a transcription from the contemporary journal Truth Seeker 1 (1845–46): 142–44. Soon after his escape from slavery, Douglass was speaking on moral issues to New Bedford's African Methodist Episcopal Zion Church, where temperance was one of the topics regularly addressed in discussion groups on "moral improvement." See William S. McFeely, Frederick Douglass (New York: W. W. Norton, 1991), p. 83. For a reading of Douglass and temperance somewhat different from mine, see John Crowley's discussion of Douglass in Temperance and American Literature, ed. David S. Reynolds and Debra J. Rosenthal (Amherst: University of Massachusetts Press, forthcoming). Crowley argues that Douglass literally was an alcoholic.

12. Douglass, "Intemperance and Slavery," 1:56, 57. Speaking as an unaccredited delegate to the 1846 World's Temperance Convention in London, Douglass had made a similar point about the racism permeating American temperance organizations; see Douglass, Bondage, p. 236. The 1842 attack on the Moyamensing Temperance Society was an important source for Frank J. Webb's The Garies and Their Friends (1857); see Robert S. Levine, "Disturbing Boundaries: Temperance, Black Elevation, and Violence in Frank J. Webb's The Garies and Their Friends," Prospects 19 (1994): 349–74.

13. On the Washingtonian movement, see Ian R. Tyrrell, Sobering Up: From Temperance to Prohibition in Antebellum America, 1800–1860 (Westport, Conn.: Greenwood, 1979), esp. pp. 159–90; and Sean Wilentz, Chants Democratic: New York City and the Rise of the American Working Class (New York: Oxford University Press, 1984), pp. 304–14. Central to the popularity of the Washingtonian movement was its shifting of power from social elites to the working and middle classes. For a fascinating discussion of the homoerotic and subversive aspects of some Washingtonian writings, see Michael Moon, Disseminating Whitman: Revision and Corporeality in "Leaves of Grass" (Cambridge: Harvard University Press, 1991), pp. 53–58.

14. Northern Star and Freeman's Advocate 1 (1842): 25; T. S. Arthur, Temperance Tales; or, Six Nights with the Washingtonians (1842) (Philadelphia: W. A. Leary, 1848), 1:3, 4, 2, 4. (Arthur, or his publisher, added the "Temperance Tales" to the title of reprintings of his 1842 best-seller.)

15. Frederick Douglass, "Principles of Temperance Reform" (1848), in Papers, 2:106–7. The "prison-house," which here refers to the tavern, also commonly referred to the institution of chattel slavery. In his preface to Douglass's Narrative of the Life of Frederick Douglass, an American Slave (ed. Houston A. Baker Jr. [New York: Penguin, 1982]), William Lloyd Garrison states that Douglass escaped from the "prison-house of bondage" (33). J. C. Hathaway, in his preface to William Wells Brown's Narrative of William Wells Brown, a Fugitive Slave (1847), calls Brown's narrative "a voice from the prison-house" (rpt. in Puttin' On Ole Massa: The Slave Narratives of Henry Bibb, William Wells Brown, and Solomon Northup, ed. Gilbert Osofsky [New York: Harper and Row, 1969], p. 177).

16. Douglass, Narrative, pp. 34–35, 38.

17. Douglass, Narrative, p. 113. For a reading suggesting that in Narrative Douglass turns against a patriarchal God, see Donald B. Gibson, "Christianity and Individualism:

(Re-)Creation and Reality in Frederick Douglass's Representation of Self," *African-American Review* 26 (1992): 591–603.

18. Frederick Douglass, "Colored People Must Command Respect" (1848), in *Papers*, 2:113. In his 1846 "The Temperance Cause in America and Britain," Douglass elaborated similarly on the importance of his own decision to resist alcoholic beverages: "I am a teetotaler, and I am so because I would elevate my race from the degradation into which they have been cast by slavery and other circumstances" (in *Papers*, 1:265).

19. For Delany's comments on temperance, see the following issues of the *North Star*: 3 March 1848, p. 3; 24 November 1848, p. 4; and 5 January 1849, p. 3.

20. *NS*, 7 January 1848, p. 3; *NS*, 28 April 1848, p. 1; "Disagreeable Breath," *NS*, 1 September 1848, p. 2; "The Humanizing Influence of Cleanliness," *NS*, 10 November 1848, p. 4. In an 1848 article on "The Temperance Cause," Douglass wrote: "We are now quite satisfied that one of the greatest hindrances to our elevation and improvement in this city [Rochester], is the too general use of ardent spirits. While the mass of colored persons in this city are sober, upright, and intelligent, there are just a sufficient number of exceptions to this rule, with the aid of the prejudice against us, to make the influence in our favor nugatory" (*NS*, 28 July 1848, p. 2).

21. Frederick Douglass, "Colorphobia," *NS*, 25 May 1849, rpt. in *Writings*, 1:385. Angered by the Evangelical Alliance's willingness to traffic with proslavery churches, to note another example from the period, Douglass in 1846 blasted Massachusetts temperance advocate James Marsh for supporting the alliance. In "Slavery in the Pulpit of the Evangelical Alliance" he rhetorically asked Marsh to explain why "if temperance had removed intemperance from the land, . . . it had not removed slavery?" ("Slavery in the Pulpit of the Evangelical Alliance: An Address Delivered in London, England, on 14 September 1846," in *Papers*, 1:411). For Douglass's comments on Father Theobald Mathew, see especially *NS*, issues of 27 July 1849, p. 3; 3 August 1849, p. 1; and 24 August 1849, p. 2. Douglass's attacks on Mathew culminated in a front-page article in the 5 December 1850 *NS*, reprinted from the *St. Louis Republican*, providing evidence of Mathew's untroubled consortings with slave traders. Douglass criticized the Sons of Temperance in *NS*, 27 June 1850, p. 3.

22. *NS*, 17 April 1851, p. 4. Douglass also printed sketches by T. S. Arthur; see the following issues of *NS*: 27 April 1849, 8 December 1848, and 3 August 1849.

23. See *FDP*, issues of 27 November 1851, p. 4, and 13 May 1852, p. 1. In 1851 Douglass reprinted in his paper the text of the proposed Maine liquor law, and between 1852 and 1855 he wrote numerous editorials supporting Gerrit Smith's efforts to pass such a law in New York State. See, for example, the following issues of *FDP*: 25 December 1851, p. 1; 18 March 1852, p. 2; 1 April 1852, p. 1; 28 January 1853, p. 3; 25 February 1853, p. 2; 9 September 1853, p. 2; 11 August 1854, p. 1; and 30 April 1855, p. 1.

24. Gerrit Smith, "Government Bound to Protect from the Dramshop: Speech of Hon. Gerrit Smith on the Sale of Intoxicating Drinks," *FDP*, 11 August 1854, p. 1; Frederick Douglass, "We Are in the Midst of a Moral Revolution," in *Papers*, 2:484 (the speech was printed in the 19 May 1854 issue of *FDP*); "The Maine Law in New York," *FDP*, 1 May 1855, p. 1.

25. "A Horrible Picture of Intemperance," *FDP*, 14 April 1854, p. 1; Frederick Douglass, "Address to My Canadian Brothers and Sisters," *FDP*, 18 August 1854, rpt. in *Papers*, 2:535.

26. Martin Robison Delany, *The Condition, Elevation, Emigration, and Destiny of the Colored People of the United States* (1852; rpt., New York: Arno, 1969), p. 193.

27. Teresa A. Goddu and Craig V. Smith, "Scenes of Writing in Frederick Douglass's *Narrative*: Autobiography and the Creation of Self," *Southern Review* 25 (1989): 839; David Leverenz, *Manhood and the American Renaissance* (Ithaca: Cornell University Press, 1989), pp. 109, 134, 129. On Douglass's complicitous relationship to the power structures of his oppressors, see also Joseph Fichtelberg, *Faith and Method in American Autobiography* (Philadelphia: University of Pennsylvania Press, 1989), pp. 116–61.

28. Gregory S. Jay argues that Douglass's deployment of conventional discourses, given that many of his readers were white, had a "rhetorical utility" ("American Literature and the New Historicism: The Example of Frederick Douglass," *boundary 2* 17 [1990]: 233). The seminal reading of the problematics of Douglass's use of public discourses is Houston A. Baker Jr., *The Journey Back: Issues in Black Literature and Criticism* (Chicago: University of Chicago Press, 1980), pp. 32–47.

29. Andrews, *To Tell a Free Story*, pp. 217, 238. As my discussion will suggest, I regard *My Bondage and My Freedom* as having achieved its own ontological status apart from *Narrative*. Hence I will be referring to the 1855 version of Douglass's life, rather than to the 1855 revision of *Narrative*. That Douglass thought of the texts as two separate texts is clear from his use of self-quotation in *Bondage*: when he conceives of his earlier version as particularly apt in its phrasings—which he does only a handful of times—he quotes from *Narrative* rather than revise; he does this most notably when discussing the significance of the slave songs (*Bondage*, ed. Andrews, p. 65), when lamenting the seemingly imminent death of his grandmother (172–74), when discussing how slavery transforms him into a brute (135–37), and when presenting his troubles with the white workers at Fell's Point (187). There are, of course, excellent reasons for Douglass to have regarded the texts as undertaking considerably different cultural work from considerably different perspectives: not only was the first written while he was under the sway of Garrison and the second after he had renounced Garrison's proslavery reading of the Constitution, but also the first was written before and the second after he emerged as an internationally prominent antislavery spokesperson, the first before and the second after he became a newspaper editor, the first before and the second after the Compromise of 1850, the first before and the second after the adoption of the Maine Law.

30. Douglass, *Bondage*, ed. Andrews, p. 89. Hereinafter, parenthetical page references are to this edition.

31. John Freccero, "Autobiography and Narrative," in *Reconstructing Individualism: Autonomy, Individuality, and the Self in Western Thought*, ed. Thomas C. Heller, Morton Sosan, and David E. Wellbery (Stanford: Stanford University Press, 1986), pp. 16–17. On Douglass and authorship, see also Sundquist, *To Wake the Nations*, pp. 90–91; and Wald, *Constituting Americans*, pp. 73–105.

32. "Speech by James McCune Smith, Delivered at the First Colored Presbyterian Church, New York, New York, 8 May 1855," in *BAP*, 4:292–93. Garrison wrote of how Douglass needed "nothing but a comparatively small amount of cultivation to make him an ornament to society and a blessing to his race" (Douglass, *Narrative*, p. 34). In *Bondage*, Douglass addresses the disturbing problem of the Garrisonians' racialist paternalism (243–45). For a useful discussion of the relationship of slave narratives to

white cultural authorities, see John Sekora, "Black Message/White Envelope: Genre, Authenticity, and Authority in the Antebellum Slave Narrative," *Callaloo* 10 (1987): 482–515; and Sekora, " 'Mr. Editor, If You Please': Frederick Douglass, *My Bondage and My Freedom*, and the End of the Abolitionist Imprint," *Callaloo* 17 (1994): 608–26.

33. As a self-help text, *Bondage* shares some qualities with not only Franklin's autobiography but also the earlier slave narrative by Venture Smith, *A Narrative of the Life and Adventures of Venture, a Native of Africa, but Resident above Sixty Years in the United States of America, Related by Himself* (1798). Venture Smith's editor, making the self-help themes explicit from the start, announced in a prefatory note that his narrative "exhibits a pattern of honesty, prudence, and industry to people of his own color; and perhaps some white people would not find themselves degraded by imitating such an example." See *Five Black Lives: The Autobiographies of Venture Smith, James Mars, William Grimes, the Rev. G. W. Offley, James L. Smith,* ed. Arna Bontemps (Middletown: Wesleyan University Press, 1971), p. 3. William Andrews terms Venture Smith the "first in a long line of black bourgeois autobiographers" (*To Tell a Free Story*, p. 52).

34. Henry Bibb, *Narrative of the Life and Adventures of Henry Bibb, an American Slave* (1849), rpt. in *Puttin' On Ole Massa*, ed. Osofsky, p. 68. For his account of slave drinking, Bibb drew on Douglass's 1845 *Narrative*.

35. Garnet's July 1846 address to the Delevan Temperance Union at Poughkeepsie, New York, is cited in Earl Ofari, *"Let Your Motto Be Resistance": The Life and Thought of Henry Highland Garnet* (Boston: Beacon, 1972), p. 28. Douglass stated similarly, in "Intemperance Viewed in Connection with Slavery: An Address Delivered in Glasgow, Scotland, on 18 February 1846," that alcohol "paralyzes [the slaves'] intellect, and in this way prevents their seeking emancipation" (in *Papers*, 1:166).

36. Sundquist brilliantly elaborates on the "countersubversive tendency (the controlled rebellion, as it were) of the slave holidays" (*To Wake the Nations*, p. 127). See also Eugene D. Genovese, *Roll, Jordan, Roll: The World the Slaves Made* (New York: Vintage, 1976), pp. 566–84.

37. Douglass, "Intemperance Viewed in Connection with Slavery," 1:166; and Douglass, "Reception Speech," in *Bondage*, pp. 251–52.

38. Eric Foner remarks on the Republican rhetoric of the 1850s, "Of all the evils of slavery, none seemed to impress Republicans more than the poverty and degradation of the mass of southern non-slaveholders" (*Free Soil, Free Labor, Free Man: The Ideology of the Republican Party before the Civil War* [New York: Oxford University Press, 1970], pp. 46–47). African American writers tended to adduce the existence of this indolent class of whites both to challenge the stereotype of the indolent black and to argue for the profound influence of social conditions on moral character. In *Slavery in the United States: A Narrative of the Life and Adventures of Charles Ball, a Black Man* (1836; rpt., Detroit: Negro History Press, 1970), editor Isaac Fisher presents the former slave Charles Ball's perspective on the poor whites' "debased and humiliated state of moral servitude": "The slaves generally believe, that however miserable they may be, in their serviled station, it is nevertheless preferable to the degraded existence of these poor white people" (224–25).

39. On the ways in which Douglass's description of Talbot County "forces the reader to gauge the various distances Douglass must have traveled in order to write such

a passage," see Barry Maxwell, "Frederick Douglass's Haven-Finding Art," *Arizona Quarterly* 48 (1992): 55.

40. Solomon Northup, *Twelve Years a Slave*, ed. Sue Eakin and Joseph Logsdon (Baton Rouge: Louisiana State University Press, 1968), p. 157.

41. Sundquist terms the whip in *Bondage* Douglass's "primary metonym" of slavery (*To Wake the Nations*, p. 110).

42. Arguably a certain class bias obtains here, as Douglass, for example, castigates Plummer for his brutal actions against a young slave woman, while letting Colonel Anthony, who refuses to help her, off the hook. Plummer is a mere brute; Anthony's cold treatment "is a part of the system, rather than a part of the man" (56). That said, because it is the master and not the overseer who possesses unlimited power over the slaves, it is the master, as Douglass observes, who is capable of going "*far beyond* the overseer in cruelty" (57). The former slave Austin Steward offers a similarly "classist" view of the overseer as especially intemperate: "If it is a fact, and certainly it is, that the master is thus affected by his costly wine; what, think you, will be the temper and condition of the coarse and heartless overseer who drinks his miserable whisky or bad brandy? It is horrible, beyond description." See Steward's *Twenty-Two Years a Slave and Forty Years a Freeman*, ed. Jane H. Pease and William H. Pease (1857; rpt., Reading, Mass.: Addison-Wesley, 1969), p. 105.

43. Black writers often portrayed the owners and overseers as in bondage to their "animal nature." William Craft's *Running a Thousand Miles for Freedom; or, The Escape of William and Ellen Craft from Slavery* (1860), for example, makes explicit the connections between drinking, sexuality, and morality by documenting the story of a young slave woman who is purchased by "an uneducated and drunken slave dealer," of whom we are told, "A long course of reckless wickedness, drunkenness, and vice, had destroyed . . . every noble impulse." When the drunken master attempts to rape her, she jumps from a window to her death. Craft remarks, "The sudden disappointment, and the loss of two thousand dollars, was more than he could endure; so he drank more than ever, and in a short time died, raving mad with *delirium tremens*." In this passage we move rather easily from intemperance to sexuality, with a sense that while the body of the slave woman has been assaulted, neither her body nor her soul has truly been violated. See William Craft, *Running a Thousand Miles for Freedom; or, The Escape of William and Ellen Craft from Slavery*, rpt. in *Great Slave Narratives*, ed. Arna Bontemps (Boston: Beacon, 1969), pp. 281, 282.

44. John Carlos Rowe, "Between Politics and Poetics: Frederick Douglass and Postmodernity," in *Reconstructing American Literary and Historical Studies*, ed. Gunter H. Lenz et al. (New York: St. Martin's, 1990), p. 204.

45. Sundquist, *To Wake the Nations*, p. 125; Nancy Bentley, "White Slaves: The Mulatto Hero in Antebellum Fiction," *American Literature* 65 (1993): 519. On beast metaphors in *Bondage*, see also Peter A. Dorsey, "Becoming the Other: The Mimesis of Metaphor in Douglass's *My Bondage and My Freedom*," *PMLA* 111 (1996): 435–50.

46. *Proceedings of the Colored National Convention, Held in Rochester, July 6th, 7th, and 8th, 1853* (Rochester: Frederick Douglass, 1853), p. 8. Garnet had proclaimed, "NEITHER GOD, NOR ANGELS, OR JUST MEN, COMMAND YOU TO SUFFER FOR A SINGLE MOMENT. THEREFORE IT IS YOUR SOLEMN AND IMPERATIVE DUTY TO USE EVERY MEANS, BOTH MORAL, INTELLECTUAL, AND PHYSICAL, THAT

PROMISE SUCCESS" (*Garnet's Address*, in *Walker's Appeal, with a Brief Sketch of His Life*, p. 93).

47. Douglass, "We Are in the Midst of a Moral Revolution," 2:482; David Walker, *Walker's Appeal*, pp. 42, 13. See also Frederick Douglass, "Is It Right and Wise to Kill a Kidnapper" (1854), wherein he proclaims, "Every slave-hunter who meets a bloody death in his infernal business, is an argument in favor of the manhood of our race" (in *Writings*, 2:287). On Douglass's increasing militancy during this period, see Blight, *Frederick Douglass' Civil War*, chaps. 3–5.

48. *Truth Stranger than Fiction: Father Henson's Story of His Own Life* (1858; rpt., New York: Corinth, 1962), pp. 88, 90, 92. For the parallel passage in his earlier narrative, see *The Life of Josiah Henson, Formerly a Slave, Now an Inhabitant of Canada, as Narrated by Himself* (Boston: Arthur D. Phelps, 1849), pp. 42–43. Henson, of course, acquired fame when rumor had it that he was the model for Stowe's Uncle Tom.

49. In quoting from his 1845 *Narrative* in describing himself as "a man transformed into a brute!" (*Bondage*, p. 136), Douglass retains the large force of the degradation, while suggesting that notions of an absolute degradation reflect his 1845 and not his 1855 perspective. On Douglass's efforts to present himself as disembodied and in this way challenge cultural conceptions of "the alleged overwhelming corporeality of blackness," see Lindon Barrett, "African-American Slave Narratives: Literacy, the Body, Authority," *American Literary History* 7 (1995): 415.

50. Frederick Douglass, "The Heroic Slave" (1853), in *Frederick Douglass: The Narrative and Selected Writings*, ed. Michael Meyer (New York: Modern Library, 1984), p. 347.

51. Delany, *Blake*, p. 93.

52. Leverenz, *Manhood and the American Renaissance*, p. 115; Bentley, "White Slaves," p. 519; Sundquist, *To Wake the Nations*, p. 123. Andrews's comments on the black Jeremiah are also relevant to this scene: "The great rhetorical task of the jeremiad is to divest self-determinative individualism of its threatening associations with anarchy and antinomianism, the excesses of the unbridled self" (*To Tell a Free Story*, p. 124).

53. Arguments along these lines have been made by Leverenz, *Manhood and the American Renaissance*; Valerie Smith, *Self-Discovery and Authority in Afro-American Narrative* (Cambridge: Harvard University Press, 1987), p. 27; Richard Yarborough, "Race, Violence, and Manhood: The Masculine Ideal in Frederick Douglass's 'The Heroic Slave,'" in *Frederick Douglass: New Literary and Historical Essays*, ed. Eric J. Sundquist (Cambridge: Cambridge University Press, 1990), pp. 178–79; Deborah C. McDowell, "In the First Place: Making Frederick Douglass and the Afro-American Narrative Tradition," in *Critical Essays on Frederick Douglass*, ed. William L. Andrews (Boston: G. K. Hall, 1991), pp. 192–214; and Smith, "Heart Attacks." James Oliver Horton argues that for antebellum blacks "the term *manhood* implied more than gender and was often used to apply to the race in general" (*Free People of Color: Inside the African American Community* [Washington, D.C.: Smithsonian Institution Press, 1993], p. 76).

54. Douglass similarly remarked in his famous "Letter to Thomas Auld" (1848): "One night, while sitting in the kitchen, I heard some of the old slaves talking of their parents having been stolen from Africa by white men, and were sold here as slaves. The whole mystery was solved at once" (see *Writings*, 1:338).

55. On the significance of Douglass's description of his mother, see Henry Louis Gates Jr.,

Figures in Black: Words, Signs, and the "Racial" Self (New York: Oxford University Press, 1987), pp. 121–23; and Peter F. Walker, *Moral Choices: Memory, Desire, and Imagination in Nineteenth-Century American Abolition* (Baton Rouge: Louisiana State University Press, 1978), esp. pp. 251–54. Because Prichard depicts what appears to be a white Egyptian prince, Walker (dubiously) suggests that Douglass had a secret desire to be white.

56. Andrews, *To Tell a Free Story*, p. 229.

57. Frederick Douglass, "Temperance and Anti-Slavery," in *Papers*, 1:207–8.

58. Douglass, "What to the Slave Is the Fourth of July?," p. 374. In the same passage he comments that in Baltimore "many a child has been snatched from the arms of its mother by bargains arranged in a state of brutal drunkenness" (374).

59. Andrews, *To Tell a Free Story*, p. 128.

60. Giles Gunn, *Thinking across the American Grain: Ideology, Intellect, and the New Pragmatism* (Chicago: University of Chicago Press, 1992), p. 32. Brook Thomas argues in a similar vein: "When previously excluded groups employ narratives of progressive emergence, they are not necessarily ironically inverting them. African-American women, for instance, may subscribe to narratives of self-assertion and autonomy . . . because their temporal logic is not identical to that of white, middle-class males for whom such narratives are worthy of ironic undercutting or deconstruction" (*The New Historicism and Other Old-Fashioned Topics* [Princeton: Princeton University Press, 1991], p. 58). See also Maggie Sale, "Critiques from Within: Antebellum Projects of Resistance," *American Literature* 64 (1992): 695–718. Cornel West has characterized American pragmatism "as a form of cultural criticism that attempts to transform linguistic, social, cultural, and political traditions for the purposes of increasing the scope of individual development and democratic operations." Central to this tradition of critical and social thought, according to West, is "a future-oriented instrumentalism" fueled by "optimism, moralism, individualism" (*The American Evasion of Philosophy: A Genealogy of Pragmatism* [Madison: University of Wisconsin Press, 1989], pp. 230, 5, 40). Douglass can be regarded as a pragmatist in just these terms.

61. Mary Louise Pratt, *Imperial Eyes: Travel Writing and Transculturation* (London: Routledge, 1992), p. 7. On capitalism and antislavery, see Thomas L. Haskell, "Capitalism and the Origins of the Humanitarian Sensibility," *American Historical Review* 90 (1985): 339–61, 547–66. Andrews sensitively addresses the issue of Douglass's complicity in the values of the dominant culture (*To Tell a Free Story*, pp. 187–88). See also Houston A. Baker Jr.'s discussion of Douglass's "fully commercial view of his situation" (*Blues, Ideology, and Afro-American Literature: A Vernacular Theory* [Chicago: University of Chicago Press, 1984], p. 48).

62. Leverenz, *Manhood and the American Renaissance*, p. 127. In an appended speech, Douglass asserts that it is the slave culture, not the culture of industrial capitalism, that "reduces man to a mere machine" ("The Nature of Slavery," in *Bondage*, p. 274). For a provocative discussion of work in Douglass's autobiographies, see Nicholas K. Bromell, *By the Sweat of the Brow: Literature and Labor in Antebellum America* (Chicago: University of Chicago Press, 1993), chap. 10.

63. The term is Carla Kaplan's. See her excellent "Narrative Contracts and Emancipatory Readers: *Incidents in the Life of a Slave Girl*," *Yale Journal of Criticism* 6 (1993): 109.

64. C. B. Macpherson, *The Political Theory of Possessive Individualism: Hobbes to Locke* (Oxford: Oxford University Press, 1962), p. 275.

65. Sacvan Bercovitch, afterword to *Ideology and Classic American Literature*, ed. Bercovitch and Myra Jehlen (New York: Cambridge University Press, 1986), p. 425. More
recently, Bercovitch describes Emersonian individualism as "a form of utopian consciousness developed within the premises of liberal culture" (*The Rites of Assent:
Transformations in the Symbolic Construction of America* [New York: Routledge,
1993], p. 345). I am arguing for a similar reading of Douglass's individualism.
66. Henry David Thoreau, "Walking," in *The Selected Works of Thoreau*, ed. Walter Hard-
ing (Boston: Houghton Mifflin, 1975), pp. 661, 662, 684, 686, 660, 685.
67. For a reading of the ladder as a figure of Jacob's ladder, see Gibson, "Christianity and
Individualism," pp. 594–95.
68. The phrase is from Houston Baker's account of blues sensibility in black texts (*Blues,
Ideology*, p. 11), a sensibility that he regards (incorrectly, I think) as lacking in Douglass's autobiographical narratives. In "Douglass's Haven-Finding Art," Maxwell talks
of Douglass's desire for "motion through actual topography" (67).
69. Henry David Thoreau, *Walden and Civil Disobedience*, ed. Michael Meyer (New York:
Penguin, 1983), p. 257.
70. Andrews, *To Tell a Free Story*, p. 239.
71. Frederick Douglass, "The Claims of the Negro Ethnologically Considered," in *Papers*,
2:522.

CHAPTER FOUR

1. *FDP*, 1 February 1856, p. 1; Harriet Beecher Stowe, "Anti-Slavery Literature," *New
York Independent*, 21 February 1856, p. 1.
2. Robert B. Stepto, "Sharing the Thunder: The Literary Exchanges of Harriet Beecher
Stowe, Henry Bibb, and Frederick Douglass," in *New Essays on "Uncle Tom's Cabin,"*
ed. Eric J. Sundquist (New York: Cambridge University Press, 1986), p. 137; Sund-
quist, *To Wake the Nations: Race in the Making of American Literature* (Cambridge:
Harvard University Press, 1993), p. 102. On Stowe's possibly harmful influence on
African American writing, see Richard Yarborough, "Strategies of Black Character-
ization in *Uncle Tom's Cabin* and the Early Afro-American Novel," in *New Essays on
"Uncle Tom's Cabin,"* ed. Sundquist, pp. 45–84. For a more sympathetic reading of
Stowe and black writers, see Harryette Mullen, "Runaway Tongue: Resistant Orality
in *Uncle Tom's Cabin, Our Nig, Incidents in the Life of a Slave Girl*, and *Beloved*," in
*The Culture of Sentiment: Race, Gender, and Sentimentality in Nineteenth-Century
America*, ed. Shirley Samuels (New York: Oxford University Press, 1992), pp. 244–64.
3. Sundquist, *To Wake the Nations*, p. 109. For a thoughtful discussion of the problematic ethics of the currently fashionable tendency to attack Stowe, see Robyn Wiegman, *American Anatomies: Theorizing Race and Gender* (Durham: Duke University
Press, 1995), pp. 193–201.
4. Toni Morrison, "Unspeakable Things Unspoken: The Afro-American Presence in
American Literature," *Michigan Quarterly Review* 28 (1989): 3, 11, 18. See also Morrison's *Playing in the Dark: Whiteness and the Literary Imagination* (Cambridge:
Harvard University Press, 1992). On the influence of Morrison's essay on American
literary and cultural studies, see Shelley Fisher Fishkin, "Interrogating 'Whiteness,'
Complicating 'Blackness': Remapping American Culture," *American Quarterly* 47

(1995): 428–67. On the importance of developing cross-racial dialogical readings, see Ann duCille, *The Coupling Convention: Sex, Text, and Tradition in Black Women's Fiction* (New York: Oxford University Press, 1993), esp. p. 24.

5. Judie Newman thus suggests that *A Key to "Uncle Tom's Cabin"* "might more properly be described as the key to *Dred*" (introduction to *Dred: A Tale of the Great Dismal Swamp*, by Harriet Beecher Stowe [Halifax, England: Ryburn, 1992], p. 14). Newman's excellent British edition promises to revive interest in *Dred*, at least overseas. For a pioneering discussion of African American influences on *Dred*, see Ellen Moers, "Mrs. Stowe's Vengeance," *New York Review of Books*, 3 September 1970, pp. 25–32.

6. *Dred* was popular (and well-received) in its own time. Stowe wrote her husband Calvin on the novel's success in the marketplace: "One hundred thousand copies of 'Dred' sold in four weeks! After that who cares what critics say? It is very bitterly attacked, both from a literary and religious point of view." Stowe's assertions to the contrary, the book had numerous admirers. Not only did Harriet Martineau find the novel "far superior to 'Uncle Tom,'" but George Eliot argued in *The Westminster Review* that those finding fault with the book "are something like men pursuing a prairie fire with desultory watering-cans." See Harriet Beecher Stowe to Calvin Stowe, 10 October 1856, *Life of Harriet Beecher Stowe: Compiled from Her Letters and Journals*, ed. Charles Edward Stowe (Boston: Houghton, Mifflin, 1889), p. 279 (Harriet Martineau's praise of *Dred* is cited on p. 308); George Eliot, "Review of *Dred: A Tale of the Great Dismal Swamp*," in *The Westminster Review*, October 1856, rpt. in *Critical Essays on Harriet Beecher Stowe*, ed. Elizabeth Ammons (Boston: G. K. Hall, 1980), p. 43.

7. Harriet Beecher Stowe, *Dred: A Tale of the Great Dismal Swamp*, 2 vol. (Boston: Phillips, Sampson, 1856), 2:274.

8. Stowe, *Dred*, 2:213.

9. In *Key*, Stowe tells of learning about slavery from discussions in the 1830s with "a very considerable number of liberated slaves" in Cincinnati (*A Key to "Uncle Tom's Cabin"; Presenting the Original Facts and Documents upon Which the Story Is Founded. Together with Corroborative Statements Verifying the Truth of the Work* [1853; rpt., Port Washington, N.Y.: Kennikat, 1968], p. 19). Stowe similarly remarks in a letter of December 1852 to an acquaintance in London: "Time would fail me to tell you all that I learnt incidentally of the workings of the slave system, in the history of the various slaves, who came into my family & of the *underground railway* which I may say ran through the barn" (Stowe to Mrs. Eliza Lee Cabot Follen, cited in E. Bruce Kirkham, *The Building of "Uncle Tom's Cabin"* [Knoxville: University of Tennessee Press, 1977], p. 137).

10. Stowe, *Key*, p. 16 (see also pp. 17–18); Stowe to Douglass, letter of 9 July 1859, in *Life and Letters of Harriet Beecher Stowe*, ed. Annie Fields (Boston: Houghton, Mifflin, 1897), pp. 133–34. William S. McFeely notes that Stowe was on the subscription list of Douglass's *North Star* (*Frederick Douglass* [New York: W. W. Norton, 1991], p. 152).

11. Stowe's 1853 letter to the American and Foreign Anti-Slavery Society is cited in Thomas F. Gossett, *"Uncle Tom's Cabin" and American Culture* (Dallas: Southern Methodist University Press, 1985), p. 294. On Stowe and the society, see also Benjamin Quarles, *Black Abolitionists* (New York: Oxford University Press, 1969), pp. 220–21. As mentioned in Chapter 2, at the same meeting Stowe's friend Leonard W. Bacon declared that she had told him that "if she were to write 'Uncle Tom' again,

she would not send George Harris to Liberia" (Gossett, *"Uncle Tom's Cabin,"* p. 294). Though Stowe had nothing positive to say about colonization after the publication of *Uncle Tom's Cabin*, critics persist in describing her and *Dred* as colonizationist. Sacvan Bercovitch, for example, refers to Stowe, along with the racist colonizationist Sarah Hale, as "mainstream Liberianists" (*The Office of the Scarlet Letter* [Baltimore: Johns Hopkins University Press, 1991], p. 102). Thomas Graham, who writes perceptively about Stowe and race, also regards *Dred* as favorable to colonization ("Harriet Beecher Stowe and the Question of Race" [1973], rpt. in *Critical Essays on Harriet Beecher Stowe*, ed. Ammons, p. 133). Yet, as we shall see, the novel rejects colonizationism in favor of the sort of halfway emigrationism championed in the mid-1850s by Mary Ann Shadd Cary and Martin Delany.

12. Stowe, *Key*, p. 252. Yarborough argues that in *Uncle Tom's Cabin* "Stowe's tragic failure of imagination prevented her from envisioning blacks (free or slave, mulatto or full-blooded) as viable members of American society" and that in *Key* she "explicitly reveals her adherence to contemporary concepts of race" ("Strategies of Black Characterization," pp. 65, 59). But however limited Stowe's reformist imagination may have been in *Uncle Tom's Cabin*, in *Key* she not only envisions but argues for the importance of blacks having full rights as U.S. citizens.

13. See Stowe's 1853 letter to the Ladies' Anti-Slavery Society of Glasgow, *Life and Letters of Harriet Beecher Stowe*, ed. Fields, pp. 209–10. During her tour of Great Britain, Stowe met William Wells Brown, William G. Allen, William and Ellen Craft, and Samuel Ward. Her initial encounter with Samuel Ward, as described by William Wells Brown in a letter of 17 May 1853 to Garrison, is especially noteworthy. At a meeting in Exeter Hall in which Stowe was "the centre of attraction," Ward delivered what Brown termed the "best speech of the evening," a scathing attack on the hypocrisy of the American pro-slavery churches . . . that caused Professor [Calvin] Stowe to turn more than once upon his seat" (*Liberator*, 3 June 1853, rpt. in *Journal of Negro History* 10 [1925]: 544–45). Though Stowe in her 1851 letter to Douglass conveyed her personal need to defend Northern ministers, by 1852 she had become more willing to criticize the sort of hypocrisy that Douglass and Ward decried. Thus in her 1854 *Sunny Memories of Foreign Lands*, 2 vols. (Boston: Phillips, Sampson, 1854), she expressed no displeasure with Ward's speech and instead used her account of Ward to refute notions of racial inferiority (even as she assented to the notion of pure racial origins): "Rev. S. R. Ward attracted attention in the company as a full-blooded African—tall enough for a palm tree. I observed him in conversation with lords, dukes, and ambassadors, sustaining himself modestly, but with self-possession. All who converse with him are satisfied that there is no native difference between the African and other men" (2:105).

The idea that there is "no native difference between the African and other men" and that blacks and whites may thus readily "converse" is central to the fund-raising volumes, *Autographs for Freedom*, that Griffiths published in 1853 and 1854 to support *FDP*. Stowe contributed a poem, an essay, and a short story to the volumes and in all likelihood read some of the contributions by the African American writers James M. Whitfield, James McCune Smith, George B. Vashon, William Wells Brown, John Langston, William J. Watkins, William J. Wilson, James Holly, and Douglass himself, who published "The Heroic Slave" in the 1853 *Autographs for Freedom*.

William Watkins's "The Evils of Colonization," published in the 1854 volume, would have further exposed Stowe to blacks' hostility to Liberia (*Autographs for Freedom*, ed. Julia Griffiths [Rochester: Wanzer, 1854], pp. 198–200).

14. William C. Nell, *The Colored Patriots of the American Revolution* (1855; rpt., New York: Arno, 1968), pp. 5, 367, 6. Nell writes of *Condition*, "In 1852, Dr. M. R. DELANY published a work with special reference to the condition of the colored people on the United States" (10). On Nat Turner, see pp. 223–27; on "The Virginia Maroons," see pp. 227–29; on David Walker and Denmark Vesey, see pp. 254–55. For useful discussions of Nell, see Dorothy Porter Wesley, "Integration versus Separatism: William Cooper Nell's Role in the Struggle for Equality," in *Courage and Conscience: Black and White Abolitionists in Boston*, ed. Donald M. Jacobs (Bloomington: Indiana University Press, 1993), pp. 207–24. *Colored Patriots* was a considerable expansion of Nell's 1851 pamphlet *The Services of Colored Americans in the Wars of 1776 and 1812*; and it was one of three black texts for which Stowe wrote introductory prefaces during the 1850s. The others were Frank J. Webb's *The Garies and Their Friends* (1857) and Josiah Henson's *Truth Stranger than Fiction* (1858). In 1855 Stowe befriended Webb's talented wife, Mary Webb, and dramatized portions of *Uncle Tom's Cabin* specifically for her, which she performed in Philadelphia, New York, and London. Stowe also wrote letters of introduction for Frank Webb and Mary Webb when they traveled to London in 1856 and helped to promote the publication of *The Garies and Their Friends* by supplying a preface. On Stowe and the Webbs, see Philip S. Lapsansky, "Afro-Americana: Frank J. Webb and His Friends," in *The Annual Report of the Library Company of Philadelphia for the Year 1990* (Philadelphia: Library Company of Philadelphia, 1991), esp. pp. 35–37. See also *The Christian Slave. A Drama, Founded on a Portion of Uncle Tom's Cabin. Dramatized by Harriet Beecher Stowe, Expressly for the Readings of Mrs. Mary E. Webb* (Boston: Phillips, Sampson, 1855).

15. Harriet Beecher Stowe, "A Brilliant Success," *New York Independent*, 30 September 1858, p. 1. On Stowe and Kinmont, see George M. Fredrickson, *The Black Image in the White Mind: The Debate on Afro-American Character and Destiny, 1817–1914* (New York: Harper Torchbook, 1972), pp. 97–129.

16. Harriet Jacobs to Amy Post, letter of 1852[?], in Harriet A. Jacobs, *Incidents in the Life of a Slave Girl*, ed. Jean Fagan Yellin (Cambridge: Harvard University Press, 1987), p. 233; Jacobs to Post, February [1853], *Incidents*, ed. Yellin, p. 233; Karen Sánchez-Eppler, *Touching Liberty: Abolition, Feminism, and the Politics of the Body* (Berkeley: University of California Press, 1993), pp. 85, 86. Yellin asserts that Jacobs "distrusted Harriet Beecher Stowe . . . because of her ideas about race" (introduction to *Incidents*, p. xviii). But if that were true, why did she pursue Stowe in the first place? On the funding of Stowe's trip, see Betty Fladeland, *Men and Brothers: Anglo-American Antislavery Cooperation* (Urbana: University of Illinois Press, 1972), pp. 352–53. Stowe may well have been right to be concerned about the ways in which the British would have patronized Louisa, who first and foremost would have been regarded less as an actual person than as a Former Slave. But for an additional critical account of Stowe's refusal to take Jacobs's daughter to England, see Deborah M. Garfield, "Vexed Alliances: Race and Female Collaborations in the Life of Harriet Jacobs," in *Harriet Jacobs and "Incidents in the Life of a Slave Girl,"* ed. Garfield and Rafia Zafar (New York: Cambridge University Press, 1996), pp. 283–85.

17. Joan D. Hedrick, *Harriet Beecher Stowe: A Life* (New York: Oxford University Press,

1994), p. 249. See also Michael Newbury, "Eaten Alive: Slavery and Celebrity in Antebellum America," *ELH* 61 (1994): esp. 181.

18. Stowe, *Key*, pp. 156, 158, 167. Stowe mentioned the escape attempt on the *Pearl* near the conclusion of *Uncle Tom's Cabin; or, Life among the Lowly*, ed. Elizabeth Ammons (New York: W. W. Norton, 1994), pp. 381–82. In his famous discussion of slaves' songs in *Bondage*, Douglass remarked that soon after their capture, the slaves of the *Pearl* found "a melancholy relief in singing" (*My Bondage and My Freedom*, ed. William L. Andrews [Urbana: University of Illinois Press, 1987], p. 66). After the escape failed and Milly Edmondson's children were confined to a slave prison, her husband, Paul, a free black, journeyed to New York to enlist the help of Henry Ward Beecher, who raised over two thousand dollars to free two of the children. In 1852 Milly herself journeyed to Beecher's home to ask for his assistance to free two more of her children. Visiting Henry at the time was Harriet, who, as Forrest Wilson condescendingly remarks, "jumped at the chance to play the role expected of the author of the great Abolition novel" (*Crusader in Crinoline: The Life of Harriet Beecher Stowe* [Philadelphia: J. B. Lippincott, 1941], p. 293). Stowe not only helped raise the funds for Milly's children but eventually helped finance the education of two of Milly's daughters at Oberlin College. Somewhat unfairly, Hedrick presents Stowe as an opportunistic "patroness" intent on getting the Edmondsons' story "for publication in the *Key*" (*Harriet Beecher Stowe: A Life*, p. 249).

19. Jean Fagan Yellin, *Women and Sisters: The Antislavery Feminists in American Culture* (New Haven: Yale University Press, 1989), pp. 82, 81.

20. Harriet Beecher Stowe, "Sojourner Truth, the Libyan Sibyl," in *Narrative of Sojourner Truth: A Bondswoman of Olden Time, with a History of Her Labors and Correspondence Drawn from Her "Book of Life,"* (1878; rpt., with an introduction by Jeffrey C. Stewart, New York: Oxford University Press, 1991), pp. 152, 154. In *"Doers of the Word": African-American Women Speakers and Writers in the North (1830–1880)* (New York: Oxford University Press, 1995), Carla L. Peterson condemns Stowe for seeking to turn Truth "into a commodity" (31), while failing to note the irony that *Truth* turned herself into a commodity by selling pictures of herself "in accordance with Stowe's . . . conception of her" (44). That commodification began, I would argue, with Truth's active decision to visit Stowe at her home. Nell Irvin Painter attacks Stowe for emphasizing "Truth's Africanness and otherness" ("Representing Truth: Sojourner Truth's Knowing and Becoming Known," *Journal of American History* 81 [1994]: 476). In *"Doers of the Word,"* Peterson emphasizes Truth's Africanness (45–55).

21. Stowe, "Sojourner Truth," p. 151; Carleton Mabee, with Susan Mabee Newhouse, *Sojourner Truth: Slave, Prophet, Legend* (New York: New York University Press, 1993), p. 65; Stowe, "Sojourner Truth," pp. 169, 161. Charles H. Foster remarks on Truth's appeal to Stowe: "Here in one person were the Negro, the Christian, and the mother separated from her child" (*The Rungless Ladder: Harriet Beecher Stowe and New England Puritanism* [Durham: Duke University Press, 1954], p. 74). Not only did Stowe write letters to abolitionists in the late 1850s recommending Truth as a speaker, she several times described her meeting with Truth to the American sculptor William Wetmore Story during her 1857 and 1860 visits to his studio in Rome, thereby inspiring him, so she claims, to create his celebrated statue of the Libyan Sibyl.

22. Sundquist, *To Wake the Nations*, p. 49.

23. Stepto writes: "In a sense, Douglass won his debate with Stowe, for he could claim some role in inducing her to write about a black revolutionary. But she won, too: When she wrote about a rebel, she wrote about one — from Virginia — who failed" ("Sharing the Thunder," pp. 151–52). Although I share Stepto's sense that a "debate" was going on between Douglass and Stowe on the issue of black heroism, I think it a bit cynical to argue that Stowe "won" by writing about a failed rebel. As I argue in my reading of *Dred*, Dred *succeeds* in spreading terror in the white community.

24. Stowe, *Dred*, 2:47. Future references to *Dred* will be supplied parenthetically in the text.

   As a single woman at the head of a plantation on a downward economic course, Nina is especially vulnerable because, as a historian of the period notes, "to be poor, female, and without the guardianship of a white male figure was to be without honor or worth in the antebellum South" (Victoria E. Bynum, *Unruly Women: The Politics of Social and Sexual Control in the Old South* [Chapel Hill: University of North Carolina Press, 1992], p. 7). At the same time, precisely because Nina is unconnected to a patriarchal figure, she has greater freedom than the typical belle of the plantation novel. From the outset of the novel, Nina is presented as a witty critic of predatory males (she aggressively defends her trifling acceptance of three marriage proposals by remarking, "Don't they [men] trifle with us girls" [1:11]) and as unconstrained by the rules of "chaperonage," which mandated that women remain in the household unless accompanied by a male guardian. On "chaperonage," see Catherine Clinton, *The Plantation Mistress: Woman's World in the Old South* (New York: Pantheon, 1982), pp. 7–9, 102.

25. Critics have been nearly unanimous in condemning Stowe's representations of blacks in the novel as "either the clichés of plantation fiction and the minstrel show . . . or representatives of the religious impulses" (Jean Fagan Yellin, *The Intricate Knot: Black Figures in American Literature, 1776–1863* [New York: New York University Press, 1972], p. 145). See also Gossett, *"Uncle Tom's Cabin" and American Culture*, p. 308. For a revisionary discussion of the progressive, *antislavery* uses of racialist discourses, see Arthur Riss's excellent "Racial Essentialism and Family Values in *Uncle Tom's Cabin*," *American Quarterly* 46 (1994): 513–44.

26. Lisette is presented as possessing a sensuality, delicacy, and airiness that is attributed to her "African and French blood" (1:62). Implicitly, that blood is credited with making her "thoughtless, unreasoning" (1:62). The embodiment of thoughtfulness and reasoning, Harry attributes the relative thoughtlessness of the slaves to their condition; and he reminds us as well that equally thoughtless is Nina herself, who, because of her own condition as fashion-conscious plantation belle, is unawares pushing the plantation toward bankruptcy. Stowe writes that Harry "inherited much of the temper and constitution of his [Scottish] father, tempered by the soft and genial temperament of his beautiful Eboe mulattress who was his mother" (1:45). Yet whatever role Stowe initially suggests "biology" may have played in the formation of his character, she comes to place a much greater emphasis on the ways in which *condition* contributes to the growth of Harry's "black" political consciousness. On Harry, see Judith R. Berzon, *Neither White nor Black: The Mulatto Character in American Fiction* (New York: New York University Press, 1978), pp. 34–35.

27. Nina's response to Tiff's singing at Sue's death helps to initiate her own conversion (1:126). On Tiff and conjure, see Gossett, *"Uncle Tom's Cabin" and American Culture*, pp. 299–300.

28. Stowe praised Henson for exemplifying "the great Christian doctrine of forgiveness" (preface to *Truth Stranger than Fiction: Father Henson's Story of His Own Life* [1858], by Josiah Henson, rpt. in *An Autobiography of the Reverend Josiah Henson*, ed. Robin W. Winks [Reading, Mass.: Addison-Wesley, 1969], p. 3).

29. Stowe, "Sojourner Truth," p. 159.

30. Alice C. Crozier errs in asserting that "none of the other characters has any relation to him [Dred]" (*The Novels of Harriet Beecher Stowe* [New York: Oxford University Press, 1969], p. 40). Stowe writes: "The negroes lying out in the swamps are not so wholly cut off from society as might at first be imagined. The slaves of all the adjoining plantations, whatever they may pretend, to secure the good-will of their owners, are at heart secretly disposed, from motives both of compassion and policy, to favor the fugitives" (1:257). As noted below, eventually Stowe reveals that even Tiff has been in contact with Dred.

31. Crozier, *Novels of Harriet Beecher Stowe*, p. 39. Gossett similarly argues that in response to the caning, Stowe "killed off her heroine Nina" and turned to other issues, making the novel into "a tale of horrors" (*"Uncle Tom's Cabin" and American Culture*, 297, 298). See also Edmund Wilson, *Patriotic Gore: Studies in the Literature of the Civil War* (New York: Oxford University Press, 1962), pp. 36–37; and Foster, *Rungless Ladder*, p. 80.

32. With near unanimity, critics have responded negatively to these initial descriptions. Sánchez-Eppler remarks, for example, that "Stowe has not so much described Dred as built his body" (*Touching Liberty*, p. 29). But it should be noted that the figure of the muscular black has an important place in African American rhetoric. Sterling Stuckey observes that David Walker believed "that the African was endowed with physical strength and fighting power clearly superior to that of the white man" (*The Ideological Origins of Black Nationalism* [Boston: Beacon, 1972], p. 12). In his famous remarks on black "double-consciousness," W. E. B. Du Bois emphasized the "dark body" and "dogged strength" of the "Negro" (*The Souls of Black Folk* [1903; rpt., New York: Penguin, 1989], p. 5). As Dorothy J. Hale notes, Du Bois regarded the black's body as "a token of veiled inner resources" and as a sign that, at the very least, "bodily strength will insure the 'Negro's' survival throughout his struggle for change" ("Bakhtin in African American Literary Theory," *ELH* 61 [1993]: 452).

33. In *Uncle Tom's Cabin*, Stowe remarks on blacks: "Their local attachments are very abiding. They are not naturally daring and enterprising, but home-loving and affectionate" (82). Later in the text St. Clare reinforces this racialist "truism" by exclaiming, "If ever the San Domingo hour comes, Anglo Saxon blood will lead the way" (234). And of course Tom rejects Cassy's request to kill Legree and "go somewhere in the swamps" (344). Dred rises to the worldly challenge that Tom chooses to reject.

34. Nell, *Colored Patriots*, pp. 227–28, 229. As historian Richard Price remarks, for Nell and other sympathetic chroniclers of maroons, "such communities stood out as a heroic challenge to white authority, and as the living proof of the existence of a slave consciousness that refused to be limited by the whites' conception or manipulation of it" (introduction to *Maroon Societies: Rebel Slave Communities in the Americas*, ed. Price [Baltimore: Johns Hopkins University Press, 1979], p. 2). R. H. Taylor notes that the "numerous slaves who sought refuge in the Great Dismal Swamp were a constant terror to the white inhabitants of the region" ("Slave Conspiracies in North Carolina," *North Carolina Historical Review* 5 [1928]: 24). On maroon communities,

see also Herbert Aptheker, "Maroons within the Present Limits of the United States" (1939), rpt. in *Maroon Societies*, ed. Price, pp. 151–67; and John W. Blassingame, *The Slave Community: Plantation Life in the Antebellum South* (New York: Oxford University Press, 1979), pp. 209–11. For interesting reflections on swamp imagery in *Dred*, see David C. Miller, *Dark Eden: The Swamp in Nineteenth-Century American Culture* (New York: Cambridge University Press, 1989), pp. 55–102. Longfellow's popular poem "The Slave in the Dismal Swamp" (1842) was in all likelihood an influence on Stowe's conception of the swamp.

35. In providing an "unofficial" account of the Vesey slave conspiracy, Stowe further aligned herself with antebellum black abolitionists; see Sterling Stuckey, "Remembering Denmark Vesey," in *Going through the Storm: The Influence of African American Art in History* (New York: Oxford University Press, 1994), pp. 19–31.

36. In a racialist moment of "explanation," Stowe states that Dred has "Mandingo" (1:253) blood on his mother's side. In her *Men of Our Times; or, Leading Patriots of the Day. Being Narratives of the Lives and Deeds of Statesmen, Generals, and Orators* (Hartford, Conn.: Hartford Publishing, 1868), Stowe, in a similarly "explanatory" moment in an admiring chapter on Frederick Douglass (380–404), asserts that Douglass's mother was from the "Mandingo tribe" (385). The Mandingo origin is significant, Stowe explains, because the "Mandingo has European features, a fine form, wavy, not wooly hair, is intelligent, vigorous, proud and brave" (385–86). Stowe was not alone in her racialist vision of African origins. The same year that Stowe published *Men of Our Times*, Rollin published her *Life and Public Services of Martin R. Delany*, wherein she linked Delany's "pride of birth" (15) to the fact that his paternal grandparents were "native Africans—on the father's side, pure Golah; on the mother's, Mandingo" (15).

37. Sundquist, *To Wake the Nations*, p. 71. The account of Dred's killing may have been inspired by the account of the vengeful "Dread" in C. G. Parsons's *Inside View of Slavery; or, A Tour among the Planters* (Boston: John P. Jewett, 1855), a text for which Stowe wrote the introduction. A white traveler in Southern slave culture, Parsons describes how the "giant slave whose name was Dread" violently resists his master's efforts to "break" him (224, 230). After his master shoots him in cold blood, he cries "to Heaven for vengeance on his murderer . . . in deep thunder tones." Vengeance against whites is exacted by another black slave, who "crept stealthily to the tent of the [slave] trader, and with one blow of the axe severed his head from his body!" (316). In her introduction, Stowe praises Parsons's book as "the work of an impartial witness" (xi). Stowe may also have had in mind Richard Hildreth, *Archy Moore, the White Slave; or, Memoirs of a Fugitive* (New York: Auburn, Miller, Orton, and Mulligan, 1855). As in *Dred*, in *Archy Moore* a maroon community lurks in the swamps waiting to take retributive vengeance on enslavers.

38. Nell, *Colored Patriots*, p. 224. Lawrence W. Levine argues that the slaves "extended the boundaries of their restrictive universe backward until it fused with the world of the Old Testament, and upward until it became one with the world beyond" (*Black Culture and Black Consciousness: Afro-American Folk Thought from Slavery to Freedom* [New York: Oxford University Press, 1977], p. 32). John Blassingame similarly observes, "The heaviest emphasis in the slaves' religion was on change in their earthly situation and divine retribution for the cruelty of their masters" (*Slave Community*, 133).

39. Stowe, *Key*, pp. 27, 28, 29. That Stowe had a personal investment in her portrayal of Dred's capacities for "supernatural perceptions" (2:5) is clear from her biography. In 1844 she experimented with mesmerism, acting as a medium. Shortly after her son Henry drowned in 1857, Stowe began to attend séances in the hopes of making contact with him in the spirit world. Calvin too had a lifelong interest in spiritualism, from time to time having visions of fairies and devils. On spiritualism and the Beecher family, see Marie Caskey, *Chariot of Fire: Religion and the Beecher Family* (New Haven: Yale University Press, 1978), pp. 287–331. Also useful is Howard Kerr, *Mediums, and Spirit-Rappers, and Roaring Radicals: Spiritualism in American Literature, 1850–1900* (Urbana: University of Illinois Press, 1972), pp. 25–36.

40. Lynn Wardley, "Relic, Fetish, Femmage: The Aesthetics of Sentiment in the Work of Stowe," *Yale Journal of Criticism* 5 (1992): 171; Alfloyd Butler, *The Africanization of American Christianity* (New York: Carlton, 1980), p. 137. See also Albert J. Raboteau, *Slave Religion: The "Invisible Institution" in the Antebellum South* (New York: Oxford University Press, 1978); and Eugene D. Genovese, *Roll, Jordan, Roll: The World the Slaves Made* (New York: Vintage, 1976), pp. 159–284. On slave religion in *Uncle Tom's Cabin*, see Hedrick, *Harriet Beecher Stowe: A Life*, pp. 214–16.

41. In her important study of religious syncretism in the South, Mechal Sobel remarks that whites, through their sharing with blacks of religious camp meeting experiences, became "more 'open' to ecstasy and spiritual life, ready and willing to have 'experience,' and to share their experience with others" (*The World They Made Together: Black and White Values in Eighteenth-Century Virginia* [Princeton: Princeton University Press, 1987], p. 203). In *My Bondage and My Freedom*, Douglass describes a week-long Methodist camp meeting at Bay Side as a ritual expression of hypocrisy in which whites from all over St. Michaels set up "a rude altar" and, in improvisatory and racist fashion, bring forth "converts" who, like Thomas Auld, continue to uphold the practice of slavery (120).

42. James M. Cox, "Harriet Beecher Stowe: From Sectionalism to Regionalism," *Nineteenth-Century Fiction* 38 (1984): 463. For a reading of *Dred* that explores the ways in which Stowe sought to link the Old and New Testaments through a dualistic conception of the novel's characters and settings, see Theodore R. Hovet, *The Master Narrative: Harriet Beecher Stowe's Subversive Story of Master and Slave in "Uncle Tom's Cabin" and "Dred"* (Lanham, Md.: University Press of America, 1989).

43. William L. Andrews, *To Tell a Free Story: The First Century of Afro-American Autobiography, 1760–1865* (Urbana: University of Illinois Press, 1986), p. 231; Harriet Beecher Stowe, "Caste and Christ," in *Autographs for Freedom*, ed. Julia Griffiths (1853; rpt., Miami, Fla.: Mnemosyne, 1969), p. 5. On the black Christian savior in Stowe, see also Wilson Jeremiah Moses, *Black Messiahs and Uncle Toms: Social and Literary Manipulations of a Religious Myth*, rev. ed. (University Park: Pennsylvania State University Press, 1993), pp. 49–66.

44. Though Judge Clayton can seem heartless in his commitment to legal formalism, there is something admirable in his willingness to speak clearly about the true nature of the master-slave relationship. His ruling echoes a famous 1829 ruling by North Carolina judge Thomas Ruffin; Stowe discusses Ruffin in *Key*, pp. 70–71. On legal issues in *Dred*, see Lisa Whitney, "In the Shadow of Uncle Tom's Cabin: Stowe's Vision of Slavery from the Great Dismal Swamp," *New England Quarterly* 66 (1993): 552–69.

45. True to her predilection for racialist ways of accounting for the actions of her characters, Stowe notes again that Harry "had inherited the violent and fiery passions of his father" (2:143), thereby partly "explaining" his anger at the decision as "white" resistance to domination. Yet the fact is that Harry never conceives of himself as white. He expresses a fraternal outrage at the implications for the slaves of Judge Clayton's decision.

46. William Wells Brown, *Clotel; or, The President's Daughter* (1853) (New York: Collier, 1970), p. 172. In linking plague to Dred's militant perspective, Stowe taps into fears of the period that linked cholera to political subversion; see Charles E. Rosenberg, *The Cholera Years: The United States in 1832, 1849, and 1866* (Chicago: University of Chicago Press, 1962). On swamps and popular notions of infection, see Miller, *Dark Eden*, p. 13. In *Bondage*, Douglass links Turner and cholera: "The insurrection of Nathaniel Turner had been quelled, but the alarm and terror had not subsided. The cholera was on its way, and the thought was present, that God was angry with the white people because of their slaveholding wickedness, and, therefore, his judgments were abroad in the land" (104).

47. Suggestive of the influence of the temperance movement on Stowe's conception of her revolutionary hero, Dred throughout the novel is described as temperate, a characterization that links him with Nat Turner, about whom Nell remarked that he never drank "a drop of spirits" (*Colored Patriots*, p. 224). In "Nat Turner's Confessions," reprinted in Stowe's *Dred*, Thomas Gray too asserts that Turner "was never known to . . . drink a drop of spirits" (2:346). Lyman Beecher argued that intemperance "obliterates the fear of the Lord, and a sense of accountability, paralyses the power of conscience, and hardens the heart, and turns out upon society a sordid, selfish, ferocious animal" (*Six Sermons on the Nature, Occasion, Sign, Evils, and Remedy of Intemperance* [Boston: T. R. Marvin, 1828], p. 52). The year before the publication of *Dred*, Catharine E. Beecher also spoke out against intemperance; see her *Letters to the People on Health and Happiness* (1855; rpt., New York: Arno, 1972), esp. p. 75. On Stowe and temperance, see Hedrick, *Harriet Beecher Stowe: A Life*, esp. pp. 133–35, 202–3.

48. Lyman Beecher, *Six Sermons*, pp. 58–59. Stowe's portrayal of the community would also have fulfilled Douglass's nightmare of white intemperance. In "Aggressions of the Slave Power: An Address Delivered in Rochester, New York, on 22 May 1856," the same day that Brooks attacked Sumner, Douglass remarked, "Lawrence was surrounded by a motley gang of ignorant invaders, blinded by the jugglery and cunning of the slaveholders; and infuriated by whiskey, threatening the people of Lawrence with fire and sword" ("Aggressions of the Slave Power," in *Papers*, 3:125).

49. According to Oliver Johnson, at a meeting in Salem, Ohio, in response to Douglass's call for blacks to resist slavery violently, Truth remarked, "Is God gone?" The implication of the question was not entirely clear to those in attendance. Was Truth asking whether God is no longer on the side of black people, or was she suggesting that violence is ungodly? In an article in an 1860 issue of the *New York Independent*, Stowe, in an account of the meeting, presents Douglass as making a fiery call for black rebellion, which Truth responds to by asking, "Frederick, is God dead?" (Mabee, *Sojourner Truth*, p. 85). The exchange probably took place in Salem, Ohio, though Wendell Phillips, Stowe's source, heard that it took place in Boston.

In his 1881 account of the incident, Douglass gave himself the final victorious statement. In response to Truth's supposedly withering " 'Frederick, is God dead?,' " Douglass declares, " 'No, . . . and because God is not dead slavery can only end in blood!' " Douglass remarks that Truth "was shocked at my sanguinary doctrine, but she too became an advocate of the sword, when the war for the maintenance of the Union was declared" (see *Life and Times of Frederick Douglass, Written by Himself: His Early Life as a Slave, His Escape from Bondage, and His Complete History* [1892; rpt., New York: Collier, 1962], p. 275).

50. Stowe, "Sojourner Truth," p. 168.

51. Sterling Stuckey, *Slave Culture: Nationalist Theory and the Foundations of Black America* (New York: Oxford University Press, 1987), p. 16. Laban was Jacob's uncle and father-in-law, father of Leah and Rachel. Jacob and Laban swore their oath of fellowship on a cairn of stones prior to sharing a ritual meal of fellowship. Their ethnic differences (Laban's language was Aramaic, Jacob's was Hebrew) had contributed to the tension that existed between them (see Genesis 31).

52. Mabee, *Sojourner Truth*, p. 89. Hedrick likewise claims that Dred's "Old Testament militancy is stilled by the words of Milly" (*Harriet Beecher Stowe: A Life*, p. 259); and Foster goes so far as to argue that the novel displays "Milly's conversion of Dred to Christian pacifism" (*Rungless Ladder*, p. 85).

53. Yearning for what Nat Turner in his "Confessions" claimed he apprehended, "a sign appearing in the heavens" (*Dred*, 2:343) that authorized him to begin his bloody rebellion, Dred had confided to Clayton his greatest fear: that he may not be one of God's consecrated prophets (2:293). That anxiety, more than Milly's argumentation, leads him to postpone his plans.

54. Hedrick asserts that it "is a measure of Stowe's failure to make him [Dred] come alive for the reader that we do not care when he dies" (*Harriet Beecher Stowe: A Life*, p. 260). Whether Hedrick and like-minded readers care or not, there is every indication that the maroon community cares, that Stowe cares, and that Stowe wants the reader to care. I find the scene affecting and unique to antebellum literature. In "Violence and Sacrificial Displacement in Harriet Beecher Stowe's *Dred*" (*Arizona Quarterly* 50 [1994]), Richard Boyd accuses Stowe of pursuing a "racist agenda" (57) in depicting Dred as an imitative version of Tom Gordon, his "white model/rival" (57). Boyd's ahistorical René Girardean reading fails to take account of Stowe's engagement with black discourses and, more crucial, fails to distinguish between the master's and slave's uses of power.

55. Raboteau, *Slave Religion*, p. 212; Stowe, *Key*, p. 250.

56. Crozier, *Novels of Harriet Beecher Stowe*, p. 37. Stowe, of course, articulated the importance of education to black elevation in her 1852–53 exchanges with Douglass. She also addressed the issue in an 1853 letter to her friend Eliza Follen: "Nothing tends more immediately to the emancipation of the slave than the education and elevation of the free" (Stowe to [Eliza] Follen, 16 February 1853, in *Life of Harriet Beecher Stowe*, ed. Charles Edward Stowe, p. 203). In *Uncle Tom's Cabin*, Eva's educational reform plan for the slaves doesn't seem to involve colonization: She hopes to "buy a place in the free states, and take all our people there, and hire teachers, to teach them to read and write" (230).

57. Crozier suggests that Anne Clayton's school constitutes "Mrs. Stowe's utopia" (*Novels of Harriet Beecher Stowe*, p. 37). On the importance of hygiene to Stowe's social and political thought, see Lora Romero, "Bio-Political Resistance in Domestic Ide-

ology and *Uncle Tom's Cabin*," *American Literary History* 1 (1989): 715–34. See also Hedrick's fine discussion of Stowe and the water cure in *Harriet Beecher Stowe: A Life*, chap. 16. Following the Civil War, Stowe sought to create an integrated school in Mandarin, Florida. When the whites of Mandarin refused to allow their children to attend classes with black children, Stowe caved in to the pressure and segregated the classrooms, hoping that whites would eventually realize the folly of their racist superiority. She remarked in 1873, "The negro children are bright; they can be taught any thing" (*Palmetto-Leaves* [Boston: James R. Osgood, 1873], p. 317). On Stowe's Mandarin school, see Alex L. Murray, "Harriet Beecher Stowe on Racial Segregation in the Schools," *American Quarterly* 12 (1960): 518–19. For a critical overview of Stowe's racial politics following the Civil War, see Gossett, *"Uncle Tom's Cabin" and American Culture*, esp. pp. 321–38.

58. Marva Banks, "*Uncle Tom's Cabin* and Antebellum Black Response," in *Readers in History: Nineteenth-Century American Literature and the Contexts of Response*, ed. James L. Machor (Baltimore: Johns Hopkins University Press, 1993), p. 219. Banks's source for her assertion would seem to be not Stowe's novel but Thomas Graham, who in 1973 wrote that "in her next antislavery novel *Dred*, [Stowe] again wrote favorably of colonization" ("Harriet Beecher Stowe and the Question of Race," p. 133). In what would seem to be an echoing of her reading of Graham and (possibly) Banks, Susan Nuerberg writes that "in her next antislavery novel, *Dred* (1856), Stowe once again embraces colonization" ("The Rhetoric of Race," in *The Stowe Debate: Rhetorical Strategies in "Uncle Tom's Cabin,"* ed. Mason I. Lowance Jr., Ellen E. Westbrook, and R. C. De Prospo [Amherst: University of Massachusetts Press, 1994], p. 262).

59. Sarah J. Hale, *Liberia; or, Mr. Peyton's Experiments* (1853; rpt., Upper Saddle River, N.J.: Gregg, 1968), p. 121. For an excellent discussion of Hale's reformist aspirations in *Liberia*, see Susan M. Ryan, "Errand into Africa: Colonization and Nation Building in Sarah J. Hale's *Liberia*," *New England Quarterly* 68 (1995): 558–83.

60. As historians of the settlement remark, "More than any other, the principle of self-help reflected the character of Elgin" (William H. Pease and Jane H. Pease, *Black Utopia: Negro Communal Experiments in America* [Madison: State Historical Society of Wisconsin, 1963], p. 92). By underscoring the importance of black participation to the success of the Claytons' community, Stowe similarly extols the value of black self-help. Richard Boyd thus overstates when he argues that Clayton's Canadian project allows him to maintain "his coercive power" over the slaves ("Models of Power in Harriet Beecher Stowe's *Dred*," *Studies in American Fiction*, 19 [1991]: 27).

61. Douglass, "The Heroic Slave," in *Frederick Douglass: The Narrative and Selected Writings*, ed. Michael Meyer (New York: Modern Library, 1984), p. 313.

62. Stowe supplies a footnote telling the reader that her depiction of Milly is informed by yet another African-American "presence," one Aunt Katy, "an old colored woman" and former slave, who "established among these destitute children the first Sunday-school in the city of New York" (*Dred*, 2:334). The image of Milly at the novel's ending argues against Gossett's reading that Stowe has lost confidence that "blacks have sufficient intelligence and will to enable them to live as equal citizens in a free society" (*"Uncle Tom's Cabin" and American Culture*, p. 303). As Stowe portrays the situation, it is the whites who lack the intelligence and will to live up to the nation's egalitarian ideals.

63. See Thomas Gray, "The Confessions of Nat Turner," in *The Nat Turner Rebellion:*

The Historical and the Modern Controversy, ed. John B. Duff and Peter M. Mitchell (New York: Harper and Row, 1971), p. 28. Stowe cuts, for example, Gray's statements that Turner was motivated by "hellish purposes" (13) and acted with "fiend-like barbarity" (27); and she cuts Gray's remarks on how his text means "to demonstrate the policy of our laws in restraint of this class of our population, and to induce all those entrusted with their execution, as well as our citizens generally, to see that they are strictly and rigidly enforced" (14).

64. Harriet Beecher Stowe, "The New Year," rpt. in Stowe, *Household Papers and Stories* (1868; rpt., Boston: Houghton Mifflin, 1896), p. 437. Patricia R. Hill argues that Stowe, in the context of the Civil War, saw Turner's militance as "too dangerous a concept for a freed slave to espouse" ("Writing out the War: Harriet Beecher Stowe's Averted Gaze," in *Divided Houses: Gender and the Civil War*, ed. Catherine Clinton and Nina Silber [New York: Oxford University Press, 1992], p. 274). In an essay in an 1861 issue of the *Atlantic*, Thomas Wentworth Higginson, to Stowe's disadvantage, noted the connection between Dred and Nat Turner: "Mrs. Stowe's 'Dred' seems dim and melodramatic beside the actual Nat Turner" (rpt. in Higginson, *Travellers and Outlaws: Episodes in American History* [Boston: Lee and Shephard, 1889], p. 321). For a good discussion of Stowe's emancipatory vision of the Civil War, see Wendy Hammand Venet, *Neither Ballots nor Bullets: Woman Abolitionists and the Civil War* (Charlottesville: University Press of Virginia, 1991), pp. 64–82.

65. Frederick Douglass, "Men of Color, to Arms!," in *Writings*, 3:319.

66. See Harriet Beecher Stowe's underrated *The Pearl of Orr's Island*, ed. E. Bruce Kirkham (1862; rpt., Hartford, Conn.: Stowe-Day Foundation, 1979), which represents slavery in the larger context of the Americas.

CHAPTER FIVE

1. When Floyd J. Miller brought out the first book publication of Martin Delany's *Blake; or, The Huts of America* (Boston: Beacon, 1970), he altered our understanding of the development of the African American novel. Some critics refer to *Blake* as the third African American novel, after William Wells Brown's *Clotel* (1853) and Frank Webb's *The Garies and Their Friends* (1857). But Brown's revised version of *Clotel, Miralda; or, The Beautiful Quadroon*, appeared in serial form in 1860–61, and Harriet Wilson's autobiographical *Our Nig* (1859) and Harriet Jacobs's novelized *Incidents in the Life of a Slave Girl* (1861) appeared before the serial publication of *Blake* in 1861–62.

The 1970 edition of *Blake* generated several fine readings of the novel. For a pioneering discussion, see Jean Fagan Yellin, *The Intricate Knot: Black Figures in American Literature, 1776–1863* (New York: New York University Press, 1972), pp. 193–211. Eric J. Sundquist's notable reading examines the novel in relation to Melville's "Benito Cereno" (*To Wake the Nations: Race in the Making of American Literature* [Cambridge: Harvard University Press, 1993], chap. 2). A number of critics have found Delany's novel to be aesthetically deficient. For example, Blyden Jackson refers to Delany's "wretchedness as a writer," concluding that "*Blake* lacks art, not mind" (*A History of Afro-American Literature*, 2 vols. [Baton Rouge: Louisiana State University Press, 1989], 1:370, 373). Wilson Jeremiah Moses condescendingly refers to the novel as "a typical exhortation to revolt by a free black pamphleteer" (*The*

Golden Age of Black Nationalism, 1850–1925 [1978; rpt., New York: Oxford University Press, 1988], p. 151). For a good (and more appreciative) later reading, see John Ernest, *Resistance and Reformation in Nineteenth-Century African-American Literature: Brown, Wilson, Jacobs, Delany, Douglass, and Harper* (Jackson: University Press of Mississippi, 1995), pp. 109–39.

2. See Yellin, *Intricate Knot*, p. 197, and Sundquist, *To Wake the Nations*, pp. 183, 193–94. On William King, see William H. Pease and Jane H. Pease, "Uncle Tom and Clayton," *Ontario History* 50 (1958): 61–73; and William H. Pease and Jane H. Pease, *Black Utopia: Negro Communal Experiments in America* (Madison: State Historical Society of Wisconsin, 1963), pp. 84–108. It is an irony of literary/cultural history that by 1861 Delany would be tying his hopes for the creation of an African American colony in Africa to the Elgin community that Stowe so greatly admired.

3. *Anglo-African Magazine*, January 1859, p. 20; M. R. Delany to William Lloyd Garrison, letter of 19 February 1859, William Lloyd Garrison Papers, Boston Public Library.

4. Miller incorrectly gives the date of the publication of the first chapter of *Blake* as 26 November 1861 (*Blake*, ix).

5. Jackson, *History of Afro-American Literature*, 1:366; Delany, *Blake*, p. 199.

6. *Provincial Freeman*, 23 February 1856, p. 163. In his 1852 *Condition* Delany had cautioned blacks against Canadian emigration because he feared U.S. "annexation" was "the inevitable and not far distant destiny of the Canadas" (*The Condition, Elevation, Emigration, and Destiny of the Colored People of the United States* [1852; rpt., New York: Arno, 1968], p. 175). By 1854, however, he had come to regard Canada's blacks as "united and powerful" ("Political Destiny of the Colored Race on the American Continent," in Rollin, p. 367), and he had run his "Call" for the Cleveland emigration convention in the *Provincial Freeman*. (In the same issue that first ran his "Call," Delany complained in a letter to the editors that Douglass had sought to make him appear "ridiculous" by deliberately letting stand the errors in the "Call" printed in *Frederick Douglass' Paper* [see Martin R. Delany to the editors of the *Provincial Freeman*, letter of 29 March 1854, in *Provincial Freeman*, 15 April 1854, p. 3].) Though the editors Isaac Shadd and Mary Ann Shadd printed the "Call," in subsequent issues they raised questions about the assumptions undergirding Delany's plan for North American blacks to become part of the "*ruling element*" of Central and South America. "Know you not that men are there before you?" they demanded ("A Word about, and to Emigrationists," *Provincial Freeman*, 15 April 1854, p. 3). Yet despite the skepticism voiced in this and other editorials, Mary Ann Shadd modified her stance shortly after Delany's 1856 arrival in Chatham, and in a July 1856 editorial she endorsed Delany's call for an August 1856 emigration convention ("The Emigration Convention," *Provincial Freeman*, 5 July 1856, p. 46). Delany's "The Cleveland Convention" appeared in the 7 June 1854 issue of *Provincial Freeman*, p. 30.

7. *Provincial Freeman*, 10 May 1856, p. 14; Martin R. Delany, "What Does It Mean?," *Provincial Freeman*, 12 July 1856, p. 50. For Douglass's earlier views on the blacks of Canada, see, for example, "The Elgin Settlements at Buxton, Canada West," *FDP*, 25 August 1854, p. 2. By 1855, perhaps because of his increasingly friendly interactions with the Shadds, Delany had come to resent Douglass's resistance to Canadian emigration, and in an essay printed in an October 1855 issue of *Provincial Freeman*, he mockingly attacked "the 'leading and great men'" of the African American community for their "studied opposition" to Canada as a "point of emigration by the

colored people of the United States." See Martin R. Delany, "Political Aspect of the Colored People of the United States: Given in a Paper, Read before the First Annual Meeting of the National Board of Commissioners, Assembled in Council in the City of Pittsburgh, on the 24th day of August, 1855, according to Art. IV of the Constitution," *Provincial Freeman*, 13 October 1855, p. 97.

8. Proclaiming as a historical truism the Byronic sentiment, "'Who would be free, themselves must strike the blow,'" Douglass, in one of his most militant antebellum lectures, "The Significance of Emancipation in the West Indies" (1857), argued for a direct link between slave insurrection and liberation (*Papers*, 3:202). Douglass delivered this speech before a predominately black audience. Given his renewed militancy, it is not surprising that he came close to collaborating with Delany on the planning stages of Brown's mission.

When Douglass first met John Brown in 1848, he described him as "a white gentleman, [who] is in sympathy a black man" (Douglass to William C. Nell, letter of 5 February 1848, *NS*, 11 February 1848, p. 2). During the 1850s Douglass printed several of Brown's antislavery writings in *FDP*, praising him as "an active and self-sacrificing abolitionist" (*FDP*, 6 July 1855, p. 2). Even after Brown's murderous raid at Pottawatomie, Kansas, on 24 May 1856, Douglass continued to praise him in his paper. For an excellent discussion of Douglass and Brown, see Benjamin Quarles, *Allies for Freedom: Blacks and John Brown* (New York: Oxford University Press, 1974).

9. In addition to Delany, among the blacks Brown had convinced to meet with him in Canada were Delany's close friend William C. Munroe and Isaac Shadd and Thomas Cary, the brother and husband, respectively, of one of Douglass's harshest critics of the 1850s, Mary Ann Shadd Cary.

10. Osborne P. Anderson, *A Voice from Harper's Ferry: A Narrative of Events at Harper's Ferry, with Incidents Prior and Subsequent to Its Capture by Captain Brown and His Men* (Boston, 1861), pp. 2, 8; "Journal of the Provisional Constitution Held on Saturday, May 8th, 1858," in "The John Brown Insurrection: The Brown Papers," in *Calendar of Virginia State Papers and Other Manuscripts from January 1, 1836, to April 15, 1869* 11 (1893): 288 (see also 272). The "Journal" was confiscated by Virginia authorities after Brown's raid. According to Daniel C. Littlefield, the Chatham document reveals that "Brown acted out of a firm commitment to American political values and Christian morality" ("Blacks, John Brown, and a Theory of Manhood," in *His Soul Goes Marching On: Responses to John Brown and the Harpers Ferry Raid*, ed. Paul Finkelman [Charlottesville: University Press of Virginia, 1995], p. 78). On the Chatham convention, see also Quarles, *Allies for Freedom*, pp. 42–54; and Robin W. Winks, *The Blacks in Canada: A History* (New Haven: Yale University Press, 1971), pp. 267–70.

According to Delany, as recorded by Rollin, "the idea of Harpers Ferry was never mentioned" at the Chatham convention (88). But Delany offered Rollin his account of the convention at a time when he would have been loathe to reveal his past insurrectionist activities. The evidence suggests that Brown had called the Chatham convention with the intention of gaining the support of black leaders for a plan to organize and lead a rebellion of the slaves of the United States.

11. Delany to J. H. Kagi, letter of 16 August 1858, in "John Brown Insurrection," pp. 291–92; Delany to M. H. Freeman, *Weekly Anglo-African*, 1 February 1862, p. 2; M. R. Delany, *Official Report of the Niger Valley Exploring Party* (1861), rpt. in *Search for a*

Place: Black Separatism and Africa, 1860, ed. Howard H. Bell (Ann Arbor: University of Michigan Press, 1969), p. 38; Delany to Henry Ward Beecher, letter of 17 June 1858, cited in Floyd J. Miller, *The Search for a Black Nationality: Black Emigration and Colonization, 1787–1863* (Urbana: University of Illinois Press, 1975), p. 178. See also Ann Greenwood Wilmoth, "Pittsburgh and the Blacks: A Short History, 1780–1875" (Ph.D. diss., Pennsylvania State University, 1975), pp. 52–56.

12. Delany, *Official Report*, p. 33. Delany explains that the reason why the delegates (and Delany himself) selected Central and South America at the 1854 emigration convention as the most suitable places for emigration was that *"Africa was held in reserve, until by the help of an All-wise Providence we could effect what has just been accomplished with signal success"* (36).

In *Official Report* Delany states that his reading of the white evangelical T. J. Bowen's *Central Africa: Adventures and Missionary Labors* (1857) had further convinced him of the need for African regeneration (36). Downplaying the influence of Bowen and other white evangelicals, Sterling Stuckey argues that Delany "broke with the view of African barbarism in modern history by arguing for the existence of luminous aspects of Africanity from which Americans were already benefiting" (*Slave Culture: Nationalist Theory and the Foundations of Black America* [New York: Oxford University Press, 1987], p. 229).

13. Frederick Douglass, "A Nation in the Midst of a Nation: An Address Delivered in New York, New York, on 11 May 1853" (1853), in *Papers*, 2:437; Douglass, "African Civilization Society," *Douglass' Monthly*, February 1859, p. 19. One of the principal backers of the African Civilization Society was Benjamin Coates, a Philadelphia white who had supported Liberian colonization and had argued in his pamphlet, *Cotton Cultivation in Africa* (1858), that black emigrants to Africa should help the natives to grow cotton in order to undermine the South's economic power and rationale for slavery. Delany would argue for a similar program in his *Official Report*. My discussion of Delany's African project draws on the following texts: Bell, *Search for a Place*; Howard Holman Bell, *A Survey of the Negro Convention Movement, 1830–1861* (1953; rpt., New York: Arno, 1969); Earl Ofari, *"Let Your Motto Be Resistance": The Life and Thought of Henry Highland Garnet* (Boston: Beacon, 1972); Victor Ullman, *Martin R. Delany: The Beginnings of Black Nationalism* (Boston: Beacon, 1971), chap. 12; Nell Irvin Painter, "Martin R. Delany: Elitism and Black Nationalism," in *Black Leaders of the Nineteenth Century*, ed. Leon Litwack and August Meier (Urbana: University of Illinois Press, 1988), pp. 156–62; Cyril E. Griffith, *The African Dream: Martin R. Delany and the Emergence of Pan-African Thought* (University Park: Pennsylvania State University Press, 1975); and especially Miller, *Black Nationality*, chap. 6.

14. Miller, *Black Nationality*, p. 198. In his *Official Report*, Delany chides but then forgives Campbell for requesting funds from the American Colonization Society (43–44).

Indicative of Delany's conflicting commitments is the fact that aboard the black-chartered *Mendi* taking him to Africa were thirty-three "emigrants sent out by the American Colonization Society" (200). Wilson Jeremiah Moses remarks: "The suspicions of Frederick Douglass and other antiemigrationists thus seemed to have been confirmed. If the African Civilization Society was not an adjunct of the American Colonization Society, its emissary to Africa was certainly a fellow traveler" (*Alexander Crummell: A Study of Civilization and Discontent* [1989; rpt., Amherst: University of Massachusetts Press, 1992], p. 128). In Delany's defense, postindependence Liberia of the 1850s was considerably different from Liberia of the 1830s and 1840s.

15. Martin R. Delany, "Liberia," *NS*, 2 March 1849, p. 2. Similarly, in his 1855 introduction to William Nesbit's blistering attack on Liberia, *Four Months in Liberia: Or African Colonization Exposed*, Delany called Liberia "pernicious, because it was originated in the South, by slave-holders, propagated by their aiders and abettors, North and South" (*Four Months in Liberia: Or African Colonization Exposed* [Pittsburgh: Shryock, 1855], p. 3). In *Four Years in Liberia* (1857), Samuel Williams, who also greeted Delany in Liberia, directly refuted Nesbit and Delany, whom he termed "a most inveterate hater of colonization" (*Four Years in Liberia: A Sketch of the Life of the Rev. Samuel Williams, with Remarks on the Missions, Manners, and Customs of the Natives of Western Africa, Together with an Answer to Nesbit's Book* [Philadelphia: King and Baird, 1857], p. 65). Facsimile reproductions of Nesbit and Williams may be found in *Two Black Views of Liberia*, ed. Edwin S. Redkey (New York: Arno, 1969).

16. E. W. B[lyden]., "Martin R. Delany in Liberia," *Liberian Herald*, rpt. in *Weekly Anglo-African*, 1 October 1859, pp. 1–2.

17. Alexander Crummell, "The Relations and Duties of Free Colored Men in America to Africa," in *The Future of Africa: Being Addresses, Sermons, Etc., Delivered in the Republic of Liberia* (New York: Scribner, 1862), pp. 216, 243, 255, 259, 245. On Delany's visit with Crummell, see Moses, *Alexander Crummell*, pp. 127–33. Henry Highland Garnet evinced similar sentiments in his "Speech Delivered at Cooper's Institute, New York City, 1860," proclaiming: "We believe that Africa is to be redeemed by Christian civilization and that the great work is to be chiefly achieved by the free and voluntary emigration of enterprising colored people" (Ofari, *"Let Your Motto Be Resistance,"* p. 183). On Crummell's sometimes patronizing views of Africa, see Kwame Anthony Appiah, *In My Father's House: Africa in the Philosophy of Culture* (New York: Oxford University Press, 1992), chap. 1.

18. Delany, *Official Report*, pp. 108–9, 115, 111, 118–19. On his meeting with Crummell, see p. 51.

19. Miller, *Black Nationality*, p. 214; Delany, *Condition*, pp. 210, 214, 213, 214.

20. Delany, *Official Report*, p. 121; Basil Davidson, *The Black Man's Burden: Africa and the Curse of the Nation-State* (New York: Times Books, 1992), p. 43; Delany, *Official Report*, p. 77. For a critical view of the "masculinist ideology" (212) informing Delany's emigration movement, see Carla L. Peterson, *"Doers of the Word": African-American Women Speakers and Writers in the North (1830–1880)* (New York: Oxford University Press, 1995), pp. 212–16. On the hazards of African diasporic thinking, see also Kenneth W. Warren, "Appeals for (Mis)recognition: Theorizing the Diaspora," in *Cultures of United States Imperialism*, ed. Amy Kaplan and Donald E. Pease (Durham: Duke University Press, 1993), pp. 392–406.

21. Frederick Douglass, "Capt. John Brown Not Insane," *Douglass' Monthly*, November 1859, in *Writings*, 2:460; Harriet Beecher Stowe, *New York Independent*, 16 February 1860, p. 1. Douglass's widely reprinted letter of 31 October 1859, in which he refuted claims that he conspired with Brown, may be found in *Blacks on John Brown*, ed. Benjamin Quarles (Urbana: University of Illinois Press, 1972), pp. 8–10.

22. Richard Blackett, "In Search of International Support for African Colonization: Martin R. Delany's Visit to England, 1860," *Canadian Journal of History* 10 (1975): 315. In a December 1860 open letter to the people of Glasgow, Delany stated that his

colony "shall not only bring the staples of commerce to British markets, but regeneration to a people who form even now an important element in the social system" (*Glasgow Examiner*, 8 December 1860, cited in Blackett, "International Support for African Colonization," p. 321). For a contemporaneous discussion of Delany's efforts to publicize his Africa project, see "Dr. Delany and Prof. Campbell in London," *Weekly Anglo-African*, 30 June 1860, p. 2. My account of Delany's British tour is indebted to Miller, *Black Nationality*, pp. 215–28; and especially Blackett, "International Support for African Colonization."

23. *Manchester Weekly Advertiser*, 21 July 1860, cited in Blackett, "International Support for African Colonization," p. 317; *Morning Post*, 23 July 1860, cited in Blackett, "International Support for African Colonization," p. 321. See also Ullman, *Martin R. Delany*, pp. 238–46. Given the highly publicized nature of this event, the incident at the congress helped to make Delany, not Douglass, the center of attention of British abolitionists, at least for the remainder of 1860. As a sign of his fame, one month after this incident he was elected chairman of the annual Peace and Temperance Festival in Buckinghamshire, where he delivered a temperance lecture to a crowd estimated at three thousand (Blackett, "International Support for African Colonization," p. 320).

24. Frederick Douglass, "Dallas and Delany," *Douglass' Monthly*, September 1860, p. 322; Rollin, p. 122. Douglass had favorably noted Delany's writings in a column titled "The Anglo-African Magazine," *Douglass' Monthly*, February 1859, p. 20.

25. Cited in Miller, *Black Nationality*, p. 252. On William King, see also Jane H. Pease and William H. Pease, *They Who Would Be Free: Blacks' Search for Freedom, 1830–1861* (New York: Atheneum, 1974), pp. 269–75. In addition to working with King, Delany made peace with Garnet and the African Civilization Society; he was named its vice president in November 1861 (Ofari, *"Let Your Motto Be Resistance,"* pp. 93–97).

26. Martin R. Delany to James Theodore Holly, letter of 15 January 1861, in *Planet* (Chatham, Canada West, 21 January 1861), rpt. in *BAP*, 2:437; "Letter from Dr. Delany," *Weekly Anglo-African*, 5 October 1861, p. 2; "Dr. Delany on Africa," *Weekly Anglo-African*, 25 January 1862, p. 2. Delany also wrote an open letter to M. H. Freeman of Avery College, printed in the *Weekly Anglo-African* of 1 February 1862, in which he attacked Haitian emigration and affirmed his commitment to "the regeneration of the African race" (2). Indicative of his commitment, during early 1862 Delany went on a lecture tour to raise funds for his African project, at times speaking to groups while wearing traditional African dress. On these tours, see *Weekly Anglo-African*, 1 March 1862, p. 2; and Miller, *Black Nationality*, pp. 260–62.

27. Delany to Dr. James McCune Smith, *Weekly Anglo-African*, 11 January 1862, p. 2; Frederick Douglass, "A Trip to Hayti," *Douglass' Monthly*, May 1861, p. 449.

28. *Weekly Anglo-African*, 12 October 1861, p. 2; *Weekly Anglo-African*, 5 October 1861, p. 3. For a sampling of Thomas Hamilton's writings on the Civil War, see the following editorials in *Weekly Anglo-African*: "What Shall Be Done with the Freedmen?," 30 November 1861, p. 2; "The Emancipation Message," 29 March 1862, p. 2; "Emancipation," 6 April 1862, p. 2.

29. Miller inexplicably failed to reprint the novel's full title in his paperback edition. In his prefatory remarks on the initial publication of chapters from *Blake* in the January 1859 issue of *Anglo-African Magazine*, Thomas Hamilton provided his readers with an overview of the novel he read in manuscript: "It not only shows the combined political and commercial interests that unite the North and South, but gives in the

most familiar manner the formidable understanding among the slaves throughout the United States and Cuba. The scene is laid in Mississippi, the plot extending into Cuba; the Hero being an educated West India black, who deprived of his liberty by fraud when young, and brought to the United States, in maturer age, at the instance of his wife being sold from him, sought revenge, through the medium of a deep laid secret organization" (*Anglo-African Magazine*, January 1859, p. 20). Hamilton's overview constitutes an excellent short plot summary of Delany's complex novel and, as is true of the novel's full title, points to its large reach.

With more recent theorists of American literary study proposing Havana as "an alternative capital of the Americas" (José David Saldívar, *The Dialectics of Our America: Genealogy, Cultural Critique, and Literary History* [Durham: Duke University Press, 1991], p. 15), Delany's novel should assume an increasingly central place in efforts to remap the boundaries of American literary study. In addition to Saldívar, see *Reinventing the Americas: Comparative Studies of Literature of the United States and Spanish America*, ed. Bell Gale Chevigny and Gari Laguardia (Cambridge: Cambridge University Press, 1986); *Do the Americas Have a Common Literature?*, ed. Gustavo Perez Firmat (Durham: Duke University Press, 1990); and Earl E. Fitz, *Rediscovering the New World: Inter-American Literature in a Comparative Context* (Iowa City: University of Iowa Press, 1991). (None of these provocative texts discusses Delany.) See also Carolyn Porter, "What We Know That We Don't Know: Remapping American Literary Studies," *American Literary History* 6 (1994): esp. 497–520.

30. Peterson writes that "Delany's protagonist [Blake] is a fictional projection of the author, recast as a picaresque hero who contemplates the possibilities of black revolution" (*"Doers of the Word,"* pp. 169–70). See also Kristin Herzog, *Women, Ethnics, and Exotics: Images of Power in Mid-Nineteenth-Century American Fiction* (Knoxville: University of Tennessee Press, 1983), p. 146.

31. Delany, *Blake*, p. 256. Future parenthetical references in the text are to Miller's 1970 edition of the novel.

32. What Delany, through Placido, is responding to, of course, is the tendency of U.S. whites to regard the liberationist desires of blacks of mixed blood as having their sources in "white" blood; he is responding, in short, to St. Clare's (and implicitly Stowe's) belief in *Uncle Tom's Cabin* that "if ever the San Domingo hour comes, Anglo Saxon blood will lead on the day" (Harriet Beecher Stowe, *Uncle Tom's Cabin; or, Life among the Lowly*, ed. Elizabeth Ammons [New York: W. W. Norton, 1994] p. 234). Delany writes in *Condition*, "The equality of the African with the European race, establishes the equality of every person intermediate between the two races" (87).

33. Moses, *Golden Age of Black Nationalism*, p. 17. Pan-African racial collectivity may prove to be difficult to achieve—witness the conflicts between Delany, Douglass, and Garnet—and, Moses warns, such assumptions may help to promote "an authoritarian collectivism, a belief that all black people could and should act unanimously under the leadership of one powerful man or group of men" (11). In the second half of the novel, with only partial success, Delany attempts to negotiate his way past such gender assumptions. For a provocative discussion quite critical of Delany's gender politics in the novel, see Robert Reid-Pharr, "Violent Ambiguity: Martin Delany, Bourgeois Sadomasochism, and the Production of a Black National Masculinity," in *Representing Black Men*, ed. Marcellus Blount and George P. Cunningham (New York: Routledge, 1996), pp. 73–94.

34. Harriet Beecher Stowe, "Caste and Christ," in *Autographs for Freedom*, ed. Julia Griffiths (1853; rpt., Miami, Fla.: Mnemosyne, 1969), p. 5. Delany uses the poem's final stanza as an epigraph to part 2 of the novel: "Hear the word! —who fight for freedom! / Shout it in the battle's van! / Hope! for bleeding human nature! / Christ the *God*, is Christ the *man*!" (6). Paul Gilroy incorrectly states that *Blake* "took its epigraph from Harriet Beecher Stowe's *Uncle Tom's Cabin*" (*The Black Atlantic: Modernity and Double Consciousness* [Cambridge: Harvard University Press, 1993], p. 27).

35. Martin R. Delany, "Domestic Economy," *NS*, 13 April 1849, p. 2. Similarly, in *Condition* he instructs that an overreliance on prayer "is a mistake, and one that is doing the colored people especially, incalculable injury" (39).

36. Guided by the book's title and to avoid unnecessary confusion, I will use the name "Blake" throughout the discussion. Delany begins calling "Henry Holland" "Blake" near the opening of part 2.

37. Delany, *Condition*, pp. 37–38.

38. In this sense the novel takes a very different narrative approach from Melville's "Benito Cereno," which much more aggressively attempts to implicate *readers* as the victims of plot (see Robert S. Levine, *Conspiracy and Romance: Studies in Brockden Brown, Cooper, Hawthorne, and Melville* [New York: Cambridge University Press, 1989], chap. 4). That said, Delany's letter to Garrison of 19 February 1859 (see n. 3 to this chap.) would suggest that he conceived of himself as writing for white readers as well.

39. M. R. Delany, *The Origin and Objects of Ancient Freemasonry; Its Introduction into the United States, and Legitimacy among Colored Men: A Treatise Delivered before St. Cyprian Lodge, No. 13, June 24th, A.D. 1853 — A.L. 5853* (1853; rpt., Xenia, Ohio, 1904), pp. 16, 39, 17, 24, 16, 18. Delany asserts that Masonic privileges are simply an impossibility for the enslaved: "The *mind* and *desires* of the recipient must be *free*; and at the *time* of his endowment with these privileges, his *person* must be unencumbered with all earthly trammels or fetters" (24). In *"Doers of the Word,"* Peterson focuses on the relationship of the novel's Masonry to capitalism (170–71), thus neglecting its Pan-African dimension. On Masonry in the novel, see also Ernest, *Nineteenth-Century African-American Literature*, pp. 128–29.

Delany implicitly suggests the Masonic character of Blake later in part 1 by describing him as a kind of astronomer (*Blake*, p. 124). As Martin Bernal has noted, nineteenth-century Africanists regularly argued that astronomy was invented by the Egyptians; astronomical and astrological figures were thus central to antebellum black Freemasonry (*Black Athena: The Afroasiatic Roots of Classical Civilization* [New Brunswick: Rutgers University Press, 1987], p. 226). Delany published two essays on astronomy in the *Anglo-African Magazine* at the time of the novel's initial serialization: "Comets," *Anglo-African Magazine*, February 1859, pp. 59–60; and "The Attraction of Planets," *Anglo-African Magazine*, January 1859, pp. 17–20.

40. On the importance of Moses to slave religion, see Lawrence W. Levine, *Black Culture and Black Consciousness: Afro-American Folk Thought from Slavery to Freedom* (New York: Oxford University Press, 1977); Albert J. Raboteau, "African-Americans, Exodus, and the American Israel," in *African-American Christianity: Essays in History*, ed. Paul E. Johnson (Berkeley: University of California Press, 1994), pp. 1–17; and Theophus H. Smith, *Conjuring Culture: Biblical Formulations of Black America* (New York: Oxford University Press, 1994), esp. chap. 2.

41. Sundquist, *To Wake the Nations*, p. 193. Blake's travels can seem a parody version of Frederick Law Olmsted's *A Journey to the Seaboard Slave States* (1856; rpt., New York: Negro Universities Press, 1968).
42. Delany, *Condition*, p. 199. For a critical account of Delany's gender politics in relation to Maggie's role in the novel, see Peterson, *"Doers of the Word,"* pp. 170–71.
43. The narrator remarks on the Brown Society: a "man with the prowess of Memnon or a woman with the purity of the 'black doves' of Ethiopia and charms of the 'black virgin of Solomon,' avails them nothing, if the blood of the oppressor, engendered by wrong, predominates not in their veins" (110). Blake encounters a similar fallen, or false, consciousness in Richmond, where "some of the light mixed bloods of Richmond hold against the blacks and pure-blooded Negroes the strongest prejudice and hatred, all engendered by the teachings of their Negro-fearing master fathers" (116). On a similar theme, see Delany, "Southern Customs — Madame Chevalier," *NS*, 22 June 1849, p. 2.
44. Frederick Douglass, *Narrative of the Life of Frederick Douglass, an American Slave: Written by Himself*, ed. Houston A. Baker Jr. (New York: Penguin, 1982), p. 119. In the context of recent historical work on African survivals in slave culture, critics want to find something more affirmative in Delany's portrayal of the conjurors in the Dismal Swamp. In *To Wake the Nations*, for example, Sundquist refers to Delany's "striking conjunction of revolution, conjure, and maroon life" (194) and asserts that the conjurors' "maroon life is . . . made a sacred preserve (a hush harbor, as it were) of the revolutionary ethos" (194). His remarks would be more appropriate to Stowe's representation of Dred's maroon community. In the cave of the "High Conjurors" (114), for example, Gamby Gholar's associate Maudy Ghamus, who invokes the deeds of Gabriel Prosser, Vesey, and Turner, reveals himself as anything but the heir of those great revolutionaries. When "a large sluggish, lazily-moving serpent . . . so entirely tame and petted that it wagged its tail" (114) approaches Blake, Maudy theatrically shouts in warning: "Go back, my chile! 'e in terrible rage! 'e got seben loog toof, any on 'em kill yeh like flash!" (114). Though Blake is too educated to be frightened by Maudy's display, Delany's point comes across quite clearly: this is precisely how the conjurors intimidate the more ignorant slaves of the nearby community. As Blake later instructs his followers Andy and Charles: "Now you see, boys, . . . how much conjuration and such foolishness and stupidity is worth to the slaves in the South. All that it does, is to put money into the pockets of the pretended conjurer" (136).
45. Andy's amazed response to Blake's definition works with (rather than against) minstrel humor and reveals once again why the slaves are so in need of intelligent black leaders: "Wy, ole feller, you is way up in de hoobanahs! Wy, you is conjure sho'nuff" (134). This is not the first time that Delany uses minstrel humor to make his point about the slaves' degradation. In a scene that, were it to appear in a white-authored novel, would be cited as evidence of the author's irredeemable racism, Daddy Joe finds that the crunchiness of the mush he had blessed — "Sumpen heah mighty crisp, ah tells yeh. . . . Sumpen heah mighty crisp in dis mush an' milk! — Mighty crisp!" (50) — comes from the "large black house roaches" (51) that had made their way into his bowl. At the revelation of this fact, there is "an outburst of tittering and snickering among the young people" (51). In his excellent study of minstrelsy, Eric C. Lott ignores this scene when arguing that Delany made "guerrilla appropriations" of minstrel stereotypes, such as those disseminated in Stephen Foster plantation songs, in order to write "black agency back into history" (*Love and Theft: Blackface Minstrelsy*

and the American Working Class [New York: Oxford University Press, 1993], p. 236).
Lott's remarks are more persuasive for part 2 of the novel.

46. See *Walker's Appeal, with a Brief Sketch of His Life. By Henry Highland Garnet. And Also Garnet's "Address to the Slaves of the United States of America"* (New York: J. H. Tobitt, 1848), p. 94. Ironically, in one of the few moments in the novel that privileges leadership other than Blake's, Delany paraphrases the words of the man with whom he was competing for funds to finance his African expedition.

47. Harriet Beecher Stowe, *Dred: A Tale of the Great Dismal Swamp*, 2 vols. (Boston: Phillips, Sampson, 1856), 2:243; Martin R. Delany, "Annexation of Cuba," *NS*, 27 April 1849, p. 2; Frederick Douglass, "Cuba and the United States," *FDP*, 4 September 1851, p. 2. The pseudonymous Demoticus Philalethes remarked in his popular 1856 "travelogue" that Cuba is "inevitably bound to become one of the States of our Confederacy" (*Yankee Travels through the Island of Cuba; or, The Men and Government, the Laws and Customs of Cuba, as Seen by American Eyes* [New York: D. Appleton, 1856], p. ii).

48. The execution of López outraged many Americans. Douglass cynically remarked on U.S. whites' support for López: "The true explanation of the present tone of the press, in regard to this occurrence is, that the ruling power of this nation which is slavery, wants a pretext for the Conquest of Cuba" ("Cuba and the United States," p. 2). Adding to desires to take control of Cuba from Spain was the Spanish seizure in Havana Bay of the American steamer *Black Warrior* in February 1854. (The steamer was released shortly thereafter.)

49. "The Ostend Report," in *The Works of James Buchanan: Comprising His Speeches, State Papers, and Private Correspondence*, ed. John Bassett Moore (1908–11; rpt., New York: Antiquarian, 1960), 9:261, 262, 265, 266. The Louisiana legislature's 1854 declaration on "Africanization" is cited in Charles H. Brown, *Agents of Manifest Destiny: The Lives and Times of the Filibusters* (Chapel Hill: University of North Carolina Press, 1980), pp. 122–23. In his inaugural address of 1852, Pierce publicly announced his desire to purchase Cuba, asserting that he would "not be controlled by any timid forebodings of evil from expansion" (Charles H. Brown, *Agents of Manifest Destiny*, p. 109). As a writer for New York's *Democratic Review* put it in 1852, "This continent is for white people, and not only the continent but the island adjacent, and the negro must be kept in slavery in Cuba and Hayti under white republican masters" (cited in Philip S. Foner, *A History of Cuba and Its Relations with the United States* [New York: International Publishers, 1963], 2:83). When Spain appointed the antislavery Marquis Juan de la Pezuela captain-general of Cuba in 1853, concerns arose among many U.S. whites about his liberalizing policies, such as the legalization of marriages between blacks and nonblacks.

My discussion of U.S.-Cuba relations and the Cuban political scene of the 1840s and 1850s is indebted to C. Stanley Urban, "The Africanization of Cuba Scare," *Hispanic American Historical Review* 37 (1957): 29–45; Robert May, *The Southern Dream of a Caribbean Empire, 1854–1861* (Baton Rouge: Louisiana State University Press, 1973); Foner, *History of Cuba*; Basil Rauch, *American Interest in Cuba, 1848–1855* (1948; rpt., New York: Octagon, 1977); Franklin W. Knight, *Slave Society in Cuba during the Nineteenth Century* (Madison: University of Wisconsin Press, 1970); Charles H. Brown, *Agents of Manifest Destiny*; and David M. Murray, *Odious Com-*

merce: Britain, Spain, and the Abolition of the Cuban Slave Trade (Cambridge: Harvard University Press, 1980).

50. Delany, "Political Aspect," p. 98; William Walker, *The War in Nicaragua* (Mobile: S. H. Goetzel, 1860), pp. 118, 265; Frederick Douglass, "Aggressions of the Slave Power: An Address Delivered in Rochester, New York, on 22 May 1856," in *Papers*, 3:116–17; Douglass, "Acquisition of Cuba," *Douglass' Monthly*, March 1859, p. 37. For Walker's discussion of the role played by Cuban Creoles in his invasion, see *War in Nicaragua*, esp. pp. 249–50, where he describes the celebration of a mass for the failed Cuban filibusterer Narciso López. Also useful is William O. Scroggs, "William Walker's Designs on Cuba," *Mississippi Valley Historical Review* 1 (1914): 198–211; and Charles H. Brown, *Agents of Manifest Destiny*, pt. 3.

51. May, *Caribbean Empire*, p. 175. In his annual message of 6 December 1858, Buchanan asked Congress for money with which to make yet another offer to Spain to purchase Cuba. When the South formed its Confederacy, Jefferson Davis declared an intention to acquire Cuba; Lincoln's rejection of the Crittendon Compromise helped to put a (temporary) halt to annexation efforts.

52. William Walker, *War in Nicaragua*, p. 134.

53. As Delany notes several times in his writings on Cuba, one of the few positive aspects of slavery in Cuba is that slaves have the legal right to self-purchase; see Martin R. Delany, "The Redemption of Cuba," *NS*, 20 July 1849, p. 2; and Delany, "Political Destiny," p. 350.

54. In making his surrogate a former slave, Delany is arguably (and probably unintentionally) conceding a point to Douglass: that the experience of slavery does help make Blake a better and more representative leader of America's blacks.

55. Henry Highland Garnet, "The Past and the Present Condition and the Destiny of the Colored Race" (1848), in Ofari, *"Let Your Motto Be Resistance,"* p. 171; Delany, *Condition*, p. 203. Consistent with his racialist view of Placido's limits as a mulatto, Delany goes on to celebrate the more obscure, "equally noble black, CHARLES BLAIR" (203), who was also executed by Cuban authorities. In an 1849 reflection on Placido, however, Delany was unconcerned about making such racial distinctions, asserting simply that "blood of the murdered Placido and his brave compatriots still cries aloud for justice, and vengeance must sooner or later overtake their guilty oppressors" ("Redemption of Cuba," p. 3). Placido was celebrated by African Americans despite the fact that he was a mulatto, that his poetry was embraced by many of Cuba's white aristocrats, and that, as Vera Kutzinski argues, he "did not care to identify himself as a 'Negro writer' " (*Sugar's Secrets: Race and the Erotics of Cuban Nationalism* [Charlottesville: University Press of Virginia, 1993], p. 84). See also Robert L. Paquette's excellent *Sugar Is Made with Blood: The Conspiracy of La Escalera and the Conflict between Empires over Slavery in Cuba* (Middletown, Conn.: Wesleyan University Press, 1988); and Frederick S. Stimson, *Cuba's Romantic Poet: The Story of Plácido* (Chapel Hill: University of North Carolina Press, 1964). The free black William Allen hailed Placido's insurrectionism: "Placido's plan in detail evinced no lack of ability to originate and execute, nor of the sagacity which should mark a revolutionary leader" ("Placido," in *Autographs for Freedom*, ed. Griffiths, pp. 260, 262). This is the same volume of *Autographs* that included Stowe's "Caste and Christ."

56. Frederick Douglass, *My Bondage and My Freedom*, ed. William L. Andrews (Urbana:

University of Illinois Press, 1987), p. 179; Delany, "Annexation of Cuba," p. 2. Sundquist suggests that Delany's portrayal of Placido conveys his "belief in the ideological function of literature" (*To Wake the Nations*, p. 208). But by quoting from one of his own poems instead of one of Placido's, Delany may be pointing to the limits of Placido's poetics and leadership. In an exchange that reflects on Placido's anachronistic status in a book set in the 1850s, Blake declares, "You, Placido, are the man for the times!" And Placido responds, given that he is no longer of "the times," "Don't flatter, Henry; I'm not" (196). As Sundquist notes (203), for Blake's and Placido's poetry, Delany also drew on his friend James M. Whitfield's *America and Other Poems* (Buffalo: James S. Leavitt, 1853).

57. Precisely what Sundquist terms "the interlocked histories" of Africa, the United States, and the Caribbean are what Delany represents in this family and foregrounds in the plotting and racial politics of the novel's second part (*To Wake the Nations*, p. 199). On the syncretic slave cultures of the Caribbean, see Herbert S. Klein, *African Slavery in Latin America and the Caribbean* (New York: Oxford University Press, 1986).

58. Unlike in "Benito Cereno," where Melville links his (white) readers with Delano so as to make them the victims of Babo's and Melville's plotting, Delany links his (black) readers to plot and offers the pleasures (available as well to sympathetic rereaders of "Benito Cereno") of observing white racists duped by the more knowing slaves. When the white captains find a fragment of a note from Placido to Blake that reads, "Faithfully yours to the end of the war" (202), one of the captains assumes the note is from Blake's wife; others are simply confused. The most knowledgeable of the captains, the Cuban Garcia, suspects that a plot may be in the works, but when the U.S. captain Royer begins to fear for their lives, Garcia counsels him against "overzealousness" (208). On the blacks' parodies of the music of the masters, see Lott, *Love and Theft*, p. 236.

59. In his 1861 *Pilgrimage*, Robert Campbell, who accompanied Delany on his Niger expedition, reported that in 1860 at Freetown, Sierra Leone, he and Delany "saw a large slaver, brought in a few days before by H.M.S.S. 'Triton.' Her officers and crew, consisting of over thirty persons, were there set at liberty, to be disposed of by the Spanish consul as distressed seamen. . . . These villains, of course, return to Havana or the United States, procure a new ship, and again pursue the wicked purpose which their previous experience enables them to accomplish with all the more impunity" (*A Pilgrimage to My Motherland: An Account of a Journey among the Egbas and Yorubas of Central Africa in 1859–60* [1861], rpt., with Delany's *Official Report*, in *Search for a Place*, ed. Bell, pp. 240–41). In *Blake*, the narrator similarly observes that slavers "frequently prepare the vessels to carry 2000 [slaves], which was the case with a slaver taken by the British cruiser, brig 'Triton,' which the writer saw at Sierra Leone, in April 1860" (213 n). In *Official Report* Delany attacks Spain and other Catholic slave powers for "persisting in holding Cuba for the wealth accruing from African Slaves stolen from their native land" (*Official Report*, pp. 103–4). In *Blake* Delany has the slave factor Draco urge the U.S. and Cuban captains to develop an "American agency in Cuba . . . to make the trade a most lucrative one" (214).

60. James Holly, *A Vindication of the Capacity of the Negro Race for Self-Government, and Civilized Progress, as Demonstrated by Historical Events of the Haytian Revolution; and the Subsequent Acts of That People since Their National Independence*

(1857), rpt. in *Black Separatism and the Caribbean, 1860*, ed. Howard H. Bell (Ann Arbor: University of Michigan Press, 1970), pp. 30, 59; Holly, "Thoughts on Hayti," *Anglo-African Magazine* 1 (1859): 365.

61. Gilroy, *Black Atlantic*, p. 25.

62. For an excellent reading of the festival occasions in the concluding chapters of *Blake*, see Sundquist, *To Wake the Nations*, pp. 209–20. Until the end of the novel, when Delany presents revolutionary black masses at the King's Day festival, he mostly ignores indigenous sources of resistance among Afro-Cuban slaves. For a more sympathetic account, see José L. Franco, "Maroons and Slave Rebellions in the Spanish Territories," in *Maroon Societies: Rebel Slave Communities in the Americas*, ed. Richard Price (Baltimore: Johns Hopkins University Press, 1979), esp. pp. 41–48. On the larger revolutionary context, see Eugene D. Genovese, *From Rebellion to Revolution: Afro-American Slave Revolts in the Making of the New World* (Baton Rouge: Louisiana State University Press, 1979).

63. Delany, "Political Destiny," p. 335. Delany asserts a politicized conception of blackness in a subsequent marriage scene calculated to offer a Pan-African image of the solidarity among free and enslaved, "pure" and mixed, blacks: the black militants Gofer Gondolier and Abyssa Soudan choose to marry at the same time as the mulatto Creoles Madame Cordora and General Juan Montego (276).

64. Gilroy, *Black Atlantic*, p. 29. On the subversive uses of black festivals, see Geneviève Fabre, "Festive Moments in Antebellum African American Culture," in *The Black Columbiad: Defining Moments in African American Literature and Culture*, ed. Werner Sollors and Maria Diedrich (Cambridge: Harvard University Press, 1994), pp. 52–63. Also useful is Robert Dirks, *The Black Saturnalia: Conflict and Its Ritual Expression on British West Indian Slave Plantations* (Gainesville: University of Florida Press, 1987); and William Luis, *Literary Bondage: Slavery in Cuban Narrative* (Austin: University of Texas Press, 1990), esp. pp. 1–119.

65. While some of the Creoles suspected of participating in La Escalera were sympathetic to the antislavery movement, others strongly supported slavery. Similarly, the "foreigners" linked to La Escalera were widely divided in their politics. The British were antislavery, while retaining an imperial ambition to gain additional colonies in the region, and of course the U.S. foreigners included proslavery and antislavery annexationists. In short, it would be imprecise simply to describe the political situation in terms of blacks versus whites. As Ann-Marie Karlsson neatly puts it, "Drawing on La Escalera for his representation of the Cuban conspiracy, Delany complicates his plot by revising the relationship between the colonizer and the colonized to suggest a break-up in the binary sense of political antagonism" ("Literary Plots, Historical Conspiracies" [paper presented at the annual meeting of the American Studies Association, Nashville, Tenn., October 1994], p. 7). On tensions between the Creoles and Peninsular Spaniards, free and enslaved blacks, whites and blacks, see esp. Knight, *Slave Society in Cuba*, pp. 92–107.

66. In an attempt to quell annexationist desires, Richard Henry Dana Jr. belittled the possibility of "Africanization," remarking in his widely read 1859 Cuban travel narrative, which was critical of slavery in Cuba and the United States, that "a successful insurrection of slaves in Cuba is impossible" (*To Cuba and Back*, ed. C. Harvey Gardiner [Carbondale: Southern Illinois University Press, 1966], pp. 127–28). In her popular 1860 Cuban travel narrative, Julia Ward Howe, on the other hand, prophe-

sied that the "enslaved race. . . , gradually conquering the finer arts of its master, will rise up to meet the hand of deliverance" (*A Trip to Cuba* [Boston: Ticknor and Fields, 1860], p. 234).

67. Delany probably made up or embellished this journalistic account. In one of the best-known descriptions of the King's Day festivities, John G. F. Wurdemann confessed to how unnerving he found a ceremony which gave "almost unlimited liberty to the negroes" and which seems "like the summons to a general insurrection" (*Notes on Cuba* [1844; rpt., New York: Arno, 1971], pp. 83, 84; Wurdemann's book was first published in Boston). Paquette writes that King's Day "provided much more than entertainment. Amid the celebration, people of color traded information, communicated ancestral beliefs, and offered emotional support to one another" (*Sugar Is Made with Blood*, p. 109).

68. Delany, "Redemption of Cuba," p. 3; Delany, "Annexation of Cuba," p. 2; Douglass, "A Nation in the Midst of a Nation," *FDP*, 27 March 1853, p. 1. Germain J. Bienvenu argues that *Blake*'s final warnings on "woe" to whites "are directed at only a specific group of whites (those who have disgraced Ambrosina) and that these portentous words are uttered by the crazy carver Gofer Gondolier" ("The People of Delany's *Blake*," *CLA Journal* 36 [1993]: 408). In fact, Gondolier is presented as admirably militant, shrewd in his antiauthoritarian duplicity, and fully worthy of marrying the African revolutionary Abyssa. Moreover, his final words speak as well to his anger at a recent attack on Placido and to his overall hatred of the white slave power.

69. Sundquist remarks, for example, that the "surprising eclipse of the novel's revolutionary import augmented its threat" (*To Wake the Nations*, p. 220); Karlsson takes that argument one step further by speculating that the ending is "inconclusive by *design* rather than by accident" ("Literary Plots," p. 8).

70. Douglass, "A Nation in the Midst of a Nation," in *Papers*, 2:437; Frederick Douglass, "The Late Election," *Douglass' Monthly*, December 1860, p. 370; Douglass, "Emigration to Hayti," *Douglass' Monthly*, January 1861, p. 386; Douglass, "Trip to Hayti," pp. 449, 450; Douglass, "Notes on the War," *Douglass' Monthly*, July 1861, p. 481.

71. Douglass wrote in August 1861, "By the simple process of calling upon the blacks of the South to rally under the Star Spangled Banner, and to work and fight for freedom under it — precisely as they are now working and fighting for slavery under the hateful flag of rebellion — we could in a few months emancipate the great body of the slaves, and thus break the back bone of the rebellion" ("The War against Slavery," *Douglass' Monthly*, August 1861, p. 498).

72. Frederick Douglass, "What Shall Be Done with the Slaves If Emancipated?," *Douglass' Monthly*, January 1862, p. 579; Douglass, "The President and His Speeches," *Douglass' Monthly*, September 1862, p. 707 (and see also Douglass's related article, "The Spirit of Colonization," pp. 705–6).

73. On the House of Representatives' *Report of the Select Committee on Emancipation and Colonization* (Washington, D.C., 1862), see Benjamin Quarles, *The Negro in the Civil War* (1953; rpt., New York: Russell and Russell, 1968), pp. 145–47; and Ullman, *Martin R. Delany*, pp. 269–77. In an anticipation of Lincoln's plan, Frank Blair, congressman from Missouri, proposed in the late 1850s that blacks be sent to what he referred to as "the vacant regions of Central and South America." Both Delany's friend James Whitfield and the prominent Haitian emigrationist James Holly supported the plan, and as Delany stated in a letter to Blair of 24 February 1858, he was

"strongly requested by Messrs. Holly and Whitfield, of New Haven and Buffalo, to communicate with you on the subject." He sent him a copy of "Political Destiny." See Frank P. Blair, *The Destiny of the Races of this Continent: An Address Delivered before the Mercantile Library Association of Boston, Massachusetts, on the 26th of January, 1859* (Washington, D.C.: Buell and Blanchard, 1859), pp. 23, 34. (Delany's letter to Blair is appended to Blair's text.)

74. Frederick Douglass, review of *The Future of Africa*, by Alexander Crummell, in *Douglass' Monthly*, July 1862, p. 674.

75. Frederick Douglass, "Dr. M. R. Delany," *Douglass' Monthly*, August 1862, p. 595.

76. Delany to Douglass, letter of 7 August 1862, in *Douglass' Monthly*, September 1862, p. 719 (Delany included with his letter a column clipped from the *Buffalo Commercial Advertiser* on Lincoln's willingness to meet with black representatives from Haiti); Delany to Edwin Stanton, letter of 15 December 1863, in *Freedom: A Documentary History of Emancipation, 1861–1867*. Ser. 2, *The Black Military Experience*, ed. Ira Berlin et al. (New York: Cambridge University Press, 1982), p. 102. See also Delany's letter of 7 December 1863 to Mary Ann Shadd Cary on his recruitment efforts in Chicago, in *BAP*, 2:520–22. In *Martin R. Delany*, Ullman mistakenly writes that Delany committed himself to the recruitment effort in 1862, after Stanton became secretary of war (see p. 283). In fact, Stanton assumed the post in January 1863. Following Ullman, Painter also incorrectly gives as 1862 the year Delany began recruiting for the black regiments of Massachusetts ("Martin R. Delany," p. 162).

According to the roster list supplied in Luis F. Emilio, *A Brave Black Regiment: History of the Fifty-Fourth Regiment of Massachusetts Volunteer Infantry, 1863–1865* (1894; rpt., New York: Arno, 1969), Lewis Douglass, who enlisted 25 March 1865, was a noncommissioned staff officer, sergeant major; Toussaint L'O. Delaney [sic], who enlisted 27 March 1863, served in Company D; and Charles R. Douglass, who enlisted 18 April 1863, served in Company F (see pp. 339, 355, 364).

77. Rollin, pp. 96, 128–29, 134. See also the letter of 2 June 1862 from William H. Johnson of Albany, New York, printed in the 19 June 1862 *Pine and Palm*, which reported: "Delany has been lecturing here with good effect. His subject has been *Africa*. He has very ably set forth the advantages to be derived by us, as a people, in emigrating" (rpt. in *A Grand Army of Black Men: Letters from African-American Soldiers in the Union Army, 1861–1865*, ed. Edwin S. Redkey [Cambridge: Cambridge University Press, 1992], p. 21). As reported in the *Liberator*, Delany was lecturing on the "Moral and Social Aspects of Africa" and the "Commercial Advantages of Africa" well into 1863; see "Lecture by Dr. Delaney [sic]," *Liberator*, 1 May 1863, p. 1.

78. Rollin, pp. 134, 15, 16, 17. On black officers in the Union army, see Berlin et al., *Freedom*, chap. 6. According to the editors of this volume, "Scarcely a hundred blacks served as commissioned officers, roughly two-thirds serving as Louisiana Native Guard officers and another quarter as chaplains and surgeons" (310).

79. William S. McFeely, *Frederick Douglass* (New York: W. W. Norton, 1991), p. 230 (see also pp. 228–35); Douglass to Abraham Lincoln, letter of 29 August 1864, in *Writings*, 3:406. (Douglass sent the letter to Lincoln ten days after their meeting.) When Douglass learned of the impending emancipation, he renewed his calls for blacks' military participation in the war. Soon after, he initiated what amounted to a two-year quest to be named a commissioned officer in the army, arguing that such an appointment would demonstrate to whites and blacks throughout the nation that the Union

was committed to antiracist policies. See Frederick Douglass, "Emancipation Proclaimed," *Douglass' Monthly*, October 1862, pp. 721–22; Douglass, "Do Not Forget Truth and Justice," *Douglass' Monthly*, April 1863, p. 818. On Lincoln's hesitations in commissioning Douglass, see Benjamin Quarles, *Frederick Douglass* (Washington, D.C.: Associated Publishers, 1948), chap. 12. For an excellent discussion of Douglass, Lincoln, and the Civil War, see David W. Blight, *Frederick Douglass' Civil War: Keeping Faith in Jubilee* (Baton Rouge: Louisiana State University Press, 1989), esp. chaps. 3–7.

80. Rollin, pp. 139, 140, 157. According to Rollin, Delany conceived of the black troops as a "corps d'Afrique," a division of blacks modeled on the "African warriors" who fought for the French in the Algerine war. As Nell Irvin Painter incisively remarks, Delany's proposed plan for a black insurrectionary war of emancipation "was the grand gesture Delany had wished for in *The Condition of the Colored People*, a realization of Henry Blake's insurrection, an action that would command the respect of the rest of the world" ("Martin R. Delany," p. 163).

81. Rollin, pp. 166, 162, 166, 168–69, 170. McFeely implicitly denies the existence of the meeting between Lincoln and Delany, as he states that Lincoln "had only two private conversations with Douglass — and none with other black leaders, except for the famous meeting with *creole de couleur* gentlemen from New Orleans just before the president's death" (*Frederick Douglass*, p. 235). For a representative statement on the pride African Americans took in Delany's commission, see the letter in the 1865 *Weekly Anglo-African* from "Jack Halliards," which rejoiced that in "the form of that spotless African and well tried veteran in the cause of right, Martin R. Delany, we have a regularly commissioned Major in the U.S. Army" (rpt. in Redkey, *Grand Army of Black Men*, pp. 278–79). In his introduction to *Blake*, Miller notes that "portraits of Delany in full regalia were sold through *The Weekly Anglo-African* for twenty-five cents" (xvi).

After Lincoln's assassination, Delany was among the first African Americans to propose a memorial. See Delany's open letter of 20 April 1865 to African Americans, rpt. in Redkey, *Grand Army of Black Men*, p. 222; and Rollin, p. 207.

82. Rollin, pp. 171, 18. Lincoln's remarks on Delany to Edwin M. Stanton, letter of 8 February 1865, may also be found in *The Collected Works of Abraham Lincoln*, ed. Roy P. Basler et al. (New Brunswick: Rutgers University Press, 1953), 8:272.

83. Rollin, pp. 300, 301. Douglass had remarked on Delany's racial pride, "He stands so straight that he leans back a little" ("Dr. M. R. Delany," p. 595).

EPILOGUE

1. Frederick Douglass, *Life and Times of Frederick Douglass, Written by Himself: His Early Life as a Slave, His Escape from Bondage, and His Complete History* (1881) (1892; rpt., New York: Collier, 1962), pp. 347, 358–59, 360. On Lincoln as Mosaic emancipator, see Theophus H. Smith, *Conjuring Culture: Biblical Formations of Black America* (New York: Oxford University Press, 1994), p. 55.

2. W. E. B. Du Bois, *The Souls of Black Folk* (1903; rpt., New York: Penguin, 1989), p. 42; Wilson Jeremiah Moses, *The Golden Age of Black Nationalism, 1850–1925*

(1978; rpt., New York: Oxford University Press, 1988), p. 54; Martin R. Delany, "True Patriotism," *NS*, 8 December 1848, p. 2; Frederick Douglass, "The Constitution and Slavery," *NS*, 16 March 1849, in *Writings*, 1:361.

3. Delany, "True Patriotism," p. 2; Lt. Edward M. Stoeber's remarks on Delany are cited in Victor Ullman, *Martin R. Delany: The Beginnings of Black Nationalism* (Boston: Beacon, 1971), p. 330; Rollin, p. 249.

4. Martin R. Delany, "Prospects of the Freedmen of Hilton Head" (1865), *New South*, rpt. in Rollin, pp. 242, 282; Ullman, *Martin R. Delany*, p. 368. By 1871 Delany had mostly given up on his plan for a "triple alliance," and in "Homes for the Freedmen" he called on Northern "philanthropic capitalists" to purchase land for poor Southern blacks (*Charleston Daily Republican*, 7 March 1871, p. 1).

5. Frederick Douglass, "Our Composite Nationality" (1869), in *Papers*, 4:245. William S. McFeely notes that Douglass's prestigious appointment in 1877 as U.S. marshal of the District of Columbia, the first to require Senate approval of a black man, "was part of [President] Hayes's shrewdly constructed screen to conceal the cessation of truly significant federal action in behalf of black people" (*Frederick Douglass* [New York: W. W. Norton, 1991], p. 289). For a useful discussion of Douglass's notion of composite American nationality, see Waldo E. Martin Jr., *The Mind of Frederick Douglass* (Chapel Hill: University of North Carolina Press, 1984), esp. pp. 199–215. On Douglass and the Republicans during Reconstruction, see David W. Blight, *Frederick Douglass' Civil War: Keeping Faith in Jubilee* (Baton Rouge: Louisiana State University Press, 1989), chap. 9.

6. Frederick Douglass, "Santo Domingo: An Address Delivered in St. Louis, Missouri, on 13 January 1873," in *Papers*, 4:344, 354, 355. (The source of the speech is a newspaper transcript.)

7. In 1868 Delany urged Southern blacks to join the American Colonization Society's *Golconda* expedition to Liberia, and in 1869 he attempted to secure a consulship to Liberia; see Floyd J. Miller, introduction to *Blake; or, The Huts of America*, by Martin R. Delany (Boston: Beacon, 1970), esp. pp. xvi–xix.

8. Frederick Douglass, "At Last, at Last, the Black Man Has a Future: An Address Delivered in Albany, New York, on 22 April 1870," in *Papers*, 4:271; Douglass, "Salutatory of the Corresponding Editor," *New National Era*, 27 January 1870, in *Writings*, 4:220. The following four articles by Delany appeared in the 1870 *New National Era*: "In and Out," 27 January 1870, p. 1; "Constitutional," 10 February 1870, p. 1; "Civil Rights," 24 February 1870, p. 1; and "Rights and Duties," 10 March 1870, p. 1. The articles were reprinted by Wilberforce University as a handbook for young blacks on U.S. citizenship: *A Series of Four Tracts on National Policy: To the Students of Wilberforce University; Being Adapted to the Capacity of the New Enfranchised Citizens, The Freedmen* (1871).

9. Rollin, pp. 281, 282, 280, 283; M. R. Delany to H. H. Garnet, letter of 27 July 1867, in the *New York Tribune*, 6 August 1867, p. 1. Delany further elaborated on his concerns about a black vice president in a letter printed in an 1867 issue of the *Christian Recorder*. Such an appointment, he argued, "would be certain to result in the overthrow of the Republican party, by driving all the conservative Negro hating elements North and South together, and end in the loss of our Cause" (cited in Ullman, *Martin R. Delany*, p. 410).

10. Major Delany to Frederick Douglass, letter of 14 August 1871, in *New National Era*, 31 August 1871, p. 3.

11. Ibid.

12. Frederick Douglass, "Letter to Major Delany," *New National Era*, 31 August 1871, p. 2. In an act of editorial control, Douglass printed his response prefatory to Delany's letter.

13. Ibid.

14. *New National Era*, 22 October 1874, p. 2; "Delany for Hampton," *Charleston News and Courier*, 26 September 1876, p. 1. On blacks' anger at Delany for campaigning in 1876 for a Democratic gubernatorial candidate, see Eric Foner, *Reconstruction: America's Unfinished Revolution, 1863–1877* (New York: Harper and Row, 1988), pp. 573–74. On the campaign, see also Dorothy Sterling, *The Making of an Afro-American: Martin Robison Delany, 1812–1885* (Garden City, N.Y.: 1971), chap. 24.

15. Frederick Douglass, "African Colonization," *New National Era*, 31 August 1871, in *Writings*, 4:302; Douglass, "The South Knows Us: An Address Delivered in Baltimore, Maryland, on 4 May 1879," in *Papers*, 4:500; Douglass, "The Negro Exodus from the Gulf States: A Paper Read in Saratoga, New York, on 12 September 1879," in *Papers*, 4:530; Douglass, *Life and Times*, p. 438; Delany to William Coppinger, letter of 18 August 1880, cited in Floyd J. Miller, *The Search for a Black Nationality: Black Emigration and Colonization, 1787–1863* (Urbana: University of Illinois Press, 1975), p. 266. For a discussion critical of Douglass's attack on the black exodus to Kansas, see Blight, *Frederick Douglass' Civil War*, pp. 206–7. On Delany and the Liberian Exodus Joint Stock Steam Ship Company, see Ullman, *Martin R. Delany*, pp. 500–506.

16. Martin R. Delany, *Principia of Ethnology: The Origin of Races and Color, with an Archeological Compendium of Ethiopian and Egyptian Civilization, from Years of Careful Examination and Enquiry* (Philadelphia: Harper and Brothers, 1879), pp. 14, 19, 9, 18, 11, 18, 27, 78.

17. Ibid., pp. 90–91, 94.

18. Frederick Douglass, "God Almighty Made But One Race: An Interview Given in Washington, D.C., on 25 January 1884," in *Papers*, 5:147; Douglass, "Our Destiny Is Largely in Our Own Hands: An Address Delivered in Washington, D.C., on 16 April 1883," in *Papers*, 5:80; Douglass, "God Almighty Made But One Race," 5:147.

19. Frederick Douglass, "The Nation's Problem" (1889), in *Papers*, 5:413; Douglass, *Life and Times*, p. 579; Douglass, "Haiti and the Haitian People: An Address Delivered in Chicago, Illinois, on 2 January 1893," in *Papers*, 5:522; Douglass, "Self-Made Men" (1893), in *Papers*, 5:567; Douglass, "The Lessons of the Hour," in *Papers*, 5:598. For a useful discussion of Douglass's writings on race, particularly late in his career, see Wilson J. Moses, "Writing Freely? Frederick Douglass and the Constraints of Racialized Writing," in *Frederick Douglass: New Literary and Historical Essays*, ed. Eric J. Sundquist (Cambridge: Cambridge University Press, 1990), pp. 66–83. Also useful is Kenneth W. Warren, "Frederick Douglass's *Life and Times*: Progressive Rhetoric and the Problem of Constituency," in *Frederick Douglass: New Literary and Historical Essays*, ed. Sundquist, pp. 253–70. On Douglass's supposed desire to be white, which his remarks on Banneker would seem to confute, see Peter F. Walker, *Moral Choices: Memory, Desire, and Imagination in Nineteenth-Century American Abolition* (Baton Rouge: Louisiana State University Press, 1978), p. 247.

20. Frederick Douglass, "Freedom Has Brought Duties: An Address Delivered in Washington, D.C., on 1 January 1883," in *Papers*, 5:55, 58–59; "The Twentieth Anniversary of Lincoln's Proclamation of Emancipation," *Washington Bee*, 6 January 1883, p. 1. The *Bee*'s comprehensive article on the dinner includes a list of the forty-one toasts offered after Douglass's address.

Index

Shaw, Lucinda, 42

Slave narratives, 21, 80, 144–45, 199, 244 (n. 7). *See also* Douglass, Frederick: *My Bondage and My Freedom*; Douglass, Frederick: *Narrative of the Life of Frederick Douglass*

Slave religion, 153–55, 156–58, 162–65, 169–70, 174–75, 194–95. *See also* Black Jeremiahs; Christ imagery; Moses

Slave resistance, 16, 28–29, 43, 82–86, 126–30, 157, 159–70, 174–76, 178, 193–94, 196–99, 210–15

Slavery: African-American perspectives on, 99–101, 147–55; and the law, 165–66. *See also* Antislavery

Smith, Craig V., 112

Smith, Gerrit, 71–72, 86; and temperance, 111, 256–57 (n. 24)

Smith, James McCune, 4, 62, 71, 114, 131, 142–43, 189

Smith, Stephen, 65

Smith, Venture, 269 (n. 33)

Sobel, Mechal, 281 (n. 41)

Sons of Temperance, 108, 110

Soulé, Pierre, 201

Spain: and Cuba, 201–2, 204, 210–14

Stanton, Edwin, 219, 220

Stanton, Elizabeth Cady, 14, 110

Stepto, Robert, 145, 155, 278 (n. 23)

Steward, Austin: *Twenty-Two Years a Slave*, 270 (n. 42)

Stewart, Maria, 13, 243 (n. 21)

Story, William Wetmore, 277 (n. 21)

Stowe, Calvin, 77

Stowe, Harriet Beecher, 6, 15, 28, 76–77, 88–90, 94, 95, 186, 207, 229, 281 (n. 39); and Martin R. Delany, 16, 143; and Frederick Douglass, 16, 143, 144–45, 146, 155, 168–69, 172, 261 (nn. 61, 62), 262 (n. 63), 278 (n. 23), 280 (n. 36), 282–83 (n. 49); and colonization, 58–60, 69–70, 71, 81–83, 148–49, 150, 151, 171–72, 259–60 (n. 46), 274–75 (n. 11); and African American abolitionists, 144–55, 274 (n. 9), 275–76

(n. 13), 276 (n. 14), 279 (n. 28), 280 (n. 37); and temperance, 146, 166–67, 282 (n. 47); and religion, 148–49, 154–59, 162–64, 168–70; and race, 150–51, 156–57, 163–64, 278 (n. 26), 279 (n. 33), 280 (n. 36); and William C. Nell, 150–51, 161, 163; and Harriet Jacobs, 151–52, 276 (n. 16); and Milly Edmondson, 152–53, 157–58, 277 (n. 18); and Sojourner Truth, 153–55, 157–59, 168–70, 277 (n. 21), 282–83 (n. 49); and slave resistance, 161–70, 174–76; and black emigration, 171–72; and black elevation, 171–74, 283 (n. 56); and Civil War, 174–75; and Nat Turner, 174–75; and John Brown, 187, 203

—Works: "Anti-Slavery Literature," 144; "A Brilliant Success," 150; "Caste and Christ," 142, 164–65, 170, 175, 177–78, 193; *Dred*, 16, 17, 142, 145, 146–49, 150, 153, 155, 156–76, 177–78, 193, 201, 274 (n. 6), 278 (n. 26), 281 (n. 39), 282 (n. 47); *A Key to "Uncle Tom's Cabin"*, 146, 148, 149, 152–53, 163, 170; *The May Flower and Miscellaneous Writings*, 144; "The New Year," 175; *Palmetto Leaves*, 284 (n. 57); "Sojourner Truth, the Libyan Sibyl," 153–54, 168, 173; *Sunny Memories of Foreign Lands*, 275 (n. 13); *Uncle Tom's Cabin*, 6, 12, 16, 31, 47, 56, 57, 58–61, 62, 63, 69, 70, 72–90, 95–96, 101, 132, 143, 145, 146, 147, 148, 149–53, 160, 163, 167, 169–73, 177, 190, 193–94, 199–200, 279 (n. 33), 283 (n. 56), 291 (n. 32)

Stowe, William S., 32–33

Stuckey, Sterling, 5, 24, 169, 245 (n. 12), 246 (n. 13), 253 (n. 5), 262–63 (n. 72), 279 (n. 32), 288 (n. 12)

Sumner, Charles, 160, 166

Sundquist, Eric J., 100, 126–27, 130, 145, 155, 162, 177, 196, 210, 293 (n. 44), 296 (nn. 56, 57), 298 (n. 69)

"The Sweetness of Home," 110

CPSIA information can be obtained
at www.ICGtesting.com
Printed in the USA
LVOW10s1344130217

524112LV00002B/83/P